WILLIAM SHAKESPEARE

A Compact Documentary Life

Convent garden   S. Clement

Arundel house   Glass house Temple stayrs Temple   Blackfryars   Bar

The Globe

Beere bayting

S. Pauwls Church

5. y Waterhouse

S. Andre in Holborne

5

Paulus wharfe

Queene hythe

The 3. Cranes

the Eel Ships

T

Winchester house

WILLIAM SHAKESPEARE

A Compact Documentary Life

S. Schoenbaum

Revised Edition
with a New Postscript

New York   Oxford
Oxford University Press
1987

Oxford University Press

Oxford   New York   Toronto
Delhi   Bombay   Calcutta   Madras   Karachi
Petaling Jaya   Singapore   Hong Kong   Tokyo
Nairobi   Dar es Salaam   Cape Town
Melbourne   Auckland

and associated companies in
Beirut   Berlin   Ibadan   Nicosia

This book is an abridged edition of *William Shakespeare: A Documentary Life* (Copyright © 1975 Oxford University Press).

First published in 1977 by Oxford University Press, Inc., 200 Madison Avenue, New York, New York 10016

First issued as an Oxford University Press paperback, 1978

Reprinted with corections and a new Postscript, 1987

Oxford is a registered trademark of Oxford University Press

Library of Congress Cataloging-in-Publication Data

Schoenbaum, S. (Samuel), 1927–
William Shakespeare : a compact documentary life.

Bibliography: p.
Includes index.
1. Shakespeare, William, 1564–1616—Biography.
2. Dramatists, English—Early modern, 1500–1700—
Biography.   I. Title.
PR2894.S33   1987   822.3'3 [B]   87-1729
ISBN 0-19-505161-0

2 4 6 8 10 9 7 5 3
Printed in the United States of America

To the memory of
James G. McManaway

Preface

For the inspiration to prepare this revised compact edition of my documentary life of Shakespeare I am obliged to Mr. Martin Dodsworth. In a generous review in *The Guardian* he observed—quite justly—that the original edition was too big for comfortable reading in bed or bath, or even on the bus. His call for a cheaper and more convenient edition 'soon' I have here sought to answer.

There must be more diverting tasks than revision so soon after the event, but the venture has yielded its dividends. In re-checking, so far as humanly possible, the data on which my original text was based, I have corrected mistakes, mostly involving points of detail, and aspired throughout to a more rigorous standard of precision. Although it is the narrative—minus most of the facsimiles and the captions—that comprises the present volume, I have included the texts of many of the facsimiles, as well as (here and there) matter from the captions. Where opportunity offered, I have enriched my narrative with additional information: sometimes by inserting a phrase or sentence, sometimes whole paragraphs or pages. Thus I have added a section on the William Shakeshafte whose presence at Lea Hall, Lancashire, is recorded in 1581. If this episode does not augment knowledge of the poet's life, it richly illustrates the perils of scholarship. I have reconsidered afresh the vexed question of the widow's portion—whether, by English common law, Anne Shakespeare would have received a life-interest of one third of her husband's estate without express testamentary provision—and I have come up with an interpretation of the evidence different from that now current in biographies of Shakespeare, including my own. There are other titbits of new information: a document naming a Richard Shakespeare, it may well be the poet's grandfather, and an account, offered as eyewitness, of a sensational murder by ratsbane in Shakespeare's Stratford, possibly in the house he bought there. This material I found among the late Tangye Lean's papers, which his widow, Mrs. Doreen Lean, graciously invited me to examine in London.

The book remains a documentary life. In this respect it differs from most of the innumerable popular biographies of Shakespeare that augment the facts with speculation or imaginative reconstruction or interpretative criticism of the plays and poems. The *Sonnets* especially have invited biographical licence. These lives are often entertaining, and sometimes instructive; but to my mind they enhance the place for a convenient narrative bringing together in up-to-date fashion all that we really know about Shakespeare, as revealed by the records. These are more numerous than generally supposed. The significance of some items is controversial, and debate—seemingly endless—has often enough generated more heat than light. Do the marriage records point to a shotgun wedding? Does the bequest of a second-best bed—an interlineation—betoken affectionate regard or derision? With what offence is Robert Greene taunting Shakespeare in his deathbed gibe? I have tried to deal with such matters dispassionately, and also with a fullness of detail not attempted in most biographies of Shakespeare. Nor have I scrupled about splitting hairs; I have worried for several pages about my protagonist's date of birth. Such minute investigations, I like to think, hold an interest of their own; but, more important, they open windows upon the quotidian life of times past, for the mundane events of Shakespeare's career— marriage, procreation, getting and spending, litigation, disposal of the estate—were also those of the ordinary mortals among whom he moved.

In threading my way through this well-explored labyrinth, I have resisted the temptation to propound new theories. I have no new Dark Lady to offer a transiently curious world; only scepticism about the credentials of those phantoms sometimes zealously championed. My aim in these pages has been distillation and synthesis rather than innovation. Because the facts are sometimes available only in mono-graphs or compilations catering mainly for specialists, I have kept paramount the needs of the general reader who is curious about the life of our supreme poet-playwright; but I rather think that the scholar will not find all the going excessively familiar.

I have viewed my domain as being spacious enough to include the apocryphal anecdotes and legendary feats that have a way of spring-ing up around the memory of great men in the times following their death. So I devote some of my pages to the deer-poaching es-capade at Charlecote, the Bidford toping contest, the bruited amour with Mrs. Davenant, and the other curious episodes that make up the Shakespeare mythos. Much of this material is quite simply good fun, but the workings of myth have a place in the historical record, and may sometimes conceal elusive germs of truth.

The uncomplicated format of this edition has made possible fuller documentation than in the previous. I have nevertheless hesitated to overwhelm the reader with notes. No matter how thick on the page, they would be insufficient to record my debts completely: one owes too much, and where so many have written on the same subject, to particularize an indebtedness may sometimes mislead rather than in-form. (Candour requires me to admit that a few times I could not remember, or track down, a source, and so left the information un-documented out of mere helplessness.) Still I should like to give a special emphasis to my primary obligations by mentioning a few here. My most important single resource was, as for all serious biog-raphers, Sir Edmund K. Chambers's triumphant synthesis, *William Shakespeare: A Study of Facts and Problems* (1930). B. Roland Lewis's *The Shakespeare Documents* (1940) has not wanted de-tractors, but is a valuable tool if used with caution. Of the more spe-cialized guides, I have turned most often to Mark Eccles's *Shake-speare in Warwickshire* (1961), a marvel of concise summation. The Stratford context has been lovingly explored by Edgar I. Fripp in a number of contributions, of which the most ambitious is his post-humous *Shakespeare: Man and Artist* (1938). Invaluable too are the four volumes of *Minutes and Accounts of the Corporation of Stratford-upon-Avon* (1921-30), which Fripp edited with Richard Savage. Of the earlier biographers I have found Malone and Halliwell-

Phillipps most enduringly useful. On education, religion, the theatres, and Elizabethan Stratford and London—topics on which I can claim no special expertise—I am especially grateful for the availability of sound guides: T. W. Baldwin on the schools, for example, and Chambers's *Elizabethan Stage* (1923) on the playhouses. Of the popular biographies I would especially cite Joseph Quincy Adams's *Life of William Shakespeare* (1923) and A. L. Rowse's *William Shakespeare* (1963). The former, although antedating Baldwin's labours, has a chapter on the poet's education that may still be consulted with profit. G. E. Bentley's *Shakespeare: A Biographical Handbook* (1961) is modest in scale and unpretentious in manner, but authoritatively informed. For particulars about minor figures I have resorted gratefully to the *Dictionary of National Biography*. The foregoing list is, as I am only too well aware, incomplete, and so I must in the last resort allow the scale and range of my indebtedness to be summed up by the dedication of this book to a humane scholar whose work represents what is best in the tradition.

Inevitably I have re-used some material from my *Shakespeare's Lives* (1970), but I have availed myself of the opportunity to reconsider what I have said previously; also, in my paragraphs on 'Sir Thomas More', I traverse some of the ground already covered (in a different context) in my *Internal Evidence and Elizabethan Dramatic Authorship* (1966). I am obliged to Penguin Books, Ltd., for permission to quote from the Introduction to William Shakespeare, *A Midsummer Night's Dream*, edited by Stanley Wells (New Penguin Shakespeare; 1967), and to Jonathan Cape Ltd. and Alfred A. Knopf, Inc., for the use of Anthony Burgess, *Shakespeare* (© Anthony Burgess, 1970).

Other debts are more personal. For generously giving of their time and wisdom, I must thank those friends and colleagues who read this book wholly or in part, in one or other of its versions: Dr. Levi Fox, Professor Roland Mushat Frye, Professor Richard Hosley, Professor James G. McManaway, Professor Kenneth Muir, Dr. Valerie Pearl, and Dr. Stanley Wells. Although I have profited from their advice, it goes without saying that they are not responsible for any faults. Others who have raised questions or answered them, or who were helpful in various ways, are Mr. Robert Bearman, Mr. Michael

Feltovic, Dr. David George, Mr. Stephen Heathcote, Mr. Arthur Keene, the Revd. Eric McDermott, S.J., Mr. Richard Proudfoot, Miss Rhoda Serlin, and Miss Katherine Williams. I have everywhere received exemplary co-operation from librarians, archivists, and staff, but would like especially to thank Mr. Horace Groves, who looked after my photographic needs at the Folger Shakespeare Library, for his perfectionist care.

For this edition I have emended some minor particulars, and here and there revised more extensively—for example, my remarks on William Shakeshafte and the Lanchashire connection, here taking into account E. A. J. Honigmann's *Shakespeare: The 'Lost Years'* (1985), which has stirred considerable interest. I have also expanded my Postscript.

The Folger Shakespeare Library   S.S.
Washington, D.C.
24 June 1986

Note on Procedures

In quoting from documents and printed texts prior to 1700, I have so far consulted the convenience of ordinary readers as to modernize spelling, capitalization, and (more lightly) punctuation; also, where appropriate, to expand abbreviations. I have not, however, tampered with proper names, as these forms sometimes have an interest of their own. Because orthography after 1700 presents fewer difficulties, I have preserved the accidentals of the originals in these extracts.

A word about dates. In this period the year (which in England was still reckoned according to the Julian calendar) began officially on Lady Day, 25 March, although popular—as distinguished from legal and governmental—practice varied. Not until the Calendar Act of 1752 was Gregorian reform instituted: eleven days were dropped from that year to correct the discrepancy that had developed between the two calendars, and 1 January became the official first day of the year. In citing dates I have followed the standard practice of revising the year (where appropriate), but not tampering with day or month. Thus in John Manningham's diary entry for a performance of *Twelfth Night* in the Middle Temple, the date appears as 2 February 1601, but in my narrative I give it as 2 February 1602. The whole question is expertly discussed by W. W. Greg, 'Old Style—New Style', in *Collected Papers*, ed. J. C. Maxwell (Oxford, 1966), pp. 366-73.

For quotations from Shakespeare I have used the Peter Alexander edition of *The Complete Works* (1951).

In the notes I have abbreviated the three most frequently cited works:

EKC   E. K. Chambers, *William Shakespeare: A Study of Facts and Problems* (Oxford, 1930), 2 vols.

ME   Mark Eccles, *Shakespeare in Warwickshire* (Madison, Wis., 1961).

SS   S. Schoenbaum, *William Shakespeare: A Documentary Life* (Oxford, 1975).

Unless otherwise noted, the place of publication is London. Although the titles of books printed before 1700 are modernized in the text, I have thought it well (for reference purposes) to preserve the original spelling in the notes. So too I have, in the text, resisted any temptation to modernize the spelling of monumental inscriptions, except for *i–j* and *u–v*.

Contents

Illustrations

Pages ii and iii: from Wenceslaus Hollar, 'Long View' of London from Bankside, 1647 (detail).

Frontispiece: The Chandos Portrait: Ozias Humphrey's version, 1783 (Folger Shakespeare Library Art Box H928 No. 1: formerly Art Inv. 323).

WILLIAM SHAKESPEARE

A Compact Documentary Life

{ 1 }

Stratford Town and Stratford Church

The story of William Shakespeare's life is a tale of two towns. Stratford bred him; London gave him, literally and figuratively, a stage for his fortune. In an unpretentious market-town he was born and reared in a house which has miraculously survived erosions by time and tourism. Before achieving his majority he took for his bride a local girl past the bloom of youth; she bore him three children, one of whom, the only son, died young. In London, Shakespeare became a common player in plays, then a popular writer of plays—the most popular in his age, although the *literati* did not universally concur in the valuation; eventually he held shares in his theatrical company, which was the foremost in the land. With the pecuniary rewards for the triumphs of his art he invested prudently in dwellings, land, and tithes. That was mostly in his native Stratford, although he had lodgings in the capital. His last years he passed in a fine house, called New Place, he had purchased in his home town. There, shortly before his death, he drew up a will in which he remembered—in addition to kin—ordinary folk, Stratford neighbours, as well as the colleagues, his 'fellows', he esteemed most in the King's troupe. He neglected to mention noble lords, although to one he had in early days dedicated two poems. In Stratford, Shakespeare died and was buried. Seven years later his collected plays were printed in a handsome folio volume. That event took place in London, which then, as now, was the centre of the publishing trade in England.

3

This simple life story, with its two vital epicentres, has been often told. Here we shall recount it again with the documentary foundation, manuscript and print, always in view, to chasten speculative elaboration or romantic indulgence. Our point of departure is Stratford town and Stratford church.

Taking its source from a spring called Avon Well in the village of Naseby in Northamptonshire, the River Avon flows westward into Warwickshire, past churches, villages, and hamlets—past Guy's Cliff, associated with the legendary earl; past Warwick, fortress of the Kingmaker, with its proud castle tower and turreted walls; past Fulbrook fields (here the waters run deep) and Charlecote, seat of the Lucys and setting for the myth of Shakespeare the Deerslayer—until, broadening, the stream reaches Stratford-upon-Avon.[1] Here the great road, or *stræt*, leading north from London to Henley-in-Arden, provided a passage, or *ford*, over the *afon*, which in Welsh signifies *river*. At this point the banks of the Avon gently ascend to a flat ground of light gravel, where early settlers built timber-frame cottages with stone foundations and thatched roofs. Southward lay the region known as Feldon, its fields ripe for pasturage, and (so the historian-cartographer John Speed remarked) 'tractable to be stirred for corn'. Beyond this stretch of flat open country, across the Vale of the Red Horse, rose the gently rolling Cotswold Hills. To the north the Forest of Arden, thick with undergrowth, sheltered abundant deer and other small game. The river, dividing champaign from woodland, supplied fresh water and a means of communication.

The settlement has a venerable history. Shortly after Christianity penetrated to the Kingdom of Mercia, we hear of a monastery established at *Stretforde*; much later, in Tudor times, local tradition held that this cloister was built where now stands the collegiate church of the Holy Trinity. In the Domesday Book, Stratford figures as an insignificant manor belonging to the pious Wulfstan, Bishop of Worcester, and extending over fourteen and a half hides—under two thousand acres—with a church and mill. For several centuries the Bishop's successors remained lords of the manor. Later, when the agricultural labourers became free tenants paying fixed money rents for their holdings under a system known as burgage tenure, individual and communal enterprise was stimulated, and Stratford developed into a thriving agricultural market-place.

'There are (as I take it)', observed the Elizabethan topographer William Harrison in his *Description of England*, 'few great towns in England, that have not their weekly markets, one or more granted from the prince, in which all manner of provision for household is to be bought and sold, for ease and benefit of the country round about.'[2] Richard I was the prince who, in the twelfth century, allowed Stratford a weekly market to be kept on Thursdays. It may well have been first held at Rother Market (*rother*, from the Anglo-Saxon, means *cattle*; the thoroughfare still bears that name), and perhaps afterwards at the place where Bridge Street, Henley Street, and High Street converge. By Shakespeare's day the ancient stone high cross at this intersection had yielded to a covered wooden Market House, open below, with four pillars supporting an upper storey, and a cupola with clock on top. In 1730 the clock was replaced; the town fathers had the whole house taken down in 1821. Today the spot where it stood is a green patch on a traffic roundabout which the visitor may glimpse, through the swirl of modern motor traffic, from the Stratford Information Office on the site where the poet's daughter Judith once lived in a house called The Cage.* The stone foundation of the original market-cross is preserved, unmarked, in the centre of the gravel path that divides the tranquil Birthplace garden. Tradesmen still display all kinds of wares every Friday in the market held at Rother Market, but the cattle market is now held on Tuesdays near the railway station.

In the thirteenth century the bishops of Worcester procured royal charters for a series of fairs. The first ran for the three days of the eve, feast, and morrow of the Holy Trinity, the festival of the parish church's dedication, a holiday which attracted many folk from neighbouring villages. A second fair (beginning on the eve of the Exaltation of the Cross) followed, and a third at Ascensiontide. The fourth, proclaimed in 1309, lasted a full sixteen days. These events wonderfully encouraged medieval commerce. Farmers mar-

---

* Until recently it housed a Wimpy restaurant.

keted their produce and livestock, while artisans—weavers, dyers, carpenters, shoemakers, and the like, of whom the town now had a full complement—displayed their wares. Not only for the benefit of locals. Travellers on their way to the cloth-making town of Coventry, famous for its cap industry, or the port of Bristol, second only to London, or industrial Birmingham might stop for refreshment at the Bear or Swan, and buy and sell merchandise at Stratford fairs.

So the town flourished. By the King's letters patent in the seventh year of Edward VI's reign, it became an independent township; a corporation possessed of a common seal and consisting of a bailiff and a council of fourteen burgesses and fourteen aldermen. Young men from the nearby villages, not content with their hereditary station as husbandmen, migrated there to learn a trade and improve their lot. The poet's father was one of these. In the sixteenth century, after the establishment of a great theatrical industry in London, the leading acting companies included Stratford in their provincial tours. The Queen's men and the Earl of Worcester's men were the first to come; they played in the Gild Hall in the summer of 1569, when John Shakespeare presided as bailiff. It is true that Stratford remained outside the mainstream of national politics, and to this day it still lies off the beaten track for the rail traveller, who must change trains at Leamington Spa; but in Tudor times the town was not, as some historians have alleged, a torpid backwater.* It was a pretty place, leafy with elms—almost a thousand of them on corporation property alone, according to a 1582 survey.

In the reign of Henry VIII, John Leland, Keeper of the King's libraries, made an antiquarian perambulation of England, to seek out the literary remains of ancient writers in monasteries and colleges. Around 1540 Leland set foot in Stratford. 'It hath 2 or 3 very large streets, beside back lanes', he noted. 'One of the principal streets leadeth from east to west, another from south to north. . . . The town is reasonably well builded of timber.'[3] (Devastating fires

---

* Rail service, limited on weekdays, is now altogether unavailable on Sundays. 'It takes longer in 1976 to get to Stratford by train than before the Second World War. . . . British rail have no apologies. "Stratford is in the wrong place—off the main line. But there's a marvellous service to Coventry." ' (*The Sunday Times Magazine,* 27 June 1976, p. 34.)

1. South-east prospect of Stratford-upon-Avon, 1746.

have long since destroyed the timbered houses Leland saw, but the medieval street grid of the old town survives intact: three arteries running parallel to the river are intersected by another three at right angles.) Leland remarks on the 'great fair' kept once each year on Holyrood Day, 14 September. In the 'right goodly chapel' in Church Street he paused to admire the Dance of Death 'curiously painted' on the walls—Reformation not having yet defaced such superstitious images.

This chapel belonged to the religious and fraternal Gild of the Holy Cross. The society's rapid growth after being formed in the thirteenth century testifies to the material prosperity of Stratford. Enriched by donations from its brethren and sisters, the Gild employed four priests to say masses in the chapel; it relieved the wants of indigent members, and supported the aged in neighbouring alms-houses. Early in the fifteenth century a flurry of Gild construction produced, among other projects, a schoolhouse near the chapel. Thus was initiated the system of free grammar-school tuition in Stratford, from which in the next century the young Shakespeare would receive the sum of his formal education. By then administration of the school had passed into the hands of the corporation, for the Gild suffered the common fate of Catholic foundations after the Acts of Suppression: lands were seized, revenues confiscated, the Gild itself dissolved,

The Gild Chapel that so impressed Leland had been improved and beautified in the reign of Henry VII by one of Stratford's most successful sons, Sir Hugh Clopton. Actually he was not born there but a mile away, at Clopton manor-house; still he always regarded Stratford as his native town. A younger brother, Clopton went off to London to seek his fortune. There, as a mercer, he amassed great wealth, and was elected alderman, sheriff, and finally in 1491 (the year he was knighted) Lord Mayor. Eventually Clopton took possession of the ancestral mansion and also—perhaps with even greater satisfaction—of his elder brother's inheritance. 'Having never wife nor children', this self-made man determined to become a great benefactor of Stratford. In addition to rebuilding the chapel, he replaced the inadequate wooden bridge, perilous at times of flood, with another, 'great and sumptuous' (in Leland's phrase). Walled on both sides, with a long stone causeway at the west end, it consists of fourteen massive segmental-pointed arches. On one of the piers was appropriately placed a stone pillar emblazoned with the arms of the city of London and the Clopton family, and beneath it this inscription: 'Sir Hugh Clopton, Knight, Lord Mayor of London, built this bridge, at his own proper expense, in the reign of King Henry the Seventh.' During the Civil War, parliamentary forces tore down one of the arches, but, restored, the bridge stands to this day, a masterpiece of Tudor engineering. The London traveller bound for Stratford by way of High Wycombe and Oxford must still cross Clopton Bridge to enter the town; so Shakespeare did almost four hundred years ago.

Sir Hugh also built for himself another fine structure, 'a pretty house of brick and timber' by the north side of the Gild Chapel. According to Leland, who so describes it,[4] Clopton in his latter days lived in this house and died there; but the King's antiquary is wrong. Clopton granted a life-interest in the dwelling to one Roger Pagett, and in his will, drawn up the day before his death in London, he bequeathed the 'great house' to his great-nephew William Clopton. At the end of the sixteenth century, when it came into the possession of another son of Stratford who had triumphed in the capital, the house was long since known as New Place.

A few years after Shakespeare's birth, William Camden, later to become the celebrated headmaster of Westminster School, toured England in Leland's footsteps, gathering material for his great topographical and antiquarian survey, *Britannia*, which he composed in choice Elizabethan Latin. Following the Avon's course, Camden arrived in Stratford, by way of Warwick and Charlecote. It made a favourable impression on him, this 'handsome small market town, which owes all of its consequence to two natives of it'. One of these great benefactors was the builder of Clopton Bridge; the other, John de Stratford. The latter figures briefly in Marlowe's *Edward II* as the implacable Bishop of Winchester who demands—and obtains— Edward's crown, and delivers it to the adulterous Queen Isabella and her paramour Young Mortimer. In the next reign John was elevated to the see of Canterbury; ultimately, in 1330, he became Lord Chancellor, an office he thrice held. When he was not preoccupied with strife of state, John de Stratford's mellower thoughts would turn to the town of his birth, and to the parish church which, as a young man, he had served as rector. This he rebuilt for the greater glory of God, and, in so doing, gave it much of the aspect it holds for the modern pilgrim. His remains however lie in an alabaster tomb in the south choir aisle of Canterbury Cathedral, near the high altar.

Holy Trinity Church, built over a span of centuries, stands hard by the Avon's banks at the southern edge of Stratford, in the neighbourhood known as Old Town.[5] A long avenue of lime trees leads to the north entrance of the church. They have stood there for centuries, their boughs 'so intermingled as to produce a solemn, yet grateful shade'; so, in 1814, wrote the author of *The Beauties of England and Wales*. The splendid edifice—almost 200 feet long by 70 wide—finds its reflection in the river's placid waters. The beauty of Holy Trinity, as well as its romantic situation, has driven beholders to strange fits of doggerel:

> Church of the Holy Cross, to God and Glory,
> Mellowed by age and just a trifle hoary;
> Christians and Clergy, blessed with light Divine,
> Still love to linger at this Sacred Shrine.[6]

In design the church is cruciform: chancel and nave, running east and west, are crossed by the north and south transepts. The square tower at their point of intersection is surmounted by a lofty octagonal stone steeple—a late improvement, for the spire that Shakespeare knew was a smaller timber one. In the eighteenth century the parishioners decided that this steeple was too mean and diminutive, and anyway it was always wanting repair; so they hired an architect to replace it with another of Warwick hewn stone.

On either side of the avenue of lime trees, Stratford folk lie buried. Here the poet's father and mother were laid to rest, as was his daughter Judith. Within the church itself are interred the more illustrious dead of Stratford, and some have imposing monuments. One of these belongs to Sir Hugh Clopton, despite the fact that he lies in London, in the parish church of St. Margaret, Lothbury. Although Jonson eulogized Shakespeare as a monument without a tomb, he was not for that reason denied his stone memorial, complete with effigy, in the north wall of the chancel. It is today the principal attraction for visitors. In medieval times the church's chief glory was the great rood loft, carved with images, and painted red and gold. It has long since disappeared—part of the toll Reformation took of the church—along with a local master's ceiling paintings that depicted St. George and the Dragon, the Last Judgement, and the history of the Holy Cross.

The church's harmonious interior proportions have, however, survived vicissitudes (the chancel fell into decay and was boarded up; two years after Shakespeare's burial there, it was declared 'ruinous'). Much of the effect we owe to John de Stratford. Parts of the ancient fabric—transepts and portions of the nave and tower—date back to the early thirteenth century, but he altered and added a good deal. The north aisle he widened, and installed in it a chapel in honour of the Holy Virgin, which after his time was wholly usurped by tombs and monuments of the Cloptons; so it is called Clopton Chapel. John also rebuilt the south aisle, and placed there a chapel to St. Thomas à Becket. In 1331 he founded a chantry of this chapel, and endowed in perpetuity five priests to chant masses at the altar for himself, his family, the Kings of England, and the Bishops of Worcester. John's nephew, Ralph de Stratford, in 1351 built for the habitation of these priests a house of square stone adjoining the western side of the churchyard. This structure came to be styled the College of Stratford, after the chapter, or college, of priests who dwelt there under a warden and served the church. That is why Holy Trinity is described as a collegiate church.

In the fifteenth century the Dean of Lichfield provided endowment for four singing boys, who were accommodated in a steep-gabled house of two or three storeys approached by steps from the chancel, through a doorway just below the Shakespeare monument. Gradually this dwelling fell into decay, and in time it became a charnel-house. An immense quantity of bones accumulated there, we learn from a late-seventeenth-century report; enough to load a great number of wagons.[7] It was already a charnel-house in Shakespeare's day. Perhaps he had it in mind when Juliet protests to Friar Lawrence,

> chain me with roaring bears,
> Or hide me nightly in a charnel house,
> O'er-cover'd quite with dead men's rattling bones,
> With reeky shanks and yellow chapless skulls.

The bone-house was demolished in 1799, but the doorway to it, now walled up, still stands.

Others who followed John de Stratford further beautified the church. Most important of these is Dr. Thomas Balshall, warden of the College in Edward IV's reign. He reconstructed the chancel from the ground up, installing the five bays on either side with their large uniform windows with cusped and crenellated transoms; also the dividing buttresses floridly ornamented in late Gothic style with angels, dragons, and grotesques. To one of Balshall's master masons we probably also owe the baptismal font. Only the shattered bowl today survives, on its new pedestal near to Shakespeare's grave, for it was in time superseded by a new font of late Renaissance design.* The original was discarded, and turned up long afterwards in the garden of a parish clerk, one Thomas Paine, who died in 1747. He was using it as a water-cistern. This is the font in which William Shakespeare and his brothers and sisters were christened.[8]

* The relic was formerly kept at the back of the nave.

A record of the baptisms was entered in the parish register, which also recorded burials and weddings. Such registers had been first instituted in 1538, when the Vicar General, Thomas Cromwell, put forth an edict for the keeping of these essential data in each parish of England. They were not, however, always regularly maintained. The order was renewed in 1547, when Edward VI was king, and some years later Queen Elizabeth enjoined every parish priest to subscribe to this oath: 'I shall keep the register book according to the Queen's Majesty's injunction.' The oldest volume of the Stratford registers—a large folio bound in brown leather, with brass corner pieces embellished with the Tudor rose—commences in March 1558, the first year of Elizabeth's reign. However, the entry for William Shakespeare's christening, as well as all the others up to mid-September 1600, is not the original but an early transcript made in the days of Richard Byfield, who became vicar of Stratford in 1597, just after the promulgation of a new provincial constitution. The Archbishop of Canterbury, acting administratively for the Crown, now required each parish to procure parchment register books at its own expense, and to transfer into them (from the paper books formerly in use) the names of those baptized, married, or buried during the reign of Elizabeth; moreover, the vicar and church-wardens were to examine and certify each page of these records. This explains why the extant registers for Stratford begin in 1558, and why the year 1600 is inscribed on the cover of the first volume.[9] Surely the most precious of such local records, they were kept on view in Holy Trinity Church until September 1966, when the Revd. T. Bland placed them for safekeeping in the Records Office a few steps down from Shakespeare's Birthplace.

These registers chronicle the most crucial events—birth, marriage, death—in the family of John Shakespeare and his descendants. Normally one might expect such records, limited to the bare citation of names and dates, to be straightforward enough, but a special problem bedevilled the earliest authorities who consulted the parish books. For a second John Shakespeare, contemporary with ours, has left his trail in the registers, as well as in other Stratford documents. This Shakespeare was a corviser, or shoemaker, from nearby Warwick who succeeded to the family business when his brother drowned in the Avon. The shoemaker married at least twice, and his offspring—Ursula, Humphrey, and Philip—duly enter the baptismal register on 11 March 1589, 24 May 1590, and 21 September 1591, respectively. Having filled some minor corporation posts and become Master of his gild, he seems to have left Stratford for good by the mid-nineties. A John Shakespeare was buried in St. Mary's in Warwick on 7 February 1624. Actually the coincidence, while curious, need not startle us, for Shakespeares, their names spelt with exotic variety, were thick on the ground in Warwickshire and the adjoining counties. (As early as 1248 a William Sakspere of Clopton in Gloucestershire was hanged for robbery; in June 1487 the Register of Merton College, Oxford, refers to a Fellow, Hugh Sawnders, whose name had been changed from *Shakspere* because it was reputed so commonplace ('Hugo Sawnder alias dictus Shakspere, sed mutatum est istud nomen eius, quia vile reputatum est').)[10] The confusions caused by the two John Shakespeares—the poet's energetic father credited with three wives and eleven children—were successfully sorted out by the close of the eighteenth century through the industry of Edmond Malone, greatest of Shakespeare scholars.

The career of John Shakespeare is amply and reliably documented. To him and to his antecedents we now turn.

❧[2]❧

The Shakespeares:
From Snitterfield to Stratford

Three and a half miles north-east of Stratford, and just north of the old turnpike road leading from the market-town to Warwick, sits, perched on a hill, the quiet little village of Snitterfield. Here Shakespeare's grandfather Richard settled some time before 1529. In those days, as now, a single structure dominated the village: the handsome, big parish church of St. James the Great with its long nave and imposing west tower. The clerestory then was new, as was the slate roof fetched (some say) from Fulbrook Castle. Within are Renaissance stalls elaborately carved with vines, and an octagonal baptismal font, still in use, dating from the fourteenth century; in all likelihood the poet's father was christened there—we do not have registers for christenings as early as that. At Hill Field the old mill by the stream has long since disappeared, and few evidences remain of the timber-frame cottages with timber-frame barns and timbered pigeon-houses. Snitterfield is situated in pleasantly rolling countryside, with scattered woodland, thickets of small trees and shrubs, heath, and yellow-blossoming gorse. Here, in several manors, Richard Shakespeare rented land, tilled the rich soil, and pastured his livestock.[1]

The court and manorial records of the area chronicle the everyday vexations and (less frequently) rewards of a farmer's life. Presumably Richard mended his hedges when ordered in 1538 to do so. A jury charged him with overburdening the common with his cattle. He paid fines for neglecting to yoke or ring his swine, and for letting his livestock run loose on the meadows—that was in 1560, when every tenant was ordered to 'make his hedges and ditches betwixt the end of the lane of Richard Shakespere and the hedge called Dawkins' hedge.' When he could not get by with an acceptable excuse, as in 1529 (our first record of him), he paid his twopence fine rather than attend the manor court held twice yearly at Warwick, a six-miles' journey from Snitterfield. A prosperous alderman of the Stratford Gild, the vintner and clothier Thomas Atwood *alias* Taylor, bequeathed Richard the team of four oxen already in his keeping. In January 1560 Richard Shakyspere—likely enough the poet's grandfather—served as one of the jury of twelve good men and true in an inquisition made by Thomas Lucy at Warwick into the estates of Sir Robert Throckmorton; Richard was no country bumpkin.[2] He helped to appraise the goods of a deceased vicar, as well as of other villagers. (This was the office of friends and good neighbours, 'persons two at the least, to whom the person dying was indebted'; so the statutes of the realm decreed, to which Henry Swinburne, the supreme Elizabethan authority on testaments, adds, 'it is not sufficient to make an inventory, containing all and singular the goods of the deceased, unless the same be particularly valued and praised [i.e. appraised] by some honest and skilful persons, to be the just value thereof in their judgements and consciences. . . .'[3]) When Richard died, before 10 February 1561, his own goods were valued at £38.17s.—almost £5 more than the vicar's. Richard Shakespeare's house abutted on the High Street, probably the high road to Warwick, and had land that stretched down to the brook which flows through Snitterfield and on down to the Avon. This property he rented from Robert Arden of Wilmcote. Arden had a daughter, Mary, who would marry John Shakespeare.

Richard had at least two sons. A Thomas Shakespeare, who paid the largest rent (£4) of all the tenants who farmed in the Hales manor in Snitterfield, may have been his issue, but proof is wanting. Henry Shakespeare, however, was certainly Richard's son. Like Thomas, he held land in the Hales manor, but he also farmed at Ingon in the nearby parish of Hampton Lucy, which lies on the left bank of the Avon and extends to the ridge dividing the fertile valley from the Forest of Arden; his brother John would also hold land in Ingon Meadow. Henry was something of a ne'er-do-well. He got into a fray with one Edward Cornwell (he became the second husband of the poet's Aunt Margaret), drew blood, and was fined, but did not show up in court to answer the charge. He was imprisoned for trespass; he incurred debts and failed to honour them. On one occasion Henry refused to pay his tithe—there was a quarrel between claimants—and for a time suffered excommunication. The authorities fined him for wearing a hat instead of a cap to church: maybe a principle was involved, for many, especially Puritans, resented the Statute of Caps, promulgated to encourage the depressed craft of cappers. He was also penalized for not labouring with teams to mend the Queen's highway, and 'for having a ditch between Red Hill and Burman in decay for want of repairing'. (These fields, still called Burman and Red Hill, may to this day be identified a short distance east of Snitterfield church, on the right-hand side of the road leading to Luscombe.) Once when he was in jail in the High Street for debt, his surety William Rounde marched over to Henry's house and appropriated two oxen which the latter had bought but characteristically not paid for. Yet when he died in his own house there was, a witness avouched, plenty of money in his coffers, corn and hay of 'a great value' in the barn, and a mare in the stable. This was the poet's Uncle Harry. In the parish church of Hampton Lucy (re-built in the early nineteenth century) he had two children baptized: Lettice in 1582 and James in 1585. Shakespeare as a boy likely enough crossed the fields to Ingon to visit his uncle and aunt and cousins. Little James died in 1589. Henry was buried in Snitterfield on 29 December 1596, and less than two months later 'Margret Sakspere, widow, being times the wife of Henry Shakspere', followed him to the grave.

Richard Shakespeare's other son John was another sort. Not content with raising crops and pasturing herds with his father in Snitterfield and his brother in Ingon, he migrated in mid-century to Stratford, where he became a glover and whittawer, or dresser of whitleather: soft white or light-coloured leather. In this craft he 'tawed' the hides of deer and horses, and also of goats and sheep and hounds (but not cattle or pigs), by imbuing the skins (after preparation) with a solution of alum—aluminium sulphate—and salt. He made and sold not only gloves but all manner of soft leather goods: belts, purses, aprons, and the like. (The dramatist recalls the glover in his shop in *The Merry Wives of Windsor*, when Mistress Quickly tries to place Master Slender—'Does he not wear a great round beard', she asks, 'like a glover's paring-knife?') It was a good trade to be in, protected against foreign competition by Act of Parliament. On market days and during fairs, the glovers commanded the most strategically located standing-place in the market square, at the Market Cross under the clock. The seventeenth-century gossip John Aubrey, celebrated for his *Brief Lives*, reports that John Shakespeare was a butcher, but this is unlikely; stringent regulations governing the wholesomeness of meat kept the two occupations separate.[4] Anyway there were local butchers—Ralph Cawdrey and Thomas Rogers—licensed by the council.

Although in those days the glovers had not yet formally organized themselves into a gild (that came about in 1606), they probably required initiates into the mystery to serve seven years as apprentices. John's entrance into the trade may have been facilitated by his father's connections. As we have seen, Richard knew Thomas Atwood, an alderman of the Gild before Stratford received its Charter. Maybe he was also acquainted with John Townsend of the Wold in Snitterfield. Townsend had a daughter Joan, who married a prominent Stratford citizen, Thomas Dickson *alias* Waterman, an alderman on the first town council, and host of the Swan Inn in Bridge Street. By trade this Dickson was a glover, and possibly the master under whom John Shakespeare served out his apprenticeship.

He enters the historical record ingloriously on 29 April 1552, when he paid a shilling fine for having amassed an unauthorized midden heap (*sterquinarium*) in Henley Street. On that occasion John was not the only offender penalized for failure to use the 'common muckhill' standing at the country end of the street, before the house of William Chambers the wheelwright; Humphrey Reynolds and Adrian Quiney were similarly fined that day. John Shakespeare's muck-hill (in the view of our foremost authority on the plague in Elizabethan England) has come to symbolize Tudor methods of sanitation.[5] Such filth spawned pestilence; at the same time, the stiff penalties imposed—equal to two days' pay for an artisan—show that the community worried about the wholesomeness of its lanes and gutters. The record has an additional interest, for it reveals that by the spring of 1552 John Shakespeare was residing as a tenant or householder in Henley Street. That must have been in the western part of the big double house; the wing which, in afterdays known as the Birthplace, has made of Stratford a secular shrine.

Soon John was acquiring more property. In 1556 he purchased from one George Turnor a freehold estate with garden and croft (*unum tenementum cum gardino et crofto*) in Greenhill Street, the road that would afterwards be called More Towns End. The same year he bought another house with adjacent garden in Henley Street from Edward West. This was to be the eastern wing, known to posterity as the Woolshop. At some time long afterwards—just when is not recorded—workmen joined together the two houses to form the present impressive structure, which gives the appearance of being a single half-timbered house of three gables. It was put up in the late fifteenth or early sixteenth century. Because of its associations, the house has not wanted fanciful appreciation. 'Shadows and weird noises are in the rafters, the wind is in the chimneys, crickets are on the hearth, fairies glisten in the light of the dying fire, through leaded windows shines the moon, without is the *to-whit, to-whoo* of the loved brown owl.'[6]

However this may be, the dwelling consists of a stone groundsill, or low foundation wall, upon which rests a sturdy oak superstructure. Wattle and daub fill in the spaces of the rectangles formed by the beams. In the centre a massive chimney stack consolidated the structure, which was covered by a timber roof—in time to come this would be replaced with tile. Late in the sixteenth century a rear wing of timber and plaster, similar to the rest, was added; it projects into the pleasant garden. John Shakespeare was still living in Henley Street in 1597, when for fifty shillings he sold a narrow strip of land —only a half-yard wide by twenty-eight yards in length—that ran along the west side of his property from Henley Street to the Gild Pits (as the royal highway was called) on the north. The purchaser, a draper named George Badger, intended, it seems likely, to put up

2. Exterior of the Birthplace, c. 1762.

a wall. Around the same time John parted with a 17-by-17-foot piece of his property on the east to Edward Willis of King's Norton, Worcestershire, who had a scheme to convert two small houses into an inn, which he would call The Bell. These conveyances show that for almost half a century of his life John Shakespeare resided in Henley Street.

Thus settled, he took for his bride Mary Arden, the prosperous farmer's daughter. The Ardens boasted one of the most venerable names in Warwickshire; Dugdale describes them as 'that most ancient and worthy family'. They had been 'lords of Warwick' before the Norman Conquest, and not many families in England could trace back their descent so far. Some Ardens had enormous wealth. In the Domesday Book, Turchillus de Eardine—Turchill of the Forest of Arden—held lands that filled over four columns; nobody else possessed so much. Our Ardens were more ordinary folk, affluent yeomen shading into minor gentry. The precise branch to which Robert Arden belonged remains obscure, despite intense genealogical zeal;[7] perhaps he was descended from some younger son of the Ardens of Park Hall, which is in Castle Bromwich in the parish of

Aston, not far from Birmingham. His grandfather may have been Robert Ardern, a bailiff of Snitterfield around the middle of the fifteenth century, and he was certainly the son of Thomas Ardern of Wilmcote. This hamlet lies in Aston Cantlow parish, stretching across the valley of the Alne, bounded on the east by the low, partly wooded hills dividing it from the Avon. This Thomas bought lands and a house in Snitterfield, and passed them on to his son. How extensive Robert Arden's Snitterfield holdings were we cannot say, but they included two farmhouses, one of which he let to Richard Shakespeare, and maybe a hundred or more acres of land.

When, shortly after 21 April 1548, Arden married Agnes Hill, *née* Webbe, the widow of a substantial farmer of Bearley grange, he was already well along in years, and had by previous marriage—or marriages—eight daughters. They must have been presentable young women, for at least six found husbands, and two of them married twice. Arden's new wife brought two sons and two daughters from her previous match, so it was a large family. The ménage lived in Wilmcote. Where precisely is not known; late in the eighteenth century, however, John Jordan, autodidact and self-appointed repository of Shakespearian lore, identified a timber-frame house in Featherbed Lane as Mary Arden's House, and by this name it is still visited by tourists. Jordan is never to be taken on faith ('one of those humble geniuses', a contemporary charitably sized him up, 'to whom a little learning, if not a dangerous thing, proved almost useless'), but Mary must have grown up, if not in these, in very similar surroundings. Situated near the village green, on the north side of the road to Stratford, the dwelling is a handsome big sixteenth-century farmhouse, two-storeyed, with stone foundation and two stone hearths on each floor (there is a large fireplace in the kitchen), inglenook in the sitting-room corner, roughly hewn oak beams for the open-timbered ceilings, and gabled dormers to light the upper storey.[8] Lately, deathwatch and furniture beetle have seriously threatened the original interior timberwork, prompting the ever-watchful guardians to commission preservative and remedial measures.

A number of years—perhaps a decade or more—must have separated John and Mary: she was the youngest of numerous siblings, he an elder son; he would live to be past seventy, and she would outlast him by seven years. Mary must have seemed a desirable match; probably her father's favourite, and practically an heiress, although (it seems) she could neither read nor write, signing documents with her mark.

In the autumn of 1556 Robert Arden lay dying. By his will made on 24 November, when he was sick in body but 'good and perfect of remembrance', he bequeathed his soul 'to Almighty God and to our blessed Lady Saint Mary and to all the holy company of heaven' —a Catholic formulation, as one would expect in a testament drawn up during Catholic Mary's reign. His wife, Robert looked after prudentially, setting conditions on his bequest of ten marks (£6.13s.4d.). But his youngest daughter inspired fonder thoughts; Arden left her, besides the customary ten marks, all of his most valuable possession: the estate in Wilmcote, called Asbyes, 'and the crop upon the ground sown and tilled as it is'.

Despite her youth, Mary was named one of the two executors, so she was present the next month for the inventory of goods and movables, which testifies to the comfortable circumstances of the deceased. His belongings included full eleven of the painted cloths in those days used in place of more costly tapestries for wall decorations; on broad strips of canvas were rudely painted in tempera scenes Biblical or mythological, with appropriately sententious mottoes beneath. (Shakespeare remembered the mottoes in *The Rape of Lucrece*: 'Who fears a sentence or an old man's saw / Shall by a painted cloth be kept in awe.') Arden's house boasted two such cloths in the hall, five in the great adjoining chamber, and four more scattered through the upstairs bedrooms. Also cupboards and oak furniture (including a little table with shelves), and enough bed linen, as well as copper pots and brass pans, a chafing dish, small handmill, and kneading trough. The inventory included too the farmer's tools and agricultural gear, a barn filled with wheat and barley, store of livestock—oxen, bullocks, colts, swine, and weaning calves—as well as bees and poultry, wood in the yard, and bacon in the roof. The Ardens had sufficient.

His body Robert asked to have buried in the churchyard at Aston Cantlow. The widow kept on in Wilmcote (apparently, as Arden hoped, she did not make trouble because of her small inheritance, but suffered his daughter Alice to live quietly with her). In 1580, 'aged and impotent' (so she described herself), she died, and was buried in the churchyard. Some time between November 1556, when Mary Arden's father drew up his will, and September 1558, when her first daughter was born, she married John Shakespeare. Very likely the ceremony took place at Aston Cantlow, in the parish church of St. John the Baptist. The registers there commence only later, and probably for that reason there is no record of John Shakespeare's marriage.

[3]

Offspring

The Shakespeares proved fruitful; so the parish registers over a period of twenty years or so, from 1558 to 1580, testify. To be sure, they chronicle burials as well as christenings, but during these decades births in the family outnumber deaths. The Shakespeares' firstborn was christened after the Catholic fashion, in Latin and with the anointing; for Mary still reigned. The rest—there were eight children in all—had Anglican baptism.

John Shakespeare's first offspring was a daughter, Joan, christened (the registers inform us) on 15 September 1558. The curate who officiated was Roger Dyos. The next year, with a new sovereign on the throne, Dyos's Romanist persuasion became unpalatable, and since he volunteered neither to resign nor to die—the usual grounds for replacement—the corporation ousted him by the simple expedient of withholding his stipend. Dyos retired to Little Bedwyn in Wiltshire, and for seventeen years nursed his grievances. Then, in 1576, he brought suit against the bailiff of Stratford for his 'yearly annuity', which he recovered with damages. Meanwhile the town managed for a time without a pastor—visiting preachers must have filled the gap—until, in January 1561, a new vicar was installed. Master John Bretchgirdle, who came from Witton, Northwich, was an M.A. of Christ Church, Oxford, and held impeccable Church of England principles. He was unmarried—a sister, perhaps two sisters, kept house for him—and bookish; his library (valued at about half his estate) included Tyndale's *New Testament in English*, Aesop, Sallust, Vergil, Horace, two works of Erasmus, a Latin-English dic-

23

tionary, and *The Acts of the Apostles, translated into English metre . . . by Christopher Tye, . . . with notes to each chapter, to sing and also to play upon the lute, very necessary for students after their study, to file their wits, and also for all Christians that cannot sing, to read the good and Godly stories of the lives of Christ his Apostles.*[1] Master Bretchgirdle performed the christening of the Shakespeares' second child, Margaret, on 2 December 1562, and witnessed her burial a few months later. On 26 April 1564, 'discreetly, and warily' (as the Prayer Book enjoins) he baptized William Shakespeare. The entry in the parish register reads 'Gulielmus, filius Johannes Shakspere'. The next spring the vicar died, leaving his dictionary to the scholars at Stratford grammar school, and was laid to rest in the parish church.

Thus we have the date of Shakespeare's baptism, but when was the poet born? Not a momentous question, perhaps, but a necessary one; for the biographer will wish to have, as his starting-point, the precise date of his hero's nativity. Traditionally, of course, we celebrate Shakespeare's birth on 23 April. That date is irresistibly attractive, coinciding as it does with the feast of St. George. Since 1222 his day has been celebrated as a national festival in Britain, and he has been patron saint of England since the time of John de Stratford. How fitting that St. George's Day should also mark the birthdate of the National Poet! We are almost tempted to forget that the wish is father of many a tradition.

This particular one goes back two centuries. In a note to his copy of Gerard Langbaine's *Account of the English Dramatic Poets* (1691), the eighteenth-century antiquary William Oldys is apparently the first to declare 23 April as Shakespeare's date of birth, although Oldys has the year wrong (1563). His contemporary Joseph Greene, curate of Stratford and master of the grammar school there, *via* James West passed along to the great Shakespearian scholar George Steevens an extract from the parish register with the note 'Born April 23, 1564'. Steevens adopted this date in his 1773 *Shakespeare*, and he has been followed by editors and biographers ever since.

But what is the evidence? We have the christening date. In Victorian times the learned Halliwell (later Halliwell-Phillipps) re-

3. William Shakespeare christened, 26 April 1564.

marked in passing that three days often elapsed between birth and baptism. This casual suggestion hardens into positive assertion in Sir Sidney Lee's *Life of William Shakespeare*, for long regarded as standard: '. . . it was a common practice at the time', Lee says, 'to baptise a child three days after birth.'[2] Actually no evidence demonstrates that such a customary interval ever obtained. The Prayer Book of 1559 offers sounder guidance. It instructs parents not to postpone christening beyond the first Sunday or Holy Day following birth, 'unless upon a great and reasonable cause declared to the curate, and by him approved'. In the latter weeks of April 1564, Sundays fell on the 16th, 23rd, and 30th, and festivals were kept on Wednesday the 19th (for Alphege, Archbishop and Martyr of blessed memory) and on Tuesday the 25th (St. Mark the Evangelist's Day); these in addition to St. George's feast. So, if Shakespeare was born on the 23rd, he should, according to the Prayer Book, have been baptized by the 25th. But perhaps superstition intervened—people considered St. Mark's Day unlucky. 'Black Crosses', it was called; the crosses and altars were almost to Shakespeare's day hung with black, and (some reported) the spectral company of those destined to die that year stalked the churchyard. Observing that Shakespeare's granddaughter Elizabeth Hall married on 22 April, De Quincey wondered whether she chose that day in honour of her famous relation. On the tablet in the poet's monument in Stratford Church, the inscription reads, *'obiit anno . . . ætatis 53'*. As he died on 23 April 1616, these words seemingly imply that his birth took place no earlier than 24 April 1563, or later than 23 April 1564; if not, Shakespeare would have expired in his fifty-second or fifty-fourth year. But this assumes that the anonymous author of the epitaph had in mind a current rather than a completed year, and that he regarded a new year as commencing with the anniversary of birth (the present legal convention) rather than with the first moment of life, if that was known. In fact we do not know what he thought, although both assumptions are reasonable enough. What we can reasonably infer is that Shakespeare was born on either the 21st, 22nd, or 23rd—Friday, Saturday, or Sunday—of April 1564. As well to celebrate his birthday on the 23rd as on either of the others.[3]

That summer the plague struck Stratford. In the burial register, alongside the entry on 11 July for Oliver Gunne, an apprentice, appears the ominous phrase, *'hic incepit pestis'*. We associate pestilence in that period mainly with the capital, with its concentrated population, huddled dwellings, and narrow back lanes; but travellers carried the bacillus into the purer air of pleasant market-towns like Stratford. When in the eighteenth century Malone studied the burial register for the latter half of 1564, he calculated that the plague had carried off more than two hundred souls—from one-sixth to one-seventh of the entire population. It is a fair estimate: the register lists 22 interments between 1 January and 20 July 1564, and then the figure leaps up to 237 for the rest of the year.[4] These statistics of course include deaths from all causes.

'Let us be thankful that "this sweetest child of Fancy" did not perish while he yet lay in the cradle . . . ,' exclaimed Malone. 'Fortunately for mankind it [the plague] did not reach the house in which the infant Shakspeare lay; for not one of that name appears in the dead list.—May we suppose, that, like Horace, he lay secure and fearless in the midst of contagion and death, protected by the Muses to whom his future life was to be devoted. . . .'[5] Such rhetorical extravagance is unusual for Malone, but one can scarcely overestimate the danger to which the infant was exposed. In plague time the bell tolled most often for the very young and enfeebled old. Richard Symons, the town clerk, buried two sons and a daughter; in Henley Street, where the Shakespeares lived, Roger Green lost four children. In August the council held an emergency session. To avoid contagion they sat in sunshine in the chapel garden, fragrant with pears and apples, rather than in the close confines of the Gild Hall, and discussed the organization of relief for the victims of pestilence. John Shakespeare attended; he was then a burgess. By December, with the coming of cold weather, the plague abated.

On 13 October 1566 the Shakespeares' second son, Gilbert, was baptized at Holy Trinity. He may have been named for Gilbert Bradley, who lived a few doors down in Henley Street, and was, like John, a glover and a member of the corporation—Bradley had become a burgess in 1565. Trade and municipal government: Gilbert Shakespeare was born into impeccably bourgeois circumstances, and his life would follow a middle-class pattern. In that respect, if no other, he resembled his brother William, who became not only a poet but also successful as the world measures success. In 1597 one 'Gilbert Shackspere' is described as a haberdasher of St. Bride's. That year, with a shoemaker from the same parish, he stood bail in Queen's Bench for £19, for William Sampson, a clock-maker of Stratford. St. Bride's is in London, but Gilbert lived in Stratford as well.[6] He was there on 1 May 1602, when he took delivery of a conveyance of land in Old Stratford on behalf of his brother William.

In November 1609 Gilbert Shakespeare was summoned to appear in the Court of Requests with Peter Ruswell, Richard Mytton, and others. What prompted the action we do not know, but feelings ran high, for when Elionor Varney, a twenty-one-year-old Stratford serving girl, presented Ruswell with the subpoena, he 'did violently snatch from her the said writ and refused to re-deliver it unto her, and delivered his staff he then had in his hand to a stander-by who therewith did assault and beat this deponent out of the house'.[7] This Ruswell (or Roswell) is mentioned along with Mytton in the only extant letter addressed to William Shakespeare:[8] we are dealing with a small town, and a limited circle of neighbours and acquaintants.

The next year, on 5 March, 'Gilbart Shakesper' witnessed a leasing of property in Bridge Street, signing his name in a fair Italian hand. Gilbert died in his forty-fifth year. On 3 February 1612 the Stratford register records the burial of 'Gilbertus Shakspeare, adolescens'. The term *adolescens* has occasioned puzzlement, but probably means 'single', for *adolocentulus* and *adolocentula* appear more than once in the registers to describe bachelors and spinsters.[9]

In April 1569 the Shakespeares gained another daughter. She was christened Joan on the 15th; so apparently the first Joan had died, probably while still an infant, in 1559 or 1560, when burial entries are sparse in the register. Of the family's four daughters, only the second Joan survived childhood, and of the eight siblings, only she—

apart from William—took a spouse. Her husband was an obscure hatter, William Hart, and their marriage, some time before 1600, is not recorded in the register; perhaps he moved to Stratford after the wedding. In 1600, and also the next year, Hart was sued for debt. His principal accomplishment seems to have been the begetting of four children: William (1600-39), Mary (1603-7), Thomas (1605-61), and Michael (1608-18). The hatter was buried on 17 April 1616, a week before his brother-in-law the dramatist. Shakespeare looked after his sister, a poor relation, in his will, for he bequeathed the widow (in addition to £20 and all his wearing apparel) a life-tenancy in the western unit of the double house in Henley Street, 'wherein she dwelleth', for the nominal yearly rent of one shilling. Joan Hart outlived her husband and her brother by thirty years. Eventually her grandson Thomas came into possession of the old homestead, both the eastern and western houses, by the terms of the testament of Lady Bernard, Shakespeare's granddaughter and last lineal descendant. The story of the Birthplace then becomes synonymous, for a long period, with that of the Harts.[10]

Of the Shakespeares' next two children we know almost nothing. One died young. The last daughter, Anne, was baptized on 28 September 1571, and buried before her eighth birthday, on 4 April 1579. The Chamberlain's Account shows that John Shakespeare paid a fee of 8*d.* 'for the bell and pall'. A son, Richard, was christened on 11 March 1574. All we know about him is the recently discovered fact that he was summoned before the Stratford ecclesiastical court on 1 July 1608 for an unspecified offence—was it Sabbath-breaking?—and fined a shilling, to be donated 'to the use of the poor of Stratford'.[11] Richard was buried on 4 February 1613.

When John Shakespeare stood at the font in Holy Trinity with his own infant for the last time on 3 May 1580, he was getting on— in just three years he would became a grandfather—and in reduced circumstances. The Shakespeares christened their last child Edmund, possibly (although the name is familiar enough) after his uncle, Edmund Lambert, to whom they had lately mortgaged part of an inheritance—a house and land in Wilmcote. (Aunt Joan, Lambert's wife, was probably godmother to the two daughters of that name.) More than anyone else in the family, Edmund seems to

4. Edmund Shakespeare buried, 31 December 1607.

have taken after his playwright brother; for, when he was old enough, he followed William to London, and became a professional actor, with which company is not recorded. In his profession he does not seem to have achieved any special eminence, but he was only twenty-seven when he died. In London he appears to have fathered an illegitimate child, buried in the cemetery of St. Giles Church without Cripplegate on 12 August 1607. The register cites 'Edward, son of Edward Shackspeere, player, base-born'; thus the christian name is wrong, but the parish clerk showed himself disinclined to make nice distinctions between similar-sounding appellations like Joan and Joanna or Orton and Horton—or Edmund and Edward.[12] Just a few months later, on New Year's Eve, the actor himself was interred in the church of St. Mary Overy (a contraction of 'over-the-river'), Southwark, 'with a forenoon knell of the great bell'. This was an expensive funeral, costing twenty shillings; burial in the church-yard could be had for only two shillings, and the lesser bell tolled for—at most—a shilling. Evidently somebody of means cared about Edmund; probably his prosperous brother William. St. Mary Overy (also called St. Saviour's) stood near London Bridge, a stone's throw from the Globe Theatre; in time to come, John Fletcher and Philip Massinger, principal dramatists for the King's men, would be buried there. Did Shakespeare arrange for a morning rather than (as customary) afternoon service so that his fellows could attend on that bitterly cold day, when children played and men and women promenaded on the frozen Thames?[13]

These were John Shakespeare's offspring—four sons and four daughters; seven ordinary mortals and one immortal—all christened and all but one buried in the collegiate church of the Holy Trinity at Stratford-upon-Avon.

[4]

Rise and Fall

When, in the winter of 1560-61, Richard Shakespeare died, his elder son was described as a husbandman (*agricola*) of Snitterfield in the letters of administration of the estate. Perhaps this is a mistake—there are many slips in the Worcester records—but we cannot be sure. At any rate he came into his father's land in Snitterfield; so we gather from a fine levied against John Shakespeare the following October for neglecting his hedges there. Shortly thereafter he parted with the copyhold, apparently to his brother-in-law Alexander Webbe, who came from Bearley to live in Snitterfield with his wife Margaret (*née* Arden) and their four small children.[1] Husbandry did not, evidently, much appeal to John.

More than once he is described in Stratford records as a glover: in 1556 Thomas Siche (or Such), a husbandman of Armscote in Worcestershire, unsuccessfully sued 'Johannem Shakyspere de Stretford . . . , glover' for £8; in 1587 'Johannes Shakspere . . . , glover', joined Thomas Jones, coppersmith, in standing bail for a local tinker indicted for felony;[2] other records, in 1573 and 1578, describe John as a 'whyttawer'. An administration bond, dated 10 October 1592, names 'John Shackspeare, glover', and bears his mark—a cross—and impressed ring seal.[3] Our only traditional anecdote about him, set down around 1657 by Thomas Plume, Archdeacon of Rochester, refers to John Shakespeare as a glover. Plume recalls that Sir John Mennis once saw the 'merry cheeked old man' in his shop; 'Will was a good honest fellow', the dramatist's father allowed, 'but

5. Thomas Plume's anecdote of John Shakespeare.

he durst have cracked a jest with him at any time.' Sir John Mennis was born in 1599, two years before John Shakespeare's death, so the two could scarcely have exchanged jests together. Maybe Plume has confused this Mennis with an older brother, Matthew, born around 1593 (although that is not too much help); or perhaps somebody told Sir John the anecdote. No matter; it shows that in the next century John Shakespeare was remembered as a glover, and associated even in old age with his shop.

That shop must have occupied what is today the eastern wing of the double house in Henley Street, the part known, from far back, as the Woolshop. But why wool, when John Shakespeare worked in leather? There is a Stratford tradition, first reported by Rowe in 1709, and confirmed by the ever-helpful Jordan, that John was 'a considerable Dealer in Wool'. Early in the nineteenth century, long after the house had become an inn, the landlord of the Swan and Maidenhead assured a visitor that 'when he re-laid the floors of the parlour, the remnants of wool, and the refuse of wool-combing, were found under the old flooring, imbedded with the earth of the foundation'.[4] The early biographers persistently refer to John Shakespeare as a wool-stapler, but only in the present century has documentary evidence of his subsidiary fleece dealings turned up: a suit in the Court of Common Pleas shows that, in Trinity Term 1599, John Shakespeare sued John Walford, clothier and thrice mayor of Marlborough in Wiltshire, for failing to pay on demand £21 for twenty-one tods of wool, a bargain agreed to thirty years earlier; a debt is a debt. Since a tod weighed twenty-eight pounds, the transaction was not trifling. How the action was resolved we cannot say, for, although its continuation is noted in the docket for the following term, the relevant plea roll has disappeared.[5] This discovery holds a salutary lesson. Tradition, often discredited and always to be regarded with scepticism, may yet conceal a kernel of truth.

On other occasions John Shakespeare sold the Stratford corporation 'a piece timber' for 3s. and brought an action against Henry Field, a tanner in Bridge Street, for eighteen quarters of barley—a lot of barley, for a quarter equalled eight bushels, or sixty-four gallons. Barley was used for what has been, until very recently, Stratford's principal industry, the manufacture of beer and ale. (Otherwise John seems to have got along amicably enough with Field; when the latter died, in the summer of 1592, John helped to appraise his goods. Field had a son Richard, with whom, as we shall see, the poet had dealings in the metropolis.) Probably John Shakespeare dealt in other agricultural commodities as well, storing them, along with his hides, in the Woolshop.

He also bought houses and let them. In October 1575 John paid Edmund and Emma Hall from Hallow in the parish of Grimley, near Worcester, £40 for two houses, with gardens and orchards, in Stratford (*duobus mesuagiis, duobus gardinis et duobus pomariis, cum pertinenciis, in Stretforde-super-Avon*). Some time before 1582 he let one of his houses to a William Burbage—was he related to the theatrical Burbages?—who later sought release from his bargain and the return of £7 he had put down. Arbiters instructed John to return the money, but Burbage had trouble collecting it (he was still trying a decade later), and perhaps never got his deposit back. John had acquired, from one of the powerful Cloptons, the lease of fourteen acres in Over Ingon meadow, in Hampton Lucy, where his brother Henry farmed. When Joyce and Alice, Mary Shakespeare's sisters, died, the Shakespeares inherited a ninth share in two houses and a hundred acres in Snitterfield.

Like others of his class John Shakespeare more than once entered the courtroom to sue and be sued. Sometimes considerable sums were at stake. In 1572 the Court of Common Pleas at Westminster awarded him the £50 he claimed a glover of Banbury owed him. The next year Henry Higford of Solihull, a former steward of Stratford, sued John for £30 in the same court. The latter did not appear. Five years later Higford sought on three separate occasions to recover the same debt in Common Pleas, and three times John failed to show on the appointed day. So it went.[6] These were mostly good years, the earlier ones anyway, for the son of the Snitterfield tenant farmer.

In 1553, just about the time that John Shakespeare settled in Stratford, the borough (as we have seen) received its Charter of Incorporation from the Crown. Now, vested with the Gild's property and authority, and possessing the power to make by-laws, a common council of burgesses and aldermen set about managing local affairs, although the Earl of Warwick, lord of the manor, retained the nomination of the vicar and the schoolmaster, and could, if he wished, veto the corporation's choice of a bailiff. Into this new Establishment the up-and-coming John Shakespeare was quickly absorbed, and by degrees he rose in the hierarchy. In September 1556 he was chosen one of the two ale-tasters, an office reserved for 'able persons and discreet'. By 'weekly and diligent search', these tasters saw that bakers made full-weight loaves, and that brewers vended wholesome ale and beer at the prescribed price in sealed pots. Offenders were summoned before the manorial court, or Leet, held twice yearly, and punished by fine, whipping, or humiliation in the stocks or pillory or on the cucking stool (a chair, sometimes in the form of an enclosed chamber pot, to which the fraudulent tradesman was tied, and which was then ducked in the river to the accompaniment of jeers from the onlooking townsfolk).[7] This was a regulated economy. The June after his appointment, John himself was fined for having missed, as taster, three sittings of the Court of Record. He had other concerns. That spring more importunate personal affairs presumably drew him from Stratford to Mary Arden's house in Wilmcote.

In the autumn of 1558 John was sworn one of the four constables: able-bodied citizens charged with preserving the peace. The Elizabethans made a standing joke of constables, their stupidity being literally proverbial—'You might be a constable for your wit', ran the familiar saw.* From this easy source of risibility the constable's son does not dissociate himself. Constable Dull in *Love's Labour's Lost* —'Most dull, honest Dull', who offers to dance or play on the tabor in the pageant of the Nine Worthies—is the slightest of preliminary sketches for the immortal Dogberry of *Much Ado About Nothing*. In his charge to Hugh Oatcake and neighbour Seacoal, stalwarts of the watch, the essential duties of the constable's office may be glimpsed through a haze of malapropism: to 'comprehend all vagrom men . . . to bid any man stand, in the Prince's name. . . . [to] make no noise in the streets; for for the watch to babble and to talk is most tolerable and not to be endured. . . . to call at all the ale-houses, and bid those that are drunk get them to bed. . . . If you meet a thief, you may suspect him, by virtue of your office, to be no true man; and, for such kind of men, the less you meddle or make with them, why, the more is for your honesty.' Despite the prudential character of Dogberry's advice, however, these guardians of law and order were entrusted with a serious enough responsibility during a volatile period in the town's history. They had to deprive angry men of their weapons, and hale into court quarrelsome types who had started bloody street brawls. This happened more than once during John Shakespeare's tenure. Constables were also responsible for fire-prevention measures in a vulnerable community.[8] As guardians of public morality, they assisted the churchwardens in bringing to book those who bowled, gamed, or tippled during times of divine service.

Other promotions quickly followed for John. The next year, in 1559, he was witnessing the minutes of the Leet as an affeeror, whose task it was to assess fines not prescribed by the statutes. Shortly afterwards—just when is uncertain—the town fathers elected him one of the fourteen principal burgesses, who met regularly at 'nine o'clock of the forenoon' in the Gild Hall.

From 1561 to 1563 the burgess served as one of the two chamberlains who administered borough property and revenues. John Taylor, a shearman of Sheep Street, was his senior colleague. At the year's end Richard Symons, the deputy steward, drew up the official

---

* Or, as a later variant (recorded in 1674) goes, 'All that are chosen constables for their wit, go not to heaven.'

6. John Shakespeare, affeeror, witnesses the Court Leet, 4 May 1561.

audit—a bare listing of receipts and outlays—and Taylor duly endorsed it on the back with his cross. John Shakespeare must have discharged this office well, for after the expiration of his term, he kept on as acting-chamberlain. The accounts presented in 1565 are described as 'made by John Shakspeyr and John Tayler'; those in 1566, as made by John Shakspeyr alone. Nobody in Stratford applied himself more devotedly to the responsibilities of local government. These were stirring years for the custodians of Stratford's purse-strings. The chapel was being Protestantized—workmen white-washed the frescoes and took down the rood-loft; they installed seats for the priest and his clerk, and perhaps a communion-table where formerly the altar stood. Vicar Bretchgirdle's house in Church Street underwent needed repair. A new classroom in the upper storey of the Gild Hall replaced the old schoolhouse in the quad. Meanwhile the pestilence came and spent itself. Through it all the acting-chamberlain kept the books, although he was slightly tardy in presenting his account for the plague year.

John Shakespeare, as we have seen, attended the session in the chapel garden when the council met to consider ways of relieving those rendered destitute by the plague. The garden stood a few yards from the door of Alderman William Bott. In May 1565 this Bott was 'expulsed' by the brethren after failing to appear before them to answer the charge of speaking abusively of the council and bailiff. On 4 July they elected John Shakespeare to replace Bott as one of the fourteen aldermen. Installation took place on 12 Sep-

7. John Shakespeare a candidate for bailiff, 4 September 1568.

tember. Henceforth he would be respectfully addressed as Master Shakespeare. At hall and in church—indeed on all public occasions—he was entitled to wear a black cloth gown faced with fur, as well as the aldermanic thumb ring ('When I was about thy years, Hal', Falstaff boasts at the Boar's Head, 'I was not an eagle's talon in the waist: I could have crept into any alderman's thumb-ring.').

Each September, on the first Wednesday, the corporation elected its bailiff by majority vote. In 1567 John Shakespeare was entered as one of the three nominees, and the next year the council chose him. He took office on 1 October. Master Shakespeare presided at the sessions (fortnightly, if required) of the Court of Record, which was a court of the Crown, and at council meetings. For his borough the bailiff was almoner, coroner, escheator, and clerk of the market. Together with one alderman annually elected to the office, he served the borough as justice of the peace. He issued warrants, dealt with cases of debt and violations of the by-laws, and carried on negotiations with the lord of the manor. Every Thursday night, when the market stalls had shut down, the bakers and brewers danced attendance on him, for it was the bailiff's prerogative to decree the weekly price of corn, and hence of bread and ale. Appropriate ceremony accompanied his exalted station. He and his deputy

wore their furred gowns in public, were escorted from their houses
to the Gild Hall by the serjeants bearing their maces before them.
They were waited on by these buff-uniformed officers once a week
to receive instructions, and accompanied by them through the market on Thursdays, through the fair on fair-days, about the parish-
bounds at Rogation, and to and from church on Sundays. At
church they sat with their wives in the front pew on the north side
of the nave. At sermons in the Gild chapel they had their seats of
honour. At plays in the Gild Hall they probably sat in the front
row.[9]

When, after his year in office and presiding at thirteen sessions of
the Court of Record, John stepped down, he was not again elected
bailiff by his brethren, although others served more than once (Robert Salisbury, a brewer, was thus honoured three times). The corporation, however, continued to take advantage of his experience.
He was in 1571 appointed Chief Alderman and deputy to the new
bailiff—Adrian Quiney, a mercer and neighbour in Henley Street.
The following January, in Hilary term, the two men rode to London
together on borough business, with permission from the aldermen
and burgesses to proceed 'according to their discretions'.

The public man who enjoyed such unqualified trust witnessed corporation minutes with his mark. Usually he employed as his sign a
gracefully drawn pair of compasses, the instrument used for measur-
ing and making ornamental cuttings in the backs of gloves. Once he
appended a different sign, which has been interpreted as a glover's
stitching clamp, or 'donkey'.[10] Legal documents (such as the inventory of Henry Field's goods and movables) he witnessed with a
cross. It is therefore natural to infer that he was illiterate. But is
this necessarily the case? Literate persons, as some authorities have
pointed out, preferred on occasion to use a mark—Adrian Quiney,
for example, whose mark or sign (an inverted upper-case Q) embel-
lishes the same page as John Shakespeare's in the council records;
that Quiney could sign his name we know, for letters written by him
have come down. A cross on a document symbolized the Holy
Cross, and avouched the piety of the signer; it was, in other words,
equivalent to an oath. It has been suggested that the compass sign
meant 'God Encompasseth Us', and the clamp had some other, un-

deciphered allegorical significance; but to this admittedly sceptical writer John Shakespeare's signs symbolize his trade and no more. It is true that he handled complicated municipal business, and that literacy is an asset to a book-keeper. It is also true that unlettered men may have shrewd business acumen. Possible light on the problem is shed by a teasing memorandum of 1596. It concerns the suit of Widow Margaret Young (she was Richard Field's sister) against another widow, Joan Perrott, over some 'deceitfully' appropriated goods, and among the items appears 'Mr. Shaxpere, one book'. Probably the entry refers to John Shakespeare rather than William, but one cannot tell for certain; and although possession of a book points to a capacity to read, it does not necessarily carry that presumption: some owners are no users. To sum up: John Shakespeare may have mastered reading and writing—there is some force to the arguments supporting that conclusion. But not a single autograph by him is extant, his civic responsibilities did not absolutely require such knowledge (a professional scrivener always stood at the ready, pen in hand), and raised as he was, a tenant farmer's son in a country village without a school, his educational opportunities were strictly limited.

We do know that after attaining the highest elective office Stratford had to offer, Master Shakespeare contemplated applying to the Heralds' College for a coat of arms. As bailiff of an incorporated town he held one of those 'divers offices of dignity and worship, [that] do merit coats of arms, to the possessor of the same offices'. Thus wrote Sir John Ferne in *The Blazon of Gentry* in 1586; and further: 'If any person be advanced into an office or dignity of public administration, be it either ecclesiastical, martial, or civil . . . the herald must not refuse to devise to such a public person, upon his instant request, and willingness to bear the same without reproach, a coat of arms: and thenceforth, to matriculate him, with his intermarriages, and issues descending, in the register of the gentle and noble.'[11] But nothing came of the application, although John received from the College a 'pattern', or sketch, for his arms. Years later, when his son applied (as it seems) in his father's behalf, the Clarenceux King-of-Arms noted: 'And the man was a magistrate in Stratford upon Avon. A justice of peace, he married a daughter and heir of Arden, and was of good substance and habileté'.[12]

What happened? The evidence suggests that John Shakespeare had fallen on hard times. Formerly punctilious about attending council meetings, he stopped coming after 1576, missing all but one session for which attendance records exist. His council brethren evidently went on hoping he would return, for year after year—longer than for any other absentee—they kept his name on the aldermanic roster. They showed consideration in other ways. When a levy for equipping soldiers was passed by the council, they asked John to pay only 3s.4d., the assessment on burgesses, rather than the double amount levied on aldermen. But, over a year later, he still owed even this reduced sum. On election day, 1578, the corporation fined one absentee, John Wheeler, stiffly (20s.) but let Master Shakespeare off. The following November they voted to have every alderman pay 4d. weekly towards poor relief, except 'Mr. John Shaxpeare and Mr. Robert Bratt, who shall not be taxed to pay anything'. Bratt was old and infirm, and anyway no longer an alderman; he would die the next year. Finally, on 6 September 1586, the council elected two new aldermen, 'for that Mr. Wheler doth desire to be put out of the company, and Mr. Shaxspere doth not come to the halls when they be warned, nor hath not done of long time'.

The picture is of a piece; John Shakespeare incurred debts and exchanged land for ready money. On 14 November 1578 he raised £40 by mortgaging part of his wife's inheritance—a house and fifty-six acres in Wilmcote—to her brother-in-law Edmund Lambert of Barton on the Heath, to whom he already owed money. On that very day Roger Sadler, a baker in High Street, drew up his will, and noted in it that Edmund Lambert and Edward Cornwell—Margaret Arden's second husband—owed him £5 'for the debt of Mr. John Shaksper'. When the borrowed £40 fell due at Michaelmas 1580, John could not pay it, so Lambert held on to the property. He was still in possession when he died seven years later. There followed litigation in the court of Queen's Bench in Westminster, as John Shakespeare tried to recover the holding from Lambert's son and heir John. In a Bill of Complaint in *Shakespeare* v. *Lambert*, 1588, the glover contended that John Lambert had on 26 September 1587 promised an additional £20 in return for delivery to him outright of the Wilmcote estate by John and Mary Shakespeare, and their eldest son William ('Johannes Shackespere et Maria uxor eius, simul-cum Willielmo Shackespere filio suo'). Lambert denied any such promise. In another suit a decade later, this time in Chancery, the Shakespeares, John and Mary, insisted that they had offered the elder Lambert the £40 for the property, only to be spurned—he wanted other money which they owed him. They never did get back this land, part of the Asbyes estate. In November 1578 John and Mary Shakespeare conveyed eighty-six more acres in Wilmcote, comprising meadow and pasture, to a Webbe relative and another for a period of years, after which the land would go back to the origi-nal possessors for Mary's heirs; again a need for cash—immediate cash—seems to have motivated the transaction. The Shakespeares were also obliged to give up their ninth part in the two houses and hundred acres in Snitterfield, the property leased to Alexander Webbe, Margaret Arden's first husband. This they sold in 1579 to Webbe's son Robert for the mean sum of £4.[13]

Troubles multiplied. In Trinity term, 1580, John was fined £20 for not appearing in the court of Queen's Bench to find security for keeping the Queen's peace. (At this time the Crown similarly penal-ized many others, more than 140 throughout England, with fines of from £10 to £200; why is not known.) The same court also fined him another £20 as pledge for a hatmaker of Nottingham who had failed his day to produce surety for good behaviour. Together the two fines amounted to the whole of the Lambert mortgage. If they were ever collected after being turned over to the Exchequer for that purpose, no record has turned up to show it. Evidently John Shake-speare did not always judge well the character of those for whom he vouched. Thus the £10 bail he stood for Michael Price, the felonious Stratford tinker, was forfeited. So too was his bond for £10 of a debt of £22 incurred by his brother Henry. On that occasion a suit fol-lowed; to escape jail John turned to his friend Alderman Hill for bail, and even swore out a writ of habeas corpus to transfer the case to another court.

Adversaries, as well as adversities, oppressed him. In the summer

8. John Shakespeare absent from church, 25 September 1592.

of 1582 he petitioned for sureties of the peace against four men—
Ralph Cawdrey, William Russell, Thomas Logginge, and Robert
Young—'for fear of death and mutilation of his limbs'.[14] Old Cawdrey, a butcher of Bridge Street, was then bailiff, but in his younger
days he had been fined more than once for frays. He and John
Shakespeare did meet again the last time the latter attended a council meeting, on 5 September 1582. Together they helped to elect a
new bailiff, so the two men had most likely patched up their differences, whatever these were.

In the autumn of 1591 the Privy Council, spurred on by the zeal
of the Archbishop of Canterbury, launched one of its periodic in-
quisitions into the spiritual health of the realm. This time the
Council ordered commissioners in every shire to ferret out and report all those who gave sanctuary to seminary priests, Jesuits, or
'fugitives', and 'all such as refused obstinately to resort to the
church'. At Stratford the following March or thereabouts, the presenters (probably the churchwardens) duly drew up a list of recusants who did not come monthly to church, as her Majesty's laws
required, and they added: 'We suspect these nine persons next ensuing absent themselves for fear of processes.' Among the names appears that of 'Mr. John Shackspeare'. In a 'second certificate' on 25
September following, the commissioners—Sir Thomas Lucy and
other justices—had the satisfaction of reporting the names of Catholics who had since conformed or undertaken to conform. The com-

missioners in the same certificate repeated what the presenters had said about the other nine: 'It is said that these last nine come not to church for fear of process for debt.'[15]

Some have viewed this episode as evidence that John Shakespeare's plight derived not from pecuniary embarrassment but his ideological waywardness. They see him as a nonconformist hero of the faith, Catholic or Puritan, valiantly—or cunningly—defying authority and partaking in forbidden ceremonies with the tacit support of other malcontents in the corporation; or as a man broken in body and spirit by that authority, and therefore retreating from the public arena. These interpretations have a romantic appeal, but John Shakespeare was a tradesman, not an ideologue. His religious views (whatever they were) need not have forced him away from the halls where his brethren—Puritans like Robert Perrott, the wealthy brewer, and Catholics like the Cawdreys—kept their faith and (unless relieved for obstinate uncooperativeness) their posts. The presenters and commissioners are alike on record as suspecting that John Shakespeare feared process for debt. None of the Stratford Nine appears in the recusant roll of 1593, and most of them were in financial difficulty—poor John Wheeler, Jr., for example: we hear several years later that his house was 'very ruinous' and his barn 'ready to fall for rottenness'. In those days sheriff's officers could make arrests on Sundays, and the church was a likely place in which to track down one's man. Did they come there to seek out John Shakespeare at the behest of William Burbage, for years frustrated in his efforts to collect the £7 plus damages due him?[16]

If the records are silent about the causes of John Shakespeare's financial difficulties, other townsmen experienced similar problems. Travellers in the west Midlands, and government officials also, noted what today we would describe as an economic recession. As the century wore on, conditions worsened rather than improved; in the year of John Shakespeare's death the poor of Stratford numbered over 700, young and old: approximately half the population. Poverty breeds other miseries. Illegitimate births, violence, and disorder increased in the borough, and the corporation duly reprimanded the ale-house keepers for contributing 'through their unreasonable strong drink, to the increase of quarrelling and other misdemeanours in their houses, and the farther and greater impoverishment of many poor men haunting the said houses, when their wives and children are in extremity of begging'.[17]

Viewed against this background, John Shakespeare's misfortunes take on a less dramatic aspect. He could still raise £10 for somebody's bail, and the court that imposed £40 in fines on him must have considered him a fairly substantial citizen. That he did not forfeit the esteem of fellow townsmen is suggested by the fact that twice during the summer of 1592 he was called upon to assist in the responsible task of making inventories of the goods of deceased neighbours—the wool-driver Ralph Shaw and Henry Field the tanner. In some ways John might count himself lucky. The wet summer of 1594—'wonderful cold, like winter', a diarist notes—was followed on 22 September, a Sunday, by a great fire that swept through Stratford. A year to a day later, on another Sunday, the town was again laid waste by conflagration, 'chiefly [as a Puritan gospeller remarked with satisfaction] for profaning the Lord's Sabbaths, and for contemning his Word in the mouth of his faithful ministers.'[18] One hundred and twenty dwellings, as well as eighty other buildings, suffered total or partial destruction in the two fires; on the south side Wood Street blazed from end to end. In Henley Street the cottage where of late Price the tinker had lived burnt to the ground, as did the tenement of William Wilson, whittawer, with its eight bays. Somehow the Birthplace escaped. If during these troubled years inexorable pressures forced John Shakespeare to part with properties, these were mostly inherited. He did sell his house in Greenhill Street some time before 1590, when his estate is described, but his double house in Henley Street, where he conducted his business and raised his family, he kept intact to his dying day and passed on to his playwright son.

In 1601, the last year of his life, the corporation was busy guarding established privileges, like the bestowing of the office of market toll-gatherer, which were being challenged by Sir Edward Greville, the grasping lord of the manor. That summer, in Trinity term, Richard Quiney (Adrian's son) rode to London to plead the borough's cause. With him he carried a declaration in his own hand naming 'Jhon Sackesper' along with other local worthies—including

9. John Shakespeare buried, 8 September 1601.

such elders as Simon Biddle the cutler and Thomas Barber, tenant of the Bear Inn, opposite the Swan in Bridge Street—as able to speak in behalf of borough rights. But John Shakespeare did not live to defend the interests of the town he had served for half a century. In early September he died at what was, for those times, a great age: he must have been in his early seventies. On the 8th he was buried in the churchyard of Holy Trinity. The stone marking his grave has long since vanished.

[5]

John Shakespeare's
Spiritual Testament

If John Shakespeare drew up a last will and testament, it would have been proved in the vicar's court; provided, that is, that his property all lay in the parish.[1] Wills, inventories, and a few grants of administration from this court now rest in the Birthplace archives, but these include no testament by the elder Shakespeare. Probably he left none, and his widow or one of their five surviving children administered the estate. More than a century and a half after his death, however, another sort of testament associated with John's name mysteriously came to light in the western house in Henley Street.

In April 1757 the then owner, Thomas Hart, fifth lineal descendant of the poet's sister Joan, was employing labourers to retile his roof. On the 29th Joseph Moseley, a master bricklayer described as of 'very honest, sober, industrious' character, found, while working with his men, a small paper-book between the rafters and the tiling. This book, or (more properly) booklet, consisted of six leaves stitched together. A Catholic profession of faith in fourteen articles, it has come to be known as the Spiritual Last Will and Testament of John Shakespeare.

With the knowledge of Hart, Moseley some time later gave the document to Mr. Payton of Shottery, a Stratford alderman. Years passed. In 1784 the ubiquitous cicerone of the Shakespeare shrines, John Jordan, was allowed to copy the manuscript, which by then lacked the first leaf. He tried to place his transcript in the *Gentleman's Magazine*. The original, Jordan informed the editor, 'is wrote in a fair and legible hand, and the spelling exactly as I have sent it you'.[2] But, unimpressed, the magazine rejected it. Meanwhile the greatest Shakespearian scholar of the day had heard of the discovery, and through the inquiries of the Revd. James Davenport, vicar of Stratford, traced it down to Payton. The latter willingly permitted Davenport to send the relic on to Edmond Malone.

In his study, surrounded by sixteenth- and seventeenth-century documents, Malone perused the testament. 'The handwriting is undoubtedly not so ancient as that *usually* written about the year 1600', Malone concluded; 'but I have now before me a manuscript written by Alleyn the player at various times between 1599 and 1614, and another by Forde, the dramatick poet, in 1606, in nearly the same handwriting as that of the manuscript in question.'[3] And so he pronounced himself 'perfectly satisfied' of its genuineness. This fragment Malone published in his 'Historical Account of the English Stage' in volume i, part 2, of his 1790 edition of *The Plays and Poems of William Shakspeare*. The Spiritual Testament includes such articles as these, beginning with the defective third attestation:

III.

"* * * * at least spiritually, in will adoring and most humbly beseeching my Saviour, that He will be pleased to assist me in so dangerous a voyage, to defend me from the snares and deceits of my infernal enemies, and to conduct me to the secure haven of His eternal bliss.

IV.

"*Item*, I, John Shakspear, do protest that I will also pass out of this life, armed with the last sacrament of extreme unction: the which if through any let or hindrance I should not then be able to have, I do now also for that time demand and crave the same; beseeching His divine majesty that He will be pleased to anoint my senses both internal and external with the sacred oil of His infinite mercy, and to pardon me all my sins committed by seeing, speaking, feeling, smelling, hearing, touching, or by any other way whatsoever.

IX.

"*Item*, I, John Shakspear, do here protest that I do render infinite thanks to His divine majesty for all the benefits that I have received as well secret as manifest, and in particular, for the benefit of my creation, redemption, sanctification, conservation, and vocation to the holy knowledge of Him and His true Catholic faith: but above all, for His so great expectation of me to penance, when He might most justly have taken me out of this life, when I least thought of it, yea even then, when I was plunged in the dirty puddle of my sins. Blessed be therefore and praised, forever and ever, His infinite patience and charity.

XII.

"*Item*, I, John Shakspear, do in like manner pray and beseech all my dear friends, parents, and kinsfolks, by the bowels of our Saviour Jesus Christ, that since it is uncertain what lot will befall me, for fear notwithstanding lest by reason of my sins I be to pass and stay a long while in Purgatory, they will vouchsafe to assist and succour me with their holy prayers and satisfactory works, especially with the holy sacrifice of the mass, as being the most effectual means to deliver souls from their torments and pains; from the which, if I shall by God's gracious goodness and by their virtuous works be delivered, I do promise that I will not be ungrateful unto them, for so great a benefit.

XIV.

'*Item*, lastly I, John Shakspear, do protest, that I will willingly accept of death in what manner soever it may befall me, conforming my will unto the will of God; accepting of the same in satisfaction for my sins, and giving thanks unto His divine majesty for the life He hath bestowed upon me. And if it please Him to prolong or shorten the same, blessed be He also a thousand thousand times; into whose most holy hands I commend my soul and body, my life and death:· and I beseech Him above all things, that He never permit any change to be made by me, John Shakspear, of this my aforesaid will and testament. Amen.

I, John Shakspear, have made this present writing of protestation, confession, and charter, in presence of the blessed Virgin Mary, my angel guardian, and all the celestial court, as witnesses hereunto: the which my meaning is, that it be of full value now

47

presently and forever, with the force and virtue of testament, codicil, and donation in cause of death; confirming it anew, being in perfect health of soul and body, and signed with mine own hand; carrying also the same about me; and for the better declaration hereof, my will and intention is that it be finally buried with me after my death.

"Pater noster, Ave Maria, credo.

"Jesu, son of David, have mercy on me.

Amen."[4]

Before the volume was printed off, Davenport forwarded to Malone a small quarto notebook belonging to Jordan, and containing the complete text of the spiritual testament. Puzzled by the sudden resurfacing of the missing first leaf, Malone put pointed questions to Jordan, whose replies, evasive and contradictory, were not calculated to allay suspicion. Nevertheless Malone went ahead and published the supplementary articles in his 'Emendations and Additions' included in the same volume:

I.

"In the name of God, the Father, Son, and Holy Ghost, the most holy and blessed Virgin Mary, mother of God, the holy host of archangels, angels, patriarchs, prophets, evangelists, apostles, saints, martyrs, and all the celestial court and company of heaven, I, John Shakspear, an unworthy member of the holy Catholic religion, being at this my present writing in perfect health of body, and sound mind, memory, and understanding, but calling to mind the uncertainty of life and certainty of death, and that I may be possibly cut off in the blossom of my sins, and called to render an account of all my transgressions externally and internally, and that I may be unprepared for the dreadful trial either by sacrament, penance, fasting, or prayer, or any other purgation whatever, do in the holy presence above specified, of my own free and voluntary accord, make and ordain this my last spiritual will, testament, confession, protestation, and confession of faith, hoping hereby to receive pardon for all my sins and offences, and thereby to be made partaker of life everlasting, through the only merits of Jesus Christ my Saviour and Redeemer, who took upon Himself the likeness of man, suffered death, and was crucified upon the cross, for the redemption of sinners.

II.

"*Item*, I, John Shakspear, do by this present protest, acknowledge, and confess, that in my past life I have been a most abominable and grievous sinner, and therefore unworthy to be forgiven without a true and sincere repentance for the same. But trusting in the manifold mercies of my blessed Saviour and Redeemer, I am encouraged by relying on His sacred word, to hope for salvation and be made partaker of His heavenly kingdom, as a member of the celestial company of angels, saints and martyrs, there to reside forever and ever in the court of my God.

III.

"*Item*, I, John Shakspear, do by this present protest and declare, that as I am certain I must pass out of this transitory life into another that will last to eternity, I do hereby most humbly implore and intreat my good and guardian angel to instruct me in this my solemn preparation, protestation, and confession of faith, at least spiritually," &c.

Later, misgivings assailed Malone, and in his *Inquiry into the Authenticity of Certain Miscellaneous Papers and Legal Instruments*, his celebrated exposure in 1796 of William Henry Ireland's forged Shakespeare papers, he retracted his earlier faith in John Shakespeare's attestation of faith. 'In my conjecture concerning the writer of that paper, I certainly was mistaken', he announced; 'for I have since obtained documents that clearly prove it could not have been the composition of any one of our poet's family; as will be fully shewn in his Life.'[5] But Malone never lived to complete the great biography to which all his previous researches comprised a prelude, and his literary executor, James Boswell the younger, could not find among Malone's papers the documentary evidence to which he had alluded. Perhaps, Boswell speculated, Malone had uncovered information to associate the testament with the other John Shakespeare. But what could the Catholic declaration of a shoemaker of Warwick be doing in the roof of the house in Henley Street?

The note-book of five leaves that Malone held in his hands has since vanished. A pity, for the techniques of modern scholarship might have answered several intriguing questions. Was the text transcribed in England (where the secretary script was favoured) or on the Continent (where the italic hand held sway)? Where was the paper manufactured? The watermark would have revealed that, and also provided a clue as to date. Was John Shakespeare's name entered in the same hand as the rest? The answer to that question would have indicated whether the copy was made locally or imported. Did the document (signed, as the last paragraph says, with the testator's own hand) bear a cross or John Shakespeare's characteristic mark of the glover's compass? These questions must remain unanswered.[6]

Another broader issue has in this century been settled. Was the whole document an invention—Jordan's invention? So that eminent Victorian Halliwell-Phillipps suspected, and in Sir Sidney Lee's biography, for long regarded as standard, this possibility has assumed the status of fact. 'Much notoriety', Lee informs us, 'was obtained by John Jordan (1746-1809), a resident at Stratford-on-Avon, whose most important achievement was the forgery of the will of Shakespeare's father. . . .'[7] Certainly Jordan was a rogue, and more than once he led Malone up the garden path; but that does not mean that the testament was a piece of his roguery.

The earlier commentators, whatever their misgivings, had no doubt that the formulary itself was authentic. Now we know that they were right. Around 1923 a Jesuit scholar, Father Herbert Thurston, found in the British Museum a Spanish version of the spiritual testament printed in 1661 in Mexico City. This 'Last Will of the Soul, made in health for the Christian to secure himself from the temptations of the devil at the hour of death',[8] was drawn up by Carlo Borromeo, the Cardinal Archbishop of Milan who died in 1584 and was canonized in 1610. His celebrated piety was fearfully tested in the late seventies, when the plague gripped Milan, carrying off (it is said) 17,000 souls. During this emergent occasion Borromeo composed the devotion which became a favoured instrument of the Counter-Reformation, and which, two centuries later, was extricated from the roof-tiles of John Shakespeare's house in Stratford.

In the spring of 1580 a team of English Jesuit missionaries, led by Fathers Edmund Campion and Robert Persons (or Parsons), stopped in Milan on their way to England from Rome, and there enjoyed the hospitality of the famous cardinal. His emaciated frame and zealous preaching in contempt of the world left a deep impression on his English guests. When they moved on, they apparently took with them copies of Borromeo's Last Will of the Soul. So we may gather from a letter written on 23 June 1581 by the rector of the English College in France to his counterpart in Rome, where the mission originated. 'Father Robert [Persons] wants three or four thousand or more of the Testaments', Dr. William Allen remarks, 'for many persons desire to have them.'[9] These persons were Catholics or likely converts in England. Into their houses the missionaries gained admission, and, once lodged, they donned the priest's vestments they always carried with them. They held secret conference, listened to confession, and celebrated Mass. They secured signatures on the testaments. Then they departed. Wandering their separate ways, both Campion and Persons passed through the Midlands. At his house, Bushwood, in Lapworth, only twelve miles from Stratford, Sir William Catesby put up Campion, and for his indiscreet hospitality was arrested and imprisoned in the Fleet. One ran a dangerous risk in harbouring popish priests, for the offence was a felony and could be punished by death. During Elizabeth's reign almost 200 Catholics suffered execution under the penal laws.

Not until 1966 did an early edition in English of the formulary come to light. *The Contract and Testament of the Soul*, printed in 1638 (probably on the Continent), closely follows Malone's text, except for the first two articles and part of the third.

I.

First, I here protest, and declare in the sight, and presence of Almighty God, Father, Son, and Holy Ghost, three persons, and one God; and of the blessed Virgin Mary, and of all the holy court of heaven, that I will live and die obedient unto the Catholic, Roman, and Apostolic Church, firmly believing all the twelve articles of the faith taught by the holy Apostles, with the interpretation, and declaration made thereon by the same holy church, as taught, defined and declared by her. And finally I protest, that I do believe all that, which a good and faithful Christian ought to believe: in which faith I purpose to live and die. And if at any time (which God forbid) I should chance by suggestion of the devil to do, say, or think contrary to this my belief, I do now for that time, in virtue of this

> 42
>
> THE TESTAMENT OF THE SOVLE.
>
> Made by S. Charles Borrom. Card. & Arch. of Millan.
>
> An Aduertisement to the deuout Reader.
>
> 1. THe deuout Person who will make vse of this spirituall Writing, for the good of his soule, let him read, or heare it read often, especially when he hopes he is in state of Grace, after Confession &

> of the Soule. 43
>
> & Comunion. And let him keep it in some place of note, & neere vnto him: & when he goeth any iourney, let him carry the same alwayes with him to haue it ready vpon all occasions. And whe he shall fall sicke, after Cofession let him renew, by reading, or hearing read, this Testamet, in presence of others, confirming finaly what he hath formerly at other times promised, & bequeathed for the good of his Soule.
>
> 2. This Testament may be made by all sorts of Persons, & at al times, writing

10. Carlo Borromeo, *The Testament of the Soule* (1638).

present act, revoke, infringe, and annul the same, and will that it be held for neither spoken, or done by me.

II.

Secondly. By this my last will I protest that, at my death, I will receive the sacraments of penance, and confession; the which if by any accident I should not be able to have, or make, I do in virtue of this present, resolve from this instant, for that time, to make it from my heart, accusing myself of all my sins committed in thought, word, and work, as well against God as against myself and my neighbour, whereof I do repent me with infinite sorrow, and desire time of penance, bitterly to bewail the same; for that I have offended my sovereign Lord and God, whom I ought to live and serve above all things. The which I now firmly purpose, with His grace, to do as long as I shall live, without ever more offending Him.

III.

Item. I do protest, that at the end of my life, I will receive the most
blessed sacrament for my *viaticum*, or last journey, that by means of
so divine a pledge, I may perfectly reconcile and unite myself unto
my Lord. The which if through any accident, I should not then be
able to perform, I do now for that time, declare, that I will receive
it. . . .[10]

So the document is genuine—there can be no question of that—except for the fabricated first leaf supplied by Jordan. But did John
Shakespeare, a miserable sinner, kneel devoutly before some impro-
vised altar, and subscribe to the profession? If he did, it is curious
that after 1580 (for the document could not have had English dis-
semination earlier) he should, in Article XII, beseech not only dear
friends and kinsfolk, but also his parents, to pray for his soul's delivery from the torments of Purgatory. His parents were then both
dead. It has been suggested that the testator was using *parents* in
the root sense of 'relations', the equivalent of *parientes* in the Italian and Spanish versions. A simpler explanation holds that John
Shakespeare signed a standardized form rather than one adapted to
particular circumstances. It has also been suggested that John Shakespeare obtained his copy of the Testament from Campion at Catesby's house in 1580, and hid it in his rafters three years later, after
the attempt of a deranged local Catholic zealot to assassinate the
Queen had instigated a wave of persecution; then did prudent
Warwickshiremen 'greatly work upon the advantage of clearing their
houses of all shows of suspicion'.[11]

But did he in fact make such a Catholic affirmation? The faith in
which William Shakespeare was reared is, after all, a matter of no
small moment, to ordinary readers as well as to theologians. But
Malone's paper has disappeared, and too many questions remain
teasingly unanswered. One circumstance in the life of the town is,
moreover, calculated to stir misgivings in the non-sectarian biographer. In 1563 the corporation moved to Protestantize the Gild
Chapel, which boasted papistical murals on such themes as the murder of Thomas à Becket, St. Helena's dream, and the Day of Judgement. The chapel had previously escaped the vandalism of zeal because it lay outside the ecclesiastical purview; perhaps the powerful

Cloptons, father and son—Catholics—protected it. But the elder Clopton died in 1560, and three years later his son, William Jr., went abroad. The council now acted. Workmen armed with sharp instruments mutilated the frescoes, especially the crosses, then whitewashed them and painted them over. Not until 1804, during restoration of the edifice, did the murals again come to light. The rape of the chapel took place when Humphrey Plymley was bailiff, with Adrian Quiney his chief alderman. John Shakespeare then served as chamberlain. He drew up the account the following January, and duly included an item of 2s. 'paid for defacing images in the chapel'. Further forays into Protestantization followed. In 1565 the corporation laid out another 2s. to have the rood loft taken down. At midsummer, 1571, a glazier replaced the stained glass in the chapel with clear panes. That year, with John Shakespeare present, the corporation agreed that the new bailiff, Adrian Quiney, should dispose of the Romanist capes and vestments gathering dust in the chapel, and yield an account of the proceeds.[12]

From these activities one may be tempted to infer a Protestant bias on the part of a prominent participating townsman, which John Shakespeare unquestionably was, and some notable authorities have so inferred: but a sceptic once again does well to resist the perils of confidence. We do not know with how much enthusiasm the council moved, and to what degree they were responding to irresistible outside pressures. Nor do the records disclose the personal emotions of any member of a corporation that still admitted Catholic sympathizers, and even professed Catholics, to its ranks. With regard to the Spiritual Last Will and Testament of John Shakespeare we can do no better than settle (as on other occasions) for a secular agnosticism, and turn to other sources for clues to the religion of his poet son.

[6]

Faith and Knowledge

If the form of faith instilled in the young William Shakespeare remains mysterious, no similar uncertainty attaches to what he experienced in church. That he worshipped at Matins and Evensong, participated at least three times a year in Communion, and was instructed by the parish priest in his catechism, we need not doubt. In Shakespeare's Stratford, on Sundays and Holy Days, shops and alehouses shut their doors; all fairs and markets ceased. The law of the realm compelled church-going, and infractions were punishable by fine. Violators found themselves hauled before the local church court. In Stratford the Act Book records that the court admonished (among others) William Flewellyn for keeping his shop windows open on the sabbath, Ralph Lorde for encouraging eating and drinking in his house during divine services, and Richard Pynke, Jr., for playing at quoits—pitching iron rings—when his neighbours worshipped. Elizabeth Wheeler, presented for brawling and not attending church, was hopelessly impenitent: 'God's wounds', she shouted in open court, 'a plague a' God on you all, a fart of ons [one's?] arse for you.' She was excommunicated.

More than half a century after the dramatist's death Richard Davies, sometime chaplain of Corpus Christi College, Oxford, and afterwards rector of Sapperton, added this terse declaration to some memoranda on Shakespeare: 'He died a papist.'[1] However intriguing, such reports belong to tradition rather than to the factual record. The religious training provided for Shakespeare by his community was orthodox and Protestant.

The moderate Protestantism of the parish churches was set forth by Queen Elizabeth's Book of Common Prayer, which her first Parliament ordered into use by the Act of Uniformity on 24 June 1559. Besides the Prayer Book, churches were instructed to furnish themselves with 'the new Kalendar, a Psalter, the English Bible in the largest volume, the two tomes of the Homilies and the Paraphrases of Erasmus translated into English'.[2] The large Bible authorized for the churches by the episcopate was the Bishops' Bible of 1568, a not very satisfactory revision of the Great Bible of 1539-41. Some churches, however, clung to the Genevan Bible, despite its association with Calvin, and this version, cheaply available in legible roman type, was favoured in most middle-class homes. Shakespeare knew it.

At services the minister appeared in 'a comely surplice with sleeves'. (This seemingly innocuous vestment occasioned distress in some quarters, where it was dispensed with as a manifesto of nonconformity. 'Though honesty be no puritan', the clown Lavache chides the Countess in *All's Well that Ends Well*, 'yet it will do no hurt; it will wear the surplice of humility over the black gown of a big heart.'[3]) For Holy Communion, administered upon the first or second Sunday of each month, there was placed 'a comely and decent table standing on a frame, . . . with a fair linen cloth to lay upon the same, and some covering of silk, buckram, or other suchlike for the clean keeping thereof'. Morning Prayer commenced early, at 7 A.M., and Evening Prayer was over by 3 P.M. In those days candles lit up the churches only at Christmas, and so services had to be conducted during daylight hours.

A passage from Scripture opened both Morning and Evening Prayer. In the course of a year all such portions of the Old Testament as were deemed 'edifying' were read; so the Prayer Book prescribed. The reading of the Old Testament was, then, selective, an appropriate passage being chosen for each service. The Apocrypha received the same treatment. Each month, however, the congregation (that is, all who attended daily) sang or said the whole of the Psalms, which in the Prayer Book appeared according to the Great (not Bishops') Bible, with the opening words of the Latin Vulgate for their titles. Over the year the whole of the New Testament—

Revelation excepted—was read three times, the Gospels and the Acts at Matins, the Catholic and Pastoral Epistles at Evensong. Proper Lessons from the New Testament were set only for the Holy Days and a few special Sundays. For the daily offices Canticles were appointed, and the choir sang the *Te Deum, Benedictus*, and *Magnificat*, and (in Lent) the *Benedicite*.[4]

After the reading and singing, a sermon; but if the priest lacked 'the gift of preaching sufficiently to instruct the people', he could instead read some of the Homilies 'distinctly and plainly'.[5] No matter how eloquent in the pulpit, however, the vicar could only defer the reading, not avoid it altogether. The Homilies were official sermons 'appointed by the Queen's Majesty [so reads the title-page of the 1582 edition] to be declared and read, by all parsons, vicars, and curates, every Sunday and Holy Day in their churches . . . for the better understanding of the simple people'. These *Certain Sermons* included appropriate set discourses for Good Friday, Easter Sunday, and Rogation week; also for the marriage service. They expounded the right use of the church, the efficacy of prayer, and the peril of idolatry. After the suppression of the rebellion in the North in 1569 and the excommunication of Elizabeth by Pope Pius V the next year, the collection, which already included 'An Exhortation to Obedience', in three parts, was enriched by 'An Homily against Disobedience and Wilful Rebellion' in six. Each instalment of the latter appropriately ended with a prayer for the Queen and the security of the realm. These Homilies on obedience and rebellion, delivered over nine Sundays and Holy Days, instilled political submissiveness in the simple people.

Before Evensong on each Sunday and Holy Day, the vicar instructed the children of both sexes in their catechism. He called on them by name, and listened while they recited. That was in English. At school the boys learnt *Nowell's Catechism* in Latin.

Thus inculcated from the formative years of early childhood, the Bible and Book of Common Prayer and Homilies profoundly nourished Shakespeare's imagination. One learned Biblical scholar, ranging through all the works with the exception of *Pericles* and the non-dramatic poems, has identified quotations from, or references to, forty-two books of the Bible—eighteen each from the Old and

New Testaments, and six from the Apocrypha.[6] Scarcely a phrase from the first three chapters of Genesis escapes allusion in the plays. Job and the apocryphal Ecclesiasticus were favourite books, but the story of Cain left an especially powerful impression—Shakespeare refers to it at least twenty-five times. Evidently he continued to consult the Bible long after his youthful indoctrination; so we may gather from certain details in the texts of *Henry V* (where he seems to have used, for the Dauphin, the de Tournes *Testament*, printed at Lyons in 1551) and *Measure for Measure*, in which the Provost's description of Barnardine—

> As fast lock'd up in sleep as guiltless labour
> When it lies starkly in the traveller's bones

—has as its source Ecclesiastes 5:11, apparently as rendered in certain revised Genevan Bibles of 1595 or later: 'The sleep of him that travelleth is sweet.'[7] Shakespeare refers more often to earlier than to later parts of books—chapters 1-4, for example, of the fifty chapters of Genesis—and shows greater familiarity with Genesis and Matthew than with any subsequent book from the Old or New Testament.[8] Not surprisingly he has lapses, mostly minor. In layman's fashion he neglects the distinction (patristic in origin) between Lucifer and Satan; he mistakes the Sabaoth—the hosts of the Lord of the *Te Deum*—with the Holy Sabbath of Shylock and his brethren. But an apparent slip may, upon closer study, merely illustrate Shakespeare's complex way with sources. Richard II, fetched forth to surrender his crown, asks, 'Did they not sometime cry "All hail!" to me? / So Judas did to Christ.' In Matthew's Gospel and Mark's, Judas salutes Jesus with 'Hail Master' (or another greeting, but not 'All hail'), and the variant has been cited as a defect in Shakespeare's Biblical knowledge. There is, however, precedent for it in Judas's greeting, 'All hail', in the play of the Agony and the Betrayal in the medieval York cycle of Mystery Plays.*

Shakespeare's range of religious reference is not limited to the

---

* Peter Milward notes that the salutation appears in the Chester play on the same theme, and he speculates that 'it may well have been used also in the Coventry play, which has unfortunately not survived' (*Shakespeare's Religious Background* (Bloomington and London, 1973), pp. 33-4).

Bible. Sometimes he quotes Scripture by way of the Prayer Book, as when the Fifth Commandment becomes 'thou shalt do no murder', and the words of the Psalmist, 'we bring our years to an end, as it were a tale that is told' ('we have spent our years as a thought', in the Genevan Bible), metamorphose into the tale told by an idiot. Nor did Shakespeare forget his catechism: in *Love's Labour's Lost* Berowne reminds the King that every man is mastered not by might but by 'special grace'; Hamlet shows his hands, 'these pickers and stealers', to Rosencrantz ('keep my hands from picking and stealing'). Our most thorough student of the Homilies takes them to be 'A New Shakespearean Source-Book', and concludes that the dramatist derived his ideas of the divine right of kings, the subject's duty to obey, and the mischief and wickedness of rebellion—ideas that so powerfully inform the English History plays—not from his narrative sources, Holinshed and the rest, but either directly or indirectly from the politico-religious creed set forth in the Homilies.[9] The services at Holy Trinity, Morning Prayer and Evening Prayer, Baptism and Holy Communion—indeed all the occasions of worship—remained with Shakespeare, and echo through the plays.

Was it, then, the Anglican faith that he embraced? Many have so concluded. One recent biographer, A. L. Rowse, is firm on this matter as on others: 'He was an orthodox, conforming member of the Church into which he had been baptised, was brought up and married, in which his children were reared and in whose arms he at length was buried.'[10] As Rowse sees it, there were for Shakespeare only two sacraments, Baptism and Holy Communion, rather than the Catholic seven. His chief exhibit of evidence is the preamble to the dramatist's will. This employs 'the regular Protestant formula', and 'one can always tell from the formula in these contemporary wills whether the person is dying a Protestant or a Catholic'.[11] But the confidence is here misplaced: testators, whether Catholic or Protestant, could use the same exordium (or their lawyers used it for them) without necessarily regarding it as an avowal of sectarian faith.[12] The baptisms and marriages and burials all within the bosom of Holy Trinity are, however, not guesses. No doubt Shakespeare did conform to the rituals of the Established Church, and attend its services. Had he neglected to do so, as a well-known theatrical figure he would with difficulty have escaped the notice of municipal authorities hostile to the stage on religious grounds. Certainly Ben Jonson's recusancy did not go unremarked. Still, the Church of England encompassed a breadth of religious experience, and to either side of the *via media* stood Puritan and neo-Catholic extremists. Moreover, one may conform outwardly as a matter of convenience, to avoid the law's importunities, and still privately nourish heterodoxy or indifference. Thus the scattering of Jews in Elizabethan London survived by conforming to the Anglican Church, but for some at least the conversion must have been prudential.

We remember the testament in the tiles, and it is a fact that Shakespeare's daughter Susanna was reported in a list of those, popishly affected, who failed to receive the Communion one Easter Sunday.[13] But of course, even if we could definitely ascertain the religious convictions of Shakespeare's father and daughter, we would still not possess a sure clue to the poet's own faith. Thus it is that theologically minded students have so industriously searched the plays for evidences of Catholic sympathies. Does not the dramatist treat his lesser Romanist clergy, a Friar Lawrence or Abbess Æmelia, more respectfully than his Protestant vicars of the villages, the Martexts and the Nathaniels? Surely his imagination did not stand aloof from the vessels and vestments of Catholicism. Nor was he unmoved by the abandoned abbeys and monasteries left crumbling in the wake of Reformation; in his 73rd Sonnet these are evoked by the poignant metaphor of the bare ruined choirs where late the sweet birds sang. In *King John*, the historical matter of which deals directly with the clash between English crown and papal authority, Shakespeare, to be sure, allows his unlovable protagonist to fulminate against the 'usurp'd authority' of the Pope—that 'meddling priest'—but such vituperation does not bulk large in the play; witness, by contrast, the Protestant controversialist John Bale's *King Johan*, or *The Troublesome Reign of King John*, by an anonymous playwright less doctrinally obsessed than Bale but more pointedly anti-Catholic than Shakespeare. (It is nonetheless the case that when an English Jesuit, William Sankey, censored Shakespeare's plays by the authority of the Holy Office in the mid-seventeenth century, he felt impelled to expunge over a score of lines and expressions from *King John*.[14])

Interested readers have discerned echoes here and there of the disused prayers and hymns of the Catholic liturgy; also a grasp of the fuller meaning of such Catholic practices as fasting and confession, and even of technical terminology. Thus, when Julia in *The Two Gentlemen of Verona* speaks of a 'month's mind', the phrase has been glossed as 'the name first used for the month of remembrance during which daily Masses were offered for the souls of the dead, and now applied to the Mass said for them a month after death'.[15] But by the late sixteenth century a 'month's mind' could signify merely a longing, such as might take a pregnant woman. Still, the Ghost of Hamlet's father uses the term *unaneled* ('Unhous'led, disappointed, unanel'd'), a reference to the Catholic Sacrament of Extreme Unction. And, if the word *purgatory* occurs only twice in the whole corpus, the concept itself is powerfully evoked by the same ghost,

> Doom'd for a certain term to walk the night,
> And for the day confin'd to fast in fires,
> Till the foul crimes done in my days of nature
> Are burnt and purg'd away.

To be sure, Shakespeare seems to err in his only overt reference to the sacrifice of the Mass—when Juliet asks the Friar whether she should come to 'evening mass'—for Pope Pius V and the Council of Trent had in 1566 done away with evening Mass; but twelve years later, recusants in the Welsh Marches were still celebrating it, and anyway the allusion appears in Shakespeare's source.[16] The facts are ambiguous: too ambiguous to justify a recent Jesuit commentator's conclusion that Shakespeare felt a positive nostalgia for England's Catholic past, although the same writer is on safer ground when he claims that Shakespeare shows much familiarity but little awkwardness in his treatment of Catholic customs and beliefs.[17]

What remains clear is that the artist takes precedence over the votary, and resists efforts on the part of sectarian apologists to put him in a convenient theological pigeon-hole. Probably Shakespeare remained a tolerant Anglican—after all, he could imaginatively comprehend, if not condone, a Shylock—but we need not find too puzzling chaplain Davies's claim that he died a papist.

His schooling, if it faithfully adhered to the law of the realm, would have inclined him to the Church of England. The forty-first item of the Injunctions given by the Queen's Majesty in 1559 decreed 'that all teachers of children, shall stir and move them to the love and due reverence of God's true religion, now truly set forth by public authority'. A noted educator of the day, headmaster of Westminster School and afterwards Dean of St. Paul's, has his ideal pedagogue thus address one of his younger charges:

> Forasmuch as the master ought to be to his scholars a second parent and father, not of their bodies but of their minds, I see it belongeth to the order of my duty, my dear child, not so much to instruct thee civilly in learning and good manners, as to furnish thy mind, and that in thy tender years, with good opinions and true religion. For this age of childhood ought no less, yea also much more, to be trained with good lessons to godliness, than with good arts to humanity.[18]

This dear child was a boy; girls from comfortable families learned to sew and sing and play upon the virginals; supervised by tutors, they mastered the rudiments of reading and writing. Some theorists—Ludovicus Vives, for example, and Richard Mulcaster—advocated formal education for women, and there existed grammar schools that admitted children of either sex. Women, however, did not go on to the universities. Warwickshire bred few Rosalinds.[19]

The curriculum of Stratford grammar school has not come down, but we can reconstruct it with some confidence on the basis of what we know of similar foundations in other parts of England. Fortunately the 'good arts' thrived better than some theorists thought sufficient. The parchment registers for Stratford pupils of this period have also, not surprisingly, perished. More than a century later, in 1709, Nicholas Rowe remarked that John Shakespeare had bred his poet son 'for some time at a Free-School, where 'tis probable he acquir'd that little *Latin* he was Master of'. This is our earliest allusion to Shakespeare's formal education, and may either record a tradition or reflect Rowe's natural inference. If an inference, it seems valid enough: we need not doubt that Shakespeare received a grammar-school education, and the only likely place for it was the King's New School of Stratford-upon-Avon. The schoolroom stood in Church Street, behind the Gild Chapel, and only a quarter-mile distant from the family house in Henley Street.

A child's education began at the age of four or five, not in the grammar school proper but in an attached petty school, under the tuition of an usher, or *abecedarius*, who also looked after the lower forms.[20] He thus spared the master 'that tedious trouble', as the council described it, of teaching the 'young youth' of the town. These ushers were not as a rule themselves especially well educated, and if the dramatist fell into the hands of a pedagogue as accomplished as his own creation Holofernes he might have accounted himself lucky.

The scholars came to class equipped with a hornbook: a leaf of paper or parchment framed in wood and covered, for protection, with a thin layer of transparent horn. On the paper was set forth the alphabet, both small letters and capitals; combinations of the five vowels with *b*, *c*, and *d*—the elements of syllabication; and the Lord's Prayer. The mark of the cross preceded the alphabet, which was hence called the 'Christ cross row'. So the Duke of Clarence, in *Richard III*, frets about King Edward's superstitious behaviour:

> He hearkens after prophecies and dreams,
> And from the cross-row plucks the letter G,
> And says a wizard told him that by G
> His issue disinherited should be;
> And, for my name of George begins with G,
> It follows in his thought that I am he.

Shakespeare also remembered his hornbook in *Love's Labour's Lost*. 'Monsieur, are you not lett'red?', Armado asks Holofernes, and Moth answers for the pedant: 'Yes, yes; he teaches boys the hornbook. What is a, b, spelt backward with the horn on his head?'—thus labelling Holofernes as a muttonhead.

Having mastered their hornbooks, the children moved on to *The ABC with the Catechism*, which reprinted the hornbook leaf, and followed it with the catechism from the Book of Common Prayer and a set of graces for praising God before and after meals. ('That is question now', catechizes the satirical Bastard in *King John;* 'And then comes answer like an Absey [i.e. ABC] book.') The third and last textbook, *The Primer and Catechism*—amounting to only two octavo gatherings—included the Calendar and Almanac, as well as the seven penitential psalms and other devotional matter. Armed with these models, the pupils were introduced to the mysteries of *prosodia*—the 'pronouncing of letters, syllables, and words with the mouth'—and *orthographia,* the 'writing of them with the hands'. In addition to reading and writing, some petty schools provided elementary instruction in the third R: numeration, the first part of arithmetic; and perhaps also the casting of accounts. *The ABC with the Catechism* furnished the nine figures 'and this circle (o) called a cipher'. After two years the scholars were ready for grammar school.

Shakespeare does not seem to have cherished especially tender memories of these days, if we may judge from the references to schools and schoolboys scattered through the plays. 'Love goes toward love as school-boys from their books', sighs Romeo beneath Juliet's balcony; 'But love from love, toward school with heavy looks.' In *The Taming of the Shrew* Gremio returns from Petruchio's disconcerting wedding 'As willingly as e'er I came from school'. Schoolboys (in *Much Ado About Nothing*) are overjoyed—but with finding birds' nests rather than with their lessons. Jack Cade, in 2 *Henry VI*, condemns Lord Say to immediate beheading for having, among other enormities, 'most traitorously corrupted the youth of the realm in erecting a grammar school'. In the second of Jaques's Seven Ages of Man, we encounter

> the whining school-boy, with his satchel
> And shining morning face, creeping like snail
> Unwillingly to school.

A less than seductive picture. All these allusions are, to be sure, made in character: Cade is the rebel leader of an ignorant and anarchic rabble; taken together, Jaques's Ages comprise, without exception, a set-piece progress of human futility. Still, these recollections of schooldays are not counterpoised in the *œuvre* by any more sympathetic opposing voice.

Nevertheless, Shakespeare was lucky to have the King's New School at Stratford-upon-Avon. It was an excellent institution of its kind, better than most rural grammar schools. According to the 1553 charter the Stratford school was to have one teacher who would receive £20 per annum and enjoy a house rent-free. This was good remuneration by the standards of the day: at Gloucester the schoolmaster, 'an ancient citizen of no great learning', drew £10, and there were other provincial pedagogues who fared no better. Enthusiasts of Stratford have pointed out that the master there commanded a higher salary than his counterpart at Eton College. Although, strictly speaking, this is true, such comparisons are not very illuminating; for the Eton master had special perquisites (such as lodgings and meals in college), whereas in Stratford £4 of the schoolmaster's stipend went to an usher 'for teaching the childer'. (That was until 1565, after which the schoolmaster received the full £20, ushers—no longer listed in the corporation records—being paid by the master out of his own pocket.) There can be no question that the pedagogues during Shakespeare's boyhood were all well qualified. They held university degrees, and when they resigned their posts, the town authorities had no difficulty in attracting able replacements.

Patient inquiry has rescued from oblivion the names and careers of the half dozen masters who came and went while Shakespeare was growing up.[21] Vicar Bretchgirdle in 1565 fetched from Warwick John Brownsword, his friend and former pupil from the Witton days (for Bretchgirdle had taught there). Brownsword wrote and published Latin verses, and a half century later was eulogized by another educator as 'that ancient schoolmaster . . . so much commended for his order and scholars'.[22] He remained in Stratford only three years before being replaced briefly by John Acton, a Brasenose College, Oxford, scholar. In 1569 Acton was succeeded by another Oxford-educated master, Walter Roche, a Lancashire man and fellow of Corpus Christi College. He had taken holy orders, and, around the same time that he was offered the Stratford post, came into a living, the rectory of Droitwich, which he held on to. Roche resigned as schoolmaster in 1571 to practise law (he on one occasion served as lawyer to Shakespeare's cousin, Robert Webbe of Snitter-field), so it is doubtful whether he taught Shakespeare, who would have been supervised in the Lower School by the usher in the same room with the older boys. Roche was later a neighbour of the Shake-speares in Chapel Street, three doors up from New Place. The next master, Simon Hunt, served from 1571 until 1575, and probably had Shakespeare as his pupil. There was a Simon Hunt who matricu-lated at the University of Douai, that continental outpost for the education of English Catholics; he became a Jesuit in 1578, and suc-ceeded the notorious Father Persons as confessor at St. Peter's. This Hunt died in Rome in 1585. He may have been the Stratford school-master, but there was another, more obscure, Hunt who died in Stratford around 1598, leaving an estate valued at £100. About the identity of the next master—Shakespeare's principal instructor—we can speak with greater certainty. Thomas Jenkins was of humble origin, the son of 'a poor man', an 'old servant' to Sir Thomas White, who was the founder of St. John's College, Oxford. At St. John's, Jenkins studied for his B.A. and M.A.; he was a fellow from 1566 to 1572, when the College granted him the lease of Chaucer's House in Woodstock. Meanwhile Jenkins had taken orders. In 1575 the Stratford burgesses paid for his removal expenses from Warwick, where he was schoolmastering. Jenkins was married: the Holy Trin-ity registers record the burial of his daughter Joan and the baptism of his son Thomas. With the consent of the corporation, Jenkins re-signed as schoolmaster in 1579, but not before finding a replacement, John Cottom, 'late of London' and a Brasenose graduate. Cottom's younger brother was a missionary priest who was arraigned (along with Edmund Campion), tortured on the rack, and in 1582 put to death, a Catholic martyr. His schoolmaster brother resigned in the previous year. Did the corporation ask him to leave? Cottom retired to Lancashire, where he came into his father's lands, acknowledged his Catholicism, and paid his recusant fines.

Thus it was possible, in Elizabethan grammar schools, to receive tuition from papists or popish sympathizers, despite the severe pen-alties to which recusant schoolmasters were subject. Presumably they maintained an outward conformity.

The next master, Alexander Aspinall, M.A., arrived on the scene too late to be Shakespeare's master, but he has a curious Shakespearian connection. In 1594 Aspinall, for many years a widower, married the Widow Anne Shaw. The Shaws were friends and neighbours of the Shakespeares in Henley Street. John Shakespeare (it will be recalled) helped to appraise Ralph Shaw's goods, and a quarter of a century later Shaw's son July (or Julyns) was one of the witnesses to the will of William Shakespeare. Long afterwards Sir Francis Fane of Bulbeck (1611-80) recorded in his manuscript commonplace book this posy:

> The gift is small;
> The will is all:
> Asheyander [i.e. Alexander] Asbenall.
> Shaxpaire upon a pair of gloves that master sent to his mistress.[23]

It has been suggested, with more sentimental fancy than plausibility, that Aspinall bought the gloves for Mrs. Shaw in the Shakespeare shop, and that the glover's son, his brain soon to catch fire with *Romeo and Juliet*, did not disdain to assist a middle-aged schoolmaster in his courtship of a Stratford wool-driver's widow.

About the sort of education that Shakespeare enjoyed—if that is the right word—under his schoolmasters, conjecture may be less waywardly pursued. The children began their long schoolday by six or seven in the morning. Lessons went on until eleven, with a short recess for breakfast; then resumed after lunch at one, and continued, usually without any respite, until five or six. (This was six days a week, most weeks of the year.) Each day began and ended with devotions. In between, the scholars plied their Latin grammar. Ornamented with a woodcut showing little boys aspiring for the tempting bidden fruit of the tree of knowledge, the authorized textbook was William Lily's *Short Introduction of Grammar*. It consisted of two parts: the first setting forth the 'accidence and principles of grammar' in English; the second, the *Brevissima Institutio*, entirely in Latin. This book the scholars memorized by rote, and thus mastered declensions and conjugations.

His own experience Shakespeare recalled with rueful amusement in Act IV of *The Merry Wives of Windsor*. There the bumbling parson-pedagogue Sir Hugh Evans—he speaks Welsh flannel, according to Falstaff, and 'makes fritters of English'—catechizes the unfortunate Master William in his accidence for the benefit of the lad's disgruntled mother. 'Sir Hugh', Mistress Page complains, 'my husband says my son profits nothing in the world at his book.' The tutor's triumphal disproof of the charge follows Lily's *Introduction* step by step, and sometimes word for word, although the contributions of Mistress Quickly owe nothing to the grammarian's expertise.

> *Evans.* Well, what is your accusative case?
> *William.* Accusativo, hinc.
> *Evans.* I pray you, have your remembrance, child. Accusativo, hung, hang, hog.
> *Quickly.* 'Hang-hog' is Latin for bacon, I warrant you.
> *Evans.* Leave your prabbles, oman. What is the focative case, William?
> *William.* O—vocativo, O.
> *Evans.* Remember, William: focative is caret.
> *Quickly.* And that's a good root.
> *Evans.* Oman, forbear.
> *Mrs. Page.* Peace.
> *Evans.* What is your genitive case plural, William?
> *William.* Genitive case?
> *Evans.* Ay.
> *William.* Genitive: horum, harum, horum.
> *Quickly.* Vengeance of Jenny's case; fie on her! Never name her, child, if she be a whore.

Some have assumed, from the name, that Shakespeare's schoolmaster Thomas Jenkins was a Welshman, and they have seen Sir Hugh as a gently satiric portrait of that pedagogue; but Jenkins was (despite his presumed ancestry) a Londoner. It is always dangerous to read Shakespeare's plays as *pièces à clef*.

As year in and year out the children toiled at their Latin, they found the precepts they needed in Lily's grammar. For examples they had to be directed elsewhere; first to a manual of brief sentences from Latin authors, such as the famous *Sententiae Pueriles* gathered together by Leonhardus Culmannus—'a Parcel of dry, moral Sayings . . .', one early educator describes it, that 'might more properly be called *Sententiae Seniles*'.[24] Further moral maxims followed

in Erasmus's *Cato*. This was read in the second form, along with
Æsop latinized and morally interpreted. To some these texts ranked
in educational value second only to Scripture. 'So far as I am able
to understand, next unto the Bible, we have no better books than
Catonis scripta, and *fabulas Æsopi*, the works of Cato, and the fa-
bles of Esop'; thus Martin Luther.[25] Terence joined the curriculum
next. Plautus was read too, although less often, and in some schools
the children acted a scene from either as a weekly exercise. Thus
was Shakespeare introduced to classical comedy and the five-act
structure of plays.

In the third form the pupils encountered modern Latin moral
poets. There was Palingenius, whose *Zodiacus Vitae* acquainted
Shakespeare with the great commonplace that all the world's a stage.
He also read Baptista Spagnuoli, called Mantuanus, the Carmelite
whose bucolic eclogues, fruits of his retirement, became a set text
for the English grammar schools. In Mantua the Duke extolled Baptista's memory with a marble statue, crowned with laurel, which he
placed alongside the monument to Vergil. Shakespeare praises Baptista in *Love's Labour's Lost*. 'Ah, good old Mantuan!' rapturously
declares Holofernes after quoting the opening lines from the *Bu-
colica*:

> I may speak of thee as the traveller doth of Venice:
> > Venetia, Venetia,
> > Chi non ti vede, non ti pretia.
> Old Mantuan, old Mantuan! Who understandeth thee not, loves
> thee not.

But, as these commendations are voiced by a pedant, they may not
be untinged by irony, and quite possibly his creator never got beyond the first eclogue. With these models the boys learned to con-
strue. Their vocabularies they enriched by memorizing Withals's
Short Dictionary or some similar compilation. This preparation en-
abled them to proceed to make their own Latins, which they began
by translating passages from the Genevan Bible. For Latin speaking
they were guided by the conversational colloquies of Corderius, Gal-
lus, or Vives, or the literary dialogues of Castalio and Erasmus: continental humanists all today forgotten, except for Erasmus and (in

England, at least) Vives. This was the work of the first three or four years.

Around 1574 or 1575 Shakespeare would have passed from the usher to the master, and from the Lower School to the advanced curriculum of the Upper. Now the students were taught rhetoric, with enough logic to make it intelligible. For texts they used Cicero's *Ad Herennium* (for general information) and *Topica* (for *inventio*), Susenbrotus (for *elocutio*, the tropes and figures of speech), Erasmus's *Copia* (for *elocutio* applied), and Quintilian, the supreme rhetorician. With these models before them, the children composed epistles, then formal themes, and ultimately—the pinnacle of grammar-school rhetoric—orations and declamations. After prose, verse. 'Though poetry be rather for ornament than for any necessary use', conceded one contemporary authority, '. . . it is not amiss to train up scholars even in this kind also. And the rather because it serveth very much for the sharpening of the wit, and is a matter of high commendation, when a scholar is able to write a smooth and pure verse, and to comprehend a great deal of choice matter in a very little room.'[26]* So the scholars were introduced to Ovid, Vergil, and Horace. Ovid, especially the *Metamorphoses*, was the favourite of the schools, and would remain the dramatist's favourite as well. To these poets were sometimes added Juvenal (Hamlet's 'satirical rogue') and Persius. For history the boys read Sallust and Caesar; the *De Officiis* of Cicero gave them moral philosophy. Thus did Shakespeare acquire the small Latin—not so small by the standards of a later age—with which Jonson credits him. In the Upper School he would also attain his less Greek, with the Greek New Testament his first source for constructions.

This then, in outline, is the education that an Elizabethan grammar school provided. It offered about as much formal belletristic in-

* In a later century John Clarke takes a more philistine view of versifying: '. . . . the best you can make of it is but a Diversion, a Degree above Fidling. . . . If I might advise therefore, I would have Boys kept wholly from this Sort of Exercise. . . . The Scribbling of paultry, wretched *Verse* is no Way for them to improve their Parts in' (*An Essay upon the Education of Youth in Grammar Schools* (1720), pp. 65-7; quoted by T. W. Baldwin, *William Shakspere's Small Latine & Lesse Greeke* (Urbana, Ill., 1944), i. 462-3).

struction as was available in those days for an incipient man of letters. The universities had little to add, for their task was to train up men for the professions: medicine, law, above all divinity. At the Inns of Court, to be sure, the students enjoyed a sophisticated literary ambience, from which some—that snarling satirist John Marston, for example—profited handsomely; but ambience is not the same thing as instruction.[27] The profession of letters, as we know it, did not then exist.

'What of It?' asks T. W. Baldwin in the title of the last chapter of his monumental study, *William Shakspere's Small Latine & Lesse Greeke*, and he offers this summing up:

> If William Shakspere had the grammar school training of his day— or its equivalent—he had as good a formal literary training as had any of his contemporaries. At least, no miracles are required to account for such knowledge and techniques from the classics as he exhibits. Stratford grammar school will furnish all that is required. The miracle lies elsewhere; it is the world-old miracle of genius.[28]

That miracle found expression in London, not Stratford, and its dimensions were apprehended not then but by succeeding generations. In schoolmaster Jenkins's eyes other pupils then in his charge may have held more conspicuous promise. Certainly none fulfilled academic expectations better than William Smith, christened half a year after Shakespeare, on 22 November 1564, the sixth son of Alderman William Smith, a mercer and linen-draper who dwelt at the New House in High Street. The Smiths were evidently favourites of Vicar Bretchgirdle, who, as he lay 'visited with the hand of God', bequeathed books from his library to five of the boys, and left a shilling to young William. (Bretchgirdle did not remember any of the Shakespeares.) Of the twenty-six male children christened in Stratford in the year of Shakespeare's birth, only one, this William Smith, would receive a university education. He was enrolled in Winchester College, and went on to matriculate at Exeter College, Oxford, in 1583. By then the family had removed to Worcester. Having taken his B.A., William Smith lived for a time in Waltham Cross before settling down as a schoolmaster in Loughton, Essex. This was the aptest scholar of Shakespeare's class.

In the next century we hear of another exceptional Stratford lad contemporary with the dramatist. The gossip Aubrey, who obtained information from 'some of the neighbours', informs us that 'There was at that time another butcher's son in this town, that was held not at all inferior to him [Shakespeare] for a natural wit, his acquaintance and coetanean, but died young.'[29] Perhaps this extraordinary natural wit graced Adrian Tyler, son of a Sheep Street butcher who had served as constable with John Shakespeare—the dramatist thought of Adrian's brother Richard when he drafted his will, so the families evidently remained friendly over the years.[30] Aubrey's anecdote, however, belongs not to the biographical record proper but to the mythos: that accretion of legend and lore which comes to surround the names of famous men. As to whether Stratford indeed nursed a second Bard who died young, history is mute, and posterity has had, perforce, to content itself with one Shakespeare.

⦃ 7 ⦄

Early Employment and Marriage

How long Shakespeare remained at the King's New School of Stratford-upon-Avon we cannot reliably say. A report from early in the eighteenth century holds that he did not complete the course: the narrowness of John Shakespeare's circumstances, 'and the want of his [i.e. William's] assistance at Home, forc'd his Father to withdraw him from thence'. Thus wrote Nicholas Rowe.[1] Even if permitted to finish his schooling (and allowing for an interval), William would have found himself, at the age of fifteen or thereabouts, confronted with the necessity of earning his living.

The 'aptest and most proper scholars', wrote Sir Thomas Elyot in his celebrated treatise on the education of the governing classes, 'after they be well instructed in speaking Latin, and understanding some poets, being taken from their school by their parents', they '. . . either be brought to the court, and made lackeys or pages, or else are bounden prentices.'[2] As regards Shakespeare, the first possibility has appealed irresistibly to those biographers who yearn to furnish the prince of poets with noble connections; usurping parental privilege, they place him for adoption in some aristocratic household, as though the sublimities of literary creation could ill spring from prosaic bourgeois soil. The second possibility—that he was bound prentice—probably comes closer to the reality, and has the support of the earliest authorities. Rowe says that the father took his eldest son into 'his own Employment'. In the previous century Aubrey had jotted in his notes: '. . . his father was a butcher, and I have been told heretofore by some of the neighbours, that when he was a boy he exercised his father's trade, but when he killed a calf, he would do it in a *high style*, and make a speech.'³ Genius will out, even from the mouths of butcher boys.

Although (as he indicates) Aubrey was in touch with local Stratford tradition, his confusion here runs deep. Glovers, as we have seen, were restrained from looking after their own slaughtering; and the picture of a poetical prodigy moved to extempore effusions in the shambles is sufficiently ludicrous. It is true that in an early play, 2 *Henry* VI, Shakespeare does indeed recall, with characteristic sympathy, the cruelty of the abattoir:

> And as the butcher takes away the calf,
> And binds the wretch, and beats it when it strays, . . .
> And as the dam runs lowing up and down,
> Looking the way her harmless young one went,
> And can do nought but wail her darling's loss. . . .

But for a lad growing up in a rural community such experience would be natural enough. He might have obtained it in Snitterfield, where his Uncle Henry farmed. Walking down to the Avon from Henley Street, he would have passed the Shambles in Middle Row, behind which the quarrelsome Ralph Cawdrey had his butcher shops. Another interpretation of the Aubrey passage has, however, suggested itself. Does there lurk in his account an obscurely disguised recollection of the boy Shakespeare taking part—with basin, carpet, horns, and butcher's knife and apron—in the Christmas mumming play of the killing of the calf? This traditional pantomime lingered into the present century in some English villages.⁴ No matter. It seems a reasonable enough supposition that William was apprenticed in his father's shop.

Reminiscences from this phase of the dramatist's career have been sought, not in vain, in the corpus; most lovingly by the Warwickshire antiquary Edgar I. Fripp:

William Shakespeare refers to the hides of oxen and horses, to calf-skin, sheep-skin, lamb-skin, fox-skin, and dog-skin, deer-skin and cheveril. He knew that 'neat's-leather' was used for shoes, sheep's

leather for a bridle. 'Is not parchment,' asks Hamlet, 'made of
sheep-skins?' Horatio replies, 'Ay, my lord, and calf-skins too.' . . .
The poet was aware that horsehair was used in bowstrings and
'calves' guts' in fiddle-strings. He notices leathern aprons, jerkins,
and bottles, the 'sow-skin bowget' or bag carried by tinkers, and he
comments humorously on the capacity of tanned leather to keep out
water. He alludes to 'flesh and fell', to the 'greasy fells' of ewes, and,
with evident pleasure, to the lamb's 'white fleece'. He knew that the
deer's hide was the keeper's perquisite, and we may believe that his
father made purchases from the keepers round Stratford. References
to cheveril (kid-skin) are much to the point. On account of its soft-
ness and flexibility it was used in the making of finer qualities of
gloves. Shakespeare speaks of 'a wit of cheveril, that stretches from
an inch narrow to an ell broad'. This is technical language, borrowed from his father's business. He mentions also a 'soft cheveril
conscience', capable of 'receiving gifts' if the owner will 'please to
stretch it', and 'a cheveril glove, . . . how quickly the wrong side
may be turned outward'.[5]

If his apprentice days were cluttered with the merchandise of his
father's shop, pungent with the aroma of leather, he nevertheless
found time—and occasion—for other pursuits. During the long summer twilights of 1582 he must more than once have found his way
along the narrow footpath that led west from his home, through
green fields, to a clump of farmhouses called Shottery, a mile distant, where the large Hathaway family dwelt. Shakespeare wooed
and bedded the farmer's eldest daughter—or did she seduce her boy
lover?—and in November they were licensed to marry. Visitors today follow the same path to the house known since 1795 as Anne
Hathaway's Cottage, but creeping suburbia, deadlier than any weed,
has blighted the pastoral loveliness of the walk.

Marriage is no doubt a crucial event in the histories of most men,
but when it occurs in the life of the National Poet it assumes a fateful significance.[6] The episode has given rise to strange reveries of biography—romantic, sentimental, misogynistic—resembling nothing
so much as 'those laborious webs of learning' which, according to
Francis Bacon, the scholastic philosophers spun out of 'no great
quantity of matter, and infinite agitation of wit'. The task of the responsible biographer is to clear away the cobwebs, and sift, as dis-

11. Anne Hathaway's Cottage.

interestedly as he may, the facts that chance and industry have brought to light. Those facts are admittedly sometimes perplexing.

Shakespeare's marriage required the official attention of the diocesan consistory court of Worcester, and the relevant records may still be examined by the curious in the muniment room there. The mere existence of such documents is itself of interest, for in Shakespeare's day a marriage certificate, as we know it, did not exist. All that was needed for a legally binding union—one which insured rights of dower and inheritance—was the proclamation of the banns three times in church on successive Sundays or Holy Days, so that anybody with knowledge of an impediment to matrimony might come forward and protest. After that, a ceremony before family, friends, and neighbours. Customarily the setting was the bride's parish, and the wedding was duly entered in the church register. But special circumstances attended this match. The groom was a minor, and his lady pregnant. Anne Hathaway's interesting condition had only lately become evident—she would not deliver until May—but haste in tying the knot was demanded anyway; for the canon law prohibited the asking of the banns during certain seasons. These included the interval from Advent Sunday until the Octave of Epiphany; in 1582, from 2 December until 13 January. That November the last three available days for publishing the banns were the Sundays of 18 and 25 November and St. Andrew's Day, the 30th. This opportunity the couple missed. Did the youth require more time to overcome his father's resistance? In any event, not until the 27th did two friends of the bride's family make the journey to Worcester, twenty-one miles to the west, there to secure the common licence required on such occasions from the consistory court, which was held at the western end of the south aisle of the cathedral. William may have come along also—'possibly with Anne on his horse behind him', one biographer helpfully suggests—but, being a minor, he had little to contribute by his presence. The then Bishop of Worcester was John Whitgift, shortly to be translated to the see of Canterbury; he was a zealous reformer of ecclesiastical abuses, and in matters of canon law a strict constructionist. Over his consistory court there presided his officers: a chancellor (Richard Cosin in 1582), assisted by a registrar, Robert Warmstry, who acted as executive officer. By the authority vested in them, they could grant exemptions from the usual regulations governing matrimony.

Such dispensations took the form of a licence addressed to the minister (sometimes named) of the church in which the wedding was to take place—this need not have been in the parish where the couple lived—and setting forth the special conditions as to banns. In some cases they were to be 'twice lawfully first asked and proclaimed'; sometimes just once, perhaps at the church door at the time of the ceremony. We even know of one licence in which the banns were dispensed with altogether. These licences were not at all uncommon; in 1582 the Worcester court granted at least ninety-eight. To secure one, the applicants had to arm themselves with several documents attesting that there were no irregularities of the sort which the banns were intended to discourage. These papers consisted of (1) a sworn allegation, giving the name, address, and occupation of the parties and of the consenting parents or guardians, and the reasons for dispensing with full publication; (2) a letter from the same parents or guardians, or from an intermediary known to the court, certifying—sometimes on oath—that no lawful impediment existed; and (3) a bond, or obligation, to indemnify the bishop and his officers should any legal action arise out of the grant of licence. These documents having been accepted, the petitioners paid a fee, anywhere from around 3s.8d. to 10s.4d., depending upon the terms of the dispensation. In return they were given a licence which was presumably kept by the vicar or curate to whom it was addressed. The clerk of the court recorded the licence in the Bishop's Register. Now the couple were free to marry. Of these several papers most biographical interest would be attached to the first, but unfortunately no sixteenth-century allegations have been preserved for Worcester diocese. Nor have any licences from this period survived. For Shakespeare's marriage we have only the bond and the entry of licence. They answer some questions and pose others.

Couched in the dry legalistic terminology of such documents, the bond (dated 28 November) specifies that William Shagspere and 'Anne Hathwey of Stratford in the diocese of Worcester, maiden' may, with the consent of the bride's side, lawfully solemnize matrimony, and thereafter live together as man and wife, after one asking of the banns—that is, they may do so, barring any obstacle of pre-contract, consanguinity, or the like. Should the validity of the union be later impeached, then the bond of £40 posted by the two sureties would be forfeited to 'save harmless the right reverend father in God Lord John, Bishop of Worcester, and his officers'. In those days £40 was a good sum of money, and would not be lightly risked. The description of Anne as a maiden has interest; some Worcester bonds make an invidious distinction between a 'maiden' and a 'single-woman', but the Bishop's officers appear not to have enquired too curiously into this bride's virginity or lack thereof.

The sureties, Fulk Sandells and John Rychardson, are described in the bond as husbandmen of Stratford ('. . . Fulconem Sandells de Stratford in comitatu Warwicensi, agricolam, et Johannem Rychardson, ibidem agricolam'). Actually they farmed in Shottery, which formed part of Stratford parish, and were friends of the bride's father. So much we gather from Richard Hathaway's will, in which he names his 'trusty' friend and neighbour Sandells as one of his two supervisors (trustees, we would say); Rychardson witnessed the testament. That no spokesmen for the Shakespeares are named in the bond has aroused dark suspicions in the suspicious. 'The prominence of the Shottery husbandmen in the negotiations preceding Shakespeare's marriage suggests the true position of affairs', writes Sir Sidney Lee magisterially:

> Sandells and Richardson, representing the lady's family, doubtless secured the deed on their own initiative, so that Shakespeare might have small opportunity of evading a step which his intimacy with their friend's daughter had rendered essential to her reputation. The wedding probably took place, without the consent of the bridegroom's parents—it may be without their knowledge—soon after the signing of the deed.[7]

Moreover, the clergyman who officiated was 'obviously' of an 'easy temper'. Confident words, 'doubtless' and 'obviously', and here used to imply irregularity and collusion for which no evidence exists. As we have seen, issuance of the licence presumed the knowledge or consent of the groom's father. If the latter wished to prevent the match, he had only to complain to the consistory court. The judge of that court might on rare occasions issue a contested licence; but no evidence of extraordinary circumstances—such as the incapacity or tyrannical obstinacy of the parent—in this case exists. Far from demonstrating an easy temper, the minister who followed his bishop's instructions, as set forth in a licence, was merely performing his duty. At that time it was the custom for the bondsmen to be friends or kinsmen of the bride, for an unmarried heiress—not her suitor—stood most in need of the law's protection against fortune-hunters.

An heiress she was. So one may gather, even today, from the spaciousness and solidity of Anne Hathaway's Cottage; rather more than a cottage, truly—this twelve-roomed rectangular farmhouse that stands, partly concealed, round the corner of the narrow lane leading from Stratford, and a few yards up from the little brook which glides through Shottery. In Shakespeare's day the house must have stood almost at the edge of the Forest of Arden. It is such a setting as Celia describes in *As You Like It*; the dwelling 'in the purlieus of this forest':

> West of this place, down in the neighbour bottom.
> The rank of osiers by the murmuring stream
> Left on your right hand brings you to the place.

—although the olive trees of Celia's Arden find no counterpart in Anne's.

The house, which remained in the Hathaways' possession until 1746, was soundly built on stone foundations, with timber-frame walls filled in with wattle and daub, and open-timbered ceiling. A pair of curved oak timbers, called 'crucks', reach from ground level to the top, where, pegged together, they support the high-pitched roof of thatch. The earliest part of the house, dating from at least the fifteenth century, consists of a hall or living-room of two twelve-foot bays, and a two-storey east wing. The stone fire-places with oak bressummers—one eight feet wide, the other eleven—were installed in the next century, when an upper floor was added to provide chambers over the hall. The massive old bake-oven in the kitchen still remains, and at the top of the narrow staircase stands the Hathaway bedstead with its elaborately carved posts (in his will Richard speaks of 'two joined beds in my parlour'). So too the dairy or buttery has been preserved intact. This was a farmhouse, and in former times other farm buildings stood nearby. To the Hathaways this property was known as Hewlands Farm, and sheep grazed on its half-yardland—anywhere from ten to twenty-three acres—of pasture and meadowland. The pasturage is gone now, but the garden, with its herbs and roses and posy peas, still flourishes, as does the orchard fragrant with wild flowers and apple trees, while jasmine clings to the Cottage walls.[8]

The Hathaways were substantial Warwickshire yeomen who had dwelt in Shottery for more than one generation. Anne's grandfather John appears as an archer in the muster-rolls, and served his parish as beadle, constable, affeeror, and one of the Twelve Men of Old Stratford (the substantial citizens, at least twelve in number, who presided twice a year at the Great Leet or Law Day).* In the subsidy of 1549-50 his goods were valued at £10, a high assessment. When he died, his son Richard carried on with the farming on the half-yardland called 'Hewland', and also on a toft and half-yardland called 'Hewlyns', as well as on a yardland with house late in the tenure of one Thomas Perkyns; in all, the holdings must have come to between fifty and ninety acres. Richard employed a shepherd, Thomas Whittington, and in his will did not forget to pay him the £4.6s.8d. he owed him; we shall be hearing again about this Whittington. The Hathaways and the Shakespeares knew one another, for in September 1566 John Shakespeare stood surety for Richard in two actions, and was called on to pay debts for him to John Page and Joan Biddle. Richard Hathaway seems to have married twice, and to have had children by both wives, seven of them still living when he drew up his will. Joan, his second wife—if she was that—survived her husband by many years; in the spring of 1601 she is described as 'the late deceased Jone Hathaway'. By then Richard lay almost twenty years in his grave.

In the will that he drew up on 1 September 1581, when he was 'sick in body but of perfect memory (I thank my Lord God)', Hathaway itemizes bequests for his three daughters and four sons. But he mentions no Anne. Yet that Shakespeare's wife had that Christian name we may hardly doubt: it appears thrice in the marriage licence bond and is inscribed on her gravestone.[9] Richard Hathaway does, however, leave ten marks—£6.13s.4d.—to his daughter Agnes, to be paid out to her on her wedding day. In this period the names Anne and Agnes were interchangeable (the latter being pronounced *Annes*), and in the same will Richard bequeathes one sheep to Agnes, Thomas Hathaway's daughter, although she was christened as Anne. There are many other examples of the same conversion; thus the great theatrical entrepreneur Philip Henslowe calls his wife Agnes in his will, but she was buried as Anne.[10]

---

* There were two such courts, one for Stratford and another for the outlying settlements of Old Stratford, Shottery, and Welcombe; see *Minutes and Accounts of the Corporation of Stratford-upon-Avon*, ed. Richard Savage and Edgar I. Fripp; Publications of the Dugdale Society (Oxford and London, 1921-30), i, p. xxiii.

The Victorian Shakespeare scholar Halliwell-Phillipps, examining the marriage licence bond, thought that the letters on the seal were R. H., for Richard Hathaway. The seal has long since disintegrated, but (if we may judge from a surviving sketch) the second letter was more likely a *K*, and this seal bearing the letters R. K. closely resembles one in common use in the Registry in the 1580s.[11] Anyway Richard Hathaway was dead when Anne married, as demonstrated by his will, which Halliwell-Phillipps discovered while his 1848 life of Shakespeare was printing. That a daughter of Richard Hathaway became Shakespeare's wife is confirmed by Rowe; he never saw the bond, yet says that 'his wife was the daughter of one *Hathaway*'. But the matter is clinched by the last will and testament of the faithful Hathaway shepherd. 'Item', declared Thomas Whittington on 25 March 1601, 'I give and bequeath unto the poor people of Stratford xls. that is in the hand of Anne Shaxspere, wife unto Mr. Wyllyam Shaxspere, and is due debt unto me, being paid to mine executor by the said Wyllyam Shaxspere or his assigns according to the true meaning of this my will.' That this is the same Whittington is apparent from his will, in which several Hathaways are mentioned, including the lately deceased Joan, and her sons John and William—Anne's brothers or half-brothers—to whom the shepherd owed money for 'a quarter of an year's board'.

Of the three daughters remembered in Richard Hathaway's will, Agnes-Anne, being the first mentioned, was probably eldest. No record of her christening has come down, for she was born, it seems, before 1558, when the baptismal registers commence. On the brass marker affixed to Anne Shakespeare's gravestone in the chancel of Stratford Church, she is described as having 'DEPARTED THIS LIFE . . . BEING OF THE AGE OF·67·YEARES'. That was on 6 August 1623. Tombstone inscriptions from this period are not invariably reliable—could the engraver have misread a carelessly formed 1 for a 7 in his script, and thus added six years to Anne's lifespan? But in the absence of other evidence we are obliged to accept this unambiguous testimony. Anne was, then, seven or eight years her husband's senior, and twenty-six in 1582; by the standards of those days, growing a bit long in the tooth for the marriage market. She took a teen-aged lover, became pregnant, and married him. Did

he reluctantly submit, to salvage the reputation of a fading siren of
Shottery with whom he had lain in an interlude of midsummer passion? Scholars (as one might expect) have ransacked the corpus for
intimations of retrospective regret, and their searches have not gone
unrewarded. Thus, Lysander and Hermia in A *Midsummer-Night's
Dream*:

> *Lysander.* The course of true love never did run smooth;
> But either it was different in blood . . .
> Or else misgraffed in respect of years—
> *Hermia.* O spite! too old to be engag'd to young.

And, more forcibly, the Duke in *Twelfth Night* to the disguised
Viola:

> Let still the woman take
> An elder than herself; so wears she to him,
> So sways she level in her husband's heart.
> For, boy, however we do praise ourselves,
> Our fancies are more giddy and unfirm,
> More longing, wavering, sooner lost and won,
> Than women's are.
>   *Viola.*   I think it well, my lord.
>   *Duke.* Then let thy love be younger than thyself,
> Or thy affection cannot hold the bent;
> For women are as roses, whose fair flow'r
> Being once display'd doth fall that very hour.

Who can deny the possibility that buried here lies wisdom purchased at the cost of personal *Angst*? Yet we do well to remind ourselves that these comments are spoken not by the author in his own
voice, but by the shadows he has created, and that they have an immediate application to the dramatic context. The Duke after all is
sentimental and more than a trifle foolish.

These perplexities are slight compared to those created by the second Shakespeare marriage record in the Worcester muniments.
When the clerk of the court entered the grant of a licence in the
Bishop's Register on 27 November 1582 (one day earlier than the
date on the bond itself), he gave the bride's name as Anne Whateley of Temple Grafton. This second Anne appears here once, and

12. The Anne Whateley entry, 27 November 1582.

nowhere else. Who is she? In the absence of any facts whatever, biographers have created a persona for the mysterious maiden from Temple Grafton, and made her a principal in a triangular drama—romantic, melodramatic, and moral—in which the passionate Will must choose between Love and Duty.

A version of the scenario full blown is to be found in Anthony Burgess's popular biography:

> It is reasonable to believe that Will wished to marry a girl named Anne Whateley. . . . Her father may have been a friend of John Shakespeare's, he may have sold kidskin cheap, there are various reasons why the Shakespeares and the Whateleys, or their nubile children, might become friendly. Sent on skin-buying errands to Temple Grafton, Will could have fallen for a comely daughter, sweet as May and shy as a fawn. He was eighteen and highly susceptible. Knowing something about girls, he would know that this was the real thing. Something, perhaps, quite different from what he felt about Mistress Hathaway of Shottery.
>
> But why, attempting to marry Anne Whateley, had he put himself in the position of having to marry the other Anne? I suggest that, to use the crude but convenient properties of the old women's-magazine morality-stories, he was exercised by love for the one and lust for the other. . . .
>
> I consider that the lovely boy that Will probably was—auburn hair, melting eyes, ready tongue, tags of Latin poetry—did not, having tasted Anne's body in the spring, go eagerly back to Shottery through the early summer to taste it again. Perhaps Anne had already said something about the advantages of love in an indentured bed, away from cowpats and the prickling of stubble in a field, and the word *marriage* frightened Will as much as it will frighten any young man. But, with the irony of things, he fell in love with a younger Anne and himself began to talk about marriage. This Anne was chaste, not wanton and forward, and there was probably no

nonsense in her family about allowing consummation of the be-
trothal. . . .

Thus rebuffed, Will—his libido 'pricking hard'—returned to his
Shottery Anne for 'a bout of lust in the August fields', an encounter
that left the lady pregnant. Sandells and Rychardson thereupon
raised their 'brawny yeomen's fists in threat'; a shotgun wedding
loomed for the post-coitally chastened Will.

> The special licence meant only two readings of the banns, not
> the three normally required. Anne, through brawny and powerful
> friends, is demonstrating that she hath a way.
> The other Anne, along with the parents on both sides, must have
> found out about this. Will had gotten a girl (well, hardly a girl) in
> the family way and had been trying to evade the penalty. Will gave
> in, with bitter resignation, and was led to the slaughter, or the mar-
> riage bed. The role of honourable Christian gentleman was being
> forced upon him. This, anyway, is a persuasive reading of the docu-
> mented facts, but no Shakespeare-lover is necessarily bound to ac-
> cept it.[12]

Colourful, if a trifle tawdry, this 'persuasive reading' certainly is; but
it is not so much biography as imaginative invention, and hence
more appropriate to a novel, which Mr. Burgess, in *Nothing Like
the Sun*, earlier gave us. Nor does it less strain credulity to surmise
(with Sir Sidney Lee) that on that remarkable November day in
Worcester a second William Shakespeare—no relation—was granted
a licence to marry a second Warwickshire Anne.[13] There are no 'documented facts' about Anne Whateley, as Mr. Burgess is well aware,
only one fact—the Register entry—and so we do not know whether
she was 'chaste, not wanton and forward', or 'sweet as May and shy
as a fawn'. We cannot even say with reasonable assurance that she
ever actually existed.

The Worcester clerk appears to have been fairly careless, for he
got a number of names wrong in the Register, or at least recorded
them differently from the way they appear in the bonds. So he wrote
'Baker' for 'Barbar', 'Darby' for 'Bradeley', 'Edgock' for 'Elcock'.
But why 'Whateley' for 'Hathaway'? These names only vaguely resemble one another. The diocesan records show that on the day the

Hathaway licence was registered, the 27th, the court dealt with forty cases, and one of these concerned the suit of the vicar of Crowle, William Whateley, in arms against Arnold Leight for non-payment of tithes. This Whateley must have been a familiar figure in the court, for his name appears in several records for 1582 and 1583. The clerk, one suspects, was copying from a hastily written temporary memorandum, or from an unfamiliar hand in an allegation; he had just been dealing with Whateley, and by a process of unconscious association made the substitution.* A prosaic as well as speculative interpretation, no doubt, of the single document, and a reading hostile to romantic yearnings. But that Anne Whateley, so nubile and blushingly chaste, should owe her very being to the negligence of a bumbling scribe perhaps has a beauty of its own.

We still may wonder how Temple Grafton enters the picture. The village lies five miles west of Stratford, and three and a half miles in the same direction from Shottery, just south of the high road leading to Alcester. From Temple Grafton, perched on a hill, one can look across the valley to Bredon Hill and the Cotswolds. Only a few of the old houses now remain, an old barn too, and an ancient stone pigeon-house with quaint conical roof; but in Shakespeare's day husbandmen farmed in the four fields of Temple Grafton, and pastured their flocks in the open common or Cow Common, while quarriers and stonemasons earned their bread from the surrounding slate deposits and limestone pits. Perhaps in the early eighties Anne Hathaway was living in Temple Grafton—the Worces-

---

* This analysis and supporting evidence are offered by J. W. Gray in his chapter, 'Hathaway or Whateley', in *Shakespeare's Marriage* (1905), pp. 21-35. E. R. C. Brinkworth thinks such a clerical error unlikely 'because the Bishop's Register is a neat fair copy written up later from notes or from files of loose documents and not on the actual day when the licence was issued' (*Shakespeare and the Bawdy Court of Stratford* (1972), p. 88). But it is not certain that the Register in this period was copied from a rough draft (see Gray, pp. 24-5); nor, in view of other, demonstrable discrepancies in the Register, is it clear why a mistake in this entry could not have been duplicated. Joseph Hill, in his edition of J. T. Burgess's *Historic Warwickshire* (1892), p. 102, suggests that the clerk's slip was of sight rather than memory, "Annamhathwey' being read as 'Annamwhateley' (cited in *Minutes and Accounts of the Corporation of Stratford-upon-Avon*, ed. Richard Savage and Edgar I. Fripp; Publications of the Dugdale Society (Oxford and London, 1921-30), iii. 111).

ter licence entries usually give the bride's residence—or the wedding ceremony may have taken place there.

A Puritan 'survey of the state of the ministry in Warwickshire', made four years later, describes the vicar of Grafton, John Frith, as 'an old priest and unsound in religion; he can neither preach nor read well, his chiefest trade is to cure hawks that are hurt or diseased, for which purpose many do usually repair to him'. Bishop Whitgift's inquisitors kept a wary eye on such wayward sympathizers with the Old Faith; in 1580 they had made Frith post bond not to marry without licence 'any persons at any times prohibited by the ecclesiastical laws', and to conduct no weddings at any other times 'without asking the banns in the church three Sundays or holidays solemnly'.[14] Did Shakespeare and his betrothed present their licence to this unsound priest? One recalls again the testament in the Birthplace rooftiles. The parish register of Temple Grafton affords no clue, for it survives only in an incomplete transcript of entries commencing in 1612.

If not in Temple Grafton, then where else might the couple have wed? St. Michael's stands hard by the registry in Worcester, but the marriage is not among those recorded there. Elsewhere in Stratford parish two other chapels (besides Holy Trinity) might have served. One was in Bishopton, slightly to the north of Shottery; the other in Luddington, three miles west of Stratford. The register for St. Peter's, Bishopton, however, begins only in 1591, and that for All Souls, Luddington, in the Bishop's transcript, in 1612. In Victorian times S. W. Fullom visited Luddington in quest of information, and in his *History of William Shakespeare* of 1862 he has a curious tale to tell:

The [old parsonage] house is occupied by a family named Dyke, respected for miles round, and here the report of the marriage can be traced back directly for a hundred and fifty years. Mrs. Dyke received it from Martha Casebrooke, who died at the age of ninety, after residing her whole life in the village, and not only declared that she was told in her childhood that the marriage was solemnized at Luddington, but had seen the ancient tome in which it was registered. This, indeed, we found, on visiting the neighbouring cottages, was remembered by persons still living, when it was in the possession of a Mrs. Pickering, who had been housekeeper to Mr. Coles, the last curate; and one cold day burnt the register to boil her kettle![15]

Fullom is elsewhere an eccentric guide,[16] but he is unlikely to have created from whole cloth an account so disarming in its particularities. Still, if this is a true report, it is odd that local tradition did not seize upon it early on. The voluble Jordan, for example, who contemplated the ruins of Luddington chapel around 1780, is silent on the subject. However, Joseph Gray, visiting Stratford shortly after 1900, heard from Edward Flower of the great Warwickshire brewing family that Luddington as the scene of Shakespeare's marriage 'was generally accepted in the neighbourhood early in the last century'.[17] Here we may let the matter rest.

Wherever the rites took place, the fact of the bride's pregnancy agitated some of the earlier biographers, who shook their heads gravely over the Bard's presumed 'antenuptial fornication'. The delinquency, if such it is, will raise few eyebrows in the permissive society; but, in his art if not in life, Shakespeare seems to place a premium on premarital continence. Romeo and Juliet bring to their single night together 'a pair of stainless maidenhoods'. 'One turf shall serve as pillow for us both', Lysander tells Hermia in the wood outside Athens; 'One heart, one bed, two bosoms, and one troth'. But she rejects such proximity to the lover she will marry:

> Nay, good Lysander; for my sake, my dear,
> Lie further off yet; do not lie so near. . . .
> Such separation as may well be said
> Becomes a virtuous bachelor and a maid,
> So far be distant; and good night, sweet friend.

'If', Prospero warns Ferdinand,

> thou dost break her virgin-knot before
> All sanctimonious ceremonies may
> With full and holy rite be minist'red,
> No sweet aspersion shall the heavens let fall
> To make this contract grow; but barren hate,
> Sour-ey'd disdain, and discord, shall bestrew

> The union of your bed with weeds so loathly
> That you shall hate it both.

In *The Winter's Tale* Florizel likens his love to that of Jupiter and golden Apollo, whose

> transformations
> Were never for a piece of beauty rarer,
> Nor in a way so chaste, since my desires
> Run not before mine honour, nor my lusts
> Burn hotter than my faith.

The desires of Florizel's creator, it seems, burnt somewhat hotter. Are we to suspect that, sated before the ceremony, he lamented with his own despoiled Lucrece—

> The sweets we wish for turn to loathed sours
> Even in the moment that we call them ours

—and embraced the cynical folk wisdom of a Parolles: 'A young man married is a man that's marr'd'? Some, not a few, have so inferred.

To interpret the episode thus, however, is to be seduced again by selective quotation. An alternative view holds that Shakespeare, far from yielding sullenly to the importunities of kin or conscience, had in fact tied the knot informally before entering into the holy bond of matrimony. Elizabethan custom recognized a troth-plight before witnesses as having the force of a civil marriage, although (then as now) issues of sexual propriety invited a spectrum of opinion. Thus William Harrington, rector of St. Anne's, Alderbury, writing early in the century, insisted that bride and groom should enter matrimony in 'clean life, that is to say, both ought to be without sin'; moreover, in lawful wedlock, 'the man may not possess the woman as his wife nor the woman the man as her husband, nor inhabit, nor fleshly meddle together as man and wife afore such time as that matrimony be approved and solemnised by our mother Holy Church, and if they do in deed they sin deadly'.[18]

Still some couples fleshly meddled together without the blessing of Holy Church, but with the sanction of troth-plight. Into such a pre-contract 'by words of the present'—*per verba de praesenti*—Alice Shaw of Hatton and William Holder of Fulbrook entered in 1585.

Before two witnesses in her father-in-law's house, she said, 'I do confess that I am your wife and have forsaken all my friends for your sake, and I hope you will use me well.' With these words she gave William her hand, and he 'used the like words unto her, in effect, and took her by the hand, and kissed together'. William and Alice used one another less well than this ritual presaged, for shortly thereafter he was suing her about the contract. There is, however, no question that in the eyes of the consistory court they had the status of man and wife.[19]

Shakespeare understood these pre-contracts well enough. They figure importantly in *Measure for Measure*, where Claudio, accused of fornication with Julietta, says in his own defence:

> upon a true contract
> I got possession of Julietta's bed.
> You know the lady—she is fast my wife,
> Save that we do the denunciation lack
> Of outward order.

Whether Shakespeare in this fashion got possession of Anne Hathaway's bed we have, of course, no way of determining, and to pursue such speculation may be merely to indulge in (as one biographer put it) a 'kindly sentiment'. But kindly sentiment has no less claim than unkindly, and troth-plight was common enough in Shakespeare's England.

Some antecedent courtship must have gone on. In the third of his Seven Ages of Man, Jaques describes the lover as

> Sighing like furnace, with a woeful ballad
> Made to his mistress' eyebrow.

If as a young lover Shakespeare composed any woeful ballads for Anne Hathaway, they no longer exist, and into this vacuum the forgers have rushed with ballads of their own, woeful in another sense. In the spacious cycle of the *Sonnets*, however, stands one anomalous amatory poem which has little connection with what has gone before or with what follows, and which is sufficiently ungainly to suggest creative adolescence. It is Sonnet 145:

> Those lips that Love's own hand did make
> Breath'd forth the sound that said 'I hate'
> To me that languish'd for her sake;
> But when she saw my woeful state,
> Straight in her heart did mercy come,
> Chiding that tongue that ever sweet
> Was us'd in giving gentle doom;
> And taught it thus anew to greet:
> 'I hate' she alter'd with an end
> That follow'd it as gentle day
> Doth follow night, who like a fiend
> From heaven to hell is flown away:
>   'I hate' from hate away she threw,
>   And sav'd my life, saying 'not you'.

In the concluding couplet could 'hate away' conceivably be a pun—one of those strained word-plays in which the Elizabethans delighted—on 'Hathaway'? So Andrew Gurr has ingeniously suggested: 'Shakespeare's future wife, so the poet says, took the meaning out of "hate" by adding its proper ending, and by so doing made it clear that she did not dislike the poet. Hate-away.'[20] *Hate-away* is not precisely equivalent to *Hathaway*, but then not all the rhymes in this sonnet are all that precise either; and the pronunciation—regarded in the context of Warwickshire dialect of the sixteenth century—makes for a better pun than might at first strike the modern ear.[21] The poem may indeed be a young poet's love token.

Naturally we yearn to visualize the object of so much biographical attention. Was Anne such an Amazonian Venus as the goddess who pursues the lovely Adonis in Shakespeare's first narrative poem? Or was she (despite her years) all yielding maidenly femininity, like Mariana at the moated grange, who plighted *her* troth to the perfidious Angelo? If Jaques's lover celebrates his mistress's eyebrow, at least one biographer has been forthcoming enough to tell us of 'the dark eyebrow of Anne Hathaway, a lovely maiden of the picturesque hamlet of Shottery'. But the dusty vellum yielded by the muniment room furnishes no intelligence as to the shade of Anne's eyebrow, nor does it even confirm her loveliness. There survives, however, in a copy of the Shakespeare Third Folio of 1664 (the second issue) in

13. Shakespeare's Consort.

the Colgate University Library in Hamilton, New York, a faded drawing of a young woman with sixteenth-century cap and ruff. Accompanying verses, parodying Ben Jonson's tribute to the Folio portrait of Shakespeare, identify the sitter:

> This figure, that thou there seest put
> It was for Shakespear's Consort cut
> Wherein the Graver had a strife
> With Nature to outdo the Life
> O had he Her Complexion shewn
> As plain as He's the outline Drawn
> The plate, believe me, woud surpass
> All that was ever made in brass.

The drawing bears the date 1708, and it seems reasonable enough to suppose that it belongs to the eighteenth century. The artist, we learn from his great grandson, was Sir Nathaniel Curzon of Kedlestone, and his handiwork is described in the Colgate Folio as a tracing. Did Curzon copy a portrait—long since vanished—of a young, soberly attractive woman of times past, and playfully offer it as an *imago vera* of Shakespeare's wife? That is more plausible (given the facetious tone of the verses) than a theory of deliberate imposition in the manner of the later fabricators; more plausible too than the infinitely more exciting hypothesis that Curzon had somehow stumbled upon an authentic portrait of Anne Hathaway. What remains certain, in the midst of so much that is questionable, is that a year before Nicholas Rowe informed the world that the poet's 'Wife was the Daughter of one *Hathaway*, said to have been a substantial Yeoman in the Neighbourhood of *Stratford*', Shakespeare-lovers had begun to wonder about the lineaments of Shakespeare's consort. That is, if one can trust Curzon's date.[22]

About the next episode in his career the record is mercifully exact. On Sunday, 26 May 1583—Trinity Sunday, the church's feast day— vicar Henry Heicroft christened the first grandchild of Alderman John Shakespeare. Her parents named the child Susanna. That spring, in April, two other infants had been baptized as Susanna, but the name, with its associations appealing to Puritans, was still rather

14. Christening of Susanna Shakespeare, 26 May 1583.

15. Christening of Hamnet and Judith, 2 February 1585.

novel in Stratford, first appearing in the parish register in 1574.[23] Less than two years later Anne gave birth to twins, a boy and a girl. The vicar had meanwhile removed to a richer benefice ten miles off in Rowington, so the twins were christened by his successor on 2 February 1585. Richard Barton of Coventry, who officiated, is described in a Puritan survey as 'a preacher, learned, zealous, and godly, and fit for the ministry'.[24] The Shakepeares named their offspring Hamnet and Judith, after their neighbours and lifelong friends the Sadlers, who lived in a house at the corner of the High Street and Sheep Street, next to the Corn Market. When in 1598 Judith and Hamnet produced a son, they called him William.

By 1585 the family of William Shakespeare was complete. Before achieving his majority he had acquired a wife and three children. They did not yet have a house of their own—that day lay a dozen years off—and the roof over their heads was probably provided by the capacious homestead in Henley Street. We do not know whether William felt, with Milton's Adam, that the world was all before him, but before long his wandering steps would take him from Stratford on his solitary way. His wife did not go with him hand in hand, but neither did he turn his back permanently on the Eden, if such it was, of his youth.

{ 8 }

The Lost Years

From 1585, when the twins were born, until 1592, when we hear about Shakespeare in a quite different context, the documentary record presents a virtual blank.* This is the interval that scholarship has designated the Lost Years. They are not, however, barren of legend, which flourishes in such voids.

Legendary heroes have legendary thirsts. If we may trust the mythos, Shakespeare quaffed deep draughts of good Warwickshire brown ale. He may well have been on intimate terms with local taps and tapsters. In *The Taming of the Shrew* Christopher Sly, 'old Sly's son of Burton Heath', urges:

> Ask Marian Hacket, the fat ale-wife of Wincot, if she know me not; if she say I am not fourteen pence on the score for sheer ale, score me up for the lying'st knave in Christendom. What! I am not bestraught. [*Taking a pot of ale*] Here's—
> 3 Servant. O, this it is that makes your lady mourn!

Certainly Shakespeare knew the little village of Barton on the Heath, situated in a stretch of barren ground fifteen miles south of Stratford, for there lived his prosperous uncle Edmund Lambert. He had married Joan Arden, one of Mary Shakespeare's seven sisters. As to whether William ever encountered a fat ale-wife in Wincot, a hamlet some five miles south-west of Stratford, history is discreetly

* The only reference to him is in *Shakespeare* v. *Lambert*, in 1588; see above, pp. 39-40.

silent; but Hackets then lived in the parish. In the eighteenth century Francis Wise, Radcliffe librarian at Oxford, journeyed to Stratford and the vicinity in search of anecdotes about the poet. One of the places he visited was Wincot, and his enquiries there supplied Thomas Warton, the Professor of Poetry at Oxford, with a note for his glossary to Shakespeare: '*Wilnecote* is a village in *Warwickshire*, with which *Shakespear* was well acquainted, near *Stratford*. The house kept by our genial hostess still remains, but is at present a mill.'[1] *The Taming of the Shrew* teases with its local allusiveness.

A grateful public first learned of the toping exploits of the young Shakespeare from the *British Magazine* in 1762. In that year an anonymous correspondent composed a 'Letter from the Place of Shakespear's Nativity' while putting up at the White Lion Inn near the top of Henley Street. His 'chearful landlord', the correspondent reports, took him to the house where the great man was born.

> From thence my landlord was so complaisant as to go with me to visit two young women, lineal descendants of our great dramatic poet: they keep a little ale-house, some small distance from Stratford. On the road thither, at a place called Bidford, he shewed me, in the hedge, a crab-tree, called Shakespear's canopy, because under it our poet slept one night; for he, as well as Ben Johnson, loved a glass for the pleasure of society; and he having heard much of the men of that village as deep drinkers and merry fellows, one day went over to Bidford, to take a cup with them. He enquired of a shepherd for the Bidford drinkers; who replied, they were absent; but the Bidford sippers were at home; and I suppose, continued the sheep-keeper, they will be sufficient for you: and so indeed they were. He was forced to take up his lodging under that tree for some hours. . . .[2]

The story surfaces too late to have more force than that of traditional anecdote. Once told, it was embroidered in the retelling. Around 1770 that doubtful repository of Stratford lore, John Jordan, furnished an account of the morning after the Bidford débâcle. Shakespeare's companions roused him, and entreated him to resume the contest, but, declining—he had had enough—the poet surveyed the adjoining hamlets, and delivered himself of an extemporaneous doggerel rhyme. 'I have drunk', he declaimed, 'with

Piping Pebworth, Dancing Marston,
Haunted Hillborough, Hungry Grafton,
Dadgeing Exhall, Papist Wicksford,
Beggarly Broom, and Drunken Bidford.'[3]

A quarter of a century later Samuel Ireland stood, overcome with emotion, before the tree which had spread its shade over Shakespeare, 'and sheltered him from the dews of the night'. The truth of the relation he did not doubt—'it is certain that the Crab Tree is known all round the country by the name of Shakespeare's Crab; and that the villages to which the allusion is made, all bear the epithets here given them: the people of Pebworth are still famed for their skill on the pipe and tabor: Hillborough is now called Haunted Hillborough; and Grafton is notorious for the poverty of its soil.'[4]

The splendid crabtree, which Ireland sketched for his *Picturesque Views*, is now long since gone, having been devoured by the souvenir hunters. On 4 December 1824 what remained was dug up and carted to the Revd. Henry Holyoakes of Bidford Grange. 'For several years previously', the Stratford antiquary Robert Bell Wheler commented mournfully, 'the Branches had entirely vanished from the further depradations of pious votaries; & the stock had mouldered to touchwood, the roots were rotten, & the time worn remains totally useless.'[5] No marker commemorates the spot for the modern pilgrim.

Perhaps it is just as well; Shakespeare's drinking exploits may have no more authoritative basis than (in Chambers's phrase) 'the inventiveness of innkeepers'. But, if we may give credence to another and much better established tradition, the Warwickshire lads amused themselves with more exciting—and dangerous—diversions than carousing tournaments. The story of Shakespeare the Deerslayer appears full blown in Nicholas Rowe's preface to his 1709 edition. It is a picturesque relation deriving, one expects, from local Stratford lore passed on to Rowe's informant, the actor Betterton. Having taken on the responsibilities of matrimony, Rowe writes,

In this kind of Settlement he continu'd for some time, 'till an Extravagance that he was guilty of, forc'd him both out of his Country and that way of Living which he had taken up. . . . He had, by a Misfortune common enough to young Fellows, fallen into ill

Company; and amongst them, some that made a frequent practice of Deer-stealing, engag'd him with them more than once in robbing a Park that belong'd to Sir *Thomas Lucy* of *Cherlecot*, near *Stratford*. For this he was prosecuted by that Gentleman, as he thought, somewhat too severely; and in order to revenge that ill Usage, he made a Ballad upon him. And tho' this, probably the first Essay of his Poetry, be lost, yet it is said to have been so very bitter, that it redoubled the Prosecution against him to that degree, that he was oblig'd to leave his Business and Family in *Warwickshire*, for some time, and shelter himself in *London*.[6]

Other versions of the story filtered down. One appears in a memorandum jotted down in Oxford late in the seventeenth century by an obscure clergyman, Richard Davies. He was perhaps then the chaplain of Corpus Christi College. Later he became curate of Sandford-on-Thames in Oxfordshire, and afterwards rector of Sapperton, Gloucestershire; he finished his days as Archdeacon of Coventry in the diocese of Lichfield, but when he died, in 1708, he was buried in Sapperton. So he never strayed very far from the Shakespeare country. The antiquary Anthony Wood, not celebrated for his benevolence, knew Davies, and described him as looking 'red and jolly, as if he had been at a fish dinner at C[orpus] C[hristi] C[ollege], and afterwards drinking—as he had been'. We do not know if Davies was in his cups when he wrote that Shakespeare was 'much given to all unluckiness in stealing venison and rabbits, particularly from Sir —— Lucy, who had him oft whipped and sometimes imprisoned and at last made him fly his native country to his great advancement'. The victim, however, took an artist's revenge by portraying his persecutor as Justice Clodpate, and identifying this 'great man' by the 'three louses rampant for his arms'. The jolly cleric's memory is not functioning very well: he cannot recall Lucy's christian name, and he has confused Clodpate—'a hearty true *English* Coxcomb' in *Epsom Wells*, a play by Davies's contemporary, Thomas Shadwell—with Justice Shallow in *The Merry Wives of Windsor*. Rowe, who cannot have known Davies's notes, gets the reference right in his passage on Falstaff:

> Amongst other Extravagances, in *The Merry Wives of* Windsor, he has made him a Dear-stealer, that he might at the same time re-

7. William Shakespeare.

William Shakespeare was born at Stratford
upon Avon in Warwickshire about 1563.4.
much given to all unluckiness in stealing venison &
Rabbits, particularly from Sr [ ] Lucy who had him
oft whipt & sometimes Imprisoned & at last made Him
fly his native Country to his great Advancemt. but
His reveng was so great that he is his Justice Clodpate
and calls him a great man & in allusion to his name bore three
From an Actor of Playes, he became a Composer.   lowses rampant for his Arms.

Ætat. 53.
He dyed Apr. 23. 1616. probably at Stratford,
for there he is buryed. and hath a Monument on   Dugd.
wch He lays a heavy curse upon any one   p. 520.
who shall remoove his bones He dyed a papist.

16. Richard Davies on Shakespeare, deer-stealer and papist.

member his *Warwickshire* Prosecutor, under the Name of Justice *Shallow*; he has given him very near the same Coat of Arms which *Dugdale*, in his Antiquities of that County, describes for a Family there, and makes the *Welsh* Parson descant very pleasantly upon 'em.[7]

In the play Falstaff has 'committed disparagements' upon Shallow, a Gloucestershire justice of the peace. 'Knight', he upbraids the fat roisterer, 'you have beaten my men, kill'd my deer, and broke open my lodge.' In retaliation Shallow has come to Windsor to make a Star Chamber case out of the affair. In the opening lines of *The Merry Wives of Windsor*, Shallow's cousin, Slender, speaks admiringly of the justice who can write himself 'Armigero', or esquire, in any legal document:

Shallow. Ay, that I do; and have done any time these three hundred years.

Slender. All his successors, gone before him, hath done't; and all his ancestors, that come after him, may: they may give the dozen white luces in their coat.

Shallow. It is an old coat.

Evans. The dozen white louses do become an old coat well; it agrees well, passant; it is a familiar beast to man, and signifies love.

Shallow. The luce is the fresh fish; the salt fish is an old coat.

Slender. I may quarter, coz.

Luces and louses; it is a predictable Elizabethan pun. From Rowe onwards commentators have noted that the Lucys of Charlecote punningly adopted as their heraldic device the luce, a fresh-water fish more familiarly known (in its fully grown state) as the pike. The Lucys bore the arms *Vair, three luces hauriant* [i.e. rising to the surface] *argent,* and on one of their tombs in Warwick the three luces on the coat are quartered, thus making up the dozen to which Slender refers. If this is what the passage in the play is about, Shakespeare, a decade or more after the event, is taking an obscurely allusive revenge upon the country justice who had invoked the rigours of the law for a venial offence indulged in by high-spirited youths of more elevated social position than the bailiff's son.[8]

A third report furnishes the ballad Rowe mentions. This Malone found late in the century, and published without attempting to conceal his scepticism:

> In a Manuscript *History of the Stage,* full of forgeries and falshoods of various kinds, written (I suspect by William Chetwood the prompter) some time between April 1727 and October 1730, is the following passage, to which the reader will give just as much credit as he thinks fit:
>
> "Here we shall observe, that the learned Mr. Joshua Barnes, late Greek Professor of the University of Cambridge, baiting about forty years ago at an inn in Stratford, and hearing an old woman singing part of the above-said song, such was his respect for Mr. Shakspeare's genius, that he gave her a new gown for the two following stanzas in it; and, could she have said it all, he would (as he often said in company, when any discourse has casually arose about him) have given her ten guineas:

"Sir Thomas was too covetous,
"To covet so much deer,
"When horns enough upon his head
"Most plainly did appear.

"Had not his worship one deer left?
"What then? He had a wife
"Took pains enough to find him horns
"Should last him during life."⁹

Joshua Barnes, who lived from 1654 to 1712, was a Greek scholar and antiquary who belonged to Emmanuel College, Cambridge.

A different version of the ballad was set down, around the middle of the eighteenth century, by William Oldys in the notes he compiled for a life of Shakespeare which, in the general disorder of his life, he never got round to writing. The notes perished along with the scheme, but not before George Steevens had seen the 'several quires of paper' covered with Oldys's 'laborious collections', and made extracts from them for his 1778 *Shakspeare*:

Mr. William Oldys . . . observes, that—"there was a very aged gentleman living in the neighbourhood of Stratford, (where he died fifty years since) who had not only heard, from several old people in that town, of Shakespeare's transgression, but could remember the first stanza of that bitter ballad, which, repeating to one of his acquaintance, he preserved it in writing; and here it is, neither better nor worse, but faithfully transcribed from the copy which his relation very curteously communicated to me."

"A parliemente member, a justice of peace,
"At home a poor scare-crowe, at London an asse,
"If lowsie is Lucy, as some volke miscalle it,
"Then Lucy is lowsie whatever befall it:
"He thinks himself greate,
"Yet an asse in his state,
"We allowe by his ears but with asses to mate.
"If Lucy is lowsie, as some volke miscalle it,
"Sing lowsie Lucy, whatever befall it."¹⁰

Before the century was out, another eminent Shakespearian, Edward Capell, had identified the aged gentleman:

—Mr. Thomas Jones, who dwelt at Tarbick a village in Worcestershire a few miles from Stratford on Avon, and dy'd in the year 1703. aged upwards of ninety, remember'd to have heard from several old people at Stratford the story of Shakespeare's robbing sir Thomas Lucy's park; and their account of it agreed with Mr. Rowe's, with this addition—that the ballad written against sir Thomas by Shakespeare was stuck upon his park gate, which exasperated the knight to apply to a lawyer at Warwick to proceed against him: Mr. Jones had put down in writing the first stanza of this ballad, which was all he remember'd of it, and Mr. Thomas Wilkes (my grandfather) transmitted it to my father by memory, who also took it in writing, and his copy is this;—"A *Parliamente member a Justice of Peace.* . . ."*

There may be confusion here, for the burial register for Tardebigge, as the village is today known, lists no Thomas Jones in 1703, or around that time, although it does record the death of an Edward Jones that year.

Having taken root, the deer-poaching legend bore strange fruits of romantic elaboration. From a note to the memoir of Shakespeare in 1763, signed 'P', and identified as the contribution of Philip Nichols, a proprietor of the *Biographia Britannica*, we learn of the unrelenting hostilities between these mighty opposites, the glover's son and the justice of the peace, and the curious means by which conciliation at last came about. The bitter ballad was not, it seems, 'the only shaft' that Shakespeare 'let fly against his prosecutor, whose anger drove him to the extreme end of ruin, where he was forced to a very low

---

* Shakespeare, *Works*, ed. Edward Capell; Note on *The Merry Wives of Windsor*, in *Notes* (1780), ii. 75. The passage is discussed by Malone, and reprinted as a note, with this prefatory comment: 'I have endeavoured to exhibit what Mr. Capel has left on this subject, in intelligible language; but am not sure that I understand him rightly. As a specimen of his style, I will add his own words, which the reader will interpret as he can' (Shakespeare, *Plays and Poems*, ed. Malone (1821), ii. 139n). The inelegancies of Capell's style did not escape remark by members of the Literary Club. 'If the man would have come to me', Dr. Johnson owned to his valued friend Bennet Langton, 'I would have endeavoured to "endow his purposes with words"; for, as it is, "he doth gabble monstrously"' (*Boswell's Life of Johnson*, ed. George Birkbeck Hill (rev. L. F. Powell; Oxford, 1934-40), iv. 5).

degree of drudgery for a support. How long the Knight continued inexorable is not known; but it is certain, that Shakespeare owed his release at last to the Queen's kindness.'[11]

Much later, in the next century, a descendant of the Lucys reported that not the Queen but her special favourite, Robert Dudley, Earl of Leicester, interceded to stay the vengeful Knight from prosecuting a crime punishable by death; subsequently Shakespeare wrote *The Merry Wives of Windsor* to please Leicester.[12] Such belated fancies, products of the myth-making imagination, need no longer detain the sober biographer; but the essential story of poaching, capture, prosecution, and flight has come down in four separate versions —those of Davies, Rowe, Barnes, and Jones (*via* Oldys and Capell) —all presumably deriving from Stratford gossip of the late seventeenth century. Does this drama have the ring of truth?

The episode, we are told, took place in Charlecote park. A century ago Henry James stood in summer twilight among the majestic oaks and ancient elms of that park, 'whose venerable verdure seems a survival from an earlier England and whose innumerable acres, stretching away, in the early evening, to vaguely seen Tudor walls, lie there like the backward years receding to the age of Elizabeth'.[13] The Great House, with its park, stands on the Avon's banks, four miles upstream from Stratford, in the level open country of the Feldon. On the west side the river's waters sweep the terrace steps; to the south a stately avenue of lime trees leads down to the old Stratford bridle road. Lucys had lived at Charlecote for generations, but not until the virus of a new malady, *la folie de bâtir*, infected the English gentry in the mid-sixteenth century did one, our Thomas (not yet knighted), rebuild his old manor house. Oaks shading the grounds furnished the open timbers for the roof of his Great Hall, from which a door opened onto the river bank. Atop the leaded cupolas crowning the octagonal turrets of the four corners of the many-gabled house, and the twin turrets of the gatehouse, gilt weather-vanes reflected the morning sun. This splendid house, completed in 1558, was the first Elizabethan mansion in Warwickshire.[14]

Surely Shakespeare would know this part of the world: tramping across the fields from his uncle's farm in Snitterfield, two miles away, he would glimpse the weather-vanes through the surrounding foliage. Today fallow deer roam the rolling grounds of Charlecote, but they were not introduced there until the eighteenth century. Nor did the estate in Shakespeare's time boast a park to lure clandestine huntsmen. ('The word *park* indeed properly signifies any enclosure; but yet it is not every field or common, which a gentleman pleases to surround with a wall or paling, and to stock with a herd of deer, that is thereby constituted a legal park: for the king's grant, or, at least immemorial prescription, is necessary to make it so.' Thus Blackstone.[15]) Not until 1618 did a Lucy apply for a royal licence to keep a park at Charlecote. What our Lucy maintained was a freewarren whose dense undergrowth sheltered rabbits and hares and foxes, wood-pigeons and pheasants, and other beasts and fowls of warren. One would class fallow deer with beasts of chase. Still, the great Elizabethan judge and legal authority Sir Edward Coke included roe deer among beasts of warren, and these may have browsed in Charlecote. The provisions of the 1563 Act for the protection of game apparently applied to deer in any enclosure, not just to those in legally empaled parks. Moreover Davies (as we have seen) mentions rabbits as well as venison. There was enough game in this warren to justify the employment of the several keepers whose names appear in Sir Thomas Lucy's Account Book: Antony and Humfrey, Robert Mathews (all three described as 'my keeper' or 'one of my keepers'), George Cox, 'keeper of my coney warren', and George Scales the falconer. Did one of these servants apprehend the poacher as he crouched over his quarry, and hale him, with ensanguined hand in bosom and downcast eye, before the imperious lord of the manor, as he sat horsed outside his gatehouse, with his lady, hawk, and hounds? So Joseph Nash evoked the historic scene for Victorian audiences in a handsome folio lithoprint for his survey of *The Mansions of England in the Olden Time*.

But Charlecote has had to compete with another setting for this melodramatic episode. Late in the eighteenth century, custodians of the mythos, aware that Sir Thomas kept no park at Charlecote, shifted the scene across the river to Fulbrook, two miles north, and midway between Stratford and Warwick.

In his *Picturesque Views* Samuel Ireland reported,

17. The Deer Barn.

Within this park is now standing, on a spot called Daisy Hill, a farm house, which was antiently the keeper's lodge. To this lodge it is reported our Shakspeare was conveyed, and there confined at the time of the charge, which is supposed to have been brought against him. This supposition, how slight soever the foundation of it may be, I yet thought sufficient to give an interest to the spot in which it is presumed to have passed. . . .[16]

In 1828 a famous visitor to Charlecote was told by a descendant of its builder that Shakespeare had stolen his deer from Fulbrook. 'The tradition went', Sir Walter Scott noted in his journal for 8 April, 'that they hid the buck in a barn, part of which was standing a few years ago but now totally decayd.'[17] Today a few nineteenth-century dwellings near the site of Daisy Hill commemorate the tradition by still bearing the name of Deer Barn Cottages.[18] The transfer does not, however, accomplish very satisfactorily the purpose for which it was designed. Henry VIII, it is true, had granted custody of the old royal park of Fulbrook, with its little castle built by the Duke of Bedford, to a progenitor of the Elizabethan Lucys. But subsequently the park fell into disrepair: weeds overran it, the palings tumbled down, and a new keeper, Sir William Compton, had the bricks carted off from the ruined castle to help create the glories of Compton Wynyates. Local sportsmen regarded the straggling remnants of the deer population as fair game. Before 1557 Fulbrook had been disparked. Not until 1615 did another Sir Thomas Lucy buy the lands and messuage (a dwelling-house with adjacent outbuildings and grounds), and enclose it with a new fence.

The setting for the story is not in any event all that crucial, for a justice of the peace could try a poacher arrested anywhere within his jurisdiction. But no officer could have ordered a whipping, because the crime (according to the operative game law) constituted a trespass, not a felony, and was punishable by a fine amounting to three times the damages, or imprisonment not exceeding three months; the offender had also to guarantee his good behaviour for seven years. If the escapade could be construed as a riot, that might bring a stiffer penalty, and if Shakespeare actually wrote a bitter ballad, that could bring into play the statutes governing criminal libels.

The legend emphasizes the severity of the magistrate, and the ballad mocks the cuckold's horns of an asinine M.P.; so it is well to consider the character of Sir Thomas. The eldest of ten children, he was only fourteen when his father arranged for him to marry Joyce Acton, aged thirteen, the sole heiress of a wealthy Worcestershire landowner. Her fortune made possible the re-building of Charlecote. In the Great Hall in 1565 the Queen's favourite Robert Dudley, deputizing for her, dubbed Thomas a knight; seven years later Elizabeth herself slept on goosefeathers in the Great Bed Chamber, and presented Lucy's daughter with a pretty jewel. This straight-nosed, square-jawed man with neatly trimmed beard (so he appears in his alabaster effigy) became a power in Warwickshire. In Parliament he busied himself with such godly works as laying down penalties for saying and hearing Mass. He also drew up a bill, left to die in committee, for 'the better preservation of grain and game' by making poaching a felony. As a Justice of the Queen's Peace, this puritanical squire exercised himself mainly over recusants, one of whom he literally uncovered, starving, in a haystack; and for his inquisitorial zeal while serving on a Privy Council commission he earned the good will of that awesomely powerful body. A grateful Parliament in 1584 passed a Private Bill assuring to Sir Thomas Lucy and others 'certain' lands which were, it seems, confiscated from *émigré* Catholics. Stratford town wined him with sack and claret at the Bear and the Swan. In public feared and respected, Sir Thomas in his domestic affairs appears to have been not unamiable. He wrote testimonial letters for an honest gentlewoman and an ailing servant. In 1584 his good offices helped to settle a lawsuit between the son of one of his servants and Shakespeare's friend, Hamnet Sadler.[19] Of his wife the squire declared, in the epitaph adorning their tomb in St. Leonard's, Charlecote,

> When all is spoken that can be saide, a wooman so furnished & garnished with vertue as not to be bettered & hardly to be equalled by any, as shee lived most vertuously, so shee died moste Godly. Set downe by him that best did knowe what hath byn written to be true
>
> Thomas Lucye.[20]

When Lucy died in 1600 the great Camden, Clarenceux King-of-Arms, arranged the funeral, and other heralds attended. In truth Sir Thomas does not sound very much like the tyrant of the tradition or the cuckold of the ballad, nor is he aptly caricatured as the dim-witted Shallow of *The Merry Wives of Windsor*.

Other considerations challenge faith. A justice of the peace should not himself have sat in judgement on the defendant he was prosecuting. If the luce was Sir Thomas's heraldic device, so was it for (among others) the Gascoynes, the Earl of Northampton, and the Worshipful Company of Stockfishmongers.[21] To some students it seems alien to Shakespeare's character and art that he should nurse a grudge for some dozen years, and then vent it by lampooning his victim in a play. And, even assuming he did so, how many in a London audience—even a Court audience—would be in a position to grasp the cryptic references to a country gentleman and something that had happened long since on his estate? If, moreover, the allusions were accessible to a knowledgeable few, would a professional dramatist like Shakespeare risk offending the well-placed friends of a man who had done the state some service? That would be foolhardy. Inconsistent too; for Shakespeare had, after all, treated respectfully Sir William Lucy, an ancestor of Sir Thomas, in 1 *Henry VI*; and the earlier Shallow of 2 *Henry IV* is depicted without malice and without, seemingly, topical allusiveness. One wonders if the legend might not have originated in Stratford long after *The Merry Wives of Windsor* was written and its author dead, among locals who read the play, recollected jests about luces and louses, and interpreted the passage in accordance with their own resentment against a powerful neighbourhood family. Time plays tricks; events merge. In 1610 another Sir Thomas Lucy, the third, did bring a Star Chamber action over the slaughter of deer by armed poachers who broke into his park at Sutton, and afterwards made an ale-house boast of their depredation.[22] Maybe by devious association this later event filtered into the tradition.

Still, the opening lines of *The Merry Wives of Windsor* are clearly allusive, and, as if matters were not already complicated enough, another model for Shallow has been proposed in our own century. This candidate, yielded by the researches of a scholar rather than by the vicissitudes of legend, is William Gardiner, a Surrey magistrate. He boasted the same fresh-water fish on his coat-armour, for his first wife was the widow Frances Wayte, *née* Luce or Lucy. This Gardiner, who had some indirect connection with the Swan Theatre, belongs to Shakespeare's London years, and so will enter this narrative in a later chapter.

Meanwhile, whatever the difficulties, the Charlecote story has not entirely lost its magic. 'The deer-stealing legend has by now a hold on popular affection that no argument can weaken,' argues a present-day occupant of Charlecote, the Hon. Alice Fairfax-Lucy.

If it were ever authoritatively disproved, children of the future would be deprived of something that for centuries has made the poet live for them. The portraits of Shakespeare are few and of debatable authenticity. In the shadowy throng of the Great he cuts an uninspiring figure. But set him against the background of Charlecote warren or Fulbroke park some night near dawn, with dangerous moonlight whitening the turf, and there you have reality. Theft, capture, punishment, flight—these are all within the compass of ordinary experience.[23]

Perhaps so, and several prominent authorities in this century—Sir Edmund Chambers, G. E. Bentley, and (more recently) A. L. Rowse—believe there may be some truth to the tradition.

Even if these legends embroider, however fancifully, a genuine escapade, they describe sports and recreation, not the serious occupations of life; Shakespeare must have provisioned his growing family with more than the odd haunch of venison. Did the young husband tick off the days and weeks and months of the apprentice's statutory seven-year sentence until the fateful day of his departure from Stratford? So one late-blooming tradition, a mutation of Aubrey's butcher-boy story, holds. When a Mr. Dowdall paused before the Shakespeare monument and epitaph at Holy Trinity in 1693, the ancient parish clerk and sexton who showed him round informed his visitor 'that this Shakespear was formerly in this town bound apprentice to a butcher; but that he run from his master to London, and there was received into the playhouse as a serviture, and by this means had an opportunity to be what he afterwards proved'.[24] Although this story does not state that the employer was William's father, it seems to have its origin in the familiar misconception about John Shakespeare's occupation, and so has no more persuasive force than implausible gossip.

Other voices, other speculations. Impressed with the dramatist's technical knowledge of the law, Malone, a barrister turned literary scholar, conjectured that Shakespeare 'was employed, while he yet remained at Stratford, in the office of some country attorney, who was at the same time a petty conveyancer, and perhaps also the Seneschal of some manor-court'.[25] Future lawyers would take up this suggestion, and not find themselves at a loss for words in arguing it. But if Shakespeare had for some years occupied a desk in some Warwickshire solicitor's office, 'attending sessions and assizes,—keeping leets and law days,—and perhaps being sent up to the metropolis in term time to conduct suits before the Lord Chancellor or the superior courts of common law at Westminster' (as a Victorian Chief Justice imagines it),[26] surely his signature would have appeared on deeds or wills he was called upon to witness; but no such signature has ever come to light.* In 1859 W. J. Thoms, a peaceable antiquary, conscripted the poet for military service in the Low Countries—a William Shakespeare, he triumphantly noted, is listed in a 1605 muster roll of trained soldiers in the village of Rowington within Barlichway Hundred, where Stratford lay.[27] But Thoms has of course confused the poet with some namesake; Rowington had its quota of Shakespeares. Other gilds—the seamen, printers, barber-surgeons, physicians, what you will—have claimed Shakespeare, but a more intriguing possibility than any of these is broached by Aubrey.

On the authority of William Beeston, he reports that 'though as Benjamin Johnson says of him, that he had but little Latin and less Greek, he understood Latin pretty well: for he had been in his younger years a schoolmaster in the country.'[28] Aubrey thought that Beeston knew most about Shakespeare, and certainly he was in a position to be well informed. An actor on both the Caroline and Restoration stages (he died in 1682), William was the son of Christopher Beeston. The latter rose from minor actor with Strange's men to become the manager of a succession of theatrical enterprises—Queen Anne's men, Queen Henrietta's men, Beeston's boys, among others—and the builder, in 1616-7, of the Phoenix playhouse. From then until his death in 1638, Christopher Beeston was the most important figure in the London theatrical scene.[29] In 1598 this Beeston belonged to Shakespeare's company, the Lord Chamberlain's men, for that year he acted with Shakespeare in Jonson's *Every Man in his Humour*. So the player and the player-poet knew one another, how intimately we cannot say.

But does it follow that Aubrey's report is trustworthy? After all, Shakespeare never went up to university, and the Stratford masters (as we have seen) held Oxford or Cambridge degrees. He might, however, have filled the humbler post of usher or *abecedarius*.[30] Aubrey merely says that Shakespeare taught 'in the country', that is,

---

* The point was made to the Victorian popularizer Charles Knight by Robert Bell Wheler, who inspected hundreds of title-deeds and other legal documents from the decade of the eighties; see S. Schoenbaum, *Shakespeare's Lives* (Oxford, 1970), p. 387.

any place outside London, and elsewhere than in Stratford the civic fathers tended to set less exacting standards. As late as 1642, in *The Holy and Profane State*, Thomas Fuller—'the great Tom Fuller', Pepys calls him—complained, of the teaching profession, that 'young scholars make this calling their refuge, yea perchance before they have taken any degree in the university, commence schoolmasters in the country, as if nothing else were required to set up this profession but only a rod and a ferule.'[31] Simon Forman, later to make his mark as physician, astrologer, and lecher, had only turned nineteen when he took up teaching—a career he shortly abandoned in order to attend Oxford, 'for to get more learning'.[32] Of course there is also the possibility that Shakespeare found employment as a private tutor in some stately home. The tradition of the poet as rural pedagogue, thumbing the Plautus he would later draw upon for one of his earliest plays, *The Comedy of Errors*, cannot be proved, nor should it be casually dismissed. It has in any event appealed irresistibly to donnish biographers.

Whatever the young Shakespeare did—whether (in Jonson's gracious phrase) he swept his living from the posteriors of little children, or clerked it for a conveyancer, or assisted his father in the glove trade—he did not do so for long. Asked what happy gale has blown him from old Verona to Padua, Petruchio replies,

> Such wind as scatters young men through the world
> To seek their fortunes farther than at home,
> Where small experience grows.

Some time before 1592 that wind carried Shakespeare to London.

He need not have waited until his arrival in London to make his first acquaintance with acting and plays. As a boy of fifteen he could have witnessed in nearby Coventry one of the last performances of the great cycle of Mystery plays acted by the craft gilds. More than once he had an opportunity, when his father held office, to watch the professional troupes that came to town. Now and then Stratford offered a chance for some amateur acting. 'At Pentecost', the disguised Julia recalls in *The Two Gentlemen of Verona*,

> When all our pageants of delight were play'd,
> Our youth got me to play the woman's part,

111

> And I was trimm'd in Madam Julia's gown;
> Which served me as fit, by all men's judgments,
> As if the garment had been made for me.

On one occasion the Stratford corporation laid out money for an entertainment at Pentecost. In 1583 they paid 13s.4d. 'to Davi Jones and his company for his pastime at Whitsuntide'. Davy Jones had been married to Elizabeth, the daughter of Adrian Quiney, and after her death in 1579 he took as his wife a Hathaway, Frances. Was Shakespeare one of the youths who trimmed themselves for this Whitsun pastime?[33]

An intriguing recent suggestion would push back Shakespeare's entrance into the player's life to before the Whitsun pastime of 1583; even to before his marriage with Anne. This reconstruction holds that, while a mere lad, Shakespeare found employment—as pedagogue and player—with the wealthy Hoghtons of Lea Hall, near Preston in Lancashire, some hundred miles distant from Stratford.

Much altered with the passage of years, Lea Hall still stands in fields near the Salwick Brook, not very far from where the ocean beats upon the northern strand. On 3 August 1581 the master, Alexander Hoghton, dying without male issue, devised a will settling annuities upon those who had served him faithfully. His brother Thomas—actually his half-brother—he 'most heartily' required to 'be friendly unto Foke Gyllome and William Shakshafte, now dwelling with me, and either to take them unto his service or else to help them to some good master . . .'. This same Thomas, in an immediately preceding bequest, is given 'all my instruments belonging to musics, and all manner of play-clothes, if he be minded to keep and do keep players'; otherwise 'the same instruments and play-clothes' shall go to the testator's brother-in-law, Sir Thomas Hesketh of Rufford, some ten miles distant. In 1914 Charlotte Stopes had drawn notice to a record, from the court rolls of the College of St. Mary in Warwick for 33 Henry VIII (1541-2), citing a Richard Shakeschafte. As the manor involved lay in Snitterfield, the reference is inescapably to the poet's grandfather Richard under a variant surname. Thus the Shakespeares—our Shakespeares—might have been referred to as Shakeschaftes; the implication is that William—

seventeen and still a bachelor—had already begun his stage career with a private household, maybe slightly changing the usual form of the family name to circumvent parental objection to this youthful adventure. Such a theory of how Shakespeare became addicted to the stage was first propounded by Oliver Baker in 1937, in his *In Shakespeare's Warwickshire,* written after he had chanced upon a printed copy of Alexander Hoghton's will in a Chetham Society publication dating back to 1860.

Plots have a way of thickening. Sir Edmund Chambers, investigating the Hoghton and Hesketh families, came up with some interesting additional data. The Sir Thomas Hesketh mentioned in the Hoghton will was on friendly terms with the powerful Stanleys, Earls of Derby. Records show Sir Thomas several times visiting the fourth Earl, Henry, and his son Ferdinando, Lord Strange, at their country houses at Lathom and Knowsley. In the household books of the Stanley steward, William Farington, Hesketh's name is bracketed with players: an entry for December 1587 reads, 'Sir Tho[mas] Hesketh, players went away.' Over the years the Stanleys patronized entertainers: tumblers and acrobats, as well as actors. The well-known Strange's men, kept by Henry, probably passed to Ferdinando, who became the fifth Earl of Derby in 1593. Touring companies, moreover, included the Stanley seats in their provincial itineraries, leaving their traces in the household accounts. Now, after Alexander Hoghton's death, William Shakeshafte possibly entered Hesketh's service. Through the latter, William may have found his opportunity to establish a connection with Lord Strange, and in this fashion gain his entrée to the London stage.

Into this intricate carpet Leslie Hotson has woven another figure. It seems that a London goldsmith, Thomas Savage, who in 1599 served as one of two trustees when Shakespeare and some of his fellows entered into an arrangement involving their ground lease for the Globe Theatre, was a native of Lancashire—in fact, obscure Rufford—and connected by marriage to the Heskeths. Moreover, several Stratford schoolmasters of Shakespeare's day similarly hailed from that northern county, and (as we have seen) one, the Catholic John Cottom, arrived in the town during Shakespeare's fifteenth year. This Cottom had dwelt nearby to the Hoghton property of Alston

Hall; Cottom's father had had business dealings with Hoghton's father. Might not this episode, as Hotson (followed by others) suggests, give a new gloss to Aubrey's remark about Shakespeare being in his younger days a country schoolmaster? Maybe he served as both assistant teacher and player to the Heskeths, taking up his post as a youth of fifteen or sixteen.

The religious dimension also has significance. Alexander Hoghton was a Catholic. So too was Sir Thomas Hesketh. The latter had a recusant son, and his widow, Lady Alice, succoured papists, on one occasion sheltering a missionary priest. Lancashire enjoyed some notoriety as a 'sink of popery'. Perhaps we have here a real clue to Shakespeare's religious sympathies. The whole affair, with its complex interconnections, has naturally appealed to Catholic apologists. Thus the Revd. Peter Milward envisages Shakespeare as being sent north by his father, perhaps after the Stratford entertainment of Derby's players, and 'bearing a letter of introduction from the schoolmaster to Alexander Hoghton. His subsequent sojourn at Rufford is said to be attested by a local tradition in the village, and confirmed by his later connection with Thomas Savage . . .'.[34]

Scholarship disports itself with such tendentious constructs, but this particular edifice alas crumbles upon close inspection. First, there is the demon of inaccuracy that pursued Mrs. Stopes. In the Snitterfield manorial record she has not only got the date wrong (it should be 1533), but has also misread Richard's surname, which appears as 'Shakstaff,' not 'Shakeschafte'. There is no evidence of anybody in the poet's family using 'Shakeshafte' as a variant. On the other hand, Lancashire had a sufficiency of Shakeshaftes, including numerous Williams. And were the play-clothes Alexander Hoghton worried about in his will actors' costumes? They could as well have decked out musicians. And what of Steward Farington's reference, 'Sir Tho[mas] Hesketh, players went away'? True, a comma has been editorially supplied, but there is no possessive. More likely Farington refers not to Hesketh's players but to the fact that both Hesketh and the players left at the same time. But in 1970 Douglas Hamer seemed to have made a crucial—indeed devastating—point respecting the bequests in the will (a sort of early non-subscription tontine arrangement), by which certain servants—eleven out of a total of thirty—were rewarded according to their seniority. The recipients drew annuities which increased with the death of each annuitant until the last drew the entire income for life. But, as E. A. J. Honigmann in 1985 noted in *Shakespeare: The 'Lost Years'*, William Shakeshafte was one of four legatees bequeathed £2; only one of the thirty annuitants received a larger amount. Thomas Barton, Hoghton's steward, was awarded no specified sum, and—according to Hamer's theory—should therefore have been one of the younger legatees; but in 1587 Barton described himself as 'about fifty'. A faithful family retainer, Thomas Coston, left £1 a year, should have been older than Barton, but was in fact younger, being twenty-nine in 1581. Hamer's argument thus collapses. Still, if Shakespeare was at seventeen in Hoghton's service, he would have had to be back in Stratford to woo, impregnate, and marry Anne Hathaway before his nineteenth birthday, not—on the face of it—the most plausible of scenarios. Most likely, when he joined his company—the Queen's, Pembroke's or another—it was as a hired man drawing wages, but before very long he was able to buy in and become a shareholder.

We are on safer ground in focusing on the records—however bare—of visiting troupes in Stratford in the late eighties. In the 1583-4 season three troupes, wearing the liveries of the earls of Oxford, Essex, and Worcester, performed in the Gild Hall and presumably also in the inn-yards of Bridge Street. But the busiest year for plays in Stratford stretched from December of 1586 to December 1587. Heralded by drum and trumpets, five companies—the Queen's, Essex's, Leicester's, Lord Stafford's, and another, unnamed—passed through the town, and left their tracks in the corporation accounts. Of these Leicester's men and the Queen's especially require notice.

Players had worn Lord Robert Dudley's badge of a bear and ragged staff since the beginning of Elizabeth's reign; with James Burbage as a leading player, they were the first company to boast a royal patent and to have a permanent playhouse, the Theatre, for their headquarters. For Shakespeare the Earl's Warwickshire connection holds a special significance. The latter kept his county ties. When in the summer of 1575 he entertained the Queen sumptuously for nineteen days at his castle in Kenilworth, twelve miles north-east of Stratford, the local populace crowded in as spectators to watch

Elizabeth as she passed in splendour, and to gape at the devices that whiled away the afternoon, or the fireworks which lit up the night sky. Some have toyed with the pleasing and not implausible notion that Alderman Shakespeare pressed in among the throng with his eleven-year-old son. On the large lake in the castle grounds a water-pageant displayed Arion on the back of a dolphin carried by a boat of which the oars simulated fins. Accompanied by instrumentalists within the dolphin's belly, Arion sang (in the phrase of an eye-witness) 'a delectable ditty of a song well apted to a melodious noise'.[35] If young William witnessed the spectacle that July 18th, he found it unforgettable. 'Thou rememb'rest', Oberon reminds Puck,

> Since once I sat upon a promontory,
> And heard a mermaid on a dolphin's back
> Uttering such dulcet and harmonious breath
> That the rude sea grew civil at her song,
> And certain stars shot madly from their spheres
> To hear the sea-maid's music.

And the Captain in *Twelfth Night* says of Viola's brother, 'like Arion on the dolphin's back, / I saw him hold acquaintance with the waves / So long as I could see'.

A decade after the princely pleasures at Kenilworth, when the Earl commanded the English forces supporting the Netherlands States-General against Spain, several of his players accompanied him to the Low Countries. On 24 March 1586 Sir Philip Sidney, writing to Walsingham from Utrecht, alludes to 'Will, my Lord of Lester's jesting player'. Such a reference is calculated to make a bardolater's heart skip a beat; but probably Sidney had in mind Will Kempe, the celebrated clown and jigmaker whom Leicester commended a few months later to the Danish Court. The Earl died in the Armada year. For a while his company soldiered on, possibly under the patronage of the Countess; then broke up. Several of the actors joined the servants of Leicester's older brother, the Earl of Warwick; others —Kempe, Bryan, Pope—took up with Strange's or the Admiral's men. Leicester's troupe may have recruited Shakespeare during the unstable period preceding their dissolution; but of course this is only guesswork.[36]

An event in the fortunes of the Queen's company opens up a more intriguing possibility. Chosen by the Master of the Revels in 1583 from among the best actors in London, and lustrous in their scarlet coats, this troupe was then in its heyday. Their stellar attraction, the peerless clown Richard Tarlton, drew throngs and laughter everywhere. In 1588 he died, and the bubble burst; but in the summer of 1587 the Queen's men were the pre-eminent troupe in the land—in Abingdon the crowd was so keen to see Tarlton and his fellows that they broke the windows in the Gild Hall. The Queen's men visited some half dozen other towns, including Stratford. On 13 June, when the company was in Thame, Oxfordshire, a melodramatic episode took place between the hours of nine and ten at night in a close called White Hound. One of the actors, William Knell—he had played Prince Hal, probably in the anonymous *Famous Victories of Henry the Fifth*—drew his weapon and assaulted his colleague John Towne, a yeoman of Shoreditch. Cornered on a mound, and fearing for his life, Towne plunged his own sword through Knell's neck. The latter died within thirty minutes. A coroner's inquest concluded that Towne had acted in self-defence, and in due course he received a Queen's pardon. Knell's widow Rebecca remarried in less than a twelvemonth, taking as her husband the actor John Heminges, who would prove so worthy a friend to Shakespeare. Meanwhile the Queen's men went about their business. We do not know precisely when they played at Stratford in 1587: the Chamberlains' account, 'from Christmas Anno 1586, Anno xxix Elizabeth Regine for one whole year', tells us only that the corporation rewarded the performers with the munificent sum of twenty shillings (the highest amount they had ever paid) and afterwards laid out sixteen pence to repair a bench, broken, one suspects, because of the press of spectators. If these players came soon after 13 June, they lacked one man. Before leaving Stratford, had they enlisted Shapespeare, then aged twenty-three, as their latest recruit?[37] A pleasing fancy, but of course no more than that, for the Queen's men might have stopped in Stratford anytime between December 1586 and December 1587. And no evidence exists of any Elizabethan company ever having recruited while on the road. London is where the action was in show business, as in so much else.

❊{ 9 }❊

London and the Theatres

History unfortunately does not record when the young husband bade his long goodbye to his family—Anne, probably already over the threshold of thirty; Susanna and the twins; his parents, now getting on, in the family house in Henley Street—and, crossing Clopton Bridge, struck out, either on his own or with a company of players, on the high road to the capital. After he became famous and a prosperous burgher of Stratford, he would hire a horse. It is a reasonable guess that the young Shakespeare went more economically, on foot.

He had two itineraries to choose from: either through Oxford or by way of Banbury. The first route was shorter and more direct; a man could manage it in four days if he covered twenty-five miles each day; at night a penny bought clean sheets in an inn. This road led the wayfarer, *via* Shipston-on-Stour and Long Compton, over the gently undulating hills dividing Warwickshire from Oxfordshire; then past the famous stone circle called 'Roll-rich stones', through bare downs to the royal park of Woodstock, thick with ancient oaks and beeches; and on to Oxford. After that, High Wycombe and Beaconsfield. The alternative itinerary, described by Aubrey as *the* road from London to Stratford, passed by Pillerton Hercy over Edgehill; thence—through Banbury ('famous for cakes, cheese, and zeal'), Buckingham, Aylesbury (approached over a little stone bridge and stone causeway), and the two Chalfonts—to Uxbridge. Here the two highways met. Shakespeare knew this latter route, if we may

trust a seventeenth-century gossip's confused report that the dramatist spent a midsummer-night at Grendon, and there encountered,
no doubt in a hail of malapropisms, the constable who furnished a
model for Dogberry; for Grendon Underwood lay on a side road
eight miles south of Buckingham.[1] From Uxbridge the single thoroughfare proceeded past Shepherd's Bush, the gallows at Tyburn,
and the Lord Mayor's banqueting house in Oxford Road. Then,
winding south, it reached a church (where Shaftesbury Avenue now
lies) in a pleasant rural village surrounded by open fields, and hence
called St. Giles-in-the-fields. Next the suburb of Holborn, and having
passed the churches of St. Andrew and St. Sepulchre, the traveller
at last entered the great city at Newgate.[2]

This was one of the seven gates through which the principal roads
led into a city encompassed, as in Chaucer's day, by 'an high and
thick wall, full of turrets and bulwarks' (so Thomas More described
it). Of rough stone and tile, capped by brick and stone battlements,
the wall stretched in a giant arc, over two miles long, round the city
on three sides. Along Thames Street the wall defending the capital
on the river side had long since yielded to the wharves, warehouses,
and quays of a thriving port. The other walls have of course vanished
too, and the portcullises and doors of the gates slammed ponderously
shut for the last time in the eighteenth century. They survive, however, as place names—Aldgate looking eastward; Bishopsgate, Moor-
gate, Cripplegate, and Aldersgate to the north; Newgate and Ludgate
(the oldest) on the west—and in this way outline for the modern
Londoner the perimeter of the old city.

If the visitor stood outside the walls on the Surrey side—say, by
the imposing tower of St. Mary Overy (now Southwark Cathedral)
—he could take in the breathtaking expanse of the metropolis, as
captured in the marvellously detailed panoramas by Visscher and
Hollar. From east to west, so far as the eye could see, stretched the
mighty artery of the great tidal river. No city in Christendom
boasted such extensive river frontage.

Sweet Thames, run softly, goes the poet's refrain. More sweet
were the waters of the Avon; ordure from the common sewer emp-
tied into the Thames, and dead dogs and other carrion floated on
the surface. But fish still swarmed in schools though the channel,

and banks of swans glided by in such profusion as to evoke the won-
derment of continental visitors.* Others plied the river too. The
great kept private boats moored to the steps that ran down from
their palatial residences to the water's edge. Ordinary folk hired
wherries at the public stairs, where the watermen shouted 'Eastward
Ho!' or 'Westward Ho!'. This clientele to a large degree consisted of
pleasure-seekers on their way to and from the Bankside theatres, bear
gardens, and bawdy-houses. In John Taylor the watermen found
their proletarian laureate, and the river its most rapturous celebrant.
The Thames, he sang unmelodiously,

> bears the lame and weak, makes fat the lean,
> And keeps whole towns and countries sweet and clean;
> Wer't not for Thames (as heaven's high hand doth bless it)
> We neither could have fish, or fire to dress it,
> The very brewers would be at a fault,
> And buy their water dearer than their malt. . . .[3]

Shakespeare must have got to know the watermen, for whether he
resided in Bishopsgate or the Clink, he would depend on them for
transport when summoned with his company for a Court performance at Whitehall or Greenwich or Richmond; he could have hailed
a water-taxi from the stairs at Blackfriars, or Paris Garden on the
opposite bank. The costumes and properties would go separately by
barge.

The river was the silver-streaming silent highway. Tall three-
masted merchant ships unloaded their cargoes at the crowded
wharves and warehouses. At Billingsgate not only fish, but all manner of victuals—groceries (spices, dried fruit, and the like) excepted
—were landed. When the Queen took to her gilt royal barge, with
pennants streaming, a spirit of festival seized the Thames. One St.
Mark's Day, John Machyn, Merchant Taylor and cheerful under-
taker, noted in his *Diary* how after supper the Queen rowed up and
down the river, with a hundred boats around her, and trumpets,

---

* With pollution now abating, fish (so the press services report) have begun to
return: some four-score species now swim in the Thames estuary, including
salmon, absent for almost a century and a half.

drums, flutes, and guns, and squibs lighting up the sky, until ten at night, when her Grace decided to call it an evening, while all along the banks a thousand people stood staring at her.[4] In 1581 Elizabeth had come aboard the Golden Hind to knight Drake; now the venerable bark that had circumnavigated the globe lay rotting out Deptford way, where Christopher Marlowe would meet his violent end.

Along the length of the river the continuous row of mansions that joined London to Westminster affirmed the wealth and power of the capital. Behind the shore pressed together rows of cottages; and, rising above the gabled roofs, the steeples of more than a hundred parish churches, some of them masterpieces of the Perpendicular style. London, the poet sings,

> like a crescent lies,
> Whose windows seem to mock the star-befreckled skies;
> Besides her rising spires, so thick themselves that show,
> As do the bristling reeds, within his banks that grow.[5]

All this the panoramas represent.

Three imposing structures dominated the scene.

London Bridge, connecting Southwark with the city at Fish Street, was the only span crossing the Thames; 'a bridge of stone eight hundred feet in length, of wonderful work'—so wrote a German visitor in 1598.[6] The Water Poet required rhyme to express *his* enthusiasm:

> Brave London Bridge claims right pre-eminence
> For strength, and architects' magnificence.

The heads of executed criminals stuck on iron spikes barbarically festooned the gate-house as one entered from the south. More inviting were the 'quite splendid, handsome, and well-built houses, which are occupied by merchants of consequence'.[7] These covered the length of the bridge, all twenty arches, and gave it the look of a continuous street rather than of a bridge. The tradesmen dwelt in the upper storeys, and displayed their wares in shops below, along both sides of a passage so narrow that (the Venetian ambassador sneered) two coaches meeting could not pass each other without danger. The pinmakers, a major attraction, kept their stalls here. Only three breaches in the lane afforded pedestrians a glimpse of the river, and of the lozenge-shaped timber frameworks, called 'starlings', built around the piers. At the tenth, or Great Pier, the starling formed, at low water, a platform to a winding flight of stone steps that led into the famous Chapel of St. Thomas, called St. Thomas of the Bridge. With its clustered columns and rich pointed-arch windows, this imposing Chapel (also accessible from the bridge street) had once honoured the memory of the Blessed Martyr; now, converted into a warehouse, it served Mammon.

To the west, St. Paul's, the largest and most magnificent cathedral in England, dwarfed the surrounding city-scape. The minster that Shakespeare knew had been shorn of some of its splendour, for in 1561 lightning destroyed the wooden steeple which soared up 150 feet and more. The devout had collected funds for restoration, but it never was replaced. The interior presented a mixed spectacle. In the Middle Aisle—called 'Duke Humphrey's Walk' or 'Paul's Walk'— lawyers at their pillars conferred with clients, masterless servants advertised for employers, coney-catchers cut the purses of coneys, and gallants exhibited their plumage, provoked quarrels, and arranged assignations with easy wenches, while tailors took note of the latest fashions and displayed their cloth and lace. Delivery men used the aisle as a short-cut to Fleet Street, although they no longer (as in former days) led their horses and mules through the cathedral. Meanwhile divine services went on in the choir. In the churchyard on Sunday mornings preachers castigated sin at Paul's Cross, which stood to the north-east. Occasionally lotteries took place in the cathedral close, but mainly this area served the book trade. Many stationers lived in the yard itself or the immediate environs and set up shop there. By the sign of the Red Lion or White Horse or Black Boy or whatever, they displayed the latest sermons or playbooks on their stalls. Most of Shakespeare's plays, those published during his lifetime, bore the imprint of stationers of Paul's Churchyard. The dramatist himself at one time had lodgings a short walk from St. Paul's, in Cripplegate ward. On more than one occasion he must there have thumbed books which provided him with sources for his plays, or simply have observed the daily re-enactment of the human comedy, in its own way no less diverting than the entertainments mounted at the Globe.

To the east another massive presence, this one more foreboding: the Tower, a vast complex of fortifications—a moat on three sides, drawbridge, thick walls, courts, and the central keep, the White Tower, with its battlements and four onion-shaped turrets surmounting the lesser towers of the stronghold. Shakespeare in *Richard II* refers to 'Julius Caesar's ill-erected Tower',[8] but he is merely echoing folklore, for William the Conqueror began the construction of the Tower. Its functions are described by John Stow in his *Survey of London*:

> This tower is a citadel, to defend or command the city; a royal place for assemblies, and treaties; a prison of estate, for the most dangerous offenders; the only place of coinage for all England at this time; the armoury for war-like provision; the treasury of the ornaments and jewels of the crown, and general conserver of the most records of the king's Courts of Justice at Westminster.[9]

This summary misses one or two features. Couples could have their marriages performed at the Tower. Holiday-makers visited the menagerie in the Lion Tower, which stood at the present main entrance; here Paul Hentzner, a tutor from Brandenburg, in 1598 viewed with interest the lions, a tiger and lynx, an 'excessively old' wolf, and an eagle and porcupine.

The mortar of the Tower walls, according to FitzStephen, the twelfth-century monk of Canterbury, was tempered with the blood of beasts. Human blood too forms part of the fabric of the Tower; not without cause was one of the towers called the Bloody Tower. Guards conveyed prisoners to it *via* a covered channel that passed beneath the Tower wharf. The entrance was called Traitors' Gate. (The young Elizabeth arrived at this gate one rainy Palm Sunday, when the river waters lapped against the steps, and protested, 'Here landeth the truest subject being a prisoner, that ever landed at these stairs.'[10]) On the narrow wharf the cannon watched impassively while cranes unloaded goods. Behind the fortress, on Tower Hill, stood the wooden scaffold and gibbet. At night ghosts haunted the corridors and staircases of the Tower; some of them the same ghosts that troubled the repose of Richard III on the eve of the battle of Bosworth Field. No other edifice figures so importantly in Shakespeare's plays.

Yet the city boasted many other buildings of exceptional interest. At Baynard's Castle, on the river bank, with an entrance in Thames Street, Richard, Duke of Gloucester, 'well accompanied / With reverend fathers and well learned bishops', waited to put by with mock humility the offer of a crown. Leicester House in the Strand, then not part of London proper but belonging to the liberty of the Duchy of Lancaster, was 'first amongst other buildings memorable for greatness'. There resided Robert Dudley, the Queen's favourite, and after him Robert Devereux. It then became known as Essex House. To this house the Earl returned after the Irish campaign saluted by the Chorus of *Henry V*, and here he plotted the abortive rebellion which brought him to disgrace and the executioner's block. Fronting upon the Cornhill stood the Royal Exchange built by Sir Thomas Gresham on the model of the Great Bourse at Antwerp. It was in the shape of a quadrangle, with enormous arched entrances at the north and south. Within, foreign merchants and traders passed along an arched cloister lined with shops on two levels. By the wax lights of this great northern bazaar they inspected armour, mousetraps, jewelry, shoe horns, and all manner of wares. At noon and at six in the evening the great bell summoned the merchants in their hundreds to congregate for the conduct of their affairs. Although Shakespeare does not allude directly to 'the eye of London' (as Munday admiringly describes the Exchange), it may have furnished him with hints for the Rialto of *The Merchant of Venice*.

As the panoramas show, to the north—beyond St. Paul's and the church steeples—stretched uncultivated fields and open country, with scattered patches of woodland. The green belt lay closer in then, and farm produce had a shorter trip to market. London ended at Clerkenwell. St. Pancras and Charing Cross were still rural villages; Islington was a hamlet on the road leading to St. Albans; trees densely covered the hills of Hampstead. But the enclosed city could ill accommodate a population swelling to 160,000 or more, so building overflowed the walls in an untidy suburban sprawl.

To the north-east, not far from Ely Place in whose gardens grew the strawberries for which the hunchbacked Richard developed his sudden longing, were situated the stews of Clerkenwell, frequented by lickerish gallants from the Inns of Court. Justice Shallow once belonged to this company, in the days when he was called 'lusty Shallow':

> There was I, and little John Doit of Staffordshire, and black George Barnes, and Francis Pickbone, and Will Squele a Cotsole man—you had not four such swinge-bucklers in all the Inns o' Court again. And I may say to you we knew where the bona-robas were, and had the best of them all at commandment.

In their Christmas revels the Inns' men offered ironical homage to 'Lucy Negro, Abbess *de Clerkenwell*', and to her choir of nuns who, with burning lamps, chanted 'Placebo' to randy gentlemen of Gray's Inn. Professor G. B. Harrison believes that possibly she chanted to Shakespeare too, and found immortality as the Dark Lady of the *Sonnets*.[11] Also intrigued by the possibility, Leslie Hotson thinks that this Lucy Negro was one Luce Morgan—Black Luce, but disappointingly not a negress—who in better days had been one of the Queen's Gentlewomen. Latterly she set up a bawdy house in St. John Street, Clerkenwell, and there 'traded in lust and gainful brothelry'.[12] She must, however, compete with other Dark Ladies.[13]

To the east, from St. Katherine's Hospital in the shadow of the Tower, to Wapping, the low-water mark of the Thames where executed pirates were left hanging until thrice washed by the tide, 'was never a house standing within these 40 years: but since the gallows being after removed farther off, a continual street, or filthy straight passage, with alleys of small tenements or cottages builded, inhabited by sailors' victuallers, along by the river of Thames, almost to Radcliff, a good mile from the Tower.'[14] Such developments made Stow, who intensely loved the city in which he lived for eighty years, long for the days described by his beloved FitzStephen:

> On all sides, without the houses of the suburbs, are the citizens' gardens and orchards, planted with trees, both large, sightly, and adjoining together. On the north side, are pastures, and plain meadows, with brooks running through them, turning water mills, with a pleasant noise. Not far off, is a great forest, a well wooded chase,

having good covert for harts, bucks, does, boars and wild bulls. The corn fields are not of a hungry sandy mould, but as the fruitful fields of Asia: yielding plentiful increase, and filling the barns with corn. There are near London, on the north side, especial wells in the suburbs, sweet, wholesome, and clear. Amongst which, Holy-well, Clerkenwell, and Saint Clemon's well, are most famous, and most frequented by scholars and youths of the city in summer evenings, when they walk forth to take the air.[15]

The air in those parts was no longer so salubrious of a summer evening as in FitzStephen's time.

For life in the capital had grown unwholesome. Pestilence hung in the clouds, and at intervals struck—in 1592-4 and again in 1603—forcing the playhouses to shut down, and the inhabitants, those who could afford to do so, to flee. Population increased not so much in the normal way, through procreation, as by an influx from outside: refugees from the religious troubles in France and The Netherlands, or country folk dispossessed of their holdings by the conversion of arable land into pasture. The poor of London were numerous. They crowded into mean slum tenements of timber eked out with mud and plaster; these dwellings devoured the flowering churchyards, spread above stables, and crept into every nook and cranny of the city. Well-to-do foreign visitors were impressed by the cleanliness of the passages. 'The streets in this city are very handsome and clean', remarked Hentzner; 'but that which is named from the gold-smiths who inhabit it, surpasses all the rest: there is in it a gilt tower, with a fountain that plays.'[16] But, like most tourists anywhere, he saw only the more attractive bits; not the overpopulated parishes and out-parishes like St. Giles, Cripplegate, or St. Leonard's, Shoreditch. So he made no notes about the squalor to which the Privy Council drew the attention of the Middlesex Justices in 1596: the 'multitudes of base tenements and houses of unlawful and disorderly resort in the suburbs', and the 'great number of dissolute, loose, and insolent people harboured in such and the like noisome and disorderly houses, as namely poor cottages, and habitations of beggars and people without trade, stables, inns, alehouses, taverns, garden-houses converted to dwellings, ordinaries, dicing-houses, bowling alleys, and brothel houses'.[17] In back alleys the lanes were too narrow to admit coaches, and the projecting upper storeys of dwellings blocked out the sunlight. Rubbish, cast from windows, lay in heaps; urine and excrement clogged the channels. In Moorfields and Finsbury Fields lay decomposing carcasses of dogs and cats and horses. The slaughter-houses of St. Nicholas-within-Newgate stood in the heart of the city; here putrefied blood ran in the streets, and offal fatted the region kites and ravens, which were (like the swans) protected birds. In Scalding Alley the poulterers publicly scalded the chickens vended in the neighbouring market of the Poultry. Running round the great wall, the Town Ditch, where fish once swam, had become a noisome source of infection. Under such conditions the black rat multiplied and, infesting tenements and hovels, spread the flea that transmitted the plague bacillus. Eventually the fiercer brown rat, which preferred to breed outside dwellings, in burrows or drains, helped to eradicate the black rat. A better standard of housing helped too. But that was not to be until after Shakespeare's time, and it required a great fire which destroyed most of the London he knew.[18]

Still, despite overcrowding, filth, and infestations of rats and disease, all manner of flowers and greenery gaily decked the capital. Along the river-bank the ancient residences (as to be expected) had spacious gardens attached, with flower beds and fruit trees. Edmund Spenser could walk forth on a spring day in 1596,

> Along the shore of silver streaming Thames,
> Whose rutty bank, the which his river hems,
> Was painted all with variable flowers,
> And all the meads adorned with dainty gems.

Wild radishes grew low in the joints of a stone wall along the Thames, by the Savoy, and could be picked when the tide receded. Under the city wall, in a garden belonging to an apothecary of London, a nettle tree flourished. Even part of the Town Ditch was filled in with gardens. There were still grassy slopes amid the ruins of dissolved priories not yet converted into tenements. In Pope Lane, in Aldersgate ward, willows (some said) once grew near the parish church of St. Anne in the Willows; no longer—'now there is no such void place for willows to grow'—but some high ashes lent beauty to the churchyard. The suburb of Holborn consisted mainly of gardens; in Hackney the village women gathered small turnips to sell at the cross in Cheapside. Cinquefoil, or five-finger, grew upon the brick wall in Liver Lane; whitlow grass climbed the back wall in Chancery Lane, and in Westminster Abbey spread over the door that led from Chaucer's tomb to the old palace.[19]

The great city of contrasts spawned stately mansions and slum tenements, gardens and midden-heaped lanes. With the Court close to hand, it was the vital nerve-centre for the professions, trade and commerce, and the arts; London nourished the English Renaissance. Only in the metropolis could a playwright of genius forge a career for himself. Anyway Stratford, a hundred miles distant, had its problems too. Older townsmen remembered the plague of sixty-four, although they would never undergo another such siege. In the summer before the Spanish Armada the Avon suddenly rose, collapsing both ends of Clopton Bridge, and washing away all the hay in the valley. Destructive fires raged three times in Stratford during Shakespeare's lifetime. Still, by the banks of the Avon one breathed a sweeter air on summer evenings. Does and bucks still found covert in the Forest of Arden, and the cornfields yielded fruitful increase; much as they did in the environs of London in the days of Fitz-Stephen. We need not wonder that (so tradition reports) the poet each year journeyed back to the town of his origin, or that he chose to buy most of his property there rather than in the capital, or that, at the height of his London fame, he elected to pass the twilight of his life in Stratford.

If a centre attracts foreign visitors, they sometimes have more to tell us than natives about principal attractions. That is certainly so with respect to the one great feature of the London scene of which we have yet to speak. No guide to the stones and streets of the capital is more painstaking than John Stow, yet he is curiously uncommunicative about the playhouses that are, for us, the glory of Elizabethan England. The defunct religious drama reminds Stow that

> Of late time in place of those stage plays hath been used comedies, tragedies, interludes, and histories, both true and feigned; for the

acting whereof certain public places as the Theater, the Curtine, &c., have been erected. [*Margin:* Theater and Curten for comedies and other shows][20]

Elsewhere, after describing Holywell, Stow casually adds: 'And near thereunto are builded two public houses for the acting and show of comedies, tragedies, and histories, for recreation. Whereof the one is called the Courtein, the other the Theatre: both standing on the south-west side towards the field.'[21] That is all, and even these laconic references he pared from his second edition of the *Survey* in 1603. By then, to be sure, the Theatre had vanished, and the Chamberlain's men had ceased playing at the Curtain. At the Globe, however, a penny bought admission to *Julius Caesar* or *Hamlet*. Stow never mentions Shakespeare's playhouse; although no Puritan, this 'merry old man' was too respectably middle-class to be drawn towards such frivolities as stage plays. For descriptions of Elizabethan theatres and the like we must turn to continental travellers. As Thomas Heywood, himself a playwright, boasted, 'playing is an ornament to the city, which strangers of all nations, repairing hither, report of in their countries, beholding them here with some admiration: for what variety of entertainment can there be in any city of Christendom, more than in London?'[22] Fortunately some of the jottings of these holiday-makers have survived.

When, in the summer of 1598, Paul Hentzner methodically did the sights, he inspected the marble tombs in St. Paul's and Westminster, as well as the armour in the Tower, and quantities of goods in the Royal Exchange. At Greenwich he gained admittance to the presence chamber (a friend made the arrangements) and caught a glimpse of the Queen, in her sixty-fifth year, with bare bosom, narrow lips, and black teeth; the English, he noted in his commonplace book, use too much sugar. For recreation Hentzner repaired to Bankside.

Without the city are some Theatres, where English actors represent almost every day tragedies and comedies to very numerous audiences; these are concluded with excellent music, variety of dances, and the excessive applause of those that are present.

Not far from one of these theatres, which are all built of wood, lies the royal barge, close to the river. . . .[23]

But Hentzner's tastes seem to have run to less sophisticated fare than stage plays, for he dwells on a different sort of amphitheatre:

> There is still another place, built in the form of a theatre, which serves for the baiting of bulls and bears; they are fastened behind, and then worried by great English bull-dogs, but not without great risque to the dogs, from the horns of the one, and the teeth of the other; and it sometimes happens they are killed upon the spot; fresh ones are immediately supplied in the places of those that are wounded, or tired. To this entertainment, there often follows that of whipping a blinded bear, which is performed by five or six men, standing circularly with whips, which they exercise upon him without any mercy, as he cannot escape from them because of his chain; he defends himself with all his force and skill, throwing down all who come within his reach, and are not active enough to get out of it, and tearing the whips out of their hands, and breaking them. At these spectacles, and every where else, the English are constantly smoaking tobacco. . . . In these theatres, fruits, such as apples, pears and nuts, according to the season, are carried about to be sold, as well as ale and wine.[24]

Other visitors too, mostly German-speaking, took down notes. Samuel Kiechel, a merchant of Ulm who sojourned in England in 1585, described the playhouses—these would be the Theatre and the Curtain—as 'peculiar (*sonderbare*, i.e. *besondere*) houses, which are so constructed that they have about three galleries one above the other.'[25] It is not clear why the galleries made such an impression—perhaps he had seen no other theatres with similar seating arrangements, or maybe had never seen any theatre. A decade later, Prince Lewis of Anhalt-Cöthen was impressed by the beautiful costumes worn by actors who personated kings and emperors in the four playhouses—*vier spielhäuser*—then operating in London. A priest of St. Mary's in Utrecht, Johannes de Witt, visited London probably in the same year, 1596, and made, in addition to notes, a unique sketch of the interior of a theatre. These have perished, but luckily De Witt's friend from his university days in Leyden, Arend van Buchell, took enough interest to copy them in his commonplace book, which, perfectly preserved, may be consulted today in the modest University Library in the centre of Utrecht. Before the century was out, Thomas Platter of Basle came to London, and a few years later he described actual stage performances he had then witnessed. The notes of Platter and De Witt, along with the latter's drawing, comprise our most valuable eye-witness information about the Elizabethan theatre. We shall be returning to them.

Dramatic art thrived in London before it had expressly designed accommodation. By the sixties we begin to get reports of troupes performing at converted inns: the Bull in Bishopsgate Street, the Bel Savage on Ludgate Hill; the Bell and the Cross Keys, near one another in Gracechurch Street; and the Red Lion and Boar's Head in Whitechapel.* Equipped with permanent stages and tiring rooms, as well as stands for spectators, these inns continued in use long after the theatres that rendered them obsolete had come into being; as late as 1594 we hear of Shakespeare's company playing 'this winter time within the city at the Cross Keyes in Gracious Street'.

Still, the erection of the first purpose-built playhouse is an immensely significant event in the history of the English drama. James Burbage, 'the first builder of playhouses', was by occupation a joiner (or craftsman-carpenter; Snug's trade) and by character 'a stubborn fellow'—so a contemporary describes him. Not thriving at his trade, he became a common player; in 1572 we hear of him as a leading member, probably the head (his name appears first in the document), of the Earl of Leicester's well-regarded troupe, and he is similarly referred to again, with the same company, in 1574 and 1576. It occurred to the itinerant actor that 'continual great profit' might accrue from a building devoted solely to dramatic entertainment. He was right. In 1576, while still not worth above a hundred marks—no mean sum then, but more, much more, was needed—he borrowed capital from his brother-in-law, the prosperous grocer John Brayne, who a decade earlier had put money into the Red Lion Inn. The next step was to find a site.

Himself a dweller in the northern suburbs, Burbage looked in that direction, fixing on the Liberty of Halliwell (or Holywell), which formed part of the Middlesex parish of St. Leonard's, Shoreditch,

---

* There is a reference in July 1587 to a play about Sampson at the Red Lion Inn; allusions to stage plays at the others are later.

and lay only half a mile outside the Bishopsgate entrance to the city. The Liberty, which took its name from an ancient holy well, had belonged to a Benedictine priory. The convent was now dissolved: the well, decayed and filthy, replenished a horsepond; and the property came within the jurisdiction of the Crown. Around the well stood undeveloped land, except for a few derelict tenements, a crumbling barn, and some gardens. Here, on a small parcel of vacant ground between the tenements and the old brick wall of the precinct, Burbage's workmen began building the Theatre in the spring of 1576. More than half a century later Cuthbert Burbage (James's son) and his family memorably described the occasion and its aftermath:

> The father of us, Cutbert and Richard Burbage, was the first builder of playhouses, and was himself in his younger years a player. The Theater he built with many hundred pounds taken up at interest. The players that lived in those first times had only the profits arising from the doors, but now the players receive all the comings-in at the doors to themselves and half the galleries from the house-keepers. He built this house upon leased ground, by which means the landlord and he had a great suit in law, and by his death, the like troubles fell on us, his sons; we then bethought us of altering from thence, and at like expense built the Globe with more sums of money taken up at interest. . . .[26]

But that event belongs to another chapter.

On the west the Theatre was bounded by a ditch dividing it from the open Finsbury Fields. As Burbage had no right of way from Holywell Lane, theatre-goers had to cross the fields, and enter by a doorway in the precinct wall. 'I would needs to the Theatre to see a play', declares Tarlton's Ghost, returned from Purgatory,

> where when I came, I found such concourse of unruly people, that I thought it better solitary to walk in the fields, than to intermeddle myself amongst such a great press. Feeding mine humour with this fancy, I stepped by Dame Anne of Cleere's well, and went by the backside of Hogsdon: where finding the sun to be hot, and seeing a fair tree that had a cool shade, I sat me down to take the air, where after I had rested me a while I fell asleep. . . .
>
> And with that I waked, and saw such concourse of people through the fields, that I knew the play was done. . . .[27]

18. A Shoreditch playhouse, c. 1597-1600.

A second theatre followed on the heels of the first. This was the Curtain, which opened its doors by the autumn of 1577, a few months after we first hear of the Theatre as operational. The house came by its name from being in the Curtain Close, some 200 yards south of the Theatre, and on the other side of Holywell Lane. The presence of two such arenas in the capital presaged the imminent triumph of Sodom, and gave a stimulus to apocalyptic rhetoric. 'Look but upon the common plays in London, and see the multitude that flocketh to them and followeth them', lamented 'T.W.', probably Thomas White (vicar of St. Dunstan's-in-the-West), in the Sunday sermon he preached at Paul's Cross on 3 November 1577: 'behold the sumptuous theatre houses, a continual monument of London's prodigality and folly.'[28] William Harrison concurred: 'It is an evident token of a wicked time when players wax so rich that they can build such houses.'[29] If, as seems likely, the man who built the Curtain was Henry Lanman or Laneman, he was not a player but a middle-aged Londoner who described himself as a gentleman. He was renting property in Curtain Close in 1581, and taking profits from the playhouse in 1585. He does not seem to have waxed especially rich from his wicked enterprise, for the Curtain never achieved the fame of Burbage's Theatre. Fencing exhibitions occasionally took place at the Curtain between 1579 and 1583. Two years later it became a supplementary house—an 'easer', the records call it—to the Theatre, and Lanman and the Burbages agreed to pool their profits, an arrangement stipulated to last for seven years. The Chamberlain's men, Shakespeare's company, were almost certainly performing at Lanman's theatre from 1597 to 1599. It was during this period that *Romeo and Juliet* 'won Curtain plaudits'. When the Prologue to *Henry V* speaks of 'this wooden O', he may possibly refer to the Curtain rather than (as often thought) to the Globe, and in this way immortalize an otherwise undistinguished house.

The Curtain must have been the Bishopsgate theatre visited by Thomas Platter in 1599, for by then the Theatre was gone:

> On another occasion, also after dinner, I saw a play not far from our inn, in the suburb, at Bishopsgate, as far as I remember. . . . At the end they danced, too, very gracefully, in the English and the Irish mode. Thus every day around two o'clock in the afternoon in the city of London two and sometimes even three plays are performed at different places, in order to make people merry [literally 'so that one make the other merry']; then those who acquit themselves best have also the largest audience. The places are built in such a way that they act on a raised scaffold, and everyone can well see everything. However, there are separate galleries and places, where one sits more pleasantly and better, therefore also pays more. For he who remains standing below pays only one English penny, but if he wants to sit he is let in at another door, where he gives a further penny; but if he desires to sit on cushions in the pleasantest place, where he not only sees everything well but can also be seen, then he pays at a further door another English penny. And during the play food and drink is carried around among the people, so that one can also refresh oneself for one's money.

> The play-actors are dressed most exquisitely and elegantly, because of the custom in England that when men of rank or knights die they give and bequeath almost their finest apparel to their serv-

ants, who, since it does not befit them, do not wear such garments, but afterwards let the play-actors buy them for a few pence.

How much time they [the people] thus can spend merrily every day at plays everyone knows well who has ever seen them [the actors] act or play. . . .[30]

The Curtain outlasted its theatrical usefulness, and (according to Malone) was in latter days employed only for prize-fights. It still stood in 1627, when a Middlesex county record refers in passing to 'the common shore near the Curtain playhouse'.

These were the theatres of the northern suburbs at the time of Shakespeare's advent to the London stage. The centre of gravity for the players was, however, shifting to the Surrey side of the river, which was well equipped for amusement-seekers. A broad meadow invited picnickers, and furnished an open area for the athletically inclined to run and wrestle, to play football and bowl. ('Was there ever man had such luck!' Cloten grumbles in *Cymbeline*. 'When I kiss'd the jack, upon an up-cast to be hit away! . . . Come, I'll go see this Italian. What I have lost to-day at bowls I'll win to-night of him.') Archery encouraged the exercise of a traditional English manly skill; that skill which Justice Shallow, sliding into senility in bucolic Gloucestershire, recalls so nostalgically: ' 'A drew a good bow; and dead! 'A shot a fine shoot. John a Gaunt loved him well, and betted much money on his head. Dead! 'A would have clapp'd i' th' clout at twelve score, and carried you a forehand shaft a fourteen and fourteen and a half, that it would have done a man's heart good to see.' Visitors could dance round the maypole. For a fee they could dance the shaking of the sheets at one of the bordellos which, licensed by tolerant authority of the Bishop of Winchester, edged the river bank, and made suburban garden-houses synonymous with harlotry. ('Dwell I but in the suburbs / Of your good pleasure?' Portia asks her husband. 'If it be no more, / Portia is Brutus' harlot, not his wife.') They could get drunk in taverns, or be fleeced in gaming houses. They could watch George Stone or Harry Hunks, their favourite bears, fight off ferocious mastiffs in amphitheatres which, as early as mid-century, are depicted in maps of Southwark; one such map, by Braun and Hogenburg (printed in 1572), shows the attached stables and kennels. The brutal pastime found its natural setting on Bankside, for the butchers dumped their offal in the Manor of Paris Garden, and thus provided ample nourishment for the beasts.[31]

The first theatre south of the river is known to historians as Newington Butts (it does not seem to have had any usual name in its own day), after the segment of the Queen's highway where the roads from Camberwell and Clapham merged leading to Southwark. There is no evidence of ancient archery butts there, as was until recently thought. The theatre, it now seems likely, was built, or converted from an existing structure, by the enterprise of Jerome Savage, the leading player for the Earl of Warwick's men, who secured their patron in 1575. The playhouse may have opened not long thereafter.[32] It was reachable on foot by the road which, continuing Southwark High Street, cut across St. George's Fields. We first hear of plays being acted at Newington Butts in 1580, after the collapse of Warwick's men; but the theatre never caught on, no doubt because of the inconvenient location. In 1592 the Privy Council directed Strange's men to play there, then rescinded the order 'by reason of the tediousness of the way and that of long time plays have not there been used on working days'.[33] When the combined Admiral's-Chamberlain's company performed at Newington Butts for an abbreviated season in 1594, their average daily takings came to a meagre 9s., despite the fact that their repertoire included *Titus Andronicus*, *The Taming of A Shrew*, and the mysterious lost play of *Hamlet*. By 1599, we are told, the theatre was 'only a memory'.[34] People no longer had to cross the fields to see a play.

For in January 1587 Philip Henslowe and John Cholmley, a citizen and grocer of London, concluded a partnership agreement in a 'playhouse now in framing and shortly to be erected and set up upon' a parcel of ground at the corner of Rose Alley and Maiden Lane. On this vacant lot, in former times, a rose garden flourished. This was the district of the stews; convenient to the river's edge, and to the city.[35] A theatre here could scarcely fail. On 19 February 1592 Strange's men opened at the Rose, under the leadership of Edward Alleyn—of all the tragedians of the age, the most formidable rival to Richard Burbage. The engagement led to the eventual partnership

of the English Roscius and the then sole landlord of the Rose
(Cholmley passes from view; probably he had died); a partnership
cemented by Alleyn's marriage to Henslowe's stepdaughter. They
reaped a great fortune from show business, and in 1613, having retired to his country estate, Alleyn munificently endowed the College
of God's Gift at Dulwich. By then the Rose had fallen into disuse—
there are no records of performances there after 1603—but it had already played its part in making Bankside the vital centre of the
London stage scene, and Henslowe the most powerful theatrical
magnate of the age. There is a Shakespearian connection with the
Rose. On 24 January 1594, when Sussex's men were playing there,
Henslowe recorded in his *Diary* a performance of *Titus Andronicus*,
which he marked as 'ne' [new],[36] a rather puzzling term that may
signify that the play was newly licensed by the Master of the Revels.
Titus is the only 'new' work which the troupe presented during their
short season at the Rose.

Hentzner refers to a theatre at the western end of Bankside, near
where the royal barge had its mooring. This must have been the
Swan in the Manor of Paris Garden. When Francis Langley, a London draper and 'goldsmith' (in this case a euphemism for money-
lender), set out to build this theatre, the Lord Mayor complained
loudly, but could do little to prevent a licence, for the land formed
part of the holdings of the dissolved monastery of Bermondsey, and
therefore fell within the purview of the Crown. Langley built in the
north-east corner of the manor grounds, east of the manor-house,
and twenty-six poles (approximately 430 feet; a pole equals 5½
yards) due south of Paris Garden stairs, where the watermen had
their wherries for hire.[37] The Swan had opened its doors to the public by the summer of 1596, for it was then (as appears likely) that
Johannes de Witt made his celebrated visit. Shakespeare had some
association with the proprietor of the Swan, for the names of the
two men appear together in 1597 in a petition for the surety of the
peace.[38]

These were the permanent public playhouses of London before
the building of the Globe. As an actor and playwright, Shakespeare
was acquainted with most of them; perhaps he knew them all. Theatre historians have painstakingly mulled over the antecedents for

these remarkable edifices, some attaching more weight than others to the animal-baiting amphitheatres or the inn-yards or the Tudor banqueting halls with their screened passageways. One learned authority has even invoked the classical authority of Vitruvius, but it is doubtful that, before setting his carpenters to work on the Theatre, James Burbage, joiner and player, struggled with the Latin of *De architectura*; nor is it appreciably more likely that he thumbed a French translation in the library of the mathematician-magus John Dee, or that Dee himself actually designed the Theatre, with Burbage as 'his collaborator and executant'.[39] These considerations need not detain us. The historians have also endlessly debated particulars, such as the dimensions of the various parts of the playhouse, or the means for effecting 'discoveries' (the curtained inner stage, a favourite construction of earlier authorities, has now lost favour). Our concern is with the generic features of the theatres, familiar from innumerable stage histories or artists' impressions or scale models. We shall not go far wrong if we take for our guide a contemporary observer, De Witt.

His notes, headed (by Van Buchell) 'Ex Observationibus Londinensibus Johannis de Witt', have been translated thus from the Latin:

There are four amphitheatres in London of notable beauty, which from their diverse signs bear diverse names. In each of them a different play is daily exhibited to the populace. The two more magnificent of these are situated to the southward beyond the Thames, and from the signs suspended before them are called the Rose and Swan. The two others are outside the city towards the north on the highway which issues through the Episcopal Gate, called in the vernacular Bishopsgate. There is also a fifth, but of dissimilar structure, devoted to the baiting of beasts, where are maintained in separate cages and enclosures many bears and dogs of stupendous size, which are kept for fighting, furnishing thereby a most delightful spectacle to men.* Of all the theatres, however, the largest and the most magnificent is that one of which the sign is a swan, called in the ver-

---

* The captive beasts, according to DeWitt's notes, included bulls, as well as bears and dogs (*multi ursi, tauri, et stupendae magnitudinis canes*).

nacular the Swan Theatre; for it accommodates in its seats three thousand persons, and is built of a mass of flint stones (of which there is a prodigious supply in Britain), and supported by wooden columns painted in such excellent imitation of marble that it is able to deceive even the most cunning. Since its form resembles that of a Roman work, I have made a sketch of it above.[40]

That sketch depicts the interior of a playhouse with three tiers of galleries surrounding a circular central yard. On either side of the yard, what some have interpreted as steps (one set labelled *ingressus*) lead apparently to the lower gallery; we cannot see the staircase that gave access to the upper tiers. A large rectangular stage (*proscænium*), improbably of greater depth than width—this is only a rough sketch—dominates the unroofed yard.* The stage rests on two hefty supports; a pair of Corinthian columns in turn sustain the 'heavens' which provide a cover. There are three figures downstage, one of whom, a woman, sits on a bench. Is it a rehearsal or an actual performance? More likely the latter, in view of the spectators in the gallery. At the rear of the stage is a tiring-house (*mimorum ædes*), in which the players changed costume and stored their properties. They entered and exited through two massive double doors in the tiring-house façade; an open door, fitted up with curtains, would do for a discovery-space—to reveal, for example, Ferdinand and Miranda at their chess game in *The Tempest*. There is no suggestion of an inner stage. Nor does De Witt's drawing show a trap door opening into the 'hell' below, although the theatre required such an aperture for ghosts and graves, as in *Hamlet*, or for the 'unhallow'd and blood-stained hole' in *Titus Andronicus*. The second storey of the façade consists of a row of six windows, apparently defining boxes in which spectators are watching the play going on below. One of these boxes could serve as a music room. They could be cleared for action aloft; this was the upper stage, used, it seems, less

* The authorities differ on the proportions (cf. Chambers, *Elizabethan Stage*, ii. 528), with the most recent student, Hosley, concluding that '[t]he stage is depicted as deeper than wide' ('The Playhouses and the Stage', *A New Companion to Shakespeare Studies*, ed. Kenneth Muir and S. Schoenbaum (Cambridge, 1971), p. 23).

19. Johannes de Witt, the Swan Theatre, as copied by
Arend van Buchell.

than earlier historians thought. Surmounting the 'heavens' is an attic loft housing the suspension-gear for flying effects, such as the descent of Jupiter in *Cymbeline*. On the roof of this hut a flagpole flies the banner of the swan, hoisted to advertise a performance that day. In the doorway to the hut stands a man; he seems to be holding to his mouth a trumpet from which hangs another, smaller flag with the sign of the swan. The top gallery has a roof designated *tectum*.

The early panoramas of London provide a glimpse of the playhouses from the outside. These views show cylindrical or polygonal structures pleasantly situated among trees, meadows, and cottages; in the later panoramas the cottages crowd in upon the theatres. It is perhaps a mistake to expect cartographical precision from such guides, but the most meticulous of them, Hollar's 'Long View' of London, depicts a circular Globe and Hope; we remember the 'wooden "O" '. Two exterior staircases, enclosed on the outside with lime and plaster, furnished entry to the galleries. Such a staircase is visible on the Shoreditch playhouse in 'The View of the City of London from the North Towards the South', *c.* 1597-1600, and on the Second Globe and the Bear Garden in the Hollar panorama. De Witt speaks of 'a mass of flint stones' or—depending upon translation—'concrete made of flintstones' used in construction (*constructum ex coacervato lapide pyrritide*), but most of the evidence—not least that of the combustibility of the playhouses—points to timber as the chief building material, the outside being finished with the usual lime and plaster. Thatched roofing covered the galleries.

Such were the essential features of the Elizabethan theatres. To a young poet-playwright of genius, they offered the advantages of their deficiencies. The absence of scenic illusion gave a spur to the creative imagination—Arden lives the more vividly because Shakespeare's theatre furnished no woodland setting, with birds and boughs and murmuring streams, for the courtship of Rosalind and Orlando. The lack of a proscenium arch made for fluidity of dramatic movement: such a stage gave scope to the immensities of *Antony and Cleopatra*. Shakespeare might have his Chorus call for a kingdom for a stage, and lament the insufficiency of his 'unworthy scaffold to bring forth/So great an object'; but these limitations did not prevent him from triumphantly undertaking the epic historical drama of *Henry* V. All this the world knows well, although the industry of editors, with their sometimes superfluous scene divisions and literary stage directions, has sometimes obscured the exhilarating freedom of Shakespeare's art.

By the late eighties, then, London boasted an incomparable theatrical establishment and audiences ready, when the trumpet sounded, to respond to poetic drama.

{ 10 }

The Upstart Crow

Shakespeare's introduction to the capital falls, frustratingly, in the void of the Lost Years, but legend has filled it with a pretty tale. The story comes under the general rubric of The Humble Origins of Great Men, and has itself a modest beginning.

The first hints emerge late in the seventeenth century, a half-century and more after Shakespeare's death. We have already encountered Mr. Dowdall, on his way back from Stratford, writing a letter filled with parish clerk's gossip about the butcher-boy who bolted and 'was received into the playhouse as a serviture'.[1] The first serious inquirer has nothing substantive to add: 'He was receiv'd into the Company then in being, at first in a very mean Rank; but his admirable Wit, and the natural Turn of it to the Stage, soon distinguish'd him, if not as an extraordinary Actor, yet as an excellent Writer.'[2] These statements affirm what we would anyway assume, that Shakespeare began his theatrical career as a hired man rather than a sharer. They do not tell us much else.

For the colourful elaboration that gives sustenance to the mythos we must wait until 1753 and the curious relation made in the memoir of Shakespeare in *The Lives of the Poets of Great Britain and Ireland*, published as by 'Mr. Cibber', but in fact largely compiled (as Dr. Johnson informed Boswell) by Robert Shiels. Johnson knew whereof he spoke, for Shiels was his amanuensis. Shiels precedes his contribution with a genealogy tracing it back to Sir William Davenant, the source of more than one dubious Shakespearian anecdote.

Despite the pedigree, the story, trailing off into unacknowledged quotation from Rowe, probably came to Shiels *via* Johnson. Shiels presents his entry thus:

> Concerning Shakespear's first appearance in the playhouse. When he came to London, he was without money and friends, and being a stranger he knew not to whom to apply, nor by what means to support himself.——At that time coaches not being in use, and as gentlemen were accustomed to ride to the playhouse, Shakespear, driven to the last necessity, went to the playhouse door, and pick'd up a little money by taking care of the gentlemens horses who came to the play; he became eminent even in that profession, and was taken notice of for his diligence and skill in it; he had soon more business than he himself could manage, and at last hired boys under him, who were known by the name of Shakespear's boys: Some of the players accidentally conversing with him, found him so acute, and master of so fine a conversation, that struck therewith, they and [*sic*] recommended him to the house, in which he was first admitted in a very low station, but he did not long remain so, for he soon distinguished himself, if not as an extraordinary actor, at least as a fine writer.[3]

To achieve marmoreal apotheosis it now required only the sonorities of the master. These Johnson in due course provided in his version for his 1765 edition of Shakespeare:

> In the time of *Elizabeth*, coaches being yet uncommon, and hired coaches not at all in use, those who were too proud, too tender, or too idle to walk, went on horseback to any distant business or diversion. Many came on horseback to the play, and when *Shakespear* fled to *London* from the terrour of a criminal prosecution, his first expedient was to wait at the door of the play-house, and hold the horses of those that had no servants, that they might be ready again after the performance. In this office he became so conspicuous for his care and readiness, that in a short time every man as he alighted called for *Will. Shakespear*, and scarcely any other waiter was trusted with a horse while *Will. Shakespear* could be had. This was the first dawn of better fortune. *Shakespear* finding more horses put into his hand than he could hold, hired boys to wait under his inspection, who, when *Will. Shakespear* was summoned, were immediately to present themselves, *I am* Shakespear's *boy, Sir*. In time

Shakespear found higher employment, but as long as the practice of riding to the play-house continued, the waiters that held the horses retained the appellation of Shakespear's *Boys*.[4]

The anecdote is clearly a pendant to the myth of the deer-poaching at Charlecote; early capitalist enterprise furnishes a heartening postlude to romantic pseudo-delinquency. If the story made any serious claim to authority, it would suggest that the Theatre or the Curtain was Shakespeare's first playhouse, for only these were reached by horseback.[5] But the story makes no serious claim. Rowe and Pope, cited by Johnson as his authorities, ignored it in their own editions of Shakespeare. The great Malone suspected that it owed something to exaggerated notions of the impoverishment of the Shakespeares—the young Will, friendless and unconnected, hanging loose upon society; and he rejected the story with Augustan finality: 'But, lastly, and principally, this anecdote is altogether unworthy of belief, because our author's circumstances and situation at this time, and the various extracts which I have just now given from the Records of Stratford, loudly reclaim against it.'[6]

Malone himself flirted with another tradition that has at least the merit of placing Shakespeare inside the playhouse rather than in its manured precincts: 'There is a stage tradition that his first office in the theatre was that of prompter's attendant; whose employment it is to give the performers notice to be ready to enter, as often as the business of the play requires their appearance on the stage.'[7] That was in 1780. By the time he got round to the life of Shakespeare he never lived to complete, Malone no longer attached much weight to the tradition, for he did not bother to repeat it. Instead his mind revolved upon the companies—Warwick's or Leicester's or the Queen's—which included Stratford in their provincial itineraries, and he closed his section on the horse-holding story with the kind of speculation that is more illuminating than the late efflorescences of tradition:

It is, I think, much more probable, that his own lively disposition made him acquainted with some of the principal performers who visited Stratford, the elder Burbage, or Knell, or Bentley; and that there he first determined to engage in that profession. Lord Leicester's servants, among whom was one of the performers just mentioned, James Burbage, the father of the celebrated tragedian, had been honoured with a royal licence in 1574. With this company, therefore, or the Queen's, or Lord Warwick's comedians, it is reasonable to suppose, that he agreed to enroll himself, and that with one or the other of them he first visited the metropolis.[8]

So we find ourselves back at the resting-point for our previous chapter.

A historian following the tracks of the metropolitan companies in the eighties risks losing the scent altogether.[9] The life of the troupes was unstable. They went off on protracted tours of the hinterland; they suffered defections and absorbed new talent; they amalgamated, divided, or expired. The records for all this activity are discouragingly incomplete. It is clear, however, that throughout most of the decade the palm for popularity went to the Queen's men—the company that was, it will be recalled, lacking a man in 1587. For a time they faced only feeble competition. Derby's men, who seem to have been distinct at least for a time from Strange's,[10] fade from view altogether. Strange's company, led by John Symons the tumbler, apparently specialized in acrobatics during much of the decade. Other troupes—Leicester's, Sussex's, Oxford's, and Hunsdon's—kept to the provinces, with only occasional forays into the capital. The Admiral's company made a bid for London favour in 1587, but stumbled on catastrophe. During a performance in November, the players tied one of their number to a post—such a column as De Witt depicts supporting the 'Heavens'—with the intention of shooting him; but the caliver (unfortunately loaded) misfired, killing a child and a pregnant woman, and wounding another spectator. The company prudently withdrew into retirement, and for over a year we do not hear of them. Meanwhile the Queen's men kept in the ascendancy. On at least seventeen occasions between the winters of 1583-4 and 1587-8 they played at Court in productions rehearsed under the practised eye of the Master of the Revels; for each of these royal command performances they received a reward of £10. No other troupe in those days acted nearly so often at Court.

But the fortunes of show business are fickle. In September 1588 death took Tarlton, the clown who was so funny that the Queen had to command his removal for making her laugh excessively. With his russet coat and buttoned hat and his tabor, Tarlton was beloved of multitudes, and quite simply irreplaceable. A John Scottowe struck the appropriate elegiac note:

> The party now is gone,
>   And closely clad in clay,
> Of all the jesters in the land,
>   He bare the praise away.[11]

Following the usual pattern of troupes under stress, Her Majesty's Players took to the road, picking up stray talent along the way, and wandering as far north as Lancashire, where in the autumn of 1588 they beguiled the Earl of Derby with a play at his seat of New Park. The next year they roamed even farther, spending ten days in Carlisle. For a while the company split up, one segment teaming up temporarily with Sussex's men. They diversified their offerings with tumblers, acrobatic routines, even a Turkish rope-dancer; all to no avail. The Queen's servants played only once at Court during Christmas 1591-2; not at all the following year. For the simple fact was that they could not compete with the young Alleyn lending his charismatic presence to the amalgamated Admiral's-Strange's men at the Rose on Bankside. The latter company had Marlowe, stirring theatre audiences with his high-astounding terms and a new drama of heroic dimensions. If the Queen's had Shakespeare, just beginning to make his presence felt in the theatre, we do not know definitely of any plays he wrote for them. For better or worse they certainly dealt with Robert Greene, experienced not only in letters but also in the hard school of Elizabethan low-life.[12]

He belonged to the brotherhood of University Wits: that small company of Bohemian intellectuals born in the provinces shortly after mid-century, and educated at Cambridge or Oxford. Footloose, they turned their backs on their origins, and gravitated to the capital, where they supplied the stationers with pamphlets and the players with plays. In London they led lives that were nasty, brutish, brilliant, and short. With Greene we cannot always separate fact from fiction in the fantasias he composed on autobiographical themes, or the legend made of him by his contemporaries. The pattern of his career—necessarily pieced together from the testimony of biased witnesses—assumes the lineaments of archetype.

He came of sound middle-class stock, the son of a Norwich saddler who educated him locally, no doubt at the Free Grammar School which, under the supervision of the mayor and aldermen, enrolled 'fourscore and four scholars'. In 1580 Greene graduated B.A. from St. John's College, Cambridge. Foreign travel provided postgraduate education; in Italy and Spain he reports seeing and practising 'such villainy as is abominable to declare'. Back in England, a restless libertine drowned in pride, he wandered one day into St. Andrew's Church in Norwich, where the preacher, John More—known as the Apostle of Norwich—laid before his imagination the terrors of God's Judgement. Greene repented. 'Lord have mercy upon me', he said to himself, 'and send me grace to amend and become a new man.' Thus reformed, he took his M.A. in 1583 from Clare Hall, Cambridge, and two years later married the virtuous and patient Dorothea. But the new man slipped back into the old: he got Dorothea with child, and, having squandered her marriage-money, shipped her off to Lincolnshire to shift for herself as best she could, then took up again with his dissolute London companions. In his own phrase, he fell again with the dog to his old vomit.

Romances issued from Greene's facile pen; he needed to keep writing to support his prodigal life style. Having pawned sword and cloak, he shifted lodgings in stews, rioted in taverns (he was a favourite of the hostess of the Red Lattise in Tormoyle Street), and hob-nobbed with a notorious ruffian, Ball—called Cutting Ball—who would eventually meet his end on the gibbet at Tyburn. For his mistress, Greene took Ball's sister. She bore him a son, ironically named Fortunatus; he would die young. His experiences Greene exploited for his own brand of superior, if sensational, journalism. In a series of pamphlets he made his notable discoveries of cosenage, laying bare the practices by which cross-biters, priggars, gripes, nips, foists, and lifts preyed upon coneys—young gentlemen, country folk, apprentices. Meanwhile he somehow managed to turn out plays also: *Alphonsus King of Aragon*, *The Scottish History of James IV*, *A Looking Glass for London and England* (with his fellow-wit, Thomas Lodge), and a minor masterpiece, *Friar Bacon and Friar*

Bungay, in the vein of wonder and romance he could still intermittently command. One episode involving the Queen's men shows him capable of the double-dealing he exposed in others. 'Ask the Queen's Players', demanded the pseudonymous Cuthbert Cunny-Catcher in 1592, 'if you sold them not *Orlando Furioso* for twenty nobles, and when they were in the country, sold the same play to the Lord Admiral's men for as much more. Was not this plain coney-catching, Master R. G.?'[13]

The charge, even if true, no longer really mattered much. In August 1592, flaunting finery his means could ill sustain, he ate a last meal with Nashe and other cronies. That evening he over-indulged in Rhenish wine and pickled herrings, and this excess (according to report) brought on his last illness. He was then lodging with his mistress, 'a sorry ragged quean', and their bastard in the house of a shoemaker of Dowgate, one Isam, and his wife. For a month Greene lingered in squalor, deserted by friends but attended by troops of lice. Mrs. Isam gave him the penny-pot of malmsey he pitifully begged, while Harvey exulted in the downfall of the wicked:

> A rakehell, a makeshift, a scribbling fool:
> A famous bayard in city, and school.
> Now sick as a dog, and ever brainsick:
> Where such a raving and desperate Dick?[14]

Between prayers Greene scribbled his last confessions, and near the end wrote piteously to his cast-off Dorothea, asking her to forgive him and pay the ten pounds he owed his host. When he died, Mrs. Isam crowned him with a garland of bays, in accordance with his last wish. Before the year was out the bookstalls of St. Paul's Churchyard displayed *The Repentance of Robert Greene, Master of Arts* and *Greene's Groatsworth of Wit, bought with a million of Repentance. Describing the folly of youth, the falsehood of makeshift flatterers, the misery of the negligent, and mischiefs of deceiving Courtesans. Written before his death and published at his dying request.*

Thus lived and died Robert Greene, the saddler's son who would not willingly let the world forget that he was a Master of Arts. His progress furnishes a direct antithesis to that of the glover's son from

Stratford who never proceeded beyond grammar school. But Greene's career holds more than an exemplary interest. In the *Groatsworth of Wit* he makes the first unmistakable reference we have to Shakespeare in London.

'The Swan sings melodiously before death, that in all his lifetime useth but a jarring sound,' the author reminds his Gentlemen Readers in the preface.

> Greene though able enough to write, yet deeplier searched with sickness than ever heretofore, sends you his swan-like song, for that he fears he shall never again carol to you wonted love lays, never again discover to you youth's pleasures. However yet sickness, riot, incontinence have at once shown their extremity, yet if I recover, you shall all see more fresh sprigs than ever sprang from me, directing you how to live, yet not dissuading ye from love.[15]

Self-pity and self-reproach here strike a comfortable alliance, sustained in the thinly disguised autobiographical fiction which follows. This recounts the adventures of Roberto, a disinherited scholar who, tricked by a whore, goes off to curse his destiny. Being a poet, he inveighs in numbers, and, while sighing sadly in Latin, is approached by a gorgeously apparelled stranger, who has eavesdropped from the other side of the hedge. The stranger, it turns out, is a player keen to book new writing talent for his company. In the old days, when the world was hard, he carried his playing fardel on his back; now he commands a wardrobe worth over £200, and gives the appearance of a gentleman of substance. He has thundered terribly on the stage (Roberto finds his voice 'nothing gracious'), and can still at a pinch indite a pretty speech; for he was 'a country author, passing at a Moral, . . . and for seven years' space was absolute interpreter to the puppets'. Seeing no alternative, Roberto joins forces with the player, and becomes a 'famoused, arch playmaking-poet', his purse now full, now empty; the darling of lewd swearing companions, the observer and unmasker of 'all the rabble of that unclean generation of vipers'.

One authority has suggested that the unnamed player with gentlemanly airs is Shakespeare: he must have spoken with a broad provincial accent; hence the ungracious voice. He was a country author, and his seven years' apprenticeship at acting covers neatly the period between the birth of the twins in 1585 and the composition of the *Groatsworth* in 1592.[16] But the hedge encounter, which must be at least partly fanciful, takes place not in 1592 but in Roberto's past; the Morals that the player boasts of having written (he mentions *Man's Wit* and the *Dialogue of Dives*) belong to the pre-Shakespearian drama; and Greene, clearly represented as junior, was actually six years older than Shakespeare.

Yet the *Groatsworth of Wit* contains—no question—a desperate shaft directed at Shakespeare. The author hurls it later, after having abandoned any pretence at fiction; he speaks as Greene, offering, while life still beats, the bitter wisdom of experience. He sets down a set of religious wholesome rules for good conduct, and then, in a letter, addresses some special advice to three of his 'fellow scholars about this city': Marlowe and (probably) Nashe and Peele. There follows the celebrated denunciation of the 'upstart crow':

> Base-minded men all three of you, if by my misery you be not warned: for unto none of you (like me) sought those burrs to cleave: those puppets (I mean) that spake from our mouths, those antics garnished in our colours. Is it not strange, that I, to whom they all have been beholding; is it not like that you, to whom they all have been beholding, shall (were ye in that case as I am now) be both at once of them forsaken? Yes, trust them not: for there is an upstart crow, beautified with our feathers, that with his *tiger's heart wrapped in a player's hide* supposes he is as well able to bombast out a blank verse as the best of you; and, being an absolute *Johannes Factotum*, is in his own conceit the only Shake-scene in a country.[17]

That Greene has singled out Shakespeare for attack is evident from the punning reference to a Shake-scene, and confirmed by a parodic allusion to one of Shakespeare's earliest plays. In *3 Henry VI* Queen Margaret has taken the Duke of York prisoner at the battle of Wakefield; she will kill him, but first she taunts him with a handkerchief dipped in his slain son's blood, and in a long tirade he responds with the only weapon left him, the rhetoric of invective. York's speech contains the line, 'O tiger's heart wrapp'd in a woman's hide!' By changing one word Greene has accused Shakespeare of cruelty.

It is not his only charge. The rest, being obscure in the best Elizabethan tradition, has inspired debate without end. The thrust of the passage as a whole is against the actors ('puppets . . . that spake from our mouths') who batten on the dramatists. A contempt for mean players came naturally to a Cambridge M.A. dependent upon these affluent inferiors for his penny-pot and lice-infested bed, and such contempt would mingle with other, equally disagreeable, emotions engendered by the accusation that he had fobbed off the same playbook on two companies. These feelings find a focus in the fable of the crow.

From antiquity the bird gifted with powers of mimicry but not of invention had intrigued poets and critics. In Macrobius, Greene found the stories of Roscius and of the cobbler's crow used in *Francesco's Fortunes*: 'Why Roscius, art thou proud with Esop's crow, being pranked with the glory of others' feathers? Of thyself thou canst say nothing, and if the cobbler hath taught thee to say *Ave Caesar*, disdain not thy tutor, because thou pratest in a king's chamber.'[18] Roscius here stands for Alleyn. Shakespeare too was an actor, and is attacked as such; the phrase about the 'upstart crow, beautified with our feathers' continues the idea expressed in 'antics garnished in our colours'. Moreover, the mere actor has the audacity to set himself up as a universal genius (*Johannes Factotum*) who can, by turning out stilted and bombastic blank verse, rival his superiors and deprive them of employment. Many have interpreted the passage in this way.

But does it harbour a more sinister charge? Perhaps the crow is not the bird taught to imitate its betters that derives ultimately from Aesop, Martial, and Macrobius; instead Greene may allude to Horace's third *Epistle*, in which the poet uses the image of a crow (*cornicula*) divested of its plundered lustre (*furtivis nudata coloribus*) in connection with the idea of plagiarism. These lines were well known in the Renaissance. In *A Strappado for the Devil* Richard Brathwait sneers at thieving crows that steal 'selected flowers from others' wit'.[19] Is Greene then maliciously suggesting that Shakespeare has appropriated the flowers of *his* wit? This is the second interpretation, and is of long standing. As far back as the eighteenth century it gave rise to the view that Shakespeare began his literary career as a Johannes Factotum in the sense of a Jack-of-all-trades who—in addition to acting—revised and adapted the plays of others, including Greene.

Few today accept this theory. It is inherently improbable that a company would entrust to a novice the task of improving the work of experienced professional dramatists. Most of the more reliable authorities now think that Greene was complaining because Shakespeare, a mere uneducated player, had the effrontery to compete as a dramatist with his betters; not because the same base fellow pilfered his wares from others. But of course it is not impossible that Greene was making a double accusation, thus conflating Aesop's crow with Horace's, which were anyway closely associated in the minds of his audience.[20]

Whatever the drift of this notorious passage, the pamphlet gave ample cause for offence; for Greene's notorious letter castigated not only Shake-scene but also two old comrades. He rebukes the 'famous gracer of tragedians'—Marlowe—for atheism and for discipleship of Machiavelli; with false delicacy he reproves 'young Juvenal, that biting satirist'—presumably Nashe—for indulging in 'too much liberty of reproof'. When the *Groatsworth* appeared the improbable rumour circulated in London that Nashe, not Greene, had written it. In his *Pierce Penniless*, printed only a month after Greene's death, Nashe recoiled in horror from the suggestion: 'Other news I am advertised of, that a scald, trivial, lying pamphlet, called *Green's Groatsworth of Wit*, is given out to be of my doing. God never have care of my soul, but utterly renounce me, if the least word or syllable in it proceeded from my pen, or if I were any way privy to the writing or printing of it.'[21] The publisher of the *Groatsworth*, William Wright, evidently anticipated a storm, for he took the unusual precaution of disassociating himself from the pamphlet; when he entered it in the Stationers' Register on 20 September 1592, he added to the licence the exculpatory clause, 'upon the peril of Henrye Chettle'.

Attention now focuses on Chettle. Of about Shakespeare's age—maybe a few years older—he was a Londoner; an easy-going sort, puffing and sweating because of his overweight. By trade a printer who had served his seven years' apprenticeship, Chettle nourished literary aspirations. For Henslowe at the Rose and Fortune he would write wholly or in part forty-eight plays over a period of five years, but his furious hack play-writing would not spare him the embarrassment of poverty and debt. Although a contemporary praised Chettle for his comedies, as a dramatist he is remembered, if at all, for his revenge tragedy of *Hoffman*. In 1592 these activities lay ahead. He was then a master printer whose partnership with William Hoskins and John Danter, two fairly disreputable members of the Stationers' Company, had lately come unstuck; Danter would go on to print the first quartos of *Titus Andronicus* and *Romeo and Juliet*. To Chettle, at loose ends, fell the task of preparing copy of the *Groatsworth* for the printers. His share in this venture brought interesting repercussions.

In 'To the Gentlemen Readers' prefacing his own *Kind-Heart's Dream*, printed by the same William Wright in the waning days of the year, or early in 1593, Chettle makes his famous apology to Shakespeare:

About three months since died M. Robert Greene, leaving many papers in sundry booksellers' hands, among other his *Groatsworth of Wit*, in which a letter written to divers play-makers, is offensively by one or two of them taken; and because on the dead they cannot be avenged, they wilfully forge in their conceits a living author: and after tossing it to and fro, no remedy, but it must light on me. How I have all the time of my conversing in printing hindered the bitter inveighing against scholars, it hath been very well known; and how in that I dealt I can sufficiently prove. With neither of them that take offence was I acquainted, and with one of them I care not if I never be: the other, whom at that time I did not so much spare, as since I wish I had, for that as I have moderated the heat of living writers, and might have used my own discretion (especially in such a case) the author being dead, that I did not, I am as sorry, as if the original fault had been my fault, because myself have seen his demeanour no less civil than he excellent in the quality he professes: besides, divers of worship have reported, his uprightness of dealing, which argues his honesty, and his facetious grace in writing, that approves his art.[22]

It is a carefully worded passage. 'Facetious [i.e. polished] grace' gracefully echoes Cicero's praise of Plautus in *De Officiis*.* Chettle's allusions are circumspect. The complainant whose acquaintance Chettle disdains while at the same time revering his learning appears to have offered threats ('him I would wish to use me no worse than I deserve'). This must have been Marlowe. Chettle reveals that he struck out from Greene's letter an aspersion which 'had it been true, yet to publish it, was intolerable'—could this have been an accusation against Marlowe of homosexuality? And who were the 'divers of worship' who sprang to Shakespeare's defence? Some enthusiasts, eager to supply their idol with the glamour of patrician connections, have suggested the intervention of noble lords. Shakespeare had not yet made the acquaintance of the Earl of Southampton—that would come the next year—but the biographer can always round up a stray aristocrat or two: perhaps the worshipful benefactor was Ferdinando, Lord Strange, patron of poets and players, and friend of the Queen's favourite, the Earl of Essex; perhaps it was the mercurial Essex himself. Dover Wilson indulges in a pleasing fancy: 'Possibly the emissary was no other than Shakespeare himself, bearing a sharply worded letter from his patron, and smoothing matters over for Chettle by his own charming manners.'[28] Should the epistle, whether carried by Shakespeare himself or delivered to Chettle afterwards, one day come to light, it is unlikely to bear a nobleman's seal. The Elizabethans made careful distinctions in their forms of address. Noblemen they would refer to as divers of honour; *worship* applied to gentlemen.[24] Anyway Shakespeare did not yet have a patron, and there is no evidence that he ever enjoyed the favour of Strange or Essex.† Who his influential supporters were we can hardly begin to guess.

The *Groatsworth* episode presents still another tantalising problem. Chettle in his preface complains about Greene's villainous scrawl, which no licenser or printer could be expected to read; and

---

* In the Bodleian and Folger copies the reading is 'fatious'. It was corrected in the course of printing, with 'which' in the same line altered to 'that' to provide space.

† The putative Strange connection stems from the assumption that Shakespeare then belonged to that nobleman's troupe.

he says that he copied it over as best he could, suppressing the scandalous tenor of the letter but not, he swears, adding a word of his own—'for I protest it was all Greene's, not mine nor Master Nashe's, as some unjustly have affirmed'. Now, almost 400 years after Chettle wrote, the spectre that he sought—successfully it seemed—to lay has been raised once again by Professor Warren Austin.[25] What if the *Groatsworth of Wit* is a fabrication after all? What if Chettle, a journeyman of letters, always needy, impersonated Greene's style and, in collusion with his colleagues in the printing trade, foisted the hoax on a public intrigued by the sensational circumstances surrounding the demise of a University Wit? The motive for the attack on Shakespeare would be a crass journalistic desire to give the pamphlet the spice of added topical interest; to stir up that tempest which in fact took place. Self-defence always arouses suspicions of culpability. Others before Austin have worried about the authorship of the *Groatsworth*, but he is the first to enlist the electronic computers in his cause.[26] The resultant formidable array of data—'Lexical Choice Variables', 'Morphological Variables', and 'Syntactical Variables'—is calculated to disarm the scruples of orthodox sceptics. It is an intriguing thesis, elaborately set forth.

Still, doubts present themselves. Greene wrote voluminously; the surviving Chettle corpus is meagre. For his inquiry, Austin has quarried five selections from Greene, and three from Chettle; a sampling not statistically overwhelming. Some of the 'Chettle' characteristics appear in Greene pieces not included in the survey. There are other problems as well.[27] This does not mean that the hypothesis is invalid, only that Austin has not proved his case. It is unlikely that such a case can be proved once and for all. In the absence of conclusive proof to the contrary, Greene must continue to bear responsibility for his mean death-bed diatribe, and we may accept, with some traces of unease, Chettle's apologia. A substitution of authors does not, in any event, resolve the interpretative problems, which are after all paramount.

Chettle's defence of Shakespeare's 'uprightness of dealing' would seem to imply that he took Greene's innuendoes as impugning the poet's honesty. Were they not so taken by R. B., Gent. (conceivably

Richard Barnfield) in one of the poems comprising the curious little collection entitled *Greene's Funerals?*

> Greene is the pleasing object of an eye:
> Greene pleased the eyes of all that looked upon him.
> Greene is the ground of every painter's dye:
> Greene gave the ground to all that wrote upon him.
> Nay more, the men that so eclipsed his fame,
> Purloined his plumes: can they deny the same?[28]

It would seem that this last contemporary reference, published early in 1594, shows some of Greene's mud still clinging to Shakespeare, here again recalled as an upstart crow decked in University Wit feathers. So, at any rate, almost everybody has thought since *Greene's Funerals* came to light almost a century and a half ago, and the passage has served to bolster the view that Greene's audience understood him to be charging Shakespeare with plagiarism. But Professor Austin has argued, this time more conclusively, that the object of R. B.'s vitriolic reproaches is not Shakespeare but Greene's enemy, Gabriel Harvey, who eclipsed Greene's fame (i.e. blackened his reputation) by traducing him, when he was yet scarcely cold in his grave, in the *Four Letters*.[29] Even the borrowed-feathers reference, which seems so clearly to echo the *Groatsworth*, has a more likely inspiration in Harvey's pamphlet: 'Thank other', he rebukes Greene, 'for thy borrowed and filched plumes of some little Italianated bravery. . . .'

So many ambiguities and perplexities attach to Greene's attack on Shakespeare and the sequel in Chettle's apology that one can sympathize with the exasperation voiced by one distinguished commentator in this century. 'This passage from Greene has had such a devastating effect on Shakespearian study', Smart complains, 'that we cannot but wish it had never been written or never discovered.'[30] Still, if the episode had not taken place, we should have been deprived of the handsome early tribute to Shakespeare in *Kind-Heart's Dream*, the first glimpse we get of him as a man, and all the more effective for being offset by the evocation, however brief and glancing, of the turbulent Marlowe, to whom no apology is forthcoming.

And what of the rancorous passage, so offensive to bardolaters, that prompted the amends? It too pays its own unpremeditated compliment to Shakespeare, for this is the tribute which envy renders to achievement. Greene's *Groatsworth of Wit* is, as the author says but not in the sense that he intended, a swan-song; the dying outcry of a generation of university-trained playwrights who were passing from the scene.[31]

{ 11 }

Plays, Plague, and a Patron

If by 1592 Shakespeare had made his mark as a playwright, we may ask with what plays. He had nothing yet in print, but this need hardly cause surprise. In that time an author retained little control over his literary creations once they left his hands. As previously noted, the profession of letters, in our sense, did not yet exist.[1] Authors were unprotected by a law of copyright—the regulations formulated and enforced at Stationers' Hall catered for the interests of the printers. Of all writers a dramatist had least to say about the publication of his works. He strove, after all, to please audiences in the theatre, not a reading public. The artefacts he sold to his theatrical company became their property, and so long as they remained viable on the stage, the actors would jealously guard them from print; for once a playbook appeared on the stalls, anybody could buy a copy, and have it produced. In Richard Brome's contract with the Salisbury Court company in Caroline times (the only such agreement of which we have knowledge, although there must have been others) the dramatist formally consented to abstain from publishing his plays without the express licence of the troupe.[2] Sometimes plays reached print anyway because of the misfortunes of the company—plague, financial stress, bankruptcy, or disbanding—or because pirated texts, inevitably corrupt, found their way into the printing-house. For one or other of these reasons, about half of Shakespeare's plays appeared in quarto editions during his lifetime; but all this came about after 1592. Clues to his earliest play-writing achievements must be sought in contemporary allusions. Fortunately the ill-will of Robert Greene in this respect renders an unintended benefaction.

The 'tiger's heart' reference in the *Groatsworth* shows that 3 *Henry VI* was then on the boards, and hence, most likely, the first two instalments of the trilogy as well. This plausible inference receives confirmation in the famous tribute paid by Nashe to the popularity of 1 *Henry VI*. 'How would it have joyed brave Talbot (the terror of the French)', he exclaims, 'to think that after he had lain two hundred years in his tomb, he should triumph again on the stage, and have his bones new embalmed with the tears of ten thousand spectators at least (at several times), who, in the tragedian that represents his person, imagine they behold him fresh bleeding.'[3] This passage, which occurs in *Pierce Penniless* (entered in the Stationers' Register on 8 August 1592), recalls Act IV, scene vii, in which old Talbot dies with his young son—his Icarus, his blossom—dead in his arms, and, frozen emblematically in the posture of a funerary sculpture, receives from Sir William Lucy his elaborate epitaph:

> . . . the great Alcides of the field,
> Valiant Lord Talbot, Earl of Shrewsbury,
> Created for his rare success in arms
> Great Earl of Washford, Waterford, and Valence,
> Lord Talbot of Goodrig and Urchinfield,
> Lord Strange of Blackmere, Lord Verdun of Alton,
> Lord Cromwell of Wingfield, Lord Furnival of Sheffield,
> The thrice victorious Lord of Falconbridge,
> Knight of the noble order of Saint George,
> Worthy Saint Michael, and the Golden Fleece,
> Great Marshal to Henry the Sixth
> Of all his wars within the realm of France.

The enthusiasm of Elizabethan theatregoers for the *Henry VI* plays—an enthusiasm evident not only from Nashe but also from their subsequent publishing history*—has moved some latter-day

---

* 2 and 3 *Henry VI* received the accolade that unauthorized publication pays to popularity (see below, p. 164). 1 *Henry VI*, on the other hand, did not achieve print until the 1623 Folio; but Henslowe, as well as Nashe, records its popularity—that is, if the play is Henslowe's 'Harey the vi' (see p. 165).

biographers to puzzlement and condescension. 'The series is unplay-able today', writes Miss Marchette Chute, 'if only for its lack of characterization and its jingoistic view of English history, but in its own day it ranked as one of the best series of productions that the London theatre had to offer.'[4] Miss Chute, having no critical pre-tensions of her own, merely reflected the consensus when she wrote, in 1951; and so her remark illustrates the ephemeral validity of such pronouncements. Shakespeare's first English history plays have since triumphantly returned to the stage in Stratford, as *The Wars of the Roses* (heavily adapted, to be sure), and elsewhere. Strictly speak-ing, the documentary biographer should stand aloof from criticism whether interpretative or judgemental, but it seems permissible to savour the fact that Shakespeare, while still in his twenties, had con-ceived and executed a sequence of historical dramas of a scale and complexity entirely novel to the London stage. If, as is certainly possible, he also wrote *Richard III* before 1593, he had extended trilogy into tetralogy, and epically transformed the amorphous ma-terials of his narrative chronicle sources. Only the Mystery plays of the cathedral towns, which he had perhaps himself witnessed as a boy in Coventry, afforded a precedent for drama on the Shake-spearian scale.

What else had he written? In the absence of a firm chronology one must speculate, and some guesses are better than others. There are critics who regard *Love's Labour's Lost* as very early work, but the problem of dating is complicated by evidence of revision, and on grounds of style a date around 1595 seems more likely. *The Taming of the Shrew*, in every way ruder, has a more convincing claim to precedence. So too *The Comedy of Errors* and *Titus Andronicus* convey an aroma of youth, and may be taken, despite startling sur-face dissimilarity, as opposite sides of the same coin: academic com-edy and academic tragedy, both transfused with the life-giving blood of the popular stage (*Titus* literally thus transfused). For *The Com-edy of Errors* Shakespeare adapted two plays of Plautus, the *Me-naechmi*—the principal source—and *Amphitruo*. In *Titus* he pays homage to his beloved *Metamorphoses*; but Seneca's *Thyestes* also provided fare to banquet on. If there is merit to the tradition that Shakespeare spent some of his Lost Years teaching in the country, he would have a pedagogue's familiarity with these classics. The Latinity of *The Comedy of Errors* and *Titus Andronicus* would moreover come naturally enough to a grammar-school man competing, at the outset of his career, with university-trained playwrights.[5]

We have one external clue to the date of *Titus*. In his Induction to *Bartholomew Fair*, performed at the Hope in 1614, Johnson has the Scrivener propose, as one of several articles of agreement with the spectators, that 'He that will swear *Jeronimo* or *Andronicus* are the best plays yet, shall pass unexcepted at, here, as a man whose judgement shows it is constant, and hath stood still, these five and twenty, or thirty years.'[6] *Jeronimo* is an alternative title for Kyd's *Spanish Tragedy*, to the resounding popular success of which Shakespeare was responding. Twenty-five or thirty years carries us back to 1584-9. Of course Jonson is not writing with the needs of future theatrical historians in mind; he rounds off his numbers, and perhaps overstates the antiquity of plays to underscore his point about the backwardness of audience taste.[7] But the reference supports a very early date for *Titus Andronicus*.

It is fair to allow that, from almost the first days of Shakespeare scholarship, connoisseurs have questioned his sole responsibility for *Titus*, and also (somewhat later) for the *Henry VI* trilogy. In 1 *Henry VI*, the irreverent treatment of Joan of Arc, depicted not as a christian martyr but as a sorceress and virago, gave offence. The same authorities thought that Shakespeare, setting out in the theatre as a play-botcher, lightly revised two anonymous plays which were the originals of 2 and 3 *Henry VI*, the former supposedly being based on *The First part of the Contention betwixt the two famous Houses of York and Lancaster*, printed in 1594, and the latter on *The True Tragedy of Richard, Duke of York*, published the next year. From as far back as 1687, readers have sought to relieve Shakespeare of the burden of *Titus*—'the most incorrect and indigested piece in all his works', Ravenscroft sneered; 'It seems rather a heap of rubbish than a structure.'[8] Such commentators allow Shakespeare a 'master-touch' or two, the occasional blossom on the dungheap, while shifting the play as a whole onto some lesser breed of playwright—a George Peele, perhaps—outside the laws of dramatic decorum; anyone but the incomparable Bard. Behind the dismissal

20. *Titus Andronicus* in performance: the Peacham drawing.

lurks, one suspects, a fastidious distaste for cannibalism, rape, and mutilation.

Yet the 'heap of rubbish' drew multitudes to the playhouse. How it appeared to a contemporary is uniquely recorded in the Longleat manuscript, with its drawing of Tamora on her knees, pleading with Titus to spare her sons. Behind her, two sons also kneel, and behind them stands, with sword drawn, the isolated figure of Aaron the Moor. (In the play the victors demand—and receive—only Alarbus, 'eldest son of this distressed queen', who is huddled mutely off to have his limbs lopped, 'And entrails feed the sacrificing fire'.) Did whoever sketched the scene—the name Henry Peacham appears in the margin—remember 'the actual action and grouping of Shakespeare's fellows in Shakespeare's theatre', as Dover Wilson has suggested?[9] Or does the drawing capture a particular moment in a private performance of the play? These questions elude solution, but the Longleat drawing makes clear that *Titus Andronicus* left a vivid impression. Vivid too, despite the disproportions, is the artist's impression, with its 'strong placing of the central figures, emphasized by the ornate spearhead of Titus's staff', and its 'variety of narrative action . . . which economically omits almost as much as it includes, suggesting the presence of the other characters solely by gesture'.[10]

In modern times revival, beginning with the celebrated Brook/ Olivier production in 1955, has once again demonstrated the stage vitality of a formerly contemned play, and revealed also how the author distances the barbarities by stylized dramaturgy and formal rhetoric. Anyway, literary connoisseurship provides no reliable instrument for resolving questions of authenticity. In 1929 Peter Alexander demonstrated that the *Contention* and *True Tragedy* are in fact corrupt texts—bad quartos—of Shakespearian originals, 2 and 3 *Henry VI*. The fact that the playwright's friends and fellows from the King's men, Heminges and Condell, included *Titus Andronicus* and all three parts of *Henry VI* in the First Folio carries powerful presumptive evidence of Shakespeare's authorship of these works. If he completed these plays by 1592, and *The Comedy of Errors* as well (not to mention *Richard III* and *The Taming of the Shrew*), he had experimented, with extraordinary success, in the three dramatic genres—comedy, tragedy, and history—recognized by his first editors.

It remains an *if*. We do not have a record of the performance of *The Comedy of Errors* until 28 December 1594. The first references to *Titus Andronicus* belong to that year too. The printer John Danter entered the latter in the Stationers' books on 6 February 1594, and in the same year Edward White and Thomas Millington were hawking it on their stalls at the sign of the Gun at the little north door of St. Paul's. In *A Knack to Know a Knave*, registered the previous month, occurs a reference to King Edgar as one as welcome

> As Titus was unto the Roman Senators
> When he had made a conquest on the Goths. . . .

Lastly, when Sussex's men produced *Titus Andronicus* at the Rose on 24 January 1594, Henslowe entered the performance as 'new' in his *Diary*. The evidence would seem to point rather conclusively to 1594 as the year of composition; that is, until one examines that evidence more closely. Although licensed by the stationers in 1594, *A Knack to Know a Knave* was acted by Strange's men two years before, on 10 June 1592; so we learn from Henslowe's *Diary*. And (as we have seen) 'new' may mean newly licensed or produced rather than newly written; a possibility supported by the title-page statement that this 'Most Lamentable Roman Tragedy' was acted by 'the Right Honourable the Earl of Darbie, Earl of Pembrooke, and Earl of Sussex their Servants'. Since the 'servants' of the Earls of Derby and Pembroke receive mention before those of Sussex, *Titus Andronicus* may have been new only to the last-mentioned in 1594. In any event, with such a production history, the play could scarcely have issued new-minted from the author's brain the same year.

One must proceed just as circumspectly in tracing Shakespeare's relations with the acting companies. If he began as a player with the Queen's men, he may have decided early to improve his prospects by moving on. Although not a single one of his pieces is known to have been produced by the Queen's, it is an intriguing fact that eventually Shakespeare got round to using three old plays from their repertoire as plot-sources: *The Troublesome Reign of King John, The Famous Victories of Henry the Fifth,* and *The True Chronicle History of King Leir, and his three daughters.* When he came to write his own versions, did Shakespeare draw upon memory of their antecedents on the stage, years past, during the Queen's men days?[11] This is mere speculation. Some Queen's plays, however, passed over into the repertoire of Alleyn's company, Strange's men; and Henslowe's *Diary*—that unique store-house of information—reveals that this troupe performed 'Harey the vi' fourteen times, with large takings, at the Rose on Bankside between 3 March and 20 June 1592. To be sure, other playwrights than Shakespeare may have felt compelled to dramatize the unedifying reign of Henry VI, just as they turned (along with Shakespeare) to Julius Caesar and to Troilus and Cressida.[12] If the Rose piece was his, it must have been, as we shall see, 1 *Henry* VI. Henslowe's dry book-keeping therefore accords with Nashe's emotive portrayal of thronged houses. But no evidence connects the dramatist himself with Strange's troupe: Alleyn is silent about Shakespeare in his correspondence, nor is the latter named in the warrant of 6 May 1593, listing members (probably sharers only) of the company; and Shakespeare does not figure in the cast list (which includes minor rôles as well as leads) for *The Second Part of the Seven Deadly Sins,* a Strange's play. From the title-pages of the debased version printed as the *True Tragedy,* we know that the Earl of Pembroke's men—the company that for a

time performed *Titus Andronicus*—had 3 *Henry* VI in their repertoire (probably 2 *Henry* VI also). *The Taming of A Shrew*, possibly
but not certainly a corrupt rendering of *The Taming of the Shrew*,
saw print in 1594 'As it was sundry times acted by the Right Honourable the Earl of Pembroke his servants'. Just possibly Shakespeare wrote the later of these plays for Pembroke's men, although
more likely the pieces passed to them from another company; certainly *Titus Andronicus* made the rounds.* Conceivably Shakespeare
for a while free-lanced as a dramatist. It is more romantically appealing, however, to imagine him as one of Pembroke's players at
around the same time that Marlowe was giving that company his
last play, *Edward II*. The two men may have been acquainted; certainly Shakespeare knew Marlowe's work, and responded to it in his
own first efforts: Tamburlaine stalks in *Henry VI*. Shakespeare
would allusively mourn Marlowe as the dead shepherd in *As You
Like It*.

Dover Wilson has given us an intriguing, admittedly conjectural,
reconstruction of the origin of Pembroke's men.[13] In 1590 Strange's
servants and the Admiral's company had merged under Alleyn, the
combined company using the two Shoreditch playhouses, Burbage's
Theatre and its 'easer', the Curtain. But the arrangement broke
down. In May 1591 Alleyn quarrelled with the elder Burbage, and
stormed off with his fellows to the rival operation on the Surrey bank, Henslowe's Rose. So much we know; the rest is hypothesis.
Wilson suggests that not everybody elected to cross the river with
Alleyn. Burbage's son Richard, at twenty-three or 'four already
envisaging himself as a rival to the laurels of 'famous Ned Allen',
induced a number of actors to stay on with him in Shoreditch and
form a new company. They then persuaded the Earl of Pembroke to
take them under his protection. Hence began the association between Burbage the player and the theatre-loving Pembrokes; an association terminated only by the tragedian's death, which in 1619
left the third Earl of Pembroke so grieved that he tender-heartedly
refrained from visiting the playhouse where his 'old acquaintance'

---

* Pinciss (see n. 11) theorizes that Pembroke's men originated as an offshoot of
the Queen's company. The previous theatrical affiliations of the players in the
will described by Mary Edmond (see n. 15) are not known.

had trod the boards. A Shakespearian connection with the Pembrokes re-emerges late, in 1623, when Heminges and Condell dedicated the First Folio of their worthy friend and fellow's plays 'To the most noble and incomparable pair of brethren', William, Earl of Pembroke, and Philip, Earl of Montgomery. The mythos adds its morsel of corroboration. In 1865 William Cory, then a master at Eton, was received at Wilton House by Lady Herbert, who told him, 'we have a letter, never printed, from Lady Pembroke to her son, telling him to bring James I from Salisbury to see *As You Like It*; "we have the man Shakespeare with us". She wanted to cajole the king in Raleigh's behalf—he came.' James did visit Salisbury at least once when he kept his court at Wilton in the autumn of 1603; but unfortunately no such letter has ever been produced.[14] Some scholars have believed that this Pembroke is the Fair Youth celebrated by Shakespeare in the *Sonnets*.

Wilson's imaginative reconstruction is pleasing, and seems plausible; but a newly discovered will by a previously unknown actor, Simon Jewell, suggests that Pembroke's men more likely began life as a touring company without Burbage or Shakespeare, and not in 1591 but in the wake of the catastrophe that overtook London the next year.[15] For that summer the plague struck. Some years previously, in a sermon preached at Paul's Cross, the Revd. T. Wilcocks had syllogistically demonstrated that 'the cause of plagues is sin, if you look to it well; and the cause of sin are plays: therefore the cause of plagues are plays'.[16] Whether plays caused plagues or no, the authorities were concerned, legitimately enough, with the dangers posed by theatres in a time of pestilence. They reasoned that public congregations including idlers, whores, and other riff-raff, not to mention many 'infected with sores running on them', were 'perilous for contagion'. When the deaths returned in the bills of mortality reached alarming proportions, the Privy Council intervened to prohibit the acting of stage plays. 'We think it fit', they informed the Lord Mayor and aldermen of London, as well as the Surrey and Middlesex justices of the peace,

that all manner of concourse and public meetings of the people at plays, bear-baitings, bowlings and other like assemblies for sports be forbidden, and therefore do hereby require you, and in her Majesty's name straightly charge and command you forthwith to inhibit within your jurisdiction all plays, baiting of bears, bulls, bowling and any other like occasions to assemble any numbers of people together (preaching and divine service at churches excepted), whereby no occasions be offered to increase the infection within the city, which you shall do both by proclamation to be published to that end and by special watch and observation to be had at the places where the . . . like pastimes are usually frequented.[17]

That was on 28 January 1593. The restraint applied to assemblies within a seven-mile radius of London. Throughout most of that year the plague raged with special ferocity. According to Stow it claimed 10,775 lives between 29 December 1592 and 20 December 1593; others give higher estimates.* But mere statistics fail to convey the human dimensions of the calamity; it is what happened to individual families that brings home the meaning of the plague. Robert Browne, formerly an actor with Worcester's men, was playing at Frankfurt fair during the long hot summer of 1593. His family remained in Shoreditch. Plague wiped them out—wife, children, the whole household. Life goes on; Browne remarried.

The following winter the visitation abated sufficiently for the playhouses to reopen for a short season, but on 3 February 1594 the Privy Council saw fit to give order 'that there be no more public plays or interludes exercised by any company whatsoever within the compass of five miles distance from London, till upon better likelihood and assurance of health farther direction may be given from us to the contrary'.[18] In the spring of 1594 the theatres opened their doors again, but the next summer the authorities were worried lest infested persons, eager for recreation after long confinement at home, should 'resort to such assemblies' and spread contagion 'through heat and throng'. This protracted closing, the longest in the brief history of the London theatrical industry, wrought havoc on the companies. The Privy Council might grant warrants to Sussex's servants or Strange's to play outside a seven-mile limit, but the troupes could hardly maintain themselves intact through a seem-

* Actually Stow gives 10,675 as his total in his *Annales of England* [1601], p. 1274, but he has incorrectly summed up his own figures.

ingly endless banishment to the hand-to-mouth existence of provincial barnstorming. When the great plague of 1592-4 at last abated, the actors were faced with the task of picking up the pieces of their lives, and reconstituting themselves as companies.

What did Shakespeare do with himself during this extended season of enforced inactivity? One pleasant hypothesis has him wandering on the Continent.* Perhaps (it is suggested) he explored the inland waterways of Northern Italy, finding his way from Ferrara on the River Po to the marshy territories of the Venetian Republic. Such experience would furnish him with his knowledge of Italian customs, ceremonials, and characteristics, and of the topography of the northern towns, as well as with his smattering of the language. Then, back in London after the plague had lifted, he conjured up the atmosphere and fragrance of Italy—of Venice and Verona, of fair Padua in 'fruitful Lombardy,/The pleasant garden of great Italy'—in a series of plays rich in local colour. In *The Merchant of Venice* Shakespeare even mentions the 'traject', or *traghetto*, 'the common ferry', as Portia describes it, 'Which trades to Venice'.[19]

But he could as well have stored his imagination with these materials of his art from books or the reports of returned travellers, or from conversing with Italians in London. The Oliphant, a Bankside inn, catered for an Italian clientele. Shakespeare must have passed it on his way to or from the playhouse; in *Twelfth Night* (admittedly set in Illyria, but no matter) the Elephant is recommended as 'best to lodge'. A Paolo Marco Lucchese, born in Lucca, ran a restaurant

---

* Charles Armitage Brown, himself an enthusiast of Italy, seems first to have publicly wondered whether Shakespeare travelled there; in 1838—arguing from the internal evidence of the plays—Brown answered in the affirmative the question posed by his chapter title, 'Did He Visit Italy?', in *Shakespeare's Autobiographical Poems*. The problem has understandably intrigued continentals. Thus the noted nineteenth-century German Shakespearean Karl Elze resisted the suggestion that Shakespeare joined a company of English comedians in Germany, but succumbed to the Italian connection: Elze theorized that in 1593 Shakespeare 'fled from the dangerous and pestilential atmosphere of the metropolis', and directly upon his return produced *The Merchant of Venice*, *Othello*, and (maybe) *The Taming of the Shrew*, 'when he was still filled with the impressions he had received, and when the whole charm of Italy and its sky unconsciously guided his pen' ('The Supposed Travels of Shakespeare', *Essays on Shakespeare* (transl. L. Dora Schmitz; 1874), pp. 254-315).

in Hart Street, in the parish of St. Olave's, and lodged Italian visitors in his house. (Did Shakespeare know Lucchese? When, in *Othello*, the reverend signiors gather in the council-chamber, the Duke asks, 'Marcus Lucchese,* is not he in town?') John Florio, compiler of the first Italian-English dictionary, was well known in aristocratic and intellectual circles; some commentators, since Warburton in the eighteenth century, have thought that Shakespeare gently mocked him as the pedant Holofernes in *Love's Labour's Lost*. The numerous Bassanos, natives of Venice, were attached to the Court as musicians in the service of the Queen. Shakespeare calls a character in *The Merchant of Venice* Bassanio, although his counterpart in the source *novella* is named Giannetto.[20] Dr. Rowse believes that Emilia Bassano, offspring of Baptist Bassano and Margaret Johnson—they lived together as man and wife—was the dark seductress of the *Sonnets*. Rowse interestingly reports that Emilia's husband was named Will, a fact which would greatly clarify the Sonnets that pun upon the word ('Whoever hath her wish, thou hast thy Will,/And Will to boot, and Will in over-plus.') He also quotes from a manuscript diary describing Emilia as 'very brown in youth'. However, Emilia's husband was, alas, not Will but Alfonso, and the critical word in the manuscript is not 'brown' but 'brave'.[21] It is useful for a Dark Lady to be demonstrably dark.

Anyway, when all is said, Shakespeare's grasp of Italian topography is not all that secure. Characters in land-locked Verona (in *Two Gentlemen*) take ship; Milan, in *The Tempest*, is conceived as connecting with the sea by a waterway. In *The Taming of the Shrew* inland Bergamo has a sailmaker, and Biondello comes ashore in Padua, one of whose citizens, Gremio, possesses an argosy. It is a harmless fantasy to imagine Shakespeare enjoying an Italian holiday while in London the bell tolled for the dead, but most likely he stayed on in England. There he tried his hand at non-dramatic composition, and found himself a patron.

He was Henry Wriothesley, third Earl of Southampton, and Baron of Titchfield. His grandfather Thomas, the first Earl, was Lord Chancellor in the days of Henry VIII, and celebrated his own

---

* *Lucchese* is Alexander's reading; see, however, note 20, p. 337.

importance by building at Titchfield the 'right stately house' so admired by the King's antiquary Leland. The second Earl, an impenitent Catholic, found himself out of his depth in political conspiracy on behalf of Mary of Scotland. He managed not to sink, but died before his son Henry—Shakespeare's patron—had turned eight. The boy's elder brother was already dead, and so, in October 1581, Henry Wriothesley succeeded to the peerage. Through most of his minority his mother remained a widow, the young peer therefore finding himself the royal ward of Lord Burghley, the Lord Treasurer. At Cecil House, along with other wards, young Southampton received the education of a courtier in the select academy maintained for the sons of the nobility. There followed four years at Burghley's college, St. John's, Cambridge, from which Southampton took his M.A. at fifteen in 1589. At Court the accomplished youth attracted the favourable notice of the Queen, and formed an attachment to her brilliant but doomed favourite, the Earl of Essex, seven years his senior. In the autumn of 1592 Southampton joined the troop of noblemen who accompanied the Queen to Oxford. No one there was more comely, according to the panegyrical pen of John Sanford, 'no young man more outstanding in learning, although his mouth scarcely yet blooms with tender down'.[22] Burghley endeavoured to marry him off to his granddaughter, Lady Elizabeth Vere, but Southampton resisted matrimony, not without vacillation.

He encouraged scholars and poets. John Florio joined his entourage as Italian tutor. One of Burghley's secretaries dedicated a Latin poem, *Narcissus*, to Southampton in 1591. In offering his *Unfortunate Traveller* to this 'ingenuous honourable Lord' two years later, Nashe complimented 'a dear lover and cherisher . . . as well of the lovers of poets, as of poets themselves'. As a boy of thirteen Southampton had favoured his guardian with a precocious essay in Ciceronian Latin on the topic, 'All men are spurred to the pursuit of virtue by hope of reward'. A worldly theme for one so young; but Wriothesley gave it an idealistic turn by identifying the reward as 'praise and reputation'. Such gifts the noble lord could receive from poet-suppliants. They in turn looked for something more tangible, which was not always forthcoming. 'Of your gracious favour I despair not, for I am not altogether fame's outcast,' Nashe wrote in

21. Southampton at twenty.

his dedication. 'Your Lordship is the large spreading branch of renown, from whence these my idle leaves seek to derive their whole nourishing. It resteth you either scornfully shake them off, as worm-eaten and worthless, or in pity preserve them and cherish them, for some little summer fruit you hope to find amongst them.'[23] Apparently the Earl did not fancy the fruit, for the epistle drops out from subsequent editions of *The Unfortunate Traveller*, and the unfortunate author had to seek his nourishment elsewhere.

In 1593 or '94 Nicholas Hilliard painted a miniature of the lovely boy with languid golden tresses. The face—with its soft features, delicately arched eyebrows, and lips curving ever so slightly upward at the corner in complacent superiority—clearly belongs to an aristocrat, and one who might fittingly receive the tribute of a poem entitled *Narcissus*. Around the time that the Earl sat for Hilliard, Shakespeare dedicated his first poem to Southampton. The poet was then almost twenty-nine, the dedicatee ten years his junior.

Venus and Adonis belongs, with *The Comedy of Errors* and *Titus Andronicus*, to Shakespeare's early classical phase. (The Adonis myth appealed to him. 'Dost thou love pictures?', the tinker Sly is asked in *The Taming of the Shrew*. 'We will fetch thee straight/ Adonis painted by a running brook. . . .') Once more Shakespeare draws upon the *Metamorphoses*, his myth-making imagination finding scope in an elaborate narrative on an erotic theme. It was a fashionable genre that produced, very possibly in the same year, its supreme exemplar in Marlowe's fragmentary *Hero and Leander*. Shakespeare might well have expected his poem to please its highborn recipient, for what youth of nineteen, cultivated in his tastes, would not find his palate gratified by the story of Adonis repudiating with adolescent masculine disdain the frenzied importunities of the goddess of love? At the same time Shakespeare was making a bid for a new audience: sophisticated, pleasure-loving, impressed by intellect without necessarily being intellectual; such an audience as Thomas Lodge, himself a gentleman of Lincoln's Inn, envisaged for his erotic epyllion, *Scylla's Metamorphosis*—'Very fit for young courtiers to peruse, and coy dames to remember'.

No author's name appears on the title-page of *Venus and Adonis*, but the dedication 'To the Right Honourable Henrie Wriothesley, Earl of Southampton, and Baron of Titchfield', is signed.

> Right Honourable, I know not how I shall offend in dedicating my unpolished lines to your Lordship, nor how the world will censure me for choosing so strong a prop to support so weak a burden. Only if your Honour seem but pleased, I account myself highly praised, and vow to take advantage of all idle hours, till I have honoured you with some graver labour. But if the first heir of my invention prove deformed, I shall be sorry it had so noble a godfather, and never after ear so barren a land, for fear it yield me still so bad a harvest. I leave it to your honourable survey, and your Honour to your heart's content, which I wish may always answer your own wish, and the world's hopeful expectation.
>
> Your Honour's in all duty,
> William Shakespeare.

The tone here—elaborately courteous but not servile, self-deprecatory but with an undertow of confidence—argues no great intimacy between poet and patron. The title-page motto, also from Ovid, qualifies the self-effacement of the dedication: 'Vilia miretur vulgus: mihi flavus Apollo/Pocula Castalia plena ministret aqua.' 'Let base conceited wits admire vile things;/Fair Phoebus lead me to the Muses' springs'; so Marlowe translated the passage from the fifteenth book of the *Amores*.

The phrase 'first heir of my invention' has given pause to the commentators. Did Shakespeare compose, or at least draft, *Venus and Adonis* as a young man in Warwickshire, and come up to London with an epyllion in his pocket, then circulate the manuscript until Southampton agreed to accept it? That kind of history would account for the vivid evocation of rural nature—the dive-dapper, the milch-doe with swollen dugs, the lustful courser and timorous snail, above all poor Wat the terrified hare fleeing his pursuers—which seems to owe more to the environs of his Uncle Henry's farm than to the Arcadia of the Roman poets. It is perilous, though, to make compositional inferences from such data; as Alexander Dyce drily observed more than a century ago, 'I have yet to learn that the fancy of Shakespeare could not luxuriate in rural images even amid the fogs of Southwark and the Blackfriars.'[24] Bucolic images might have appealed with special potency to a poet whose 'idle hours' (in the dedication phrase) were enforced by the plague closing of the theatres. Maybe Shakespeare described *Venus and Adonis* as the first heir of his invention simply because it marked his début as a published author. Or perhaps he was distinguishing between a serious literary venture, properly launched in a printed book with a dedication, and those ephemeral entertainments which the masses admired in Shoreditch and on Bankside. As an aspiring man of letters he may have accepted, as a fact of life, his age's condescending valuation of plays and playwrights. He would go to his grave not knowing, and possibly not caring, whether *Macbeth* or *The Tempest* or *Antony and Cleopatra* ever achieved the permanence of print.

Venus and Adonis was another matter. Shakespeare took pains with the first offspring of his dedicating muse. The 1593 quarto is exceptionally free from misprints and like misdemeanours; it seems clear that, whether or not the author himself corrected proof, he supplied the printer with a fair copy of his manuscript. And he picked an excellent printer.

He was Richard Field, a fellow townsman who operated a shop in the Blackfriars.[25] Three years Shakespeare's senior—the Stratford register lists his baptism on 16 November 1561—he was the son of Henry Field, a tanner in Bridge Street. The elder Field figures in the early town records: in 1560 he was fined, with fifteen others, 'for having and suffering their dogs and bitches going at large in the streets'. When Henry died in 1592, John Shakespeare helped to appraise the old bedsteads and other household stuff comprising Field's modest estate. Though unprosperous himself, Field had given his son a good start by apprenticing him to the printing trade in London. The stationer George Bishop, to whom Richard was originally bound, handed him over for a six-year term to Thomas Vautrollier, a Huguenot with a shop in the Blackfriars. An accomplished master-printer, Vautrollier did justice to such demanding assignments as De Beau Chesne and Baildon's *Book Containing Divers Sorts of Hands*. The Huguenot's energetic wife, Jacqueline, was capable of looking after the shop when her husband was in Edinburgh managing another flourishing printing business. In 1587 the master died, and the following year his widow married their only apprentice. He was then twenty-seven, and had only lately been made free of the Stationers' Company. In Jacqueline Field, Mrs. Charlotte Stopes thinks she has found Shakespeare's Dark Lady: '. . . she was a Frenchwoman, therefore likely to have dark eyes, a sallow complexion, and that indefinable *charm* so much alluded to.'[26] For *charm*, read loose morals. Mrs. Stopes's reasoning is not impeccable.

Richard Field entered *Venus and Adonis* in the Register at Stationers' Hall on 18 April 1593. Less than two months later, an elderly gentleman, Richard Stonley, Esq., saw the poem on the stalls at the sign of the White Greyhound in Paul's Churchyard, and bought a copy for sixpence. One of the four tellers of the Exchequer, Stonley had a London house in Aldersgate, but spent his weekends on his Doddinghurst estate in Essex; at the advanced age of seventy-seven this civil servant who had spent his whole career dealing with Crown finances found himself imprisoned in the Fleet because of massive

22. *Venus and Adonis* in the Stonley Diary Account Book, 1593.

personal debt. A figure of some consequence in his own day, but later forgotten, Stonley has the minor distinction of being the first recorded purchaser of Shakespeare's first publication.*

Multitudes bought *Venus and Adonis*; the poem went through sixteen editions before 1640. No other work by Shakespeare achieved so many printings during this period. Readers thumbed it until it fell to pieces; so we may infer from the fact that for most of the editions only a single copy has survived.

At the turn of the seventeenth century the students of St. John's College, Cambridge, mounted an amateur play, *The Return from Parnassus*, in the course of which one of the characters expresses his enthusiasm for Shakespeare. 'Let this duncified world esteem of Spencer and Chaucer', Gullio rhapsodizes: 'I'll worship sweet Mr. Shakspeare, and to honour him will lay his *Venus and Adonis* under my pillow, as we read of one (I do not well remember his name,

* Stonley's Diary and the *Venus and Adonis* entry were known in the eighteenth century. On 7 May 1794 the antiquary Francis Douce wrote to George Steevens about the item (Folger Shakespeare Library, MS. C.b.10). Douce must be the acquaintance referred to in the note included by Malone in his *Inquiry into the Authenticity of Certain Miscellaneous Papers and Legal Instruments* (1796): 'the following entry [has] been found in an ancient MS. Diary, which some time since was in the hands of an acquaintance of Mr. Steevens, by whom it was communicated to me: "12th of June, 1593. For the Survay of Fraunce, with the Venus and Athonay p^r Shakspere, xii.d."' (p. 67n). The reference is also cited in Isaac Reed's 1803 Variorum edition of Shakespeare (ii. 152). Thereafter the Diary disappeared from view until it resurfaced in San Francisco and was acquired by the Folger in 1972. While routinely reading through the three volumes, Mrs. Laetitia Yeandle, the Library's Curator of Manuscripts, discovered the entry, which the Folger announced on 23 April 1973. It is *Survey* and *Adhonay* (not, as in Malone, *Survay* and *Athonay*) in the entry. The Diary is now Folger Shakespeare Library MS. V.a.460, and the entry appears on f. 9.

but I am sure he was a king) slept with Homer under his bed's head.' 'O sweet Mr. Shakspeare', he sighs elsewhere, 'I'll have his picture in my study at the Court.'[27] Biographers have interpreted Gullio's testimonial as recognition from the university,[28] but, if so, it is back-handed recognition. The applause after all comes from a fool, as signified by his name, his philistine dismissal of Chaucer and Spenser, and his inability to recall that the king who admired Homer was Alexander the Great. Still, this allusion and others testify to the continuing popularity of *Venus and Adonis* with a certain class of readers: university students, courtiers, Inns of Court men, witlings, and gallants about town. Field may well have viewed the commercial success of the poem with some chagrin, for he had parted early with it. After printing two editions, he relinquished his rights in the work to John Harrison, who had been selling the book without owning the copyright. Perhaps Field would have mistrusted the potential of any poet who hailed from his own market town, more celebrated for malting than the arts.

The 'graver labour' promised by the author in his first dedicatory epistle found fruition the following spring in another elaborate Ovidian narrative, a companion piece to *Venus and Adonis*. If the latter explores the theme of Eros denied through the failed seduction of a coy youth, *The Rape of Lucrece* treats the subject of Eros gratified through the successful violation of a sober matron. The complaining females make an oddly contrasting pair. Once again Field did the printing, and in accordance with his usual high standard. This time, however, Master Harrison held the copyright from the first, as is shown by the entry to him, in the Stationers' Register on 9 May 1594, of a book 'entitled *The Ravishment of Lucrece*'.

There is again a dedication to Southampton:

The love I dedicate to your Lordship is without end; whereof this pamphlet, without beginning, is but a superfluous moiety. The warrant I have of your honourable disposition, not the worth of my untutored lines, makes it assured of acceptance. What I have done is yours; what I have to do is yours; being part in all I have, devoted yours. Were my worth greater, my duty would show greater; meantime, as it is, it is bound to your Lordship, to whom I wish long life still lengthened with all happiness.

Your Lordship's in all duty,
William Shakespeare.

As is to be expected, the authorities have minutely compared Shakespeare's two dedications. Interpretations differ. 'A super-subtle criticism', writes Sir Edmund Chambers, 'detects a great advance in the poet's intimacy with his patron between the two addresses, which I am bound to say is not apparent to me.'[29] But Chambers belongs to a minority; most students (including this one) do discern a progression of warmth. This is a matter that each reader, with the text of the dedications before him, may decide for himself.

The Rape of Lucrece enjoyed a less spectacular success than its predecessor, but nevertheless gathered a more than respectable eight editions before 1640.* The two poems, embellished with all the flowers of Renaissance rhetoric, established Shakespeare as a poet of love. In the last of the *Parnassus* plays, the *Second Return*, acted in the same Cambridge hall during the Christmas revels of (probably) 1601-2, Judicio expresses the verdict of the judicious:

> Who loves not Adon's love, or Lucrece' rape?
> His sweeter verse contains heart-robbing lines,
> Could but a graver subject him content,
> Without love's foolish lazy languishment.[30]

Evidently word of *Julius Caesar* and *Henry V* had not yet found its way to cloistered Cambridge. Or, being plays, perhaps they did not count.

As to how the young Earl responded to the two dedications, contemporary report is silent. Tradition, however, first coming to light in Rowe's memoir, fills the gap:

> There is one Instance so singular in the Magnificence of this Patron of *Shakespear*'s, that if I had not been assur'd that the Story was handed down by Sir *William D'Avenant*, who was probably very well acquainted with his Affairs, I should not have ventur'd to have

---

* My tally of editions of this poem, as of *Venus and Adonis*, derives from the *Short-Title Catalogue* (rev. ed., 1976).

inserted, that my Lord *Southampton,* at one time, gave him a thousand Pounds, to enable him to go through with a Purchase which he heard he had a mind to.[31]

Although any intelligence transmitted on the authority of Davenant—playwright, poet laureate, theatrical entrepreneur, and self-promoting embellisher of the Shakespeare mythos—must awaken suspicions in the wary, a recent biographer of both Shakespeare and Southampton inclines to acceptance.[32] The sum mentioned, described by Dr. Rowse as 'goodly', would have done justice to an Elizabethan Maecenas, but it is unlikely that Shakespeare had the luck of Horace or Vergil. In the nineties Southampton was under financial pressure. Rumour had it that the Earl was obliged to part with £5,000 for going back on an ill-advised promise to marry the Lord Treasurer's granddaughter; it is a fact that in November 1594 he was feeling sufficiently pressed to lease out the porter's lodge, as well as other buildings and rooms, of his London residence, Southampton House.[33] So far as we know, Shakespeare's property investments over a lifetime did not in their aggregate exceed £1,000. It has been suggested that he used the money to buy an interest in the Chamberlain's company in 1594; but this is no more than an attempt to rationalize an outlandish figure. Shakespeare did not again dedicate one of his writings to a noble lord. Southampton now departs from the biographical record.

He does not, however, drop out of speculation. Many commentators, perhaps a majority, believe that the Earl is the Fair Youth urged to marry and propagate in the *Sonnets,* and there immortalized by the poet who addresses him in the extravagant terms of Renaissance male friendship. The object of this devotion, the Master-Mistress of the sonneteer's passion, has 'a woman's face' but (worse luck for his heterosexual celebrant) a man's phallus. Nature, Shakespeare ruefully declares in Sonnet 20,

> as she wrought thee, fell a-doting,
> And by addition me of thee defeated
> By adding one thing to my purpose nothing.
> But since she prick'd thee out for women's pleasure,
> Mine be thy love, and thy love's use their treasure.

The portrait here does not accord ill with Hilliard's miniature of the feminine youth. A dating of the *Sonnets* during the Southampton period, say 1592-5, would help with the identification. Several topically allusive poems—the so-called 'dating sonnets'—support (according to some enthusiasts) this putative chronology; but the ambiguous language of poetry resists the fragile certitude of interpreters. And even if we might confidently date individual sonnets, we could not therefore rule out the possibility that the sequence as a whole occupied its creator over an extended period; sporadic entries, as it were, in a poet's rhyming diary. Some of the impassioned later sonnets manifest a psychological and metaphorical—not to say metaphysical—complexity unparalleled in what we know Shakespeare was writing in the early nineties. To the greatest authority on the *Sonnets* in this century, Hyder Rollins, writing in 1944, the solution to the question of chronology, on which depend solutions to the other questions, 'has been and remains an idle dream'.[34] So it still remains, despite the best and brightest efforts. Nor can we rest secure that the printed order of the *Sonnets* is correct. It is not clear to what extent the personages of these poems—Fair Youth, Dark Lady, Rival Poet—represent real individuals: the imperatives of Art, no less than the circumstances of Nature, dictate their rôles. And what of the rôle of the speaker himself, the naked 'I' which we here encounter for the first and only time in the entire Shakespeare corpus? 'With this key', Wordsworth said of the cycle, 'Shakespeare unlocked his heart.' But the doubt haunts us that the speaker may be, at least in part, another dramatic characterization. If the persona of the *Sonnets* addresses us with the resonance of authenticity, so do Shylock and Hamlet. Here as elsewhere, the biographer, in his eagerness for answers to the unanswerable, runs the risk of confusing the dancer with the dance.

The mystery is not lightened by the cryptic poem entered in the Stationers' books on 3 September 1594, and printed the same year with the title *Willobie his Avisa, or The True Picture of a Modest Maid, and of a Chaste and Constant Wife*. This curious work seems to have something to do with the *Sonnets*. In a prefatory epistle one Hadrian Dorrell reveals how the *Avisa* came to be printed. Dorrell shared a chamber, presumably at the university, with a promising young scholar, Henrie Willobie, who entrusted his friend with the key to his study before going abroad in the Queen's service. Among Willobie's papers Dorrell found the *Avisa*, which he so fancied that he had it published without his room-mate's knowledge. A Henry Willobie of West Knoyle, Wiltshire, matriculated at St. John's College, Oxford, in 1591, but transferred to Exeter College, where he took his degree in 1595. This must be the Willobie of the *Avisa*. There was no Hadrian Dorrell at Oxford during those years, although a Thomas Darell was enrolled in Brasenose College; perhaps Hadrian is a Willobie pseudonym—it is one of many puzzles.

The poem describes how Avisa—'This Britain bird' that 'outflies them all'—repels assaults upon her chastity by a motley succession of suitors. While yet of 'tender age' she fends off a Nobleman of mature years; after matrimony she resists, in turn, a 'Caveleiro' (afflicted by piles or pox), 'D.B. a Frenchman', 'Dydimus Harco. Anglo-Germanus', and 'Henrico Willobego. Italo-Hispalensis'. This last, referred to as 'H.W.', has a 'familiar friend W.S. who not long before had tried the courtesy of the like passion, and was now newly recovered of the like infection. . . . and in viewing afar off the course of this loving comedy, he determined to see whether it would sort to a happier end for this new actor, than it did for the old player.'[35] *H.W., W.S., new actor, old player*—the veiled references tease; and the situation vaguely resembles that of the *Sonnets*. Moreover, one can trace a tenuous Shakespearian connection with Willobie. The latter's elder brother William in 1590 married Eleanor Bampfield; her sister Katherine in the same month married Thomas Russell. There is evidence that Henry Willobie was on amiable terms with his sister-in-law's husband. Russell was a friend of Shakespeare, although we do not know how long they knew one another; the dramatist named him an overseer of his will, and left him £5. If (as tradition holds) Shakespeare stopped over in Oxford when he took the road that led from London to Stratford, he might possibly have there met Willobie through Russell. This is all speculative, no doubt; but one can appreciate the temptation to identify 'W.S.' with William Shakespeare, and 'H.W.' with Henry Wriothesley, the proposed Fair Youth of the *Sonnets*.

There is the lady too, dwelling in a house 'where hangs the badge/

Of England's Saint'. Shall we then knock on the door of an inn
called the George or the St. George in Oxford, and there inquire
after the Dark Lady in the guise of the landlord's beautiful wife? So
several, most notably Arthur Acheson, have done.[36] But these possibilities, at first so tantalizing, dissolve upon closer acquaintance.
H. W. are also of course the initials of Henry Willobie, a candidate
closer to home than the Baron of Titchfield. The invincible chastity
of Avisa doubtfully qualifies her for the part of the promiscuous
temptress of the *Sonnets*. In 1970 Professor B. N. De Luna argued,
rather strangely, for identifying Avisa with the Virgin Queen, and
her house with Elizabeth's palace at Greenwich, flying (during her
residence) banners bearing the Cross of St. George.[37] With so much
doubtful in this obscure allegory, all that emerges clearly is that *Willobie his Avisa* does not help us much with the *Sonnets*.

The poem has nevertheless an indisputable Shakespearian interest, for the commendatory verses prefacing it include this stanza,
with our first printed reference by name to Shakespeare as a poet:

> Though Collatine have dearly bought,
> To high renown, a lasting life,
> And found, that most in vain have sought,
> To have a fair, and constant wife,
>   Yet Tarquin plucked his glistering grape,
>   And Shake-speare paints poor Lucrece' rape.[38]

By the autumn of 1594, when *Willobie his Avisa* appeared on the
stalls, the plague had for several months relaxed its grip on the capital, and normal patterns of life reasserted themselves. On 8 October
1594, 'the time being such as, thanks be to God, there is now no
danger of the sickness', Henry Carey, first Baron Hunsdon, re-
quested the Lord Mayor of London to suffer Hunsdon's 'now company of players' to exercise their quality that winter at the Cross
Keys inn in Gracious Street. Now an old man, Hunsdon was the
Lord Chamberlain who had championed the players in their skir-
mishes with the municipal authorities. According to the widely acquainted astrologer Simon Forman, he had formerly kept as his mistress Emilia Bassano—Dr. Rowse's Dark Lady—and she had borne
his child. He had now less than two years to live. Hunsdon's new

troupe had performed for a brief season in June 1594 for Henslowe at Newington Butts: our first record of the Chamberlain's men. During the Christmas festivities the following December the company played twice at Court. On 15 March 1595 the Accounts of the Treasurer of the Queen's Chamber list William Shakespeare as joint payee, with William Kempe and Richard Burbage—all three 'servants to the Lord Chamberlain'—for plays performed before her Majesty the previous St. Stephen's Day (26 December) and Innocents' Day (28 December) at the royal palace at Greenwich. The Innocents' Day citation is probably a mistake; a payment to the Admiral's men for the 28th appears in the same Accounts, and the Chamberlain's players seem to have had another date that day.[39] But that is a trifling detail. This record is the first to connect Shakespeare with an acting company, and the only official notice of his name with respect to a theatrical performance. The entry shows that Shakespeare had become a leading member of the Lord Chamberlain's men. He would stay with that company, which eventually passed under royal patronage, until he retired from the stage altogether.

{12}

The Lord Chamberlain's Man

The record of payment for the two royal performances at Greenwich in 1594 shows Shakespeare as now set on his professional course. The lineaments of his career at last emerge from the shadows; debate and speculation, never entirely absent, recede; events fall into place. In his entry the Treasurer of the Queen's Chamber brackets Shakespeare with the Chamberlain's foremost clown—'Monsieur du Kempe', Nashe eulogized him, 'Jest-monger and vicegerent general to the ghost of Dicke Tarlton'—and with the great tragedian who would create the title rôles of *Hamlet*, *Othello*, and *King Lear*. Although Shakespeare achieved no comparable thespian preeminence, it is as a player that the Treasurer by implication classes him, and certainly he served his troupe in this capacity. Shakespeare moreover became a shareholder in his company, unlike most Elizabethan dramatists who eked out their precarious livelihoods—*vide* Greene—as employees of the players. Probably he helped stage his own plays and also those of others. Above all, he was his troupe's regular dramatist, in the sense that he wrote exclusively for them; their 'ordinary poet', in Elizabethan theatrical parlance. The entire period produced only a handful of like professional writers, among them Heywood, Fletcher, and Dekker, who were even more prolific than the poet who, according to his awe-struck fellows, never blotted a line. *Professional* is in this context a key term. Shakespeare's combined achievements as actor, sharer, and playwright made him, as our greatest living authority on the Elizabethan and Jacobean stage observes, 'the most complete man of the theater of his time'.[1] Few in any age have served the stage so variously. Not Racine or Ibsen or Shaw; only Molière, besides Shakespeare, among playwrights of world stature.[2]

Posterity, understandably enough, reserves veneration for the dramatist—not the player or manager whose triumphs, however applauded, were transitory—and accords to the book of his plays that immortality which the author, if he dreamed of it at all, envisaged as forthcoming in recognition of the poems he dedicated to a noble lord. Yet, despite the ephemerality of performance, a special interest attaches to an evening in the mid-nineties when a Shakespearian play was acted under unusual circumstances. An eyewitness recorded the event.

On 28 December 1594 professional players hired for the occasion—no doubt these were the Chamberlain's men—performed *The Comedy of Errors* as part of the Christmas 'law-revels' at Gray's Inn. This was the largest of the four Inns of Court where young gentry studied for the bar and disported themselves in their leisure hours with literature, theatricals, and the ladies. The first Yuletide festivities after the great plague, when too many invitations were issued and accepted, produced the pandemonium on Innocents' Day described in *Gesta Grayorum*:

> The Ambassador [of the Inner Temple] came . . . about nine of the clock at night. . . . When the Ambassador was placed, . . . and that there was something to be performed for the delight of the beholders, there arose such a disordered tumult and crowd upon the stage, that there was no opportunity to effect that which was intended. . . . The Lord Ambassador and his train thought that they were not so kindly entertained, as was before expected, and thereupon would not stay any longer. . . . After their departure the throngs and tumults did somewhat cease, although so much of them continued, as was able to disorder and confound any good inventions whatsoever. In regard whereof, as also for that the sports intended were especially for the gracing of the Templarians, it was thought good not to offer anything of account, saving dancing and revelling with gentlewomen; and after such sports, a *Comedy of Errors* (like to Plautus his *Menechmus*) was played by the players. So that night was begun, and continued to the end, in nothing but

confusion and errors; whereupon, it was ever afterwards called, *The Night of Errors*.[3]

'The next night . . .', the narration continues, in the pompously facetious style affected for the occasion, 'we preferred judgements thick and threefold, which were read publicly by the Clerk of the Crown, being all against a sorcerer or conjurer that was supposed to be the cause of that confused inconvenience.' The arraignment charges that this sorcerer had (among other misdemeanours) 'foisted a company of base and common fellows, to make up our disorders with a play of errors and confusions; and that that night had gained to us discredit, and itself a nickname of "Errors" '.

Another early comedy by Shakespeare has also been associated with a particular festive occasion. By virtue of its brevity, special casting requirements, and (in Sir Edmund Chambers's phrase) 'the hymeneal character of the theme', *A Midsummer-Night's Dream* would appear to be well suited to grace a wedding celebration. The many female and fairy parts required boy actors—would the Chamberlain's men have the resources to fill them without special recruitment for the nonce? The text seemingly provides alternative endings for public presentation in a theatre, and private performance at a great house. 'Lovers to bed', Duke Theseus decrees after the fifth-act dance;

> 'tis almost fairy time.
> I fear we shall out-sleep the coming morn,
> As much as we this night have overwatch'd.
> This palpable-gross play hath well beguil'd
> The heavy gait of night. Sweet friends, to bed.

The comedy might well thus end in the playhouse. But with midnight struck and the stage cleared, Puck enters, broom in hand, and the fairies steal through the house to bless the bridal bed with fortunate increase, and hallow each chamber with 'sweet peace'. How appropriate to a hymeneal occasion!

Biographers and editors have suggested a number of aristocratic weddings as the setting for the first night of *A Midsummer-Night's Dream*. These range over a decade, from the marriage of Robert Earl of Essex and Frances Lady Sidney in the spring of 1590, to that of

Henry Lord Herbert and Anne Russell in June 1600; but most now prefer, by reason of date and circumstance, the wedding of Sir Thomas Heneage, the elderly Treasurer of the Chamber, to the mother of Shakespeare's patron, Mary Countess of Southampton—although the bride would perhaps have found doubtfully flattering the allusion to '. . . a dowager,/Long withering out a young man's revenue'. One recent biographer goes so far as to state as a fact that Shakespeare composed his fantasy for the festivities at Southampton House on 2 May 1594.

But the suggestion, at first so beguiling, becomes less appealing under rigorous scrutiny. Dr. Stanley Wells puts the negative case most cogently:

There is no outside evidence with any bearing on the matter. The theory has arisen from various features of the play itself. It is, certainly, much concerned with marriage; but so are many comedies. It ends with the fairies' blessing upon the married couples; but this is perfectly appropriate to Shakespeare's artistic scheme, and requires no other explanation. . . . A *Midsummer Night's Dream* (like *Love's Labour's Lost*) appears to require an unusually large number of boy actors. Hippolyta, Hermia, Helena, Titania, Peaseblossom, Cobweb, Moth, and Mustardseed would all have been boys' parts. Puck and Oberon too may have been played by boys or young men. But the title page of the first edition, printed in 1600, tells us that the play was 'sundry times publicly acted by the Right Honourable the Lord Chamberlain his servants'. If Shakespeare's company could at any time muster enough boys for public performances, we have no reason to doubt that it could have done so from the start. Thus the suggestion that the roles of the fairies were intended to be taken by children of the hypothetical noble house seems purely whimsical. The stage directions of the first edition, which was probably printed from Shakespeare's manuscript, show no essential differences from those in his other plays; a direction such as '*Enter a* Fairie *at one doore, and* Robin goodfellow *at another*' (II.i.0) suggests that he had in mind the structure of the public theatres. Furthermore, although noble weddings in Shakespeare's time were sometimes graced with formal entertainments, usually of the nature of a masque, the first play certainly known to have been written for such an occasion is Samuel Daniel's *Hymen's*

Triumph. This was performed in 1614, some twenty years after the composition of *A Midsummer Night's Dream.* By this time the tradition of courtly entertainments had developed greatly; and *Hymen's Triumph* does not appear to have been played in a public theatre.[4]

Although Shakespeare did not seek the publication of his plays (for reasons noted earlier), publication came anyway. In this respect 1594 is again a landmark year. Two of his pieces, and perhaps a third, reached print. *Titus Andronicus,* entered in the Stationers' Register on 6 February, was the first to be published, followed quickly by *The First Part of the Contention betwixt the two famous Houses of York and Lancaster* (Stationers' Register: 12 March)— the debased text, assembled from actors' recollections, of *2 Henry VI.* If *The Taming of A Shrew* indeed represents a corrupt redaction of *The Taming of the Shrew,* which differs from it radically, then that play too was initially printed in 1594; the authentic version, familiar to all readers and playgoers, did not appear until seven years after the dramatist's death. In none of these three quartos of 1594 is Shakespeare mentioned by name. Nor does he receive billing on the title-pages of plays printed, evidently without his consent, during the next three years. These pieces are *The True Tragedy of Richard, Duke of York* (the Bad Quarto of *3 Henry VI*) in 1595, and *Romeo and Juliet* (another Bad Quarto), *Richard II,* and *Richard III* in 1597. The last three enjoyed immense popularity. In 1599 appeared a second edition of *Romeo and Juliet* which, despite the title-page boast that it was 'Newly corrected, augmented, and amended', contains numerous errors. This edition too was anonymous. But the second quartos of *Richard II* and *Richard III,* both of 1598, bore Shakespeare's name. In 1598 too *Love's Labour's Lost* was published as 'By W. Shakespere'; this is the earliest extant impression, although the title-page describes it as 'Newly corrected and augmented'. The year 1598 also saw the publication of *1 Henry IV* without the author's name, the oversight being remedied on the title-page of the third edition ('Newly corrected by W. Shakespeare') in 1599. Thus, by 1598 at least eight, and possibly nine, of Shakespeare's plays had made their appearance on the booksellers' stalls. He had written more than that, as the informative Francis Meres makes clear.

A scion of the Lincolnshire Mereses, famous in the Fens, Francis was born one year after Shakespeare. The title-page of Meres's first publication, a sermon entitled *God's Arithmetic*, describes him succinctly as 'Master of Art of both Universities, and Student in Divinity'. In London, where he dwelt in Botolph Lane and enthusiastically familiarized himself with the literary and theatrical scene, Meres undertook to contribute to a series of volumes initiated in 1597 by Nicholas Ling's *Politeuphuia: Wit's Commonwealth*. These consisted of collected apophthegms, or pithy precepts, on morals, religion, and the arts—printed counterparts to the commonplace books in which thoughtful Elizabethans jotted down observations of life and tit-bits of wisdom from authors ancient or modern, mostly the former, to be hauled out when a public or literary occasion called for the seasoning of discourse with authority. Meres's *Palladis Tamia. Wit's Treasury. Being the Second Part of Wit's Commonwealth* follows his own dictum that 'all the source of wit . . . may flow within three channels, and be contrived into three heads; into a sentence [i.e. maxim], a similitude, and an example'.[5] Nourished by euphuism, Meres revelled above all in similitudes, and packed thousands into his squat little octavo volume of almost seven hundred pages. 'As A . . ., so B . . .,' runs his endlessly repeated formula, applied to a range of subjects that begins with God and ends with Death. Thus, 'As a cock croweth in the darkness of the night, so a preacher croweth in the darkness of this world.' Meres is no women's liberationist: 'As pigeons are taken with beans, and children enticed with balls; so women are won with toys.' Nor is he especially enterprising; despite his lengthy list of acknowledgements to sacred and profane writers, his similitudes are mostly Erasmus's *Parabolae sive Similia* Englished, and for his historical examples he cheerfully ransacked Ravisius Textor's popular and encyclopaedic *Officina*.[6] Along the way, however, Meres finds space for a sixteen-page 'Comparative discourse of our English poets, with the Greek, Latin, and Italian poets'. On this section, and to a lesser degree on the brief chapters that follow on painting and music, his fame rests.

For by comparing the best among his contemporaries with the ancients and with the masters of Renaissance Italy, he provides a unique indication of how a patriotic Elizabethan, not himself artistic, evaluated the cultural life of his day. There is nothing in the age comparable to Meres's comparative discourse in the *Palladis Tamia*. This work behind him, he retired into provincial obscurity, and passed the remainder of his long life (he died in 1647) as rector and schoolmaster of Wing in Rutland.

It is Meres's commendations of Shakespeare that principally engage interest. He lauds the poet for 'mightily' enriching the English language, and gorgeously investing it 'in rare ornaments and resplendent habiliments'. Shakespeare is one of the best for lyric poetry, comedy, and tragedy, as well as one of 'the most passionate among us to bewail and bemoan the perplexities of love'. Sandwiched between praise of Shakespeare as the 'mellifluous and honey-tongued' Ovidian poet and deviser of 'fine filed' phrases comes the celebrated passage enumerating Shakespeare's writings:

> As Plautus and Seneca are accounted the best for comedy and tragedy among the Latins, so Shakespeare among the English is the most excellent in both kinds for the stage. For comedy, witness his *Gentlemen of Verona*, his *Errors*, his *Love Labour's Lost*, his *Love Labour's Won*, his *Midsummer's Night Dream*, and his *Merchant of Venice*; for tragedy, his *Richard the 2.*, *Richard the 3.*, *Henry the 4.*, *King John*, *Titus Andronicus* and his *Romeo and Juliet*.[7]

Meres's reference (just preceding) to Shakespeare's 'sugared sonnets among his private friends' shows that at least some of these poems were in existence by 1598. *The Comedy of Errors* had entered the record earlier, in the account of the boisterous revels at Gray's Inn, but for five of the plays—*The Two Gentlemen of Verona*, *Love's Labour's Won*, *A Midsummer-Night's Dream*, *The Merchant of Venice*, and *King John*—Meres furnishes our earliest external evidence of date. For the investigator faced with the daunting task of charting the sequence of Shakespeare's works, his testimony can scarcely be overvalued.

Surely the most intriguing entry is *Love's Labour's Won*. Has

Meres simply made a mistake? Or does he refer to a lost play of Shakespeare's? Or is *Love's Labour's Won* an alternative title for an extant piece? The first possibility—that of error—was ruled out by a London bookseller's discovery, as recently as 1953, of a manuscript scrap which bookbinders used more than three centuries ago to make the back hinge of a volume of sermons. The paper contains a stationer's notations of books he had in stock in August 1603. Among the items listed is 'Love's Labour Won', which follows (logically enough) 'Love's Labour Lost'. Most likely *Love's Labour's Won* is an alternative title for a known play. If so, it is unlikely to be one of the other comedies cited by Mères. Some authorities have favoured *The Taming of the Shrew*, in which love's labour is unmistakably won; although early, the play is omitted from *Palladis Tamia*. But the stationer includes 'Taming of A Shrew' as a separate entry in his inventory. The fact that most comedies have a love interest and end in prosperity does not facilitate the task of identification. *Much Ado About Nothing*, straining against the outer time-limit of Meres's range, is a possibility.* Professor T. W. Baldwin, who with a whole slender volume on the subject is our leading authority on a non-existent play, leans to *All's Well that Ends Well*, in which Helena 'wins' her obnoxious husband by the bed trick; but such reasoning presupposes, without adequate evidence, a lost early draft of the Jacobean problem comedy.[8] A more adventurous authority interprets 'love's labour's won' to mean 'love's pains earned', and opts for *Troilus and Cressida*;[9] but nobody seems to have seconded this unlikely nomination. *Love's Labour's Won* remains a minor Shakespearian enigma.

Because of the accident of chronology that made him the earliest recorded enthusiast of Shakespeare, Francis Meres begins the story of the poet's reputation. According to one historian of Shakespearian criticism, the encomiums in *Palladis Tamia* show 'how early the conception of Shakespeare as a universal genius had dawned'.[10]

---

* Robert F. Fleissner has lately suggested that *Much Ado About Nothing* was originally a subtitle for *Love's Labour's Won*, titular wit being deployed in a Won/Nothing quibble ('*Love's Labour's Won* and the Occasion of *Much Ado*', *Shakespeare Survey* 27 (Cambridge, 1974), pp. 105-10). Doubters will no doubt remain doubtful.

Meres occupies his niche of honour in biographies bearing such chapter headings as 'Rise in Fame and Social Dignity'. But this pretender to, and admirer of, wit is himself a writer of disarming witlessness. Sometimes the strain in finding an apt simile shows. Thus, 'As Anacreon died by the pot: so George Peele by the pox', where the sound, not sense, yokes the comparison. Meres is a remarkably undiscriminating panegyrist. He lavishes praise on Sidney ('our rarest poet') and on *The Faerie Queene* ('I know not what more excellent or exquisite poem may be written'), but Shakespeare must share praise for comedy with such decidedly lesser talents as 'Master Rowley, once a rare scholar of learned Pembroke Hall in Cambridge', and 'Anthony Mundye, our best plotter', not to mention a quartet of Henslowe's impecunious journeymen: Porter, Wilson, Hathaway, and Chettle. As a tragedian Shakespeare competes with his Warwickshire neighbour Michael Drayton. If the former is 'honey-tongued', Drayton is 'golden-mouthed', and there does not seem to be much to choose between the two epithets. Drayton is, with Shakespeare, a bewailer of the perplexities of love. The former also wins praise for his moral virtue, an attribute that Meres overlooks mentioning for Shakespeare, who was not in this respect deficient. Drayton is clearly the compiler's favourite, being cited a record thirteen times, although Meres lists more titles for Shakespeare than for anyone else. In all, Meres commends 125 English writers, painters, and musicians. C. S. Lewis best sums up his status as a critic. 'Meres's patterned equivalences', Lewis writes, 'bear about the same relation to real criticism as Fluellen's comparison of Macedon and Monmouth bears to real geography.'[11]

One of the plays listed by Meres, *Henry IV*—he does not distinguish between parts—was newly composed in 1598. This drama created a fortuitous stir that would not entirely subside for half a century and more. In his *Church-History of Britain* Thomas Fuller writes:

> Stage-poets have themselves been very bold with, and others very merry at, the memory of Sir John Oldcastle, whom they have fancied a boon companion, a jovial roister, and yet a coward to boot, contrary to the credit of all chronicles, owning him a martial man of merit. The best is, Sir John Falstaffe hath relieved the mem-

ory of Sir John Oldcastle, and of late is substituted buffoon in his place, but it matters as little what petulant poets, as what malicious papists have written against him.[12]

'Of late is substituted buffoon': a curious phrase, in view of the almost sixty years separating *Henry IV* and the *Church-History*. In his *Worthies of England*, published posthumously in 1662, Fuller grumbles again. 'Now as I am glad that Sir John Oldcastle is put out', he declares, 'so I am sorry that Sir John Fastolfe is put in. . . .'[13] Originally, as these remarks indicate, Shakespeare had called his fat knight Oldcastle. The choice of a name was a blunder, as the repercussions quickly proved.

The historical Oldcastle, styled Lord Cobham, was a distinguished and tragic figure. A Wycliffite who denounced the Pope as anti-Christ, he was hanged and burnt for his heretical faith on the Lollard gallows in St. Giles's Fields, and afterwards enrolled by John Foxe in his *Book of Martyrs*. Needless to say, Catholics viewed Oldcastle somewhat differently. In his *Examen of the Calendar or Catalogue of Protestant Saints*, the Jesuit Persons wrote, 'The second month of February is more fertile of rubricate martyrs, than January, for that it hath 8 in number, two Wickliffians, Sir John Oldcastle, a ruffian-knight as all England knoweth, and commonly brought in by comedians on their stages: he was put to death for robberies and rebellion under the foresaid King Henry the Fifth.'[14] (Persons in due course drew a contorted riposte from John Speed, who interestingly assumes that the playwright who transformed a Protestant martyr into a comic buffoon must have been a Catholic apologist. In his *History of Great Britain* (1611) Speed writes: 'That N. D. [Nicholas Dolman, Persons's pseudonym] . . . hath made Oldcastle a ruffian, a robber, and a rebel, and his authority, taken from the stage-players, is more befitting the pen of his slanderous report, than the credit of the judicious, being only grounded from this papist and his poet, of like conscience for lies, the one ever feigning, and the other ever falsifying the truth . . . I am not ignorant.') Complaint about the slur on a name revered by Protestants was most likely lodged by William Brooke, seventh Lord Cobham, or by his successor—after his death in 1597—Henry, eighth

Lord Cobham; they were lineally descended, on the mother's side, from Oldcastle. It has been suggested that Shakespeare's original choice of a name was deliberately provocative, an act of retaliation against a dynasty hostile to the stage; but there is no evidence of the Cobhams' puritanical leanings, and more likely the dramatist took the name, without a second thought, from his source play, *The Famous Victories of Henry the Fifth*. A second thought would have been advisable.

The Brookes wielded power at Court. William, a Privy Councillor and Lord Chamberlain, could have ordered the change directly or used his influence with the Master of the Revels. His son Henry— the brother-in-law of Sir Robert Cecil and intimate of Raleigh—was an adversary of Essex and of Shakespeare's patron Southampton. No matter that the Essex faction mocked Brooke as 'my lord Fool'; he had successfully weathered the opposition to his appointment, in 1596, as Lord Warden of the Cinque Ports. Identification of the Cobham who remonstrated (assuming one did remonstrate) depends on the precise dating of *1 Henry IV*, which may have reached the boards before or after William's death.

The protest, whatever its source, carried weight. Shakespeare changed Oldcastle to Falstaff, a name suggested by the cowardly bit-player in *1 Henry VI* who takes to his heels from the battlefield without 'having struck one stroke'. For good measure the playwright also altered the names of Oldcastle-Falstaff's tavern mates, Harvey and Russell, to Bardolph and Peto—best not to offend the Earls of Bedford, who bore the name Russell, or Sir William Harvey, shortly to marry the dowager Countess of Southampton, who had already survived two husbands. (Harvey is thought by some to be the mysterious 'Mr. W. H.' of the *Sonnets* dedication.[15]) Shakespeare covered, as best he could, the traces of references that would grate on proud sensibilities, but Harvey and 'Rossill' surface in Boar's Head intrigue, and Oldcastle lingers in a metrically deficient line, a botched pun ('my old lad of the castle', i.e. roisterer), and a surviving speech prefix, 'Old'. But most telling of all is the author's humble Epilogue disclaimer in *2 Henry IV*: '. . . Falstaff shall die of a sweat, unless already 'a be kill'd with your hard opinions; for Oldcastle died a martyr and this is not the man.'

In 1599 a team of dramatists from the rival Admiral's men—Drayton, Munday, Wilson, and Hathaway—produced *The True and Honourable History, of the Life of Sir John Old-castle, the Good Lord Cobham*.

> It is no pampered glutton we present,
> Nor aged counsellor to youthful sin,
> But one, whose virtue shone above the rest,
> A valiant martyr and a virtuous peer.

Thus speaks the Prologue, not without smugness; and concludes: 'Let fair truth be graced, / Since forged invention former time defaced.' Still, despite such protestation, these professionals twice pay allusive tribute to Shakespeare's Falstaff, curiously disengaged from Oldcastle. 'Where the devil are all my old thieves', the King asks, 'that were wont to keep this walk? Falstaffe, the villain, is so fat, he cannot get on's horse, but me thinks Poins and Peto should be stirring here abouts.' And, some lines later, Sir John the parson of Wrotham refers to 'that foul, villainous guts, that led him to all that roguery . . . that Falstaffe'. By a nice irony *Sir John Oldcastle* came to be associated with Shakespeare's name, and found a place in the Third Folio (second issue) of his plays in 1664. Such are the vagaries of show business.

The earliest mention of the behind-the-scenes brouhaha comes in a letter written, around 1625, by Dr. Richard James. 'A short, red-bearded, high-coloured fellow' (so an enemy described him), James was a divine whose appetite for travel took him as far as Russia; he was also a small poet who trailed in the tribe of Ben, and—not least —the antiquary in charge of Sir Robert Cotton's great library. In his letter, addressed to Sir Harry Bourchier, James considers the question put to him by a young gentlewoman of Bourchier's acquaintance: how could Sir John Falstaff die in the reign of Henry V, and live again to be banished for cowardice in Henry VI's time? To which James replies:

> That in Shakespeare's first show of Harrie the Fifth, the person with which he undertook to play a buffoon was not Falstaffe, but Sir Jhon Oldcastle, and that offense being worthily taken by personages descended from his title, as peradventure by many others

also who ought to have him in honourable memory, the poet was put to makc an ignorant shift of abusing Sir Jhon Fastolphe, a man not inferior of virtue though not so famous in piety as the other. . . .[16]

A late embellishment of the episode draws no less a personage than the sovereign herself into the intrigue: '. . . this Part of *Falstaff*, according to Rowe, 'is said to have been written originally under the Name of *Oldcastle*; some of that Family being then remaining, the Queen was pleas'd to command him to alter it; upon which he made use of *Falstaff*.'[17]

A royal command also figures in the sequel story of how Shakespeare came to write the last of his Falstaff plays. This famous tradition first reaches print in the defensive apologia prefixed in 1702 by John Dennis to his *Comical Gallant*. An adaptation of *The Merry Wives of Windsor*, Dennis's play had just failed on the stage, there being no way the hapless author could placate his two camps of detractors, one of which (he lamented in his dedicatory epistle) believed the original play 'to be so admirable, that nothing ought to be added to it; the others fancied it to be so despicable, that any ones time would be lost upon it'. Thus caught between Scylla and Charybdis, Dennis defends his own meddling pen by invoking a more glorious past:

> That this Comedy was not despicable, I guess'd for several Reasons: First, I knew very well, that it had pleas'd one of the greatest Queens that ever was in the World, great not only for her Wisdom in the Arts of Government, but for her knowledge of Polite Learning, and her nice taste of the Drama, for such a taste we may be sure she had, by the relish which she had of the Ancients. This Comedy was written at her Command, and by her direction, and she was so eager to see it Acted, that she commanded it to be finished in fourteen days; and was afterwards, as Tradition tells us, very well pleas'd at the Representation.[18]

In his prologue the adaptor again alludes to the fourteen days of composition time.

Two years later, however, in replying with heavy sarcasm to Jeremy Collier's *Dissuasive from the Play-House*. Dennis improved upon the anecdote by contracting the fortnight into ten days: 'Nay the poor mistaken Queen her self, encouraged Play-Houses to that degree, that she not only commanded *Shakespear*, to write the Comedy of the *Merry Wives*, and to write it in Ten Days time; so eager was she for the wicked Diversion. . . .'[19] Next Rowe, speaking of the 'many gracious Marks of her Favour' that Queen Elizabeth gave Shakespeare, adds an appealing circumstantial detail:

> She was so well pleas'd with that admirable Character of *Falstaff*, in the two Parts of *Henry* the Fourth, that she commanded him to continue it for one Play more, and to shew him in Love. This is said to be the Occasion of his Writing *The Merry Wives of* Windsor.[20]

Finally, just a year later, the publisher's hack Gildon (doubtfully immortalized by Pope in *The Dunciad*) retells the tradition in the *Remarks on the Plays of Shakespear* which, without benefit of an invitation from the editor, he published as a supplement to Rowe:

> The *Fairys* in the fifth Act makes a Handsome Complement to the Queen, in her Palace of *Windsor*, who had oblig'd him to write a Play of Sir *John Falstaff* in Love, and which I am very well assured he perform'd in a Fortnight; a prodigious Thing, when all is so well contriv'd, and carry'd on without the least Confusion.[21]

The assurances of which Gildon boasts probably have as their source the printed remarks of Dennis and Rowe, but the citation of the Fairies is (as we shall see) pertinent.

A report unremarked for over a century, and then exhumed for special pleading, must arouse sceptical misgivings. How Dennis came upon the story we do not know; possibly, as Malone supposed, from Dryden who may have had it from Davenant. The tradition, however, receives some confirmation from the fact that *The Merry Wives of Windsor* is described on the title-page of the 1602 Quarto as having been acted 'before her Majesty'. Apparently none of these early authorities—Dennis, Rowe, or Gildon—had seen the Quarto.[22]

A royal occasion conceivably inspired the original production. Shakespeare sets the scene for *The Merry Wives* at Windsor, where the installation of the Knights of the Garter took place each year in the chapel of St. George, the patron saint of the order. In Act V the Fairy Queen's speech—with its gracious allusions to the stalls in the choir chapel, the crests, blazons, and coat-armour of the Garter knights, and the motto of the order, *Honi soit qui mal y pense*—underscores the Garter connection of the play. Some hold that *The Merry Wives of Windsor* had its first performance in 1597, not at the formal installation (unattended by the Queen) in St. George's chapel at Windsor, but at the Garter Feast in the royal Whitehall Palace a month earlier, on St. George's day, 23 April. That year George Carey, Lord Hunsdon, was one of the five newly elected Knights. Upon his father's death in 1596 Hunsdon had taken over the sponsorship of Shakespeare's company—it was briefly known as Hunsdon's men—and the next year, in mid-April, his Queen, who had a dear regard for him, appointed him Lord Chamberlain. What more natural, in view of this double recognition, than that the Lord Chamberlain, who lavished large sums on the Garter celebration, should commission his leading dramatist to produce, on the spur, a play on the theme of Falstaff in love, for presentation by the Chamberlain's servants at the magnificent Feast honouring the new Knights? It is an appealing enough hypothetical reconstruction of the events leading up to the first night of *The Merry Wives of Windsor*, and not implausible as such hypotheses go.[23]

The year before the Garter Feast there took place on Bankside a puzzling episode which its modern discoverer would connect with the composition of *The Merry Wives of Windsor*. In the autumn of 1596 William Wayte petitioned for sureties of the peace against William Shakspere, Francis Langley, Dorothy Soer wife of John Soer, and Anne Lee, '*ob metum mortis*'—'for fear of death', a conventional legal phrase in such documents. The writ of attachment, issued to the sheriff of Surrey, was returnable on the last day of Michaelmas Term, 29 November. To obtain such a writ, the complainant swore before the Judge of Queen's Bench that he stood in danger of death, or bodily hurt, from a certain party. The magistrate then commanded the sheriff of the appropriate county to produce the accused person or persons, who had to post bond to keep the peace, on pain of forfeiting the security.

Of the *dramatis personae* in this minor legal drama, we have already encountered Langley. A money-broker fifteen years Shakespeare's senior, he had built the Swan playhouse in Paris Garden. (It has been suggested by Leslie Hotson that Shakespeare's company was at the Swan in 1596, but there is no adequate evidence to show that it was.) Dorothy Soer and Anne Lee are otherwise unknown; it is a minor solace that nobody has yet cast either for the part of Dark Lady. About Wayte we have more information. These writs of attachment were often retaliatory, and in fact Langley had earlier in the same term sworn the peace against Wayte and Wayte's stepfather William Gardiner, a Surrey justice of the peace with jurisdiction in Paris Garden and Southwark. A deposition in another case sneeringly describes Wayte as 'a certain loose person of no reckoning or value, being wholly under the rule and commandment of the said Gardiner'.[24] This Gardiner was known and detested by many in the district. Through money-lending and sharp practices (he married a prosperous widow, and proceeded to defraud her son and brothers and sisters), the justice had risen to wealth and civic dignity. He made numerous enemies, including his own son-in-law John Stepkin. On his death-bed Stepkin darkly suspected that Gardiner was responsible for his fatal illness; was he not, after all, a sorcerer who kept two toads? In the spring of 1596 Gardiner quarrelled with Langley, who denounced him as 'a false perjured knave'. The justice in turn sought to put the Swan out of business.

Somehow Shakespeare was drawn into this feud. Dr. Hotson believes that Gardiner, not Sir Thomas Lucy, was satirized as Justice Shallow in *The Merry Wives of Windsor*, and also in *2 Henry IV*; and that the dramatist lampooned Wayte in the figure of Slender. The Surrey justice owned an enclosed deer park in Godstone. By virtue of his marriage he was entitled to impale upon his coat of arms—a golden griffin—three white luces; hence the allusion to luces/louses in *The Merry Wives of Windsor* (I. i). Gardiner arranged an advantageous match for his kinsman Wayte; in the play Shallow tries to mate his simpleton cousin Slender with Anne Page, who possesses (in addition to brown hair and a small womanly voice) £700 and possibilities. These parallels between life and art are intriguing, but the edifice of argument rests on a fragile foundation. Shallow—foolish, ancient, essentially harmless—will hardly pass muster as a caricature of the overbearing Justice Gardiner. There is no evidence that Shakespeare ever set eyes upon Gardiner. For all we know the poet may have been an innocent bystander (he lived in the neighbourhood),[25] although Langley's theatrical associations suggest a more direct involvement. But all that has come to light is the single laconic record. The rest is speculation.

One can readily imagine Shakespeare present, as a leading member of his troupe, in Whitehall Palace at Westminster for the Garter Feast which coincided (if we may accept the traditional anniversary) with his thirty-third birthday, and anxiously watching the première of his play. It is a harmless fancy to toy with. Perhaps he acted in *The Merry Wives of Windsor*; he must have done a good deal of acting, especially in the earlier years.

About his life as a mime Shakespeare seems to have entertained ambivalent feelings. The *Sonnets* reveal that he chafed at the social inferiority of actors; he confesses having made himself 'a motley to the view', and arraigns Fortune

> That did not better for my life provide
> Than public means which public manners breeds.
> Thence comes it that my name receives a brand,
> And almost thence my nature is subdu'd
> To what it works in, like the dyer's hand.

But such passing moods must have yielded to a dominant professionalism. The First Folio that gathers together Shakespeare's plays also pays tribute to the player. His old fellows, Heminges and Condell, place him—appropriately enough, given the occasion—at the head of their catalogue of 'the Principal Actors in all these Plays' on the ninth preliminary leaf to the Folio. *All* is a big number; we should welcome more precise information.

The epigram addressed 'To our English Terence Mr. William Shake-speare', and included by John Davies of Hereford in his *Scourge of Folly*, if cryptic, has at least the merit of being contemporary:

> Some say (good Will)—which I, in sport, do sing—
> Hadst thou not played some kingly parts in sport,

> Thou hadst been a companion for a king,
> And been a king among the meaner sort.[26]

In what sense was Shakespeare 'a king among the meaner sort'? How was he fitted to be 'a companion for a king'? And which kingly parts did he play? Some biographers believe that Shakespeare donned the sceptre and crown of Duncan, Henry IV, and Henry VI; even the self-dramatizing Richard II. These are guesses. He is not thought to have taken the stellar roles of Lear and Macbeth,* which Burbage made famous.

In 1699 an anonymous enthusiast of the stage, perhaps the antiquary and play-collector James Wright, remarked in a vague but not unreasonable parenthesis that 'Shakespear . . . was a much better poet, than player'.[27] Rowe, gathering material for his memoir of Shakespeare, tried to find out more, with little success:

> His Name is Printed, as the Custom was in those Times, amongst those of the other Players, before some old Plays, but without any particular Account of what sort of Parts he us'd to play; and tho' I have inquir'd, I could never meet with any further Account of him this way, than that the top of his Performance was the Ghost in his own *Hamlet*.[28]

The Ghost in *Hamlet*; that at least tells us something.

To this traditional intelligence the disorderly antiquary Oldys adds another morsel a half-century later. This item appears in the rag-bag of notes which the great Shakespearian scholar Steevens rescued from oblivion:

> One of Shakespeare's younger brothers, who lived to a good old age, even some years, as I compute, after the restoration of K. *Charles II.* would in his younger days come to London to visit his brother *Will*, as he called him, and be a spectator of him as an actor in some of his own plays. This custom, as his brother's fame enlarged, and his dramatic entertainments grew the greatest support of our principal, if not of all our theatres, he continued it seems so long after his brother's death, as even to the latter end of his own life.

---

* An elegy on Burbage in 1619 refers to him in the part of Lear; it is a reasonable assumption that he also played Macbeth (see Dennis Bartholomeusz, *Macbeth and the Players* (Cambridge, 1969), pp. 9-11).

. . . this opportunity made them [the actors] greedily inquisitive into every little circumstance, more especially in his dramatick character, which his brother could relate of him. But he, it seems, was so stricken in years, and possibly his memory so weakened with infirmities (which might make him the easier pass for a man of weak intellects) that he could give them but little light into their enquiries; and all that could be recollected from him of his brother *Will*, in that station was, the faint, general, and almost lost ideas he had of having once seen him act a part in one of his own comedies, wherein being to personate a decrepit old man, he wore a long beard, and appeared so weak and drooping and unable to walk, that he was forced to be supported and carried by another person to a table, at which he was seated among some company, who were eating, and one of them sung a song.[29]

So, if this report is true, Shakespeare played Adam in *As You Like It*, as well as Hamlet's Ghost; characters with either one or both feet in the grave. Dignified parts. Oldys's authority is not very reassuring, however, for none of Shakespeare's three brothers lived into the Restoration.

A while later in the eighteenth century Edward Capell, justly celebrated for his editorial labours on Shakespeare, retailed the same anecdote, but the source has now become a senile ancient of Stratford.

A traditional story was current some years ago about Stratford,— that a very old man of that place,—of weak intellects, but yet related to Shakespeare,—being ask'd by some of his neighbours, what he remember'd about him; answer'd,—that he saw him once brought on the stage upon another man's back; which answer was apply'd by the hearers, to his having seen him perform in this scene the part of Adam: That he should have done so, is made not unlikely by another constant tradition,—that he was no extraordinary actor, and therefore took no parts upon him but such as this: for which he might also be peculiarly fitted by an accidental lameness, which,— as he himself tells us twice in his "*Sonnets*," v. 37, and 89,—befell him in some part of life; without saying how, or when, of what sort, or in what degree; but his expressions seem to indicate— latterly.[30]

In Sonnet 37 the poet complains of being 'made lame by Fortune's dearest spite', and in 89 he threatens, 'Speak of my lameness, and I straight will halt'. Metaphor, it seems, is not Capell's strong suit, but in his descent into literalism he has good company. The idea of a hobbling Bard appealed to Sir Walter Scott, himself lame. 'He is a stout man at quarterstaff, and single falchion', Sussex describes Shakespeare (a 'gamesome mad fellow') in *Kenilworth*, 'though, as I am told, a halting fellow; and he stood, they say, a tough fight with the rangers of old Sir Thomas Lucy of Charlecote, when he broke his deer-park and kissed his keeper's daughter.'[31] Here Sussex stands at the crossroads where legends meet.

Despite the imaginary afflictions he owes to the unimaginativeness of his critics, Shakespeare managed to act in the plays of fellow dramatists for the Chamberlain's men, as well as in his own. When Ben Jonson brought his plays together in 1616 for the first of the great dramatic folios of the age, he gave Shakespeare pride of place in the list of 'principal comedians' in *Every Man in his Humour*, acted in 1598. Did Shakespeare take the part of the elder Knowell? He presumably did not act in the sequel *Every Man out of his Humour*, for his name fails to appear in the cast-list. He is, however, numbered among the tragedians who enacted the same dramatist's *Sejanus*—a box-office failure—in 1603. The company's leading actor, Richard Burbage, appears in both lists, as do Shakespeare's friends and fellows Heminges and Condell.

According to a late tradition, Shakespeare gave Jonson, eight or nine years his junior, his start with the Chamberlain's men. Rowe tells the story:

His Acquaintance with *Ben Johnson* began with a remarkable piece of Humanity and good Nature; Mr. *Johnson*, who was at that Time altogether unknown to the World, had offer'd one of his Plays to the Players, in order to have it Acted; and the Persons into whose Hands it was put, after having turn'd it carelessly and superciliously over, were just upon returning it to him with an ill-natur'd Answer, that it would be of no service to their Company, when *Shakespear* luckily cast his Eye upon it, and found something so well in it as to engage him first to read it through, and afterwards to recommend

Mr. *Johnson* and his Writings to the Publick. After this they were profess'd Friends; tho' I don't know whether the other ever made him an equal return of Gentleness and Sincerity.[32]

The dark connotations of the last sentence evoke the familiar picture of Shakespeare and Jonson as mighty opposites, with Gentle Will inspiring envious passions in rare and rivalrous Ben. Such images, belonging to the mythos, will in due course occupy us, as will Jonson's comments on Shakespeare.

The mythos, to which we owe so many small pleasures, outdoes itself in the legendary playhouse encounter of the actor and the Queen. Much repeated, the story achieves definitive statement in a bookseller's compilation, the *Dramatic Table Talk* of Richard Ryan, published in 1825:

> It is well known that Queen Elizabeth was a great admirer of the immortal Shakspeare, and used frequently (as was the custom with persons of great rank in those days) to appear upon the stage before the audience, or to sit delighted behind the scenes, when the plays of our bard were performed. One evening, when Shakspeare himself was personating the part of a King, the audience knew of her Majesty being in the house. She crossed the stage when he was performing, and, on receiving the accustomed greeting from the audience, moved politely to the poet, but he did not notice it! When behind the scenes, she caught his eye, and moved again, but still he would not throw off his character, to notice her: this made her Majesty think of some means by which she might know, whether he would depart, or not, from the dignity of his character, while on the stage.—Accordingly, as he was about to make his exit, she stepped before him, dropped her glove, and re-crossed the stage, which Shakspeare noticing, took up, with these words, immediately after finishing his speech, and so aptly were they delivered, that they seemed to belong to it:
>
> > "And though now bent on this high embassy,
> > Yet *stoop* we to take up our *Cousin's* glove!"
>
> He then walked off the stage, and presented the glove to the Queen, who was greatly pleased with his behaviour, and complimented him upon the propriety of it.[33]

So agreeable is it to have this glimpse of the courtly Warwickshire provincial exercising his extempore wit with his sovereign that one is almost tempted to overlook a few considerations hostile to romance.[34] In Elizabethan theatres performances took place in the afternoon, not at night; the stage afforded no scenery for eavesdroppers to conceal themselves behind; the Queen is not known to have professed admiration for Shakespeare; she was disinclined to expose herself to the multitude by visiting the playhouse; and she restrained herself publicly (as in private) from flirtations with subjects of inferior station. These details unfortunately impair faith in a story which, in its naïve way, shows Shakespeare in a kingly part and as a fit companion for a monarch.

Burbage had his female admirers too, if we may trust the scurrilous anecdote that Edward Curle, a student at the Middle Temple, related to his room-mate John Manningham, and which the latter jotted down in his manuscript *Diary* on 13 March 1602. When (according to Manningham) Burbage was playing Richard III, a citizeness became infatuated with him, and they arranged an assignation; but Shakespeare overheard the conversation, arrived first, and 'was entertained, and at his game ere Burbage came'. When the message arrived that Richard III was at the door, the triumphant lover, with some relish, returned word that William the Conqueror preceded Richard III. 'Shakespeare's name William', Manningham helpfully adds.[35]*

---

* The story had currency long before Manningham's *Diary* surfaced, and appears, already elaborated, in Thomas Wilkes's *A General View of the Stage* (1759), pp. 220-1. As Wilkes's version (offered 'for the sake of the entertainment it may afford the reader') is not noticed in EKC or SS, and is earlier than the others, it will perhaps repay quotation in full:

> One evening when Richard III. was to be performed, Shakespear observed a young woman delivering a message to Burbage in so cautious a manner as excited his curiosity to listen to. It imported, that her master was gone out of town that morning, and her mistress would be glad of his company after Play; and to know what signal he would appoint for admittance. Burbage replied, three taps at the door, and it is I, Richard the Third. She immediately withdrew, and Shakespeare followed 'till he observed her to go into a house in the city; and enquiring in the neighbourhood, he was informed that a young lady lived there, the favourite of an old rich merchant. Near

If this anecdote, which carries more weight than legendary accretions, is true, and the leading playwright of the Chamberlain's men competed for the favours of stage-struck ladies of the town, the company also (and this admits of no question) co-operated wholeheartedly to maintain their pre-eminence. In 1597 the troupe faced its most dangerous crisis, for on 13 April James Burbage's lease on the Theatre, their regular house, expired.[36]

Negotiations for a new agreement had got under way between Burbage and the ground landlord, Giles Allen. For a while it looked as though they might be able to come to terms. Burbage agreed to a higher rent—£24 a year instead of £14—and even, reluctantly, to allowing the landlord to take eventual possession of the building. But when Allen demanded permission to convert the playhouse to his own uses after a period of only five years, Burbage drew the line. He now prudently cast about for an alternative theatrical site, and thought he had found it in the old frater, or refectory, of the dissolved Blackfriars monastery which, although within the city walls, was subject to the Crown, not to the Lord Mayor and aldermen of London. Burbage committed £600 for the frater, and at the cost of several hundred pounds more refurbished the structure for theatrical use. But the aristocratic residents of the fashionable district, alarmed at the prospect of a common playhouse in their midst, protested to the Privy Council. They had their way, although in the fullness of time Shakespeare's company would put their Blackfriars property to good use.

Meanwhile troubles crowded in on the Chamberlain's men. In

---

the appointed time of meeting, Shakespear thought proper to anticipate Mr. Burbage, and was introduced by the concerted signal. The lady was very much surprised at Shakespear's presuming to act Mr. Burbage's part; but as he (who had wrote Romeo and Juliet) we may be certain did not want wit or eloquence to apologize for the intrusion, she was soon pacified, and they were mutually happy till Burbage came to the door, and repeated the same signal; but Shakespear popping his head out of the window, bid him be gone; for that William the Conqueror had reigned before Richard III.

The Manningham entry first reached print in 1831, when J. Payne Collier reported his discovery of the *Diary* in *The History of English Dramatic Poetry to the Time of Shakespeare*.

late January 1597 James Burbage died. April came and went without
a new lease. In July, reacting to the scandal caused by the seditious
Isle of Dogs at the Swan, the Privy Council assented to the Lord
Mayor and aldermen's petition for the 'final suppressing of . . .
stage plays', and further ordered the dismantling of the Shoreditch
and Bankside playhouses; the Curtain and the Theatre are specifically named. Fortunately the final solution was not final, and the
acting companies were soon back in business. The Chamberlain's
servants played for a while longer at the Theatre, at the landlord's
sufferance, but by the end of the year they had moved to the Curtain. Their old playhouse now stood empty, and provided a minor
satirist of the day with an image of desolation:

> But see yonder,
> One like the unfrequented Theatre
> Walks in dark silence, and vast solitude.[37]

Shakespeare's company found itself without a permanent home.

It was now the task of Burbage's son Cuthbert to resume discus-
sions with a landlord at once avaricious and puritanical. When Allen
came to town and put up at the George Inn in Shoreditch, as he did
four times a year to receive his rents, Cuthbert pleaded with him to
grant a new lease, and in the autumn of 1598 capitulated to terms he
viewed as grossly exorbitant—only to have Allen refuse to accept
Richard Burbage as security. Sanguine that 'the right and interest of
the said Theatre was both in law and conscience absolutely vested'
in him, Allen made plans 'to pull down the same, and to convert
the wood and timber thereof to some better use. . . .' *To some better use*; the phrase sufficiently indicates his prejudice. But he never
had a chance to visit his righteous wrath on the playhouse; for report
of what was afoot reached the Burbages.

On 28 December 1598, with Allen away in the country, a determined party gathered at the Theatre under cover of darkness. While
Widow Burbage looked on approvingly, her sons Cuthbert and
Richard, along with their friend and financial backer William Smith
of Waltham Cross, their chief carpenter Peter Street, and ten or
twelve workmen, proceeded to dismantle the Theatre: an action specifically permitted them by a covenant of the expired lease. The epi-

sode is described by Giles Allen, still impotently furious three years after the event. Cuthbert Burbage and his crew, he deposed, did

> riotously assemble themselves together and then and there armed themselves with divers and many unlawful and offensive weapons, as namely, swords, daggers, bills, axes, and such like, and so armed did then repair unto the said Theatre. And then and there, armed as aforesaid, in very riotous, outrageous, and forcible manner, and contrary to the laws of your Highness's realm, attempted to pull down the said Theatre, whereupon divers of your subjects, servants and farmers, then going about in peaceable manner to procure them to desist from that their unlawful enterprise, they, the said riotous persons aforesaid, notwithstanding procured then therein with great violence, not only then and there forcibly and riotously resisting your subjects, servants and farmers, but also then and there pulling, breaking, and throwing down the said Theatre in very outrageous, violent and riotous sort, to the great disturbance and terrifying not only of your subjects, said servants and farmers, but of divers others of your Majesty's loving subjects there near inhabiting.[38]

The timber from the dismantled Theatre these riotous men then ferried across the river to Bankside, where they erected a new play-house more splendid than any London had yet seen. This they called the Globe.

They built on garden plots and grounds in St. Saviour's parish, in the environs of the Rose and the Bear Garden, and the handsome big church of St. Mary Overy;[39] west of Dead Man's Place on the south side of old Maiden Lane (now Park Street)—'a long straggling Place', Stow's eighteenth-century editor describes it, 'with Ditches on each side the Passage to the Houses being over little Bridges, with little Garden Plotts before them, especially on the North side which is best both for Houses and Inhabitants'.[40] Shakespeare and his fellows must have watched the work progress. Allen did not stand by; instead he brought suit against carpenter Street, Burbage's agent, in the Queen's Bench, claiming £800 damages, a sum that included £700 for the Theatre and 40s. for trampling on the grass. Among other charges, Allen accused the Burbages of not having spent £200 (as the old lease required) in improvements of tenements on the property; but James Burbage had years earlier anticipated this tactic by commissioning an expert craftsman to take before-and-after 'views' giving proof of repairs and of the erection of new tenements. Not surprisingly, Allen failed in his attempt at legal harassment. The Court of Requests ordered him to desist from bringing any further suits respecting the demolition of the Theatre. He sued anyway, and got nowhere.[41]

Meanwhile the Chamberlain's men were playing at the Globe. In a post-mortem inventory (dated 16 May 1599) of the property of Sir Thomas Brend, whose son Nicholas had leased the site, the Globe is described as newly erected—'de novo edificata'—and in the occupation of William Shakespeare and others ('in occupacione Willielmi Shakespeare et aliorum'). If it was not by then yet ready for use, it was by autumn. Thomas Platter of Basle records the visit made that September, on the 21st:

> . . . after dinner, at about two o'clock, I went with my party across the water; in the straw-thatched house we saw the tragedy of the first Emperor Julius Caesar, very pleasantly performed, with approximately fifteen characters; at the end of the play they danced together admirably and exceedingly gracefully, according to their custom, two in each group dressed in men's and two in women's apparel.[42]

If, as is most likely, this was Shakespeare's *Julius Caesar*, it is the first recorded performance at the Globe.

The competitive presence of a new theatre on Bankside was most acutely felt by the Admiral's men, under Alleyn and Henslowe, at the Rose a few hundred feet away. Although only a dozen years old, the house was dangerously decayed, and, because of its position on swampy ground, uninviting in bad weather. Sensibly, the Admiral's company decided to decamp. Alleyn leased a plot of ground on the other side of the Thames, near the fields of St. Giles without Cripplegate, in the Liberty of Finsbury; an up-and-coming district that met the essential condition of being outside City jurisdiction. Alleyn and Henslowe then contracted with the Globe carpenter, Peter Smith, to build a playhouse between Whitecross Street and Golding (or Golden) Lane, about a half-mile west of the old Curtain. The agreement, which survives among the Henslowe papers at Dulwich

College, calls for a structure generally modelled on the Globe, but square: 80 feet by 80 on the outside, and 55 feet each way within. The stage projecting into the yard was 43 feet wide. The Fortune (as the house was called) is the only Elizabethan public theatre for which we have authenticated specifications, and these help us to visualize the dimensions of the Globe. Henslowe and Alleyn supplied their carpenter with a 'plot', or drawing, of the stage and staircases, but this has disappeared. The playhouse, flying the flag of Dame Fortune, opened in the autumn of 1600, and remained a fixture of Finsbury for two decades.

The men who built the Globe had formed a syndicate. Jointly they bore the expense of leasing the site, and of putting up and operating the playhouse. Together they shared in the profits that accrued to them from their investment. The original agreement drawn up by the solicitors and formally signed on 21 February 1599 was a 'tripartite lease', the three parties being Nicholas Brend, the Burbage brothers, and five members of the Chamberlain's troupe: William Shakespeare, John Heminges, Augustine Phillips, Thomas Pope, and William Kempe. Of these players only Shakespeare was a playwright as well. His four partners all excelled in their quality. Most famous was Kempe, who inherited Tarlton's mantle; he played Peter in *Romeo and Juliet* and Dogberry in *Much Ado About Nothing*, and enthralled London by his exuberant feat of dancing the morris to Norwich. These five Chamberlain's men held half of Brend's lease, the other half belonging to the Burbages. With the co-operation of two nominal trustees—the Lancashire-bred goldsmith Thomas Savage and Merchant-Adventurer William Leveson (also churchwarden of St. Mary's, Aldermanbury)—the actors now converted their joint tenancy into a tenancy in common, which made separate estates of their shares; otherwise their rights would pass in survivorship. (The legal considerations are these: when a participant in a joint-tenancy scheme dies, his share goes to his associates rather than descending to his heirs, the last joint-tenant becoming sole possessor; in a tenancy in common, the shares devolve upon the heirs of the individual partners.) Shakespeare thus held one fifth of a moiety, or half-interest, in the Globe enterprise; ten per cent of the whole. The value of a share fluctuated as the original

23. John Ward on Shakespeare's spending, 1661-3.

shareholders decreased or augmented their number. Kempe withdrew by 1602, making Shakespeare's holding one eighth of the total. But the latter's interest fell to a twelfth when Condell and Sly became shareholders, *c.* 1605-8; one fourteenth after the incorporation of William Ostler in 1612. When Shakespeare's company began, around 1609, to use the Blackfriars as their winter playhouse, he had (as we shall see) a stake in that operation too. These facts are known because Heminges and Condell set them forth when they testified as defendants in a suit brought in the Court of Requests three years after Shakespeare's death.[43]

Attempts to calculate the poet's earnings have produced widely divergent figures. The earliest report derives from the mythos: a diary entry made sometime between 1661 and 1663 by the Revd. John Ward, who was vicar of Stratford in the days when Shakespeare's daughter Judith still lived. For supplying the stage with two plays a year, Ward notes, the dramatist had 'an allowance so large' that 'he spent at the rate of a 1000*l.* a year, as I have heard'.[44] The amount is extraordinary, and Ward does not claim for it more than the status of rumour: 'as I have heard'.

But how much *did* Shakespeare earn? Malone estimated about £200 a year from the theatre. In our own century Sir Sidney Lee concluded, on the basis of elaborate computations, that 'Shakespeare, during fourteen or fifteen years of the later period of his life, must have been earning at the theatre a sum well exceeding 700*l.* a year in money of the time'.[45] Sir Edmund Chambers disagrees; Shakespeare's professional income, he estimates, came to roughly a third as much. That would seem closer to the mark. Of course a sharer's proceeds fluctuated, depending upon the size of his holding, and the house's takings. A plague season would be ruinous. An average annual return of £200 was excellent by Elizabethan standards—ten times what a well-paid schoolmaster could hope for. In his excellent *Shakespeare: His World and his Work*, M. M. Reese assumes that at some time, presumably during retirement, Shakespeare sold his theatrical interests for 'a substantial capital sum'.[46] Quite possibly; but we do not actually know whether he disposed of his shares or held on to them until the end. Eventually they passed to the families of Heminges and Condell. These shares commanded substantial sums on the open market. In 1634, when the Blackfriars was the principal house of Shakespeare's company, one Blackfriars and two Globe shares went for £350.

The profits made by the Chamberlain's men after they settled in at the Globe were the rewards for golden achievement; the company dominated the theatrical scene. Ward was right in putting Shakespeare's production at two pieces a year. That was, of course, on average. Chronology blurs at the edges, but between 1598 and 1601 he seems to have composed *Henry V*, *Much Ado About Nothing*, *Julius Caesar*, *As You Like It*, *Twelfth Night*, and *Hamlet*. The Chamberlain's servants twice played at Court during the Christmas season in 1598-9; twice also in 1599-1600 and 1600-1, and three times in 1601-2. Which plays the records fail to show—the troupe acted favourites from their repertoire as well as new pieces. Sometimes their patron laid on a special performance at Hunsdon House in the Blackfriars precinct as part of the entertainment for a visiting dignitary. 'All this week the Lords have been in London, and passed away the time in feasting and plays', Rowland Whyte reported in a letter to Sir Robert Sidney on 8 March 1600, 'for Vereiken* dined upon

* Lodovick Vereiken (or Verreyken), secretary of Albert, Cardinal Archduke of Austria, and Isabel Clara Eugenia, Infanta of Spain. Vereiken had lately arrived in England on a delicate mission 'to revive the ancient league between England and Burgundy', Albert being Duke of Burgundy. The play performed for the secretary's delectation was likely enough 1 *Henry IV*.

Wednesday, with my Lord Treasurer, who made him a royal dinner; upon Thursday my Lord Chamberlain feasted him, and made him very great, and a delicate dinner, and there in the afternoon his players acted, before Vereiken, *Sir John Old Castell*, to his great contentment.'[47] Two years later, on 2 February, John Manningham attended a feast in the Middle Temple. The comedy mounted by the Chamberlain's men that night took his fancy; he made a note in his *Diary*. Much like the *Menaechmi* of Plautus, Manningham observed, and even more like the Italian play called *Inganni*. To make the steward believe, by means of a counterfeit letter, that 'his lady widow' was in love with him, and to tell him how to smile and dress, 'and then when he came to practise making him believe they took him to be mad'—that was a 'good practice'. There was laughter in the Middle Temple that night of *Twelfth Night*.[48]

Most dramatists for the popular stage at some time or other wrote in collaboration. The amiable Dekker, who (in Lamb's phrase) had poetry enough for anything, shared his poetry with Middleton and Webster, and later with Ford; Heywood boasted that he had had 'either an entire hand, or at the least a main finger' in 220 plays. Even the imperious Jonson joined forces with Chapman and Marston on *Eastward Ho*, which caused an uproar and almost

24. John Manningham sees *Twelfth Night*, 2 February 1602.

cost him his ears. Shakespeare was unusual in holding aloof from joint authorship, at least until towards the end of his play-writing career, when he seems to have worked together with the young dramatist who would succeed him as the 'ordinary poet' of the company. Being a shareholder helped him to keep his independence. On one occasion, however—so the evidence indicates—he was called upon to doctor a play written by other hands, for which company is uncertain.

That play survives, in damaged and chaotic shape, in a manuscript with the title 'The Book of Sir Thomas Moore'. In its original form a fair copy by Anthony Munday, the playbook had been submitted by the company to Sir Edmund Tilney, the Master of the Revels, who exercised the prerogatives of censorship. Subsequently the manuscript underwent extensive alteration, with passages marked for deletion, and scenes removed or inserted. The text contains additions in no fewer than five hands. If Shakespeare made any of these revisions, they would hold extraordinary interest as the only extant specimen of dramatic manuscript in his hand. A number of authorities in fact believe that he wrote the three pages of the Ill May-Day scene of 'Sir Thomas More', the pages of British Library MS. Harley 7368 occupying folios 8 and 9, and labelled as in hand D.

A play on the life of More required extraordinary tact, for, although a great man, and recognized as such, he was a steadfast Catholic who brought on his own martyrdom by refusing to bow to the Tudor monarch who demanded acknowledgement of his supremacy. This critical issue the authors tiptoe gingerly round; we hear of 'articles' to which More cannot in conscience subscribe, but their significance is not explored. Originally this evasive historical drama had been put together by Chettle and the Munday admired by Meres as 'our best plotter'; Dekker had a hand in it too, but whether from the first is not clear. Something went awry. Either the script ran foul of the censor or dissatisfied the company, maybe both. A directive at the beginning of one deleted scene reads, 'This must be new written', but the injunction is not in Tilney's hand, and may reflect playhouse rather than Revels Office intervention. Anyway much of the play was new written. Dekker supplied additions; possibly Heywood too. Finally (if this conjectural reconstruction has merit) the company turned to Shakespeare. He contributed the scene in which More, as sheriff of London, deploys his homely eloquence to pacify the apprentices in their May-Day rebellion against the foreigners in their midst. This attempt by three poets to rescue a sinking play failed. Not until the present century did 'Sir Thomas More' achieve performance.

The Ill May-Day scene parallels a memorable episode in a later play: Menenius Agrippa using his eloquence and cajolery to calm the plebs in Coriolanus's Rome. Actually a broad spectrum of evidence supports the Shakespearian attribution. Palaeographers, most notably Sir Edward Maunde Thompson, have minutely compared the three pages in hand D with the six authenticated Shakespeare signatures, and concluded that in every instance the same penman wielded the quill. Thompson's most interesting exhibit is the unusual spurred *a* found in one of the signatures, and most closely approximated in the word *that* at line 105.* In both *a*'s 'the pen, descending in a deep curve from the overhead arch, is carried to the left into the horizontal spur and then to the right *horizontally* till it ascends to form the second minim'.[49] Palaeographical confidence is qualified, however, by the fact that the sampling of Shakespeare's hand is so small, and most of what we have abnormal because of illness (a dying man signed the will) or the cramping confines of conveyancing seals. Spelling affords another kind of evidence. At line 50 *scilens*, for *silence*, is most unusual, but also appears eight times in the speech prefixes for Justice Silence in the Quarto of *2 Henry IV*. For the comfort of modern readers, editors have regularized away such orthographic idiosyncrasies, behind which almost certainly lies the author's original draft or foul papers.

Most striking, though, are the likenesses of style and thought. The dark forebodings of chaos, the commitment to the values of an ordered, hierarchic society, the complexly ambivalent attitudes towards the mob—these strike a familiar note. More's metaphorical identification of the rioters with a surging flood recalls the 'bounded waters' lifting 'their bosoms higher than the shores' in *Troilus and Cressida*; his apocalyptic vision of the consequences of rebellious in-

---

* In the facsimile (illustration 25), l. 10 from the top.

25. 'Ill May-Day': Addition IIc, 'Sir Thomas More'.

solence—his prophecy of a time when 'men, like ravenous fishes, / Would feed on one another'—brings to mind the universal wolf devouring himself in Ulysses's touchstone speech on degree. The specific image comparing devouring men to the devouring fishes is, to be sure, a commonplace traceable back to the Church Fathers; but the concatenation of parallel figures and ideas is nevertheless impressive.[50] The cumulative evidence for Shakespeare's hand in the 'More' fragment may not be sufficient to sweep away all doubts—but who else in this period formed an *a* with a horizontal spur, spelt *silence* as *scilens*, and had identical associative patterns of thought and image? All roads converge on Shakespeare.*

When he turned to 'Sir Thomas More', if he did turn, presents another problem. Munday, Chettle, and Dekker were not Chamberlain's men, but in fee to Henslowe. Some think the revision took place in 1593, when the Lord Strange's men, with Shakespeare possibly one of them, were temporarily amalgamated with the Admiral's company. The palaeographical evidence, it must be granted, favours such dating. But, in the view of others, stylistic considerations point to a later date for the Ill May-Day scene, 1600 or early 1601. In the summer of 1600 the Admiral's men, biding their time until their new playhouse the Fortune opened, went on tour, and Henslowe for a while made few diary entries of payments to his chronically indigent playwrights. What more natural than that they should, for the nonce, offer their wares to the rival Chamberlain's men? If 'Sir Thomas More' was written then—and this is only speculation—its theme of rebellion and execution would assume an ominous topical significance.

For on 8 February 1601 the charismatic but unstable Earl of Essex, once the Queen's darling, made his bid for supreme power. With his fellow conspirators he marched on the Court, but finding the way barred, marched back through the city in a desperate bid to enlist the support of the populace. But the people held prudently aloof, and the Earl barricaded himself in Essex House, then surrendered. The prime movers of the insurrection were executed in

---

* Scholarly opinion now also favours ascription to Shakespeare of a shorter addition, a twenty-one-line speech by More, which is, however, in the hand of a professional playhouse scribe.

February and March of 1601. 'God for his pity help these troublous times', beseeches a sheriff of London in 'Sir Thomas More' after the collapse of the May-Day insurrection:

> The streets stopped up with gazing multitudes.
> Command our armed officers with halberds
> Make way for entrance of the prisoners.
> Let proclamation once again be made,
> That every householder, on pain of death,
> Keep in his prentices, and every man,
> Stand with a weapon ready at his door,
> As he will answer to the contrary.[51]

These lines would have special reverberations in the winter of 1601. Somebody in the censor's office or the playhouse marked them for deletion.

Shakespeare's patron and Shakespeare's company played their parts in the February adventure, and both fared better than they might reasonably have hoped. Southampton, still under the Essex spell, had joined in the conspiracy and was tried and condemned to death with his idol. But Southampton moved compassion by virtue of his demeanour and (although no stripling, having turned twenty-seven) his youth. The dowager Countess pleaded piteously with Secretary Cecil for mercy to her miserable son, led astray by bad company. She prevailed, the sentence was commuted, and Southampton spent the remaining years of Elizabeth's reign incarcerated in the Tower, where he had his books, a room with a view, and a black and white cat which (legend holds) joined him by climbing down the chimney. As for the Chamberlain's men, money—not allegiance—enticed them into the web. One of the plotters, Sir Gelly Meyrick, seduced them with a bonus of 40s. beyond 'their ordinary' to perform the afternoon before the *putsch*, against their better judgements, a stale play depicting the deposition and murder of a king. *Richard II*, Shakespeare's friend and fellow Augustine Phillips testified, was 'so old and so long out of use' that the players felt 'that they should have small or no company at it'. But Meyrick had his way—'So earnest he was to satisfy his eyes with the sight of that tragedy which he thought soon after his lord should bring from the

stage to the state, but that God turned it upon their own heads.'
Thus wrote the Crown's most effective prosecutor, Francis Bacon, in
his *Declaration of the Practises and Treasons* of the Earl of Essex.
At Tyburn, Meyrick suffered the hangman's noose 'with a most un-
daunted resolution'. On the eve of Essex's execution, 24 February,
the Chamberlain's men amused the Queen with a play—the title is
not recorded—at Court. So they suffered not at all. 'How this happened history does not tell us', Dover Wilson speculates, 'but if the
Lord Chamberlain was a sensible man, a few words of explanation
from the author of the play [i.e. *Richard II*] as to its exact tenour
and purport should have placed matters in a proper light.'[52] This
is perhaps to overestimate the importance of playwrights in the
Elizabethan scheme of things.

Forgiveness did not erase bitter memories. Summer came. In her
Privy Chamber at East Greenwich, in the presence of the Keeper
of the Records of the Tower, William Lambarde, 'her Majesty fell
upon the reign of King Richard II, saying, "I am Richard II, know
ye not that? . . . He that will forget God, will also forget his benefactors; this tragedy was played 40 times in open streets and
houses." '[53] Some believe that the fall of Essex, the meteor Shakespeare had saluted in *Henry V*, left an enduring imprint on the
poet's imagination. Did he, in the enigmatic Prince of Denmark, set
up for spectators in the Globe Theatre a mirror of the inmost part
of the enigmatic Earl who was 'th'observ'd of all observers' and (to
his followers) 'th'expectancy and rose of the fair state'?[54] However
that may be, and it is probably no more than romance, few will
doubt that with *Hamlet*, written while the old Queen still ruled, we
have intimations of a new mood. The Jacobean Shakespeare is in
the wings.

[13]

A Gentleman of Means

If Shakespeare was indifferent to the ultimate fate of the plays that immortalized him, he showed no similar nonchalance about assembling and passing down intact his estate. As early as 1737 Alexander Pope made the point in the elegant couplets of *The First Epistle of the Second Book of Horace*:

> Shakespear, (whom you and ev'ry Play-house bill
> Style the divine, the matchless, what you will)
> For gain, not glory, wing'd his roving flight,
> And grew Immortal in his own despight.[1]

'Habits of business are not incompatible with the possession of the highest genius', observed the most indefatigable nineteenth-century student of the Shakespeare records, J. O. Halliwell (later Halliwell-Phillipps), and he concluded: 'No doubt . . . can exist in the mind of any impartial critic, that the great dramatist most carefully attended to his worldly interests; and confirmations of this opinion may be produced from numerous early sources.'[2] What Halliwell says with the complacent assurance of Victorian philistinism is in fact true, and Shakespeare's non-theatrical activities—more especially his pursuit of means and dignities—supply the principal burden of this chapter.

By the mid-nineties Shakespeare was a householder in London; so the Subsidy Rolls and other accounts in the Exchequer office reveal.[3] From time to time Parliament granted subsidies to the Crown, in fixed amounts, on land and personal property. The last of three such subsidies voted in 1593 was at the rate of 2s.8d. in the pound on the value of goods, and collectable in two instalments; the first at 1s. 8d. in the pound, the second at 1s. The modesty of the assessment failed to discourage evasion. Local commissioners, served by Petty Collectors, had the responsibility for rounding up the taxes. They reported defaulters to the Exchequer, which in turn instructed the sheriffs of the counties to recover the arrears and answer for them at the annual inspection of their accounts. On 15 November 1597 the Petty Collectors for Bishopsgate ward swore that certain persons, whose names followed, had either died, vacated the ward, or avoided payment. The list for St. Helen's parish, which had seventy-three rateable residents, includes the name of William Shackspere, assessed 5s. on goods valued at £5 (the property of the most prosperous inhabitant of the parish, 'Sir John Spencer, knight, a commissioner', was valued at £300). The assessment, made in October 1596, had fallen due the following February.

Shakespeare's ward straddled Bishopsgate Street, the main thoroughfare leading from London Bridge, past Moorfields and Finsbury Fields, to the Theatre and Curtain in windswept Holywell. A cosmopolitan, mostly upper-middle-class neighbourhood, Bishopsgate boasted 'divers fair inns, large for receipt of travellers' (the Bull, the Angel, and, outside the gate, the Dolphin were especially notable), as well as some fine houses. On the right-hand side of the newly constructed conduit, which supplied the district with fresh water, stood Crosby Place, handsomely built of stone and timber. There, where Richard Crookback had once lodged, the Lord Mayor held court. Another mansion celebrated the worldly achievement of Sir Thomas Gresham; this house would shortly become a school for

26. Shakespeare a tax defaulter in Bishopsgate ward, 15 November 1597.

London merchants. Bishopsgate had pockets of squalor too. In Petty France, on the bank of the Town Ditch, the French community crowded into tenements, and polluted the ditch, here running into a narrow channel, 'with unsavoury things'. Bethlehem Hospital, popularly known as Bedlam, housed the lunatics who provided Sunday diversion for amusement seekers. Within the parish church of St. Helen's, its Gothic spire dominating the scene, Gresham and other distinguished parishioners had their tombs and monuments. Shakespeare presumably worshipped in St. Helen's on Sundays. During the week he could easily get to the playhouse on foot.[4]

Whether he ever paid his 5s. tax is not known. When the Parliament of 1597 voted a new subsidy, Shakespeare was again assessed, on 1 October 1598, this time 13s.4d. on goods valued at £5. Although the assessment had gone up, the rate remained the same, for this subsidy was collected in one instalment. Once more the due date passed, and the Petty Collectors—Thomas Symons, skinner, and the engagingly named Ferdinando Clutterbook, a draper—reported the delinquent. The abbreviation *Affid*, for *Affidavit*, written in the left-hand margin alongside Shakespeare's name, means that the collectors certified he had not paid his tax. They next list him, in copies of accounts prepared for the Exchequer, with persons who do not answer because they have no goods, chattels, lands, or tenements in the district. These delinquents, Shakespeare among them, were entered by the Exchequer in the residuum, or back-tax, accounts for London. The marginal note *Surrey*, and the reference to 'Residuum Sussex', added later, signify that Shakespeare had migrated across the river to the Surrey Bankside. (At that time Surrey and Sussex managed with one sheriff between them.)

In the last Exchequer notice of Shakespeare, dated 6 October 1600, the tax bill of 13s.4d. is still outstanding. The notation *Episcopo Wintonensi* in the left-hand margin indicates that the Court of Exchequer had referred the dramatist's arrears to the Bishop of Winchester, whose liberty of the Clink in Surrey lay outside the sheriff's jurisdiction. The natural inference is that Shakespeare now lived in the Clink, although it is a curious fact that his name has not been traced in any of the annual lists of residents of the Clink parish (St. Saviour's) compiled by the officers who made the rounds to collect tokens purchased by churchgoers for Easter Communion, which was compulsory.[5] In his accounts for 1600-1 the Bishop reported, without naming names, a sum collected from the rate-payers referred to him. It has been assumed that the amount includes Shakespeare's 13s.4d.

If he found his way onto any other subsidy rolls, these have not come to light. In 1796, however, Edmond Malone mentioned documents with information about Shakespeare's London residences:

> From a paper now before me, which formerly belonged to Edward Alleyn, the player, our poet appears to have lived in Southwark, near the Bear-Garden, in 1596. Another curious document in my possession, which will be produced in the History of his Life, affords the strongest presumptive evidence that he continued to reside in Southwark to the year 1608. . . .[6]

Malone never alludes to these curious papers anywhere else, and they have since vanished without trace; but it is (as we shall see) unlikely that Shakespeare was still in Southwark as late as 1608.[7]

To sum up: Shakespeare was living in St. Helen's parish, Bishopsgate, at some date before October 1596; perhaps as early as the winter of 1596-7, but certainly no later than 1599, he had taken up residence in the Liberty of the Clink in Southwark. In other words Shakespeare crossed the river around the time that his company did. So we would have guessed had we no records at all; but the documents, so laboriously sought and studied, do provide certainty in place of plausible assumption, and yield more precise addresses for Shakespeare in the nineties.

London addresses. In the great metropolis, which catered for every taste and aspiration, he ordered his life according to his professional needs, with first the Theatre and afterwards the Globe as the fixed foot of his compass; but he maintained and over the years strengthened his ties with his native Stratford, where he had left behind a wife and three children. If they ever visited him in St. Helen's parish or the Clink, no record shows it. In Stratford his daughters married and bore offspring, and in Stratford they were laid to rest, as were their parents, in Holy Trinity Church or the churchyard divided by the avenue of lime trees. 'He was wont to go to his native

27. Hamnet Shakespeare buried, 11 August 1596.

country once a year,' Aubrey noted for his Brief Life. It is reasonable to suppose that Shakespeare was there on 11 August 1596, when the parish register records the burial of his son Hamnet, aged eleven and a half. His death doomed the male line of the Shakespeares to extinction.

On occasion, according to the mythos, Shakespeare found solace at the sign of the bush in Oxford, where he would break the journey between London and Stratford. This wine-house was called the Taverne, rechristened the Crown half a century after the poet's death; an unpretentious two-storey house with twin gables, fronting on the Cornmarket, just a few yards from the High Street, and convenient to the main highway running to Warwickshire and the north. The landlord, John Davenant, was a melancholy sort, never seen to laugh; yet his fellow townsmen so well esteemed him that in 1621 they made him the mayor of Oxford. He had a wife and seven children, of whom one, Robert, remembered years later (when he had become a parson) being showered with a hundred kisses by the acclaimed playwright from London. The vintner's wife was reputedly very beautiful, 'and of a very good wit and of conversation extremely agreeable'. She had less discretion than her husband, though, if there is truth to the salacious gossip that began making the rounds late in the seventeenth century. This held that Mistress Davenant shared her bed with the poet who had extricated himself from the meshes of the Dark Lady.

Ordinarily a wine-shop offered neither lodging nor stabling, but these amenities were available at the Cross Inn bounding the Taverne on the north, with which it shared a common courtyard. Of course an overnight guest could at a pinch sleep upstairs at the Taverne. There a fire roared in winter in the huge brick hearth; an interlacing pattern of vines and flowers adorned the walls, and along the top a painted frieze exhorted the pious to 'Fear God above all thing'. When these decorations came to light in 1927, a newspaper described the Painted Chamber as 'the room in which Shakespeare slept'.[8] Did he indeed here take his leave of the landlord's beautiful and witty wife, and proceed refreshed, if not edified, on the road to Stratford, where Anne, eight years his senior, bided his return?

The legend of Shakespeare's liaison with Mistress Davenant originates with her poet son. When merry over his wine with Samuel Butler, the celebrated author of *Hudibras*, and other cronies, Sir William would own to being the literal—as well as the poetical—son of Shakespeare. Perhaps Davenant was jesting, not very tastefully, in his cups; possibly he wished merely to claim membership in the tribe of Will, as others belonged to the tribe of Ben. Aubrey, however, who first reports the story in his Brief Life of Davenant, took it as a profession of illicit paternity, and that is how the age took it. 'That notion of Sir William's being more than a poetical child only of Shakespeare was common in town', Alexander Pope observed to Joseph Spence; 'and Sir William himself seemed fond of having it taken for truth.'[9] In his diary Thomas Hearne, a keeper of the Bodleian Library and knowledgeable local antiquary, recorded the episode as an Oxford tradition. 'Mr. Shakespear was his God-father & gave him his Name', Hearne notes, then adds in a parenthesis: 'In all probability he got him.'[10]

That was in 1709. More than thirty years later, at a dinner party given by the Earl of Oxford, Pope—who would not have known Hearne's diary—regaled the guests with the same anecdote. William Oldys, present that night, made a note of the conversation:

If tradition may be trusted, Shakespeare often baited at the Crown Inn or Tavern in Oxford, in his journey to and from London. The landlady was a woman of great beauty and sprightly wit; and her husband, Mr. John Davenant, (afterwards mayor of that city) a grave melancholy man, who as well as his wife used much to delight in Shakespeare's pleasant company. Their son young Will Davenant (afterwards Sir William) was then a little school-boy in the town, of about seven or eight years old, and so fond also of Shakespeare, that whenever he heard of his arrival, he would fly from school to see him. One day an old townsman observing the boy running homeward almost out of breath, asked him whither he was posting in that heat and hurry. He answered, to see his *god*-father Shakespeare. There's a good boy, said the other, but have a care that you don't take *God's* name in vain. This story Mr. Pope told me at the Earl of Oxford's table, upon occasion of some discourse which arose about Shakespeare's monument then newly erected in Westminster Abbey; and he quoted Mr. Betterton the player for his authority. I answered that I thought such a story might have enriched the variety of those choice fruits of observation he has presented us in his preface to the edition he had published of our poet's works. He replied—"There might be in the garden of mankind such plants as would seem to pride themselves more in a regular production of their own native fruits, than in having the repute of bearing a richer kind of grafting; and this was the reason he omitted it."[11]

When Pope repeated the story to Spence a year or so later, in 1742-3, the schoolboy's interlocutor had become 'a head of one of the colleges (who was pretty well acquainted with the affairs of the family)'.[12] A pleasant jest, and one that evidently could bear repetition; but it does not originate in the Davenant-Shakespeare context. As the learned Oldys recalled, John Taylor the Water Poet had included the anecdote in his *Wit and Mirth* in 1629.[13] In that version the godfather is not Will Shakespeare but goodman Digland the Gardener. For what it is worth, an Oxford connection remains, for (Oldys reports) Taylor picked up other jests for his collection there.

The story filtered into print. In 1698 Gildon coyly intimated, in *The Lives and Characters of the English Dramatick Poets*, that Shakespeare on his numerous journeys into Warwickshire had much frequented the Davenant tavern, 'whether for the beautiful mistress of the house, or the good wine, I shall not determine'.[14] A half century later the former prompter of Drury Lane, William Rufus Chetwood, of whom Chambers observed, not unjustly, that 'his ignorance is certain and his *bona fides* improbable', was more direct. 'Sir *William Davenant*', Chetwood tersely reports, 'was, by many, supposed the natural Son of *Shakespear*.' He scrutinized the frontispiece portrait of Davenant in the 1673 folio of his *Works* for resemblances to

Shakespeare, but found himself handicapped by the fact that Davenant had lost his nose as the result of mercury treatment for the pox. 'The Features', Chetwood concluded, 'seem to resemble the open Countenance of *Shakespear,* but'—and with this part of the verdict it is difficult to quarrel—'the want of a Nose gives an odd Cast to the Face.'[15]

Once broadcast, the piquant tale was endlessly repeated. Sir Walter Scott found a place for it in *Woodstock.* 'Out upon the hound!' Colonel Everard explodes when told of Davenant's boast; 'would he purchase the reputation of descending from poet, or from prince, at the expense of his mother's good fame?—his nose ought to be slit.' The colonel is reminded that such an operation would prove difficult.

A wise child knows his own father, but Davenant showed small wisdom in his eager efforts to legitimatize the offspring of his muse by proclaiming the dubiety of his own origins. Still, even if his revelation bears all the earmarks of questionably self-serving invention, it seems likely enough that Shakespeare knew the Taverne and the Cross Inn in Oxford, and that he was there (in Aubrey's phrase) 'exceedingly respected'. Not only as an admired writer. After 1596 Shakespeare could command the respect due to a gentleman.

It will be recalled that his father had made a preliminary approach to the Heralds' College, probably at some time after he became bailiff of Stratford in 1568, but then, as troubles closed in on him, let the matter drop. The heralds commanded heavy fees when the Shakespeares, beset by creditors, could ill afford them. Then, in 1596, John Shakespeare renewed his application—or, more likely, his son did so in his father's name. John was in his sixties, an old man for those days, and he would think twice before making the long and tiring journey by horse to London. On the other hand, William was there on the spot. If he started from scratch with a new application in his own name while his father still lived, the College of Arms would have regarded such a course as irregular: it was proper that the grant be made to the oldest male in the direct line, and to the member of the family who enjoyed the more dignified social position (former bailiffs rated higher than playwrights).[16] There was nothing, however, to prevent the eldest son from setting into motion the machinery for a grant in which the entire family would take pride.

Preserved at the College are two rough drafts of a document, dated 20 October 1596 and prepared by Sir William Dethick, Garter King-of-Arms, granting the request of John Shakespeare for a coat of arms. A note at the foot of one of these drafts describes 'This John' as having received a 'pattern' on paper 'under Clarent Cook's hand . . . xx years past'. That is how we know of the earlier application. The twenty years alluded to, carrying us back to 1576, may be taken as approximate. A 'pattern' was a trick, or pen-and-ink sketch, of a coat of arms. Robert Cook, then Clarenceux King-of-Arms, would for a fee have drawn it on paper, reserving parchment for the approved design. That stage was never reached when John first applied.

These heraldic documents often yield interesting genealogical details, but the 1596 draft grant is not in this respect especially communicative. Garter states that he has been 'by credible report informed'—this is sufficiently vague—that the petitioner's 'parents and late antecessors' had been rewarded for valiant service by King Henry VII of famous memory, and that 'the said John hath married the daughter and one of the heirs of Robert Arden of Wilmcote in the said county, esquire'.[17] (In this second draft Dethick has inserted 'Grandfather' above 'antecessors', and 'esquire' replaces 'gent.'.) That is all; references to past service and John's marriage. Four soldiers surnamed Shakespeare are known to have held the rank of archers a half-century after the battle of Bosworth Field, but Garter's haziness has led some to wonder whether he is not implying, with heraldic courtesy, that the earlier Shakespeares were socially acceptable but undistinguished as the College of Arms measured distinction. However, the note appended to the document furnishes a few supporting facts about the applicant himself—that 'xv or xvi years past' (a mistake for xxv and xxvi?) he was a justice of the peace and bailiff, and a Queen's officer; that he had 'lands and tenements of good wealth, and substance', worth £500; and that he had taken for his wife the daughter of a gentleman of worship. John Shakespeare was indeed the Queen's officer, for as bailiff he held the fortnightly Court of Record—a Crown court—and as coroner, almoner, and the like, also represented the Crown.

In consideration of these claims of honour, the Garter King-of-Arms declares that he has assigned and confirmed this shield: 'Gold, on a bend sables, a spear of the first steeled argent, and for his crest or cognizance a falcon, his wings displayed argent, standing on a wreath of his colours, supporting a spear gold, steeled as aforesaid, set upon a helmet with mantles and tassels as hath been accustomed and doth more plainly appear depicted on this margent.' In the upper left-hand corner of both drafts appears, as Garter indicates, a rough sketch of the trick of arms. At a time when heraldry tended towards fussiness and over-elaboration, the Shakespeare arms have a classic simplicity.[18]

Above the shield and crest the clerk has written 'non, sanz droict'. The phrase gave him trouble. He scored it through, then repeated it, above, with initial capitals: 'Non, Sanz Droict'. At the head of the document he had a third go, this time putting the words in capitals and omitting the comma: 'NON SANZ DROICT'. Could the phrase conceivably signify an endorsement of heraldic correctness? Probably not—more likely it represents a motto, 'the invention or conceit of the bearer' (as one contemporary remarks), which required no *imprimatur* from the heralds. 'Non sanz droict'—*Not without right*—makes better sense than 'Non, Sanz Droict'—*No, without right*. In his *Poetaster* Jonson sneers at common players who aspire to heraldic distinctions—'They forget they are i' the statute, the rascals; they are blazoned there, there they are tricked, they and their pedigrees: they need no other heralds, iwis'—and some have seen mockery of Shakespeare's motto in *Every Man out of his Humour*, in which the rustic clown Sogliardo, fresh from having laid out £30 for his arms, is mocked with the 'word', *Not without mustard*. The parallel is suggestive, but Sogliardo is not an actor, and his coat-armour, which flaunts a boar's head, is unlike Shakespeare's. If the latter did choose 'Non sanz droict' as his motto, neither he nor his descendants seem ever to have used it. No motto appears above the arms displayed in relief on the Shakespeare monument in Stratford church, nor was the phrase included on the gravestone of his daughter Susanna.

A fair copy of the draft of 1596 has never come to light, and John Shakespeare was still described as a yeoman in January 1597, when he sold a strip of land to George Badger; but there is no reason to doubt (with Sir Sidney Lee) that the grant was executed. Did he find that new honours, 'Like our strange garments, cleave not to their mould / But with the aid of use'? Three years later John again applied to the heralds. This time they are a little more specific about the petitioner: they speak of John as a Queen's officer and bailiff of Stratford, and describe his ancestor as having been 'advanced and rewarded with lands and tenements given to him in those parts of Warwickshire where they have continued by some descents in good reputation and credit'. The document confirms and exemplifies the Shakespeare arms—hence Lee's misgivings—but the applicant's real purpose was to obtain allowance to combine his arms with those of his wife's family. The grant authorizes the Shakespeares to divide their shield vertically, with the Shakespeare bearings on the dexter half, and the Arden on the sinister. (Helena, in *A Midsummer-Night's Dream*, describes her closeness to Hermia as 'an union in partition . . . with two seeming bodies, but one heart . . . like coats in heraldry, / Due but to one, and crowned with one crest'.) But the heralds worried about the Ardens of Wilmcote (misspelt *Wellingcote* by the clerk). Did they trace their descent from the prestigious Ardens of Park Hall in Warwickshire? That would entitle them to 'Ermine, a fess checky gold and azure', a coat derived from the "Newburgh" earls of Warwick.* At first the heralds opted for this device, and sketched it impaled with the Shakespeare arms, then changed their minds, scratched it out, and alongside drew a differentiated form of the ancient Arden coat, 'Gules, three cross-crosslets fitchées gold, and on a gold chief a martlet gules.'† Evidently they felt, on second thought, that the Wilmcote Ardens rated only the less illustrious old coat. The latter, it has recently been suggested, may indicate a connection with the Cheshire and Staffordshire Ardens.[19] In the end the Shakespeares decided not to impale their arms.

A few years later their honours contributed to a heraldic tempest in a teacup. In the restricted and self-contained society of the College of Arms quarrels and rivalries flourished. These the personality

---

* *Fess*: in heraldry, a broad horizontal band drawn across the centre of a shield.
† *Fitchées*: in heraldry, pointed at the lower extremity; applied to crosses.

*Shakespear y' Player
by Garter*

28. The York Herald's complaint, 1602.

of Sir William Dethick abetted. The greedy and despotic Garter King-of-Arms was easily vexed. Once he had struck his own father with his fist; he stabbed his brother with a dagger, and raised eyebrows at the funeral of Sir Henry Sidney by assaulting the minister in the church. In the Heralds' College he berated, reviled, and sometimes beat his colleagues. Such a man makes enemies, and in the person of the less violent but no less contentious York Herald, Ralph Brooke, *alias* Brokesmouth, he found almost—but not quite—his match. In 1602 Brooke accused Dethick of elevating base persons, and assigning devices already in use. (Earlier in his career Sir William had aroused criticism for granting the royal arms of England, slightly differenced, to a plasterer named Daukins.) Brooke drew up a list of twenty-three cases where, he alleged, Dethick and his associate Camden, Clarenceux King-of-Arms, had abused their authority. Shakespeare's name appears fourth on the list. Elsewhere, beneath a rough sketch of the familiar arms, Brooke has written,

'Shakespear the Player, by Garter'. The appellation *player* is no doubt pejoratively intended.

Apparently the York Herald compiled these notes in preparation for a formal hearing by the commissioners for the Office of Earl Marshal. The particulars of Brooke's complaint are not recorded, but may be inferred from the joint reply of Garter and Clarenceux. They defended the eligibility of John Shakespeare—a magistrate 'of good substance and habileté' who had married an heir of Arden—and insisted that the device prepared for him did not infringe upon the arms of Lord Mauley, *Gold, a bend sable:* 'the spear on the bend', after all, was 'a patible [i.e. acceptable] difference'. Other families displayed a black bend with gold on their shields, for example (as Dethick and Camden pointed out), the Harleys and Ferrers. So too did Shakespeare's Stratford neighbours the Quineys, whose arms sealed the only surviving letter to the poet. Anyway some devices were bound to resemble one another, so many had been conferred. Dethick, for all his faults, knew his business. The charges came to nothing.

In 1597 Shakespeare bought a fine house for himself and his family. This was New Place, built by Stratford's greatest benefactor, Sir Hugh Clopton, at the corner of Chapel Street and Chapel Lane (otherwise known as Walker's Street or Dead Lane). It had a chequered history. Across the road stood the chapel re-edified by Sir Hugh, where priests chanted prayers for the repose of his soul, but, despite these spiritually satisfying environs, the Cloptons do not seem to have used New Place much. Sir Hugh died in London, and his heirs preferred to live at Clopton Manor, two miles distant from Stratford, and on the edge of the Welcombe Hills. Around 1540 (it will be recalled) New Place sufficiently impressed the King's antiquary for him to make a note of the 'pretty house of brick and timber'. A Quiney had been dwelling there in 1532. Towards mid-century the mansion found a distinguished tenant when Dr. Thomas Bentley, the King's physician and former president of the College of Physicians, leased it from a Clopton. But when Bentley died in 1549, his landlord complained in Chancery that the doctor had 'left the said manor place in great ruin and decay and unrepaired'.[20] In 1563 another Clopton, pressed for cash, gave up the title of New Place to William Bott, whom the next year he accused of defrauding him of rents, and forging a deed related to Clopton lands.

A sometime undersheriff, and formerly of Snitterfield, this Bott in 1564 took his seat on the aldermanic council (apparently without prior service as a principal burgess), and the next year was ousted for indiscreetly allowing 'that there was never a honest man of the council or the body of the corporation of Stratford'. Others besides the council and William Clopton complained about Bott—a false harlot and a false villain, as Roland Wheler told him to his face at the Swan. His own son-in-law, John Harper of Henley-in-Arden, described Bott as 'void of all honesty and fidelity or fear of God, and openly detected of divers great and notorious crimes, as namely felony, adultery, whoredom, falsehood, and forgery'. Bott had secured a match, in April 1563, between his daughter Isabella and Harper, the latter 'being a plain and a simple person', and then a minor; he had also by 'policy' assured the Botts of Harper's inherited lands should Isabella die without issue. The next month there followed (if report is true) a lurid crime: murder of kin, by poison, for the estate. Roland Wheler, who now and then performed services for Bott in return for some odd shillings and a cow, provides an eyewitness account of the murder, none the less harrowing for the dry legal phrasing:

> the said Bott having in this wise forged the said deed and so conveyed the said lands, the said Bott's daughter, wife of the said John Harper, did die suddenly and was poisoned with ratsbane, and therewith swelled to death. And this deponent knoweth the same to be true, for that he did see the wife of the said Bott in the presence of the same Bott deliver to the said Harper's wife in a spoon mixed with drink the said poison of ratsbane to drink, which poison she did drink in this deponent's presence, the same William Bott by and at that time leaning to the bed's feet. And this deponent saith that the said William Bott did see this when it was done. And this deponent saith that after the wife of the said William Bott had so given the said drink to the said Harper's wife, the said Harper and this deponent did see her lay a thing under a green carpet. . . .

This 'thing' Harper offered to taste, thinking it brimstone, 'but by the persuasion of this deponent, who suspected it to be ratsbane, he did forbear'. It is curious, assuming the deposition true, that Bott never stood trial for murder, although divers persons knew of the crime; but Wheler deposes that it was hushed up because, were Bott hanged, 'Mr. Clopton and the said John Harper should both lose all their lands, which the said Bott had beguiled them of. . . .' The Stratford parish register records the burial, on 7 May 1563, of 'Isabella, uxor Johannis Harper de Henleyarden'. (Wheler, deposing eight years after the purported event, seems to think the murdered woman's name was Lettice. The latter was Isabella's sister. By then both women were dead.) Bott was residing at New Place before he acquired it that year. The murder may have taken place there.[21]

Four years later Bott sold New Place to an Inner Temple lawyer, William Underhill, who was clerk of assizes at Warwick and a substantial property holder in the county. New Place passed to his son and heir William—described as 'a subtle, covetous, and crafty man'—who sold the house to Shakespeare. The foot of fine—a summary record—of the deed transferring the dwelling to William Shakespeare is dated 4 May 1597, and records the payment to Underhill of £60 in silver (*sexaginta libras sterlingorum*). For Sir Hugh Clopton's Great House, however decayed, the figure may well seem absurdly low; but in fines of this period the consideration mentioned is customarily a legal fiction. We do not know how much Shakespeare actually laid out.

Two months later Underhill died at Fillongley, near Coventry, after orally bequeathing 'all his lands' to his first-born Fulke. In 1599 Fulke, still a minor, was hanged at Warwick for poisoning his father. The law took the forfeit of the Underhill estate for felony, but it was regranted to Fulke's younger brother Hercules when he came of age in 1602. In Michaelmas term of that year, Hercules Underhill confirmed the sale of New Place to Shakespeare, who paid the prescribed fee, equal to one quarter of the yearly value of the property, to clear the title.

The house that he bought was the second largest in Stratford.* It

---

* The most imposing house was the old College, Crown property leased in 1596 to Thomas Combe.

29. George Vertue, sketch of New Place, 1737.

had a frontage of over sixty feet in Chapel Street, a depth (along Chapel Lane) of at least seventy feet in some parts, and a height of over twenty-eight feet at the northern end, which abutted the residence known, since 1674, as Nash House. No fewer than ten fireplaces warmed New Place in winter, and there were probably more rooms than fireplaces, the latter being a taxable luxury.[22] In the eighteenth century George Vertue made two pen-and-ink sketches of Shakespeare's house, as someone, perhaps a descendant of the poet's sister Joan Hart, remembered it. One drawing depicts a handsome big house of three storeys and five gables, with ornamental beams (the timber Leland mentions). The other shows the gate and entrance, the courtyard before New Place, and, on either side of the court, buildings, one being the servants' quarters. In 1767 Richard Grimmitt, a former Stratford shoemaker then in his eighties, recalled having played as a child with a Clopton lad in the Great House called New Place—there was a brick wall, 'with a kind of porch', at the end next to the chapel, and the boys would cross 'a small kind of Green Court before they enter'd yᵉ House which was bearing to yᵉ left, & fronted with brick, with plain windows, Consisting of com-

235

mon panes of Glass set in lead, as at this time'. This testimony supplements Vertue on the position and aspect of the house.

Shakespeare's house stood in ample grounds. In 1565 Bott sued a neighbour for removing twelve pieces of sawed timber from 'le barn yard' near 'le Newe Place garden' in 'Dede Lane'. That garden is first mentioned in the 1563 indenture. The fine of 1597 speaks of a messuage with two barns and two gardens (*uno mesuagio, duobus horreis et duobus gardinis*); the second fine adds two orchards (*duobus pomariis*). The garden must have been fairly small at first, before the addition (when we do not know) of land to the east, in Chapel Lane. This land, on which a cottage once stood, had in former times belonged to the dissolved priory of Pinley, and was afterwards part of the estate of a John Gilbert. The combined gardens, stretching over three-quarters of an acre, came to be known as the Great Garden. A tradition, better than most, holds that Shakespeare planted the mulberry tree that grew in the Great Garden until 1758, when it was cut down and fashioned into more authentic relics than a single mulberry tree—even one with a stock six inches in diameter—might be thought capable of yielding. New Place was also famous for its vines. Fifteen years after the poet's death, Sir Thomas Temple, Baronet, commissioned one of his men, Harry Rose, to ride to Stratford at his first opportunity and gather from the vines of New Place '2 or 3 of the fairest of those buds on some few shoots of the last year's vines'.[23] Sir Thomas's sister-in-law had much commended the vines—they were probably grape-vines. She lived across the road from Shakespeare's house, at the corner of Chapel Street and Scholar's Lane. Her house, with numerous modern improvements and extensions, now welcomes visitors to Stratford as the Falcon Hotel.

Shakespeare moved into New Place before the year was out or, at the latest, early in the new year. We know because, in a survey of corn and malt made on 4 February 1598, he is listed as a resident of Chapel Street ward, in which New Place was situated. The inventory gives his holding as ten quarters (equivalent to eighty bushels), presumably of malt; so other entries in the survey, and final totals, suggest. Three successive wet summers had resulted in shortage of grain, inflated prices, and (inevitably) hoarding. The town fathers responded by limiting the quantity of malt a household could store for their own brewing. (Malting, as previously noted, was Stratford's principal industry.) The Shakespeares' ten quarters represented an average holding. Of their thirteen neighbours in Chapel Street ward, two stored more: Thomas Dyxon and schoolmaster Aspinall. Sir Thomas Lucy of Charlecote, listed as a 'stranger', hoarded the most, sixteen quarters in Richard Dixon's barn, and twelve and a half quarters with Abraham Sturley, of whom we shall be hearing more.

The house described as run down a half-century earlier underwent restoration by its new owner. In his 1733 edition of Shakespeare, Lewis Theobald, who knew Sir Hugh Clopton (a scion of the family that built New Place), reports that Shakespeare had 'repair'd and modell'd it to his own Mind'. The corporation in 1598 paid 'Mr. Shaxspere' ten pence for a load of stone, which it used (fittingly enough) to mend Clopton Bridge. The import of the record is not certain—it might, in the absence of a christian name, conceivably refer to the dramatist's father—but most likely the stone was left over from the repairs executed at New Place.

What did fellow townsmen make of the distinguished playwright of the Chamberlain's company and admired poet of love's languishment who sojourned each year in their midst? They probably troubled their heads little enough about the plays and poems. Business was another matter; they saw Shakespeare as a man shrewd in practical affairs, and approachable (if need be) for a substantial loan on good security. Anyway the Quineys so regarded him. Shortly after William Shakespeare bought his own house in Stratford, Adrian Quiney, John Shakespeare's old neighbour and fellow trades-man, told Abraham Sturley that the master of New Place might have a mind to make some investments. This Sturley hailed from Worcester; he had studied at Queens' College, Cambridge, and after a spell in the service of Sir Thomas Lucy had come to Strat-ford, where he thrived—in 1596-7 he was bailiff. On 24 January 1598 Sturley wrote to Richard Quiney, who was then in London. 'It seemeth by him [Adrian Quiney]', Sturley informed Richard, 'that our countryman Mr. Shaksper is willing to disburse some money upon some odd yardland or other at Shottery or near about us; he thinketh it a very fit pattern to move him to deal in the matter of our tithes.' A purchase of tithes would bring perquisites as well as income. Did his Stratford neighbours guess that Shakespeare, who now signed himself gentleman, was keen to improve his status in other respects? In any event, if they dangled land and tithes before him, he was not ready to bite. Not yet.

October came, and Richard Quiney was again in London, this time to petition the Privy Council for a corporation charter on better terms and for relief from the latest subsidy voted by Parliament. With the bad weather and two devastating fires, Stratford had fallen on hard times; so Quiney had a good case. But he was forced to cool his heels in London for four months. He looked for support from the lord of the manor, Sir Edward Greville, who had promised money 'for prosecuting the cause' (as Sturley put it). Meanwhile, on 25 October, Quiney thought it prudent to get off a letter from his inn, the Bell in Carter Lane, to his 'Loving good friend and countryman Mr. Wm. Shackespere'. In his small, rapid hand, Quiney asked his loving countryman's help with a loan of £30 upon his own security and that of Master Bushell or Master Mytton. 'Mr. Rosswell', on whom he had counted, 'is not come to London as yet and I have especial cause.' Richard Mytton and Peter Roswell were gentlemen in Greville's service. 'You shall friend me much', the letter continues, 'in helping me out of all the debts I owe in London, I thank God, and much quiet my mind, which would not be indebted. I am now towards the Court'—the watermen would ferry him to Richmond—'in hope of answer for the dispatch of my business.' Shakespeare never received this anxious communication, for Quiney took it back with him to Stratford, and when he died in office as bailiff in 1602, after being wounded while trying to calm down a drunken brawl involving Greville's men, the letter found a place among the Quiney papers in the corporation archives.

Why did he not dispatch it? Perhaps Quiney decided to get together personally with Shakespeare; maybe the playwright called on his countryman at the Bell, near St. Paul's. A distinguished biographer of Shakespeare, Joseph Quincy Adams, has concluded: 'By whatever means they met, Shakespeare good-naturedly agreed to secure the money for Quiney, for before the day was over Quiney

30. Richard Quiney's letter to Shakespeare, 25 October 1598.

had written the news to his brother-in-law.'[24] This is to make facts of possibilities. Quiney did indeed write that day; on 4 November Sturley speaks of this communication, importing 'that our countryman Mr. Wm. Shak. would procure us money'—but he comments, 'which I will like of as I shall hear when, where, and how; and, I pray, let not go that occasion if it may sort to any indifferent conditions.'[25] The phrasing does not suggest a mission accomplished. Around the same time, Adrian Quiney advised his son and partner Richard that, if he bargained with Shakespeare or received money from him, he would do well to buy some knit stockings at Evesham for their mercer's shop. This seems to refer to a business deal rather than to the loan. In fact we do not know whether Shakespeare came to Richard Quiney's aid, although he likely enough did. The sequel is happy. Eventually the Queen agreed to relieve 'this town twice afflicted and almost wasted by fire', and the Exchequer reimbursed Quiney for his expenses in London. The Quineys and the Shakespeares continued on cordial terms, Richard's son Thomas marrying Shakespeare's younger daughter, although it was not (as things turned out) a fortunate union.[26]

There were deaths as well as marriages. In March 1601 Thomas Whittington, the Hathaway shepherd, died after drawing up a will in which he remembered the 40s. owed him by the Shakespeares.[27] Sentimental biographers have envisaged Whittington as an archetype of the noble shepherd, rather like the loyal Adam of *As You Like It*, who had helped Anne out with a loan while her husband was preoccupied with play-writing in the indifferent metropolis; but the sum might equally well have represented Whittington's uncollected wages or savings held for safe-keeping. On 8 September 1601 John Shakespeare was buried in the churchyard of Holy Trinity. In the absence of a will the double house in Henley Street would pass to his eldest son William. No doubt Mary Shakespeare stayed on at the family domicile she had known for almost half a century. Some of her children kept her company, grandchildren too—her daughter Joan, married to the hatter Hart, lived there with her growing family. The widow survived another seven years. On 9 September 1608 the Stratford register records the burial of 'Mayry Shaxspere, widow'.

Of how Shakespeare spent his days away from London the records reveal little. They merely chronicle, in dry legalistic fashion, petty disputes over money matters that found their way into court. A man with more than sufficient malt for his domestic brewing sometimes parted with a few bushels on credit, and, when the bill went unpaid, he would resort to litigation. Shakespeare was in this respect no different from others. In the spring of 1604 he (or some-

31. Mary Shakespeare buried, 9 September 1608.

240

one else in his household) sold his neighbour Philip Rogers twenty bushels of malt, and on 25 June lent him 2s. Rogers was an apothecary who (by licence) sold ale as well as drugs and tobacco; we hear of him dispensing his potables in Chapel Street and the High Street, not far from New Place. His whole obligation to Shakespeare came to a little over £2, of which Rogers had returned 6s., leaving a balance of 35s.10d. With William Tetherington as his lawyer, Shakespeare brought Rogers to the Court of Record, which sat fortnightly, the bailiff presiding, and heard cases representing debts not in excess of £30. The plaintiff demanded his 35s.10d., plus 10s. damages. How the court ruled is not known.

It was not the only time the poet sued. A few years later he was back in the same court seeking the recovery of £6, plus damages, from John Addenbrooke. He may have been the Addenbrooke who sold licences for starch in Warwickshire around 1600. The action dragged on for almost a year, from 17 August 1608 until 7 June 1609, leaving a trail of records more numerous than interesting. The court issued a summons which the serjeant served, a jury was empanelled, the defendant was cited to appear, the jury reached a verdict favourable to the plaintiff, the court ordered John Addenbrooke to appear and this time to satisfy William Shackspeare for both debt and damages, and finally, when he failed to come, asked Addenbrooke's surety, Thomas Horneby, to show cause why he should not pay the £6 plus 24s. for costs and damages. Horneby was a blacksmith (as was his father) who kept an ale-house in Henley Street. Whether Shakespeare ever collected is not recorded. His persistence may strike moderns as heartless, but the course Shakespeare followed was normal in an age without credit cards, overdrafts, or collection agencies.[28]

Such vexations were infrequent. Shakespeare must have passed his time mainly with his family or cultivating the gardens of New Place, with their mulberry tree and flourishing vines. Formal records neglect the unsensational events of quotidian life, although the mythos does now and then gratify curiosity with an informal glimpse of the playwright in his provincial setting. George Steevens preserves a tradition, plausible enough, that Shakespeare enjoyed his weekly cup at his local: 'The late Mr. James West, of the Treasury, assured me, that at his house in Warwickshire he had a wooden bench, once the favourite accommodation of Shakspeare, together with an earthen half-pint mug, out of which he was accustomed to take his draughts of ale at a certain publick house in the neighbourhood of Stratford, every Saturday afternoon.'[29] When crossed, he availed himself of the exquisite revenges of art: 'Old Mr. Bowman the player reported from Sir William Bishop', Oldys notes, 'that some part of Sir John Falstaff's character was drawn from a townsman of Stratford, who either faithlessly broke a contract, or spitefully refused to part with some land, for a valuable consideration, adjoining to Shakespeare's, in or near that town.'[30]

The mythos is crueller to John Combe, the wealthiest bachelor—indeed the wealthiest citizen—in Stratford, who reputedly amassed his fortune by exacting his usury at the legally acceptable rate of ten in the hundred. This Combe, the tale went round, served as a butt for Shakespeare's extempore wit. Amongst 'the Gentlemen of the Neighbourhood', Rowe records,

> it is a Story almost still remember'd in that Country, that he had a particular Intimacy with Mr. *Combe*, an old Gentleman noted thereabouts for his Wealth and Usury: It happen'd, that in a pleasant Conversation amongst their common Friends, Mr. *Combe* told *Shakespear* in a laughing manner, that he fancy'd, he intended to write his Epitaph, if he happen'd to out-live him; and since he could not know what might be said of him when he was dead, he desir'd it might be done immediately: Upon which *Shakespear* gave him these four Verses.
>
> > *Ten in the Hundred lies here ingrav'd,*
> > *'Tis a Hundred to Ten, his Soul is not sav'd:*
> > *If any Man ask, Who lies in this Tomb?*
> > *Oh! ho! quoth the Devil, 'tis my* John-a-Combe.
>
> But the Sharpness of the Satyr is said to have stung the Man so severely, that he never forgave it.[31]

Rowe's version brings to a climax a long development. In 1634, while touring in Warwickshire, a Lieutenant Hammond 'of the military company in Norwich' examined the monuments in Stratford

Church, and after pausing, suitably impressed, over the 'neat monument of that famous English poet, Mr. Wm. Shakespeere', turned to another—'one of an old gentleman, a bachelor, Mr. Combe, upon whose name the said poet did merrily fan up some witty and facetious verses, which time would not give us leave to sack up'.[32] (A comb was a measure, equal to four bushels or half a quarter of grain; hence the word-play on fanning up (= winnowing) and sacking up (= collecting).) Hammond did not trouble to set down the verses, but the oversight was remedied (with an unanticipated bonus) by Nicholas Burgh, a Poor Knight of Windsor, who around mid-century included in his commonplace book not only the poet's epitaph on 'John A Combe', the Devil's son, but also Shakespeare's handsome verse amends to the bachelor who made 'the poor his issue'. Aubrey too found a place for anecdote and epitaph in his jottings.

A tradition so variously reported might, at first glance, seem worthy of credit, but the doggerel rhyme itself, so un-Shakespearian in flavour, invites scepticism. Doubts are reinforced by the fact that similar epitaphs, but on an unnamed usurer, had appeared earlier in *The More the Merrier* (1608) by 'H. P.', and also in Camden's *Remains, Concerning Britain* (1614 ed.), among a group of 'conceited, merry, and laughing epitaphs, the most of them composed by Master John Hoskines when he was young'. Later in the century other renderings substituted names—Stanhope, Spencer, or Pearse—for Combe. Among the 'divers select epitaphs and hearse-attending epodes' annexed to his *Remains after Death*, printed in 1618, Richard Brathwait included the familiar verses 'upon one John Combe of Stratford upon Aven, a notable usurer, fastened upon a tomb that he had caused to be built in his lifetime'. No matter that Combe built no tomb in his lifetime; Brathwait has the right usurer. But he neglects to mention Shakespeare. Only later did the oft-repeated epitaph become attached, through the machinery of myth, to a celebrated Stratford name.

The episode had an aftermath much later, in 1740, when Francis Peck, a Leicestershire parson and dilettante antiquary, reported another Shakespearian epitaph on a different Combe:

Every body knows *Shakespeare*'s epitaph for *John a Combe*. And I am told he afterwards wrote another for *Tom a Combe*, alias *Thin-Beard*, brother of the said *John*; & that it was never yet printed. It is as follows.

> 'Thin in *beard*, & thick in purse;
> 'Never man beloved worse:
> 'He went to th' grave with many a curse:
> 'The Devil & He had both one nurse.'

This is very sour. . . .[33]

All that now remained was for the inimitable Jordan to join together the epitaphs for the Combe brothers in a single immensely unreliable anecdote. The episode now shelters under the roof of the Bear:

Mr Combe and the Bard of Stratford were intimately aquainted, the former one day in a tavern [Said to be the sign of the Bear in the Bridge Street in Stratford] said to the other, 'I suppose you will write my Epitaph when I am dead you may as well do it now that I may know What you will say of me when I am gone immediately he replied it shall be this. . . . The company instantly burst into a loud laugh perhaps from the justness of the idea, and the hatred that all men have to the character of a miser and usurer, the violence of the mirth somewhat subsiding they desired to hear what he had to say of Mr Thomas Combe brother of the former gentleman, when he instantly said

> "But thin in beard, tho' thick in purse,
> "He's gone to hell, with many a curse,
> "The Devil and he, suck'd both one nurse,
> "For never man was loved worse.

This brother was remarkable for the thinnes of his Beard and no doubt also for his covetuous disposition, therfore the Poignancy of the sarcasm afforded no small diversion among the convivial meeting; but it is said the severity of the satire made so deep an impression upon the two brothers that they never forgave the Author of their Epitaphs; whether this is true is not now to be known, tho' it is by no means improbable. . . .[34]

But Shakespeare did not nourish a hatred for the Combes, nor did the latter go to the grave with bitterness in their hearts towards their witty tavern companion. John Combe remembered Shakespeare in his will by leaving him £5, and in his own will the poet bequeathed his sword as a keepsake to Combe's nephew and heir Thomas.* Shakespeare (as we shall see) amicably did business with John Combe, and the two men remained friends until the end.

'He hath much land, and fertile . . .', Hamlet says of the contemptible Osric. ' 'Tis a chough; but, as I say, spacious in the possession of dirt.' Earlier the Prince had pondered the fate of another landholder. 'This fellow', he muses, contemplating the skull in his hand, 'might be in's time a great buyer of land, with his statutes, his recognizances, his fines, his double vouchers, his recoveries. Is this the fine of his fines, and the recovery of his recoveries, to have his fine pate full of fine dirt?'[35] The author of these lines himself became, shortly after writing them, spacious in the possession of dirt. On 1 May 1602 William Shakespere, gentleman, turned over £320 in cash to William Combe and his nephew John for four yardlands of arable land in Old Stratford, with rights of common for livestock in the outlying fields. A yardland varied in size, according to locality, but usually came to about thirty acres. The deed describes the parcel as 'containing by estimation one hundred and seven acres, be they more or less' of arable. Old Stratford was farming country to the north of the borough, of which it originally formed part. William Combe gave his address as Warwick, which he had represented in Parliament. In 1593 he had bought the Old Stratford freehold to the west of Welcombe. Now, almost a decade later, the parties present interchangeably set their hands and seals to the conveyance. The purchaser did not attend the formalities, but left his younger brother Gilbert to take possession in front of the witnesses: Anthony Nash, Humphrey Mainwaring, and others. The prolix document speaks of the premises as being 'now or late in the several tenures or occupations of Thomas Hiccoxe and Lewes Hiccoxe'. These were tenants of the freehold; whether they stayed on after the ownership changed hands is not known. The name Hiccoxe is ordinary enough.

* In fairness to Jordan it should be noted that he was aware of this bequest.

After 1603 a Lewis Hiccox with his wife Alice—'old Goody Hicox'—kept an inn in Henley Street; probably the eastern house of the Birthplace, which (as later records show) was converted into the Maidenhead Inn.[36] Did Hiccox exchange the plough for the tap?

(In 1610, as provided by the original contract, a fine was entered in the Court of Common Pleas to confirm Shakespeare's title. It describes the freehold as consisting of 107 acres of land, and 20 of pasture. Some biographers have thought that the pasturage represents an addition to the original purchase, but these twenty acres formed part of the parcel bought by William Combe in 1593.)

Five months after he bought his land in Old Stratford, on 28 September 1602, Shakespeare acquired the copyhold title to a quarter-acre of land, comprising a garden with cottage, on the south side of Chapel Lane (*alias* Dead Lane or Walker's Street), facing the garden of New Place. This property, plus one or two other parcels in Stratford, belonged to the manor of Rowington, held by the dowager Countess of Warwick, the lady of the manor. In accordance with the feudal custom still in force, Walter Getley, deputy seneschal in the court baron of the Countess, surrendered the cottage with its appurtenances to Shakespeare and his heirs forever. No doubt the cottage came in handy as quarters for a servant or gardener. A survey of Rowington manor on 24 October 1604 recorded that William Shakespere held 'there one cottage and one garden, by estimation a quarter of one acre', and paid a nominal annual rent of 2*s*.6*d*. Shakespeare is also listed—this time as a customary tenant in Rowington manor—on 1 August 1606 in the books of the Auditors of the Land Revenue. The year after his decease his daughter Susanna, upon payment of the 2*s*.6*d*. fine, was admitted tenant of the cottage.

On 24 July 1605 Shakespeare made his most ambitious investment. For £440 he procured a half-interest in a lease of 'tithes of corn, grain, blade, and hay' in three nearby hamlets—Old Stratford, Welcombe, and Bishopton—along with the small tithes of the whole of Stratford parish, with certain exceptions honouring former rights: the minister of Luddington chapel, for example, continued to garner the tithes of his village.[37] As drawn up in 1544 between the warden of the College of Stratford and William Barker, the lease had a duration of ninety-two years. But after the Dissolution the property of the College, as of other religious foundations, passed to the Crown, which in turn reassigned a parcel of the tithes to the corporation of Stratford. Barker's lease remained valid, however, although it would eventually revert to the corporation. In 1580 he sold the lease to Ralph Hubaud[38] of Ipsley, formerly a sheriff of Warwickshire, at the same time reserving a rental income for himself and his heirs. It was from Hubaud that Shakespeare bought his moiety in a lease that now had thirty-one years left to run. Shakespeare's friend Anthony Nash of Welcombe served as a witness, as he had three years before on the occasion of the Old Stratford freehold transaction. Shakespeare's lawyer Francis Collins, who drew up the indenture, witnessed it too.[39] A member of the town council from 1602 to 1608, Collins was a personal friend, and some years later would be named an overseer of the poet's will. When Hubaud died shortly after the tithes transaction, the inventory of his lands and goods included a debt of £20 'Owing by Mr. Shakespre'.

The latter agreed to pay yearly rents of £5 to John Barker, a lifelong gentleman usher to the Queen (his monument is in Hurst in Berkshire), and another £17 to the bailiffs and burgesses of Stratford. A Chancery bill of 1611(?) reveals that Shakespeare's interest in the tithes brought him £60 per annum net. When his heirs sold most of their share back to the corporation in 1625, they valued it at £90, or £68 clear, for £22 still went into rents. Shakespeare did not farm his own tithes, but entrusted collection to Anthony Nash. A respected gentleman of substance, Nash had a son Thomas, who would marry Shakespeare's granddaughter.

Other townsmen had larger tithe interests than Shakespeare, and were richer. But by 1605 he had more than restored his family's decayed fortunes. In addition to his tithe income he owned arable and pasture lands, the Birthplace in Henley Street, and the Great House of New Place with its extensive gardens and cottage. All this in addition to his theatrical earnings. The applause of multitudes no doubt gratified the creator of *Hamlet*; but after four captains had borne the Prince from the stage, accompanied by the peal of ordnance, the applause died away and the audience streamed into the Bankside dusk. Such rewards were transient. An entailed estate, passed down successively from generation to generation, represented permanence. So perhaps he thought. But his direct line was extinguished before the century was out, the corporation repossessed the tithes, a later owner razed New Place, the fields of Old Stratford are now traceable only in long-expired conveyances.* Only the art, as he prophesied in his *Sonnets* when the eternizing mood was on him, endures. A somewhat later poet makes the point with lyrical grace:

> Trust to good verses then;
> They only will aspire,
> When pyramids, as men,
> Are lost, i' th' funeral fire.

* Dr. Levi Fox, Director of the Shakespeare Birthplace Trust, informs me that the Trust acquired the 107 acres in 1930.

ᖁ[14]ᖃ

His Majesty's Servant

While folk in Stratford went about the ordinary affairs of life, great events were taking place on the national stage. Inevitably, the Queen declined. She had ruled for almost half a century; most of her subjects had never known another sovereign. Towards the end a heavy dullness and irritability, the infirmities of advanced age, overtook her. She had the coronation ring, symbolizing her marriage to England, filed from her finger: her attendants could not twist it off, so deeply embedded was it in her flesh. Still she was fit when the Chamberlain's men played before her for the last time on 2 February 1603; but soon after she fell irrecoverably ill. As Elizabeth sat dying—she refused to lie down, for fear she would never rise—her ministers crowded round to hear a successor named. She procrastinated, as she always had, but finally whispered to Cecil, 'I will that a king succeed me, and who but my kinsman the King of Scots.' On 24 March she died, the Privy Council at once proclaimed the accession of James VI of Scotland as James I of England, and Sir Robert Carey took horse to bear the tidings to Edinburgh. In London bonfires blazed in the streets. Thus ended the Tudor dynasty, and thus began the reign of the house of Stuart, amidst popular rejoicing over the peaceful change of crowns.

The new monarch began his leisurely month's progress from Scotland to London. At Newark-upon-Trent, on 21 April, he made a great impression when a cutpurse in the throng was apprehended 'doing the deed'. The King immediately ordered 'this silken base

32. *Measure for Measure* at Court, 26 December 1604.

thief' hanged, but before leaving Newark he also set free all the wretched prisoners held in the castle. By these acts he demonstrated both his justice and his gracious mercy, in accordance with the theories 'Of a King's Duty in his Office' he had set forth in his *Basilicon Doron*. At Christmastide the next year, on St. Stephen's night (26 December), Shakespeare's company entertained the Court in the Banqueting House at Whitehall with a new comedy probably first acted during the previous summer season. *Measure for Measure* dealt with themes of justice and mercy in a way calculated to strike a responsive chord in the new sovereign; the character of Duke Vincentio, who like James abhors crowds, offered an idealized authority figure with whom he could easily sympathize. To suggest that *Measure for Measure* was a royal play planned and written expressly for Court performance is no doubt to strain interpretation.[1] Still, the universalities of Shakespeare's art have their topical aspect, and it is a fact that a special relation was established early on between his company and the new monarch. They became his players.

Only ten days after his arrival in the capital, James had through his secretary instructed the Keeper of the Privy Seal, 'our right trusty and well-beloved counsellor' Lord Cecil, to prepare for Shakespeare's company letters patent under the Great Seal of England. The royal warrant, dated 17 May 1603, furnished the Keeper of the Privy Seal with the form and also the actual wording of the formal Patent enrolled two days later. In Polonius's vein, the latter licenses and authorizes

these our servants Lawrence Fletcher, William Shakespeare, Richard Burbage, Augustyne Phillippes, John Heninges, Henrie Condell, William Sly, Robert Armyn, Richard Cowly, and the rest of their associates, freely to use and exercise the art and faculty of playing comedies, tragedies, histories, interludes, morals, pastorals, stage plays, and such others like as they have already studied or hereafter shall use or study, as well for the recreation of our loving subjects as for our solace and pleasure when we shall think good to see them during our pleasure. . . .

And whether these servants are publicly exercising their quality 'within their now usual house called the Globe', or in any city, university town, or borough of the realm, the Patent instructs all justices, mayors, other officers, and loving subjects 'to allow them such former courtesies as hath been given to men of their place and quality, and also what further favour you shall show to these our servants for our sake', for such favour 'we shall take kindly at your hands'.

The royal Patent (renewed in 1619 and again, after the king's death, in 1625) testifies to the pre-eminence of the company now known as the King's men. The other regular London troupes—the Admiral's company and Worcester's—passed under the patronage of less illustrious members of the royal family, and were henceforth called Prince Henry's men and Queen Anne's men.

The Lawrence Fletcher heading the names on the Patent calls for a comment, for he is there mentioned for the first time as Shakespeare's associate. Fletcher had acted before James in Scotland as 'comedian to his Majesty'. As Fletcher does not appear in the list of 'Principal Players' included in the First Folio, he apparently did not long continue as a member of the company. In his will another King's man, Augustine Phillips, remembered his fellow Fletcher, and the latter was himself buried in Southwark in 1608.

None of the troupes was playing when James entered the metropolis, for once again the plague gripped London. Such was the virulence of the epidemic that, when James was crowned in July 1603, the public was barred from the ceremony, and the royal procession through London cancelled. The triumphal arches erected for the occasion were dismantled, but they rose again when the processional entry belatedly took place on 15 March 1604.[2] For that occasion each of the King's men named in the Patent was entitled to receive, as a Groom of the Chamber and hence a member of the royal household, four and a half yards of scarlet-red cloth for his livery.

This issue of cloth Sir George Home, Master of the Great Wardrobe, recorded in his account. Shakespeare's name, second in the Patent, this time heads the list. On such occasions the Crown lavishly distributed red cloth. Not all the recipients, however, joined in the solemn procession which, commencing at the Tower, wended its way—to the accompaniment of music, song, and orations—past symbolic pageants and through triumphal arches to Whitehall. Mainly the marchers consisted of noblemen and courtiers and government functionaries arranged in appropriate order by the heralds. No players receive mention in the elaborate accounts, some written by theatre men, of the Magnificent Entertainment of King James.[3]

The players were, however, in attendance on a sensitive diplomatic occasion the next summer. For eighteen days in August they waited upon the new Spanish ambassador and his train at the Queen's palace, Somerset House, which James had placed at the ambassador's disposal. The payment of £21.12s. recorded in the Declared Accounts of the Treasurer of the King's Chamber specifically cites only Augustine Phillips and John Heminges, but Shakespeare, as a senior member of the company, must have been one of the 'ten of their fellows' who were also rewarded. England had not enjoyed diplomatic relations with Spain since the defeat of the Armada in 1588. Now, with a peace treaty in the air, the distinguished emissary from Madrid, Don Juan Fernandez de Velasco, no doubt received courtesies befitting his titles: Constable of Castile and Legion, Duke of the City of Fryas, Earl of Haro, Lord of the Towns of Villapano and Pedraca de la Syerra, Lord of the House of Velasco, and of the Seven Infants of Lara, Great Chamberlain unto Philip III King of Spain, Counsellor of State, and War, and President of Italy.[4]

No troupe acted more often before James than his own men. They played, according to one reckoning, 187 times between the issuance of the Patent and the year of Shakespeare's death. For the year commencing 1 November 1604 and ending 31 October 1605, the account of the Master of the Revels, Sir Edmund Tilney, lists eleven performances by his Majesty's players. There would have been a twelfth, but the play laid on for that night was cancelled. Of the ten pieces shown, seven were by Shakespeare, most of them past favourites from the repertoire—*The Comedy of Errors, Love's Labour's Lost, The Merry Wives of Windsor*, etc.—but the king also watched the newish *Othello* and (as mentioned) *Measure for Measure*. *The Merchant of Venice*, almost a decade old, he saw twice.* The trial scene especially must have arrested his attention; justice and mercy again. The impressive number of Court performances contrasts with former days, when the Chamberlain's men played now and then before the old Queen, and it is indicative of the new dispensation. G. E. Bentley makes the point statistically: 'In the ten years before they became the King's company, their known performances at court average about three a year; in the ten years after they attained their new service their known performances at court average about thirteen a year, more than those of all other London companies combined.'[5]

The first decade of the seventeenth century represents the high tide in the artistic fortunes of the King's men. These years saw the first productions by them of (among others) *Othello, King Lear, Macbeth*, and *Antony and Cleopatra*. Shakespeare's foremost rival gave the same company *Volpone* and *The Alchemist*. *King Lear*, perhaps for our time the quintessential Shakespearian tragedy, was first acted (as seems likely) in early 1605 at the Globe, with Burbage in the title role and Armin as the Fool. On 26 December 1606 it was played before King James at Whitehall: thus much we learn from the Stationers' Register entry and the title-page of the first Quarto, both of which give the author deferential prominence. Such acknowledgement was unusual in an age in which dramatic publication was as often as not anonymous. Shakespeare also received the more equivocal compliment of having foisted upon him plays for whose paternity the tests of evidence absolve him. Earlier editions of apocryphal plays—*Locrine* in 1595, *Thomas Lord Cromwell* in 1602—had borne the initials 'W. S.', but *The London Prodigal*

---

* In the Revels account the scribe considerately lists in the margin the poets who made the plays, but his spelling of Shakespeare—*Shaxberd*—is odd. Perhaps he was a newly arrived Scot who indulged his burr orthographically. The then Clerk of the Revels was William Honyng, but diligent investigation has not yet succeeded in determining whether he was a native of Scotland, or even whether he drew up this particular account.

(1605) and *A Yorkshire Tragedy* (1608) broadcast Shakespeare's name unabashedly. The King's servant now stood at the height of his celebrity as well as of his powers.

The mythos ratifies fame after its own fashion. Once again Davenant is the ultimate source. An advertisement to an anonymously edited *Collection of Poems . . . By Mr. William Shakespeare*, printed for the stationer Bernard Lintot about 1709, offers this information: 'That most learn'd Prince, and great Patron of Learning, King *James* the First, was pleas'd with his own Hand to write an amicable Letter to Mr. *Shakespeare*; which Letter, tho now lost, remain'd long in the Hands of Sir *William D'avenant*, as a credible Person now living can testify.'[6] In his marginalia Oldys identified this 'credible Person' as John Sheffield, Duke of Buckingham (1648-1721), and reported that Buckingham had it from Davenant himself.[7] It is a pity that the latter never published the 'amicable Letter', for nobody has since managed to produce it.

In the spring of 1605 Augustine Phillips died. He and Shakespeare had worked together for over a decade, ever since the formation of the Chamberlain's troupe after the great plague of 1592-4. Like Shakespeare and a handful of other players, Phillips was one of the original sharers in the company. He and Shakespeare acted together in Jonson's *Every Man in his Humour* and *Sejanus*. Phillips also performed in Shakespeare's plays; which parts we do not know, but his name appears fourth in the First Folio in the list of 'the Principal Actors in all these Plays'. During these active years Phillips and his family—his wife Anne and their four daughters (a son, Augustine, died young)—lived close to the Bankside theatre district in Horseshoe Court in St. Saviour's, Southwark, but shortly before he drew up his will in May 1605 they had moved into a newly purchased house in Mortlake, Surrey. In his testament, proved 13 May, the player remembered his fellows in the King's company. To the hired men he left £5 to be distributed equally amongst them. His 'late apprentice' Samuel Gilborne inherited (along with other bequests) Phillips's purple cloak and mouse-coloured velvet hose. Shakespeare heads the list of King's men: 'Item. I give and bequeath to my fellow William Shakespeare a thirty shillings piece in gold.' Only one other fellow (Condell) received as large an individual bequest. It testifies to Shakespeare's warm personal relations with a valued colleague.

Literary geniuses are not, on the whole, celebrated for their amiable dispositions—'Nice people are two a penny', George Mikes consoles himself; 'great writers are few and far between'—yet, in an age of sharp-toothed satire, almost everyone seems to have thought well of Shakespeare. Only Greene, dying without room for magnanimity in his heart, speaks harshly of him, to be followed immediately by Chettle's report that divers of worship commended Shakespeare's uprightness of dealing. One 'An. Sc.' (Anthony Scoloker?), in his epistle to *Daiphantus, or The Passions of Love*, remarks on 'friendly Shakespeare's tragedies'. Did the two men know one another, as the phrase suggests? This reference excepted, Scoloker—if it is he—is utterly unknown. John Davies of Hereford calls Shakespeare 'good Will' in *The Scourge of Folly*; in *Microcosmos* Davies owns to loving players, and sees 'W. S.' as one transcending, by his qualities of character, the baseness of the quality:

> And though the stage doth stain pure gentle blood,
> Yet generous ye are in mind and mood.[8]

A poet and minor playwright for a rival company describes Shakespeare as 'so dear loved a neighbour'.[9] In this period the impressions of contemporaries sometimes find their distillation in a single apt epithet that clings to a name. Jonson, who aspired to be remembered as Honest Ben, is instead known as Rare Ben Jonson, *honest* falling to the unassuming Tom Heywood. Man proposeth, but posterity disposeth. Shakespeare is enshrined in consciousness as Gentle Will Shakespeare. One cannot imagine a more fitting designation for the innate gentleman who was not gently born.

These miscellaneous testimonials of the minnows who swam in the Elizabethan literary and theatrical stream receive confirmation from the mythos. Aubrey, in touch with a living tradition through the actor Beeston, admired Shakespeare the more because 'he was not a company keeper' in Shoreditch—he 'wouldn't be debauched', excusing himself when approached ('and if invited to, writ: he was in pain'). So Aubrey jotted down, helter-skelter, on a miscellaneous

33. The Aubrey scrap, 1681.

scrap. One cannot say with absolute certainty that these notes apply to Shakespeare—so disordered is the manuscript at this point—rather than to the biographer's informant, William Beeston; but most responsible authorities, including Chambers, believe that Shakespeare is the subject. In his comparatively polished Brief Life of Shakespeare, Aubrey makes the point more affirmatively: 'He was a handsome, well-shaped man: very good company, and of a very ready and pleasant smooth wit.'[10] In the next century Rowe once more summed up a tradition: 'Besides the advantages of his Wit, he was in himself a good-natur'd Man, of great sweetness in his Manners, and a most agreeable Companion; so that it is no wonder if with so many good Qualities he made himself acquainted with the best Conversations of those Times.' That was in London. In Stratford, 'His pleasurable Wit, and good Nature, engag'd him in the Acquaintance, and entitled him to the Friendship of the Gentlemen of the Neighbourhood.'[11]

Nowhere, one suspects, was Shakespeare's good nature more severely tested than in his complexly ambivalent relationship with Jonson; ambivalent at least on the latter's side.[12] The mythos fastens upon the rivalry between the two masters. In the seventeenth century, hearsay anecdotes found a place in the notations of Sir Nicholas L'Estrange, Nicholas Burgh, and Thomas Plume. These anecdotes (with one exception) show agile Will overcoming ponderous Ben. In a merry tavern meeting Jonson begins his own epitaph

('Here lies Ben Johnson that was once one'), then passes the pen to Shakespeare, who completes it:

> Who while he lived was a slow things [*sic*],
> And now being dead is nothing.

Shakespeare, standing godfather to one of Jonson's children, and faced with the necessity of thinking of an appropriate christening gift, comes out of 'a deep study' inspired. 'I'll e'en give him a dozen good latten spoons', he tells Ben, 'and thou shalt translate them.' For modern readers this feeble jest requires a gloss: *latten* was a brass or brass-like alloy. In Plume's version of the latten spoon anecdote, the roles are reversed; so Shakespeare does not invariably have the last word.

The rivalry finds most memorable expression in the famous passage in Thomas Fuller's brief memoir of Shakespeare for his *History of the Worthies of England*:

> Many were the wit-combats betwixt him and Ben Johnson, which two I behold like a Spanish great galleon, and an English man-of-war; Master Johnson (like the former) was built far higher in learning; solid, but slow in his performances. Shake-spear with the Eng-

34. L'Estrange's anecdote of Shakespeare and Jonson, 1629-55.

lish man-of-war, lesser in bulk, but lighter in sailing, could turn with all tides, tack about and take advantage of all winds, by the quickness of his wit and invention. He died *Anno Domini* 16... and was buried at Stratford upon Avon, the town of his nativity.[13]

'Which two I behold', writes Fuller. The picture he had formed exists only in the mind's eye; this is a literary evocation, not a reminiscence derived from report. The rest of Fuller's short biography, starkly devoid of concrete data, confirms the impression. Although he perambulated the countryside in quest of matter for his *Worthies*, he failed to dig up the year of Shakespeare's death, for which he leaves a pathetic blank in his text. Yet the date is plain to see on the monument in Stratford Church.

The anecdotes, however dubious, suggest a good-natured competition between these antithetical giants—the handsome, well-shaped Shakespeare; corpulent Jonson with his mountain belly—who conceived and fashioned their art on mutually exclusive principles. The tradition of Jonson's malevolence derives from the scattered aspersions in his writings. In his Prologue to the revised version of *Every Man in his Humour* he glances scathingly at a contemporary playwright so indifferent to the neo-classical unities as to have a swaddled child metamorphose into a bearded sexagenarian, or a few rusty swords enact the Wars of the Roses, or a Chorus waft audiences over the seas. The Induction to *Bartholomew Fair* sneers at 'those that beget tales, tempests, and such like drolleries'. It is not difficult to guess the object of these shafts. Still Shakespeare's closest friends in the King's men invited Jonson to contribute the principal eulogy to the First Folio, and he responded with one of the most admired commendatory poems in the language. When not under encomiastic obligations, in notebooks that lay unpublished until after his death, Jonson recalls affectionately—but not uncritically—his friend already dead probably a decade and more. Ben's tribute gains rather than loses force from the stubborn reservations, dictated by artistic conscience, about Shakespeare's fluency. These after all pertain to the craft, not the craftsman.

I remember, the players have often mentioned it as an honour to Shakespeare, that in his writing (whatsoever he penned) he never blotted out line. My answer hath been, would he had blotted a thousand. Which they thought a malevolent speech. I had not told posterity this, but for their ignorance, who choose that circumstance to commend their friend by, wherein he most faulted, and to justify mine own candour, for I loved the man, and do honour his memory (on this side idolatry) as much as any. He was indeed honest, and of an open, and free nature; had an excellent phantasy, brave notions, and gentle expressions, wherein he flowed with that facility, that sometime it was necessary he should be stopped: *Sufflaminandus erat*, as Augustus said of Haterius. His wit was in his own power; would the rule of it had been so too. Many times he fell into those things could not escape laughter, as when he said in the person of Cæsar, one speaking to him, 'Cæsar thou dost me wrong'—he replied: 'Cæsar did never wrong, but with just cause,' and such like, which were ridiculous.* But he redeemed his vices with his virtues. There was ever more in him to be praised, than to be pardoned.[14]

'He was indeed honest. . . .' From Jonson there can be no higher praise.

A romantic legend brings Jonson and Shakespeare together, along with Raleigh, Donne, Beaumont, and other men of talent and genius, at the Mermaid Tavern in Bread Street, where flowed rich canary wine and words nimble and full of subtle wit. A tradition so firmly entrenched in literary folklore no doubt renders analysis impotent, but the unconvivial biographer must nevertheless observe that the Mermaid sessions were a belated invention of the nineteenth-century biographical imagination. (Raleigh was imprisoned in the Tower from 1603 until after Shakespeare's death.)[15] Shakespeare did, however, know the tavern and its genial host, William Johnson, a 'common vintner' who in 1613 got into trouble with the law by letting his customers have a morsel of meat on fish days. Johnson was a party to Shakespeare's last property transaction.[16] For a while

---

* The passage does not appear in *Julius Caesar*, but instead: 'Know, Caesar doth not wrong; nor without cause/Will he be satisfied' (III.i.47-8). Presumably Shakespeare or the players altered the passage in response to Jonson's voiced objections, and removed what may seem to some not an absurdity but a revealing paradox. The play was first printed in the 1623 Folio in a text apparently deriving from the prompt-book.

the poet had lodgings not far from Bread Street, to the east of St. Paul's.

In 1604, and for a time before and perhaps after, 'one Mr. Shakespeare . . . lay in the house' of Christopher Mountjoy, a French Huguenot tire-maker (i.e. manufacturer of ladies' ornamental headgear) in Cripplegate ward, an enclave within the north-west corner of the city walls. Perhaps Shakespeare heard of the Mountjoys from his friends the Fields. Jacqueline Field would know Mme Mountjoy from the French church in London; besides, from 1600 the Fields lived in Wood Street, close to the Mountjoy house. The latter, a substantial dwelling with shop on the ground floor and lodgings above, was situated at the north-east corner of Monkswell (Muggle) and Silver Streets. A map drawn a half-century earlier depicts, in conventionalized fashion, the twin-gabled house with its eaves extending over the shop front.

On the opposite corner stood the 'great house builded of stone and timber, now called the Lord Windsor's house, of old time belonging to the Nevels'.[17] Silver Street, so named from the silversmiths dwelling there, had 'divers fair houses'. Just down the road was the parish church of St. Olave's, 'a small thing, and without any noteworthy monuments'. Several of the city companies had their halls in the area—the Barber-Surgeons, the Haberdashers, and (a little farther off) the Wax-chandlers—and maintained alms-houses providing a roof and pittance for decayed members. Shakespeare could handily stroll over to his friends Heminges and Condell in the adjoining parish of St. Mary's, Aldermanbury, where the actor-sharers lived as pillars of the community: Condell a churchwarden, and Heminges a sidesman. If the middle-class respectability of Silver Street became oppressive, the playwright could escape, down Wood Street or Foster Lane, to Paul's Churchyard, with its displays of the latest books, or listen in the Middle Aisle of St. Paul's to the 'strange humming or buzz, mixed of walking, tongues and feet'—the 'still roar or loud whisper' of humanity.

Christopher Mountjoy did a flourishing business creating his tires of gold and silver and precious stones for high-born ladies (the Queen herself once patronized him). Silver Street was the centre of the wig trade—'All her teeth were made in the Blackfriars', Jonson's

35. The Belott-Mountjoy suit: Shakespeare cited to testify, 1612.

Captain Otter remarks in *Epicoene*: 'both her eyebrows in the Strand, and her hair in Silver Street'. Meanwhile Mme Mountjoy, like the wives in Elizabethan city comedies, carried on an amour with a tradesman. He was Henry Wood, a mercer and cloth trader in Swan Alley, a short distance (along Coleman Street) from Silver Street. We know about the affair because Mme Mountjoy consulted the physician-magus Simon Forman when she became pregnant. A note in a Forman case-book reads, rather mysteriously, 'Mary Mountjoy alained [i.e concealed]'; matter here for a sequel to *The Merry Wives of Windsor*.

The pregnancy proved a false alarm, Mme Mountjoy and Mrs. Wood did not (as they for a time considered doing) keep a shop together, the Mountjoys' union remained intact.[18] They had an only child, a daughter Mary, who helped in the shop along with the apprentices. In March 1598 Mountjoy visited Forman to ask how his apprentices would do, and the wise man recorded their names in his fractured French: Gui Asture and Ufranke de la Coles. There was a third apprentice, Stephen Belott. He was the son of a French widow whose second husband, Humphrey Fludd, described as 'one of the King's trumpeters', had bound him to Mountjoy. After completing his apprentice term in 1604, Stephen went off to see the world, but he soon returned to Silver Street, this time on a fixed salary. Shakespeare, then living in the house, was drawn into a domestic drama involving the Mountjoys and their former apprentice. We know because eight years afterwards, in the late spring of 1612, the poet came up to London from Stratford to testify in a Court of Requests suit, *Belott* v. *Mountjoy*.

The depositions unravel the history of a courtship and its aftermath. Belott was an eligible bachelor who, everybody agreed, conducted himself irreproachably in the Mountjoy ménage. Shakespeare testified that Stephen 'did well and honestly behave himself' and was 'a very good and industrious servant in the said service'—although he did not (in Shakespeare's hearing) avouch 'that he had got any great profit and commodity by the service'. Mountjoy, however, did 'bear and show great good will and affection' to the young man. The tire-maker and his wife fancied their industrious former apprentice for a son-in-law, and encouraged the 'show of goodwill'—the words are those of Joan Johnson, then a servant in the house—'between the plaintiff and defendant's daughter Mary'. She goes on: 'And as she remembereth, the defendant did send and persuade one Mr. Shakespeare that lay in the house to persuade the plaintiff to the same marriage.' The services of a match-maker were needed because Belott, a practical sort, was holding out for a more advantageous marriage settlement. Daniell Nicholas, a friend of the family, furnishes some details:

> Shakespeare told this deponent that the defendant told him that if the plaintiff would marry the said Marye, his daughter, he would give him, the plaintiff, a sum of money with her for a portion in marriage with her. And that if he, the plaintiff, did not marry with her, the said Marye, and she with the plaintiff, she would never cost him the defendant, her father, a groat; whereupon and in regard Mr. Shakespeare had told them that they should have a sum of money for a portion from the father, they were made sure by Mr. Shakespeare by giving their consent, and agreed to marry.

The wedding took place on 19 November 1604, in the parish church of St. Olave in Silver Street. The records do not show whether Shakespeare attended.

Complications followed upon conjugality. Instead of staying on in the Silver Street shop, as Mountjoy expected, the couple set up a rival establishment with an apprentice of their own. Belott had looked forward to a portion of £60 with Mary, and, after her father's death, an inheritance of £200. Instead the old man fobbed them off with £10 for their purse, and some paltry household stuff: old furniture and an old feather bolster, worn blankets, coarse napkins, a bobbin box, and two pairs of scissors—small scissors at that. When Mme Mountjoy, who had urged her husband to be more generous, died in 1606, the Belotts moved back to Silver Street to keep house for the widower and become partners in the business. But arguments over money followed, Stephen and Mary packed up and left, Mountjoy sank into dissipation. These vicissitudes took place over a space of years. Finally rumours circulated that Mountjoy intended to cut off his daughter and her husband penniless. Hence the suit.

The court had the task of determining what financial settlement had been agreed upon at the time of the marriage. Belott persuaded Nicholas to go with his wife to Shakespeare to ascertain the truth about 'how much and what' Mountjoy had promised. 'And asking Shakespeare thereof, he [Shakespeare] answered that he promised if the plaintiff would marry with Marye, his the defendant's only daughter, he, the defendant, would by his promise, as he remembered, give the plaintiff with her in marriage about the sum of fifty pounds in money and certain household stuff.' Such evidence was of course hearsay; vague hearsay, at that. Only Shakespeare himself could resolve the question, and the two sides must have looked forward, with hope or apprehension, to his testimony. But Shakespeare's memory of the precise details of events long since past failed him. Why should he have recalled? He had no personal stake in the matter. Mountjoy had promised Belott a dowry of some sort, and there had been many conferences, but what the portion was, or when it was to be paid, Shakespeare could not say, nor could he vouch that 'the defendant promised the plaintiff two hundred pounds with his daughter Marye at the time of his decease'. The witness likewise professed ignorance of 'what implements and necessaries of household stuff' Mountjoy gave with Mary.

That was on 11 May 1612. The court appointed a second hearing for 19 June, and Shakespeare's name appears in the margin for a set of interrogatories; but he did not testify again. Others did—Nicholas, William Eaton (then an apprentice in Silver Street), Mountjoy's tire-maker brother Nowell—and although they all agreed that Shakespeare had acted as honest broker in the match, nobody could remember the sums discussed. The court in the end referred the case for arbitration to 'the reverend and grave overseers and elders of the French church in London', who decided that both father and son-in-law were a bad lot—'tous 2 pere et gendre desbauchéz'—but awarded Belott twenty nobles (£6.13s.4d.). A year later Mountjoy had still not paid the sum, but (according to later church registers) he was able to afford to keep up his licentious life: 'sa vie desreglée, et desbordée'.

Of all the Shakespeare records, only the Belott-Mountjoy suit shows him living amidst the raw materials for domestic comedy. The proceedings, for all their mercenary or sordid overtones, reveal the poet-dramatist of superhuman powers as a somewhat baffled mortal, or (in the discoverer's words) as 'a man among men'.[19] One biographer has even envisaged Shakespeare buying a beginner's conversational manual in Paul's Churchyard, and with Mary alongside to help him in his halting efforts, learning the elements of spoken French he would put to such good use in the scene of Princess Katherine's English lesson.[20] 'Comment appelez-vous la main en Anglais?' 'La main? Elle est appelée de hand.' A pretty thought; but Shakespeare seems to have written *Henry V* before lodging with the Mountjoys.

Meanwhile important events were taking place in the fortunes of his company. In August 1608 the King's men assumed the lease of the Blackfriars theatre. As a principal sharer, Shakespeare would have a voice in this crucial decision. The Blackfriars, it will be recalled, was the disused monastery hall that James Burbage had in 1596 selected for a projected playhouse, only to be forced to abandon the scheme after investing heavily in renovations. His sons leased the property to Henry Evans, a Welsh scrivener turned entrepreneur of the children's troupes. Evans used the Blackfriars as a private showcase for the boy actors—the 'little eyases' to whom Hamlet refers. They had a tumultuous history. More than once Blackfriars children incurred the displeasure of the authorities, and finally, with their production in 1608 of Chapman's *Conspiracy and*

Tragedy of Charles, Duke of Byron, they so scandalized the French ambassador that the king ordered their suppression. Evans now surrendered his lease to Richard Burbage. The playhouses were anyway closed because of the plague. By the late autumn of 1609, however, the King's men had probably begun operations in their new house in the heart of London, less than three hundred yards south-west of St. Paul's.

It was, compared with the Globe, an intimate theatre. The rectangular auditorium into which James Burbage had converted the upper-storey Parliament Chamber of the Upper Frater measured 46 feet by 66 feet. At one end the tiring-house extended across the full breadth of the hall; on the second storey of the façade three boxes served for music room, Lord's room, and (when required) action above. Candles suspended in branches illuminated the stage. The house accommodated around 700 spectators, only a fraction of the number—estimated at from 2,500 to 3,000—on Bankside. The whole audience—whether in pit, galleries, or boxes—sat, and for this privilege they paid a minimum admission of sixpence: six times the price of the cheapest entry to the Globe. At Blackfriars, in a glittering and hushed atmosphere, the King's men catered for a sophisticated clientele of courtiers, hangers-on, professional types, and intelligentsia, rather than the heterogeneous masses who frequented the Globe, and who (it may be said for them) did not find *Hamlet* or *King Lear* over their heads.[21]

Theatre historians have seen the transfer as profoundly influencing the stagecraft of Shakespeare's last plays: henceforth, Professor Bentley suggests, Shakespeare wrote 'with the Blackfriars in mind and not the Globe'.[22] An intimate theatre, without unruly groundlings, invited intimate scenes; sentiment rather than passion would now reign. So the theory goes. Act II, scene ii, of *Cymbeline* may be said to exemplify the new mode. Iachimo emerges from the chest in Imogen's bedchamber, lit by a single flickering taper; he makes notes of the surroundings—the window, the adornment of the bed, the painted arras—and, more especially, of the sleeping girl with the mole on her left breast; then he removes her bracelet and tiptoes back into the chest, closing the lid over his head. It is easier to imagine such a scene in the enclosed, candle-lit Blackfriars than in the open-air vastness of the Globe.

Although the notion is intriguing, the actual stage provenance of *Cymbeline, The Winter's Tale*, and *The Tempest* is not clear; *Henry VIII*, we know, was performed at the Globe as a 'new' play. For the King's men did not quit their Bankside theatre after 1609. The Blackfriars served as their winter house; come spring, they were playing at the Globe again. There, in 1611, Simon Forman saw *Macbeth* on 20 April, and *The Winter's Tale* on 15 May. He also caught a performance of *Cymbeline* but neglected to specify either date or theatre, although one guesses it was the Globe. In his *Book of Plays*[23] the astrologer has left for posterity his unique eyewitness accounts of these productions.* Autolycus's roguish antics pointed a useful moral: 'beware of trusting feigned beggars or fawning fellows.' The bedchamber scene in *Cymbeline* made an impression of a different sort. 'Remember . . .', Forman writes, 'in the deepest of the night she being asleep, he opened the chest and came forth of it, and viewed her in her bed, and the marks of her body; and took away her bracelet. . . .'

Whether they acted in small or large regular theatres like the Blackfriars and Globe, or on temporary stages at Court or while on provincial tour, the King's men adapted the plays in their repertoire to changing conditions of performance. Such was the fabled flexibility of Elizabethan dramaturgy. The significance of the Blackfriars move lies more in its social and economic dimension, from which (needless to say) the aesthetic is not entirely separable. Sensing which way the wind was blowing, the company opted for the Court, not the city. Of course they could not have predicted that the fissures already present in society would eventually so widen as to plunge the nation into a civil war which would put an end to all but surreptitious theatrical activity. They did not need to make such predictions; the move made sense as a business gamble, and paid off handsomely. The King's men knew how to please the new, more

---

* Forman also saw a performance of *Richard II* at the Globe on 30 April 1611, but his description does not accord with Shakespeare's play, and suggests that the King's men had another piece on the same reign.

narrowly based, audience. Tragedy now gives way to tragi-comedy as the dominant genre.

The Blackfriars lease of 9 August 1608 created a syndicate of seven owners or 'housekeepers': Richard and Cuthbert Burbage, Thomas Evans (about whom nothing is known), Shakespeare, Heminges, Condell, and Sly. Each member made his contribution of £5.14s.4d. towards the annual rent of £40. Within a week Sly died, so Shakespeare's share (and assessment) rose to one-sixth. The Blackfriars house proved much more profitable than the Globe. Twenty years after Shakespeare's death a share in the former was almost twice as remunerative as one in the latter, an interest of one-eighth in the Blackfriars returning £90 a year as opposed to £25 from a one-sixteenth interest in the Globe.[24]

In 1609 *Troilus and Cressida* was published under unusual circumstances. The play had been entered in the Stationers' Register for 'Master Robertes' six years earlier, with a note to forestall publication until 'he hath gotten sufficient authority for it'. The King's men protected their playbooks. But on 28 January 1609 another two stationers—Richard Bonian and Henry Walley—entered *Troilus and Cressida* on the Register, and issued it the same year, with a title-page advertising the play as 'Written by William Shakespeare' and 'acted by the King's Majesty's servants at the Globe'. A second issue later the same year removed the reference to performance from the title-page, and added an unsigned preface which includes some intriguing assertions:

> Eternal reader, you have here a new play, never staled with the stage, never clapper-clawed with the palms of the vulgar, and yet passing full of the palm comical. . . . Take this for a warning, and at the peril of your pleasure's loss, and judgements, refuse not, nor like this the less, for not being sullied with the smoky breath of the multitude; but thank fortune for the scape it hath made amongst you, since by the grand possessors' wills I believe you should have prayed for them rather than been prayed.[25]

The play could have been 'new' only to readers. The 'grand possessors' wills' thus insouciantly flouted must have been those of

Shakespeare's company. Had the publishers got hold of a transcript in private hands? And what of the references to a comedy 'never staled with the stage' or 'sullied with the smoky breath of the multitude'—in direct contradiction of the statement on the first title-page? Are we to infer that *Troilus and Cressida* had never seen performance, or that it was acted privately? More likely the latter. One of the Inns of Court would suit this ratiocinative drama. There are some interesting biographical implications. 'A special audience of this sort would allow one to discount any idea that the play reflects some deep-rooted cynicism in its author's attitude at this time; the satiric strain would be in part at least explained by the quality of persons in the audience and the time and place of the performance.'[26] However beguiling, this is, of course, mere speculation.

Vexing as they are, the problems surrounding the first publication of *Troilus and Cressida* pale into insignificance alongside those visited upon Shakespearian scholarship by Thomas Thorpe in the same year with his quarto edition of the *Sonnets*. Some, if not all, of these poems had circulated in manuscript since at least 1598, when Meres refers to Shakespeare's 'sugared sonnets among his private friends'. Versions of two (138 and 144) had appeared in 1599 in *The Passionate Pilgrim*, a collection of short, mostly amorous, poems printed by William Jaggard with a catchpenny title-page ascription to W. Shakespeare—despite the fact that most of the items, including the well-known song, 'Crabbed age and youth', belonged to other hands. Ten years later Thorpe brought out his edition of the *Sonnets*.

All the signs point to unauthorized publication; unauthorized, that is, by the writer, not by Stationers' Hall. The numerous misprints indicate that the poet who took such pains with *Venus and Adonis* and *The Rape of Lucrece* had no part in supervising the printing of his most important body of non-dramatic verse. Few close students believe that all 154 poems of the cycle follow the sequence that their creator intended, although nobody has succeeded in rearranging them persuasively.

But the most mystifying problems of this edition are those posed by the dedication, supplied not in the usual downright fashion by the author, but by the publisher:

TO.THE.ONLY.BEGETTER.OF.
THESE.ENSUING.SONNETS.
Mr.W.H. ALL.HAPPINESS.
AND.THAT.ETERNITY.
PROMISED.
BY.
OUR.EVER-LIVING.POET.
WISHETH.
THE.WELL-WISHING.
ADVENTURER.IN.
SETTING.
FORTH.
T.T.

More than a century ago Richard Grant White wrote, 'Mr. Thomas Thorpe appears in his dedication as the Sphinx of literature; and thus far he has not met his Œdipus.'[27] He has yet to meet his Œdipus, although there has been no appreciable falling off in the number of well-wishing adventurers attempting to solve the riddle—or riddles—of the *Sonnets*.

Interest centres on the dedicatee. If Mr. W. H. is the 'only begetter' in the sense of inspirer of the *Sonnets*, then in identifying him we identify the Fair Youth who—cajoled, adored, chided—is, the speaker excepted, the principal personage of the drama. Is he Henry Wriothesley, third Earl of Southampton, with his initials reversed to deter the uninitiated? Not very likely. No strained ingenuity, however, is required to attach the initials to William Herbert, third Earl of Pembroke. Rich and handsome, liberal as a patron ('a most magnificent and brave peer, and loved learned men', Aubrey said of him), he was susceptible to feminine allurement, although stand-offish about matrimony. Moreover, this nobleman has a Shakespearian connection as one of the two brothers to whom Heminges and Condell dedicated their fellow's plays: those 'trifles' which their Lordships valued as something, and 'prosecuted both them, and their author living, with so much favour'. Herbert has attracted distinguished favourers, including Dover Wilson and Sir Edmund Chambers. In recent years, however, his star has declined. Born in 1580, he makes a precocious friend and lover, unless one assigns a later date to the cycle than most readers think likely. And it is doubtful that the obsequious Thorpe would insolently address a noble lord by the unhonorific 'Mr.'.

The other candidates are mostly non-starters. As early as the eighteenth century W. Hughes was put forward by Tyrwhitt (the great editor of Chaucer), and found favour with Malone. They detected a clue in Sonnet 20: 'A man in hue all *hues* in his controlling', and created the non-existent Hughes. Oscar Wilde resuscitated Hughes for his sublimated homo-erotic fantasy *The Portrait of Mr. W. H.* Should one prefer a more recent entry in the Thorpe sweepstakes, one may mull over the qualifications of William Hatcliffe, Prince of Purpoole—the Lord of Misrule—at the Gray's Inn Christmas revels of 1587-8. Dr. Hotson believes that this obscure Lincolnshire man, chronically in debt, journeyed to London in 1609 and there arranged with Thorpe for publication of the *Sonnets*.[28] But Hatcliffe's claims have failed to generate much enthusiasm. Dr. Hotson's theory is perhaps less endearing than that of a German, D. Barnstorff, who proposed that Mr. W. H. is Master William Himself. The Variorum editor of the *Sonnets* is correct in saying that this is in fact not the most idiotic guess ever made.

Another school of interpretation, going back as far as George Chalmers in the *Supplemental Apology* of 1799, holds that *begetter* means *procurer*, and that the dedicatee has merited his ambiguous glory not as the inspirer of the *Sonnets* but as the unpoetical middleman who furnished Thorpe with his copy-text. Again we have a choice of candidates. Sidney Lee is drawn to the stationer William Hall, who has the right initials, and, indeed, whose name stares at us from the dedication directly we remove the point after the *H* of 'Mr. W. H. ALL'. Another nominee is Shakespeare's brother-in-law William Hathaway. Most plausible of all, however, is Sir William Harvey, who in 1598 became the third husband of the Countess of Southampton. When she died in 1607, Sir William (this hypothesis holds) assented to the publication of a poetical testament which his wife regarded as too intimate to share with the public during her lifetime. The 'ETERNITY.PROMISED.BY.OUR.EVER-LIVING.POET' would be the dedicatee's progeny, for in 1608 Harvey took another wife, the young Cordelia Annesley. Precedent exists for addressing a knight as Mr.; Lady Southampton herself did so in her letters. On the other hand, the reading of *begetter* as *procurer* strikes some, understandably enough, as strained. The problem persists.

Indeed the entire dedication, not really punctuated at all but festooned with arbitrary points, is so syntactically ambiguous as to defeat any possibility of consensus among interpreters. Some would divide the lines into two sentences; others see 'Mr. W. H.', not Thorpe, as the subject of *wisheth*. All the riddles of the *Sonnets*—date, dedication, sequence, identity of the *dramatis personae*—elude solution, while at the same time teasing speculation. This writer takes satisfaction in having no theories of his own to offer.

In 1612 William Jaggard brought out a new edition of *The Passionate Pilgrim*, augmented by two long poems from Thomas Heywood's *Troia Britannica*. As Jaggard did not consult Heywood, or even give him credit on the title-page, the latter naturally felt offended, and vented his spleen, with more indignation than clarity, in an epistle to the printer following *An Apology for Actors*, also published in 1612. The passage holds interest for its Shakespearian allusion:

> Here likewise, I must necessarily insert a manifest injury done me in that work, by taking the two Epistles of Paris to Helen, and Helen to Paris, and printing them in a less volume, under the name of another, which may put the world in opinion I might steal them from him; and he to do himself right, hath since published them in his own name. But as I must acknowledge my lines not worthy his patronage, under whom he hath published them, so the author I know much offended with M. Jaggard (that altogether unknown to him) presumed to make so bold with his name.[29]

Apparently Shakespeare complained too, but privately and to the printer, for Jaggard cancelled the title-page and substituted a new one omitting Shakespeare's name. It survives in a single copy in the Bodleian Library. Thus the two sonnets, Heywood's poems, and the other bits and pieces now comprised an anonymous rather than falsely ascribed volume. Whether Heywood felt mollified is not known, but may be doubted.

The leading playwright of the age's leading company did not disdain to try his hand at trifling assignments no sooner completed than forgotten. For a fee Shakespeare devised the *impresa* to be borne by Francis Manners, sixth Earl of Rutland, as one of the contenders in the tourney at Court marking the King's Accession day, 24 March 1613. These *imprese* were insignia, allegorical or mythological, with appropriate mottoes, the whole painted on paper shields. The devices displayed at this tilt baffled at least one of the spectators, Sir Henry Wotton, who complained that 'some were so dark, that their meaning is not yet understood, unless perchance that were their meaning, not to be understood'.[30] Wotton thought that the Herbert brothers carried the best *imprese* that day. No matter; on 31 March, at Rutland's seat, Belvoir Castle, his steward Thomas Screvin recorded the payment of 44s. 'to Mr. Shakspeare in gold about my Lord's *impresa*', and another 44s. 'to Richard Burbadge for painting and making it'. Burbage was a talented amateur painter whose familiar portrait, probably by himself, today hangs at Dulwich College. The linking of his name with Shakespeare's effectively eliminates any doubt that it was the poet rather than some other Shakespeare—John Shakespeare, the royal bit-maker, for example—who created the Earl's *impresa*.*

In the same month, March 1613, Shakespeare made his last investment. This time the house he bought was in London, not Stratford, and he seems not to have lived in it. Situated in the desirable Blackfriars district, the property was once, like the theatre, part of the vast Dominican priory complex. After the Dissolution the residence had been in the tenure of James Gardyner, Esq., and, after him, of John Fortescue, Gent.; in 1604 it was leased to William Ireland, a haberdasher, for twenty-five years. The owner was 'Henry Walker, citizen and minstrel of London'. The 'dwelling house or tenement', part of which was built over 'a great gate', was right up against the King's Wardrobe on the east, and abutted a street leading down to Puddle Wharf, where the Thames narrowed into a creek. On the west side the parcel included a plot of ground that the widow Anne Bacon had lately boarded up on two sides; an old

* The Rutland papers record payment to Burbage for another *impresa* on 25 March 1616.

36. The Earl of Rutland's *impresa*, 31 March 1613.

brick wall enclosed the third side. The purchaser was entitled to free entry through the gate and yard, and also to 'all and singular cellars, sollars [i.e. upper rooms or lofts], rooms, lights, easements, profits, commodities, and hereditaments whatsoever to the said dwelling house or tenement belonging, or in any wise appertaining'. These details the conveyance sets forth. There are two copies, one for Shakespeare and the other for Walker. The transfer took place on the 10th. For the Blackfriars gate-house Shakespeare paid £140, of which £80 was in cash. He now had a house within a couple of hundred yards of the Blackfriars theatre; and at Puddle Wharf, just a few steps down the road, wherries were moored that could whisk him to Bankside. But this proximity would hardly matter much if, as seems likely, the dramatist had begun to contemplate giving up the London stage for Stratford retirement, although, to be sure, the last plays—*Pericles* and the others—hardly testify to artistic disengagement. In purchasing the gate-house was he merely following the example of his friend, Richard Burbage, who had bought several parcels in the district? The transaction may have been a real-estate investment pure and simple.

In some ways perhaps not so simple. According to the title-deed, Shakespeare had three co-purchasers: William Johnson, John Jackson, and John Hemming. Hemming (or Heminges) was almost certainly the dramatist's old associate from the King's men.* Johnson

---

* Some biographers have without sufficient cause doubted the identification; e.g. J. O. Halliwell-Phillipps, *Outlines of the Life of Shakespeare* (7th ed., 1887), i. 239.

presided as landlord of the Mermaid. The name Jackson is common enough, although he may be (as Dr. Hotson believes) the shipping magnate of Hull who enjoyed the company of 'noble wits' at the Mermaid, and was married to the sister-in-law of Elias James, a brewer at the foot of Puddle Dock Hill.[31] Despite the involvement of these parties in the transaction, Shakespeare was evidently the sole buyer. He put up the purchase-money; the others merely acted as trustees in his interest. The day after the sealing of the deed, Shakespeare mortgaged the gate-house back to Walker for the remaining £60. That sum fell due on 29 September next. If the buyer failed to pay it, the agreement stipulated that the seller would regain possession of his property 'from the feast of the Annunciation of the blessed Virgin Mary next coming' for the term of one hundred years at the rent of 'a pepper corn, at the feast of Easter yearly'.

These elaborate arrangements, calling for trustees and a mortgage, place the Blackfriars purchase in a different category from Shakespeare's other investments. The mortgage, at any rate, is easily explained as a temporary expedient allowing the buyer some time to raise the balance of the purchase price. But why the trusteeship? The practical effect would be to deprive Shakespeare's widow of presumed dower right to a third share for life in this part of the estate; for in a joint tenancy, Chancery would not recognize Anne's privilege unless her husband had survived the other trustees.[32] Some biographers see dark overtones of marital discord; Sidney Lee remarks, 'Such procedure is pretty conclusive proof that he had the intention of excluding her [his wife] from the enjoyment of his possessions after his death.'[33] But, at the very least, this is to confuse the part with the whole: although (as we shall see) interpretation is vexed, Shakespeare did not demonstrably exclude Anne from the enjoyment of his other possessions. In his will other considerations than the widow's right to dower moved him. In fact we do not know why he enlisted Heminges, Johnson, and Jackson as trustees.

A few subsequent developments respecting the gate-house require notice. Shakespeare let it to a John Robinson. In the spring of 1615, 'Ann Bacon being lately dead', Shakespeare joined several other property owners in the Blackfriars in petitioning the Court of Chancery to give the widow's son and executor, Mathias Bacon, authority to surrender the 'letters patents and other deeds' pertaining to the said 'messuages, tenements and premises' (the documents in the case are dated 26 April (Complaint), 5 May (Answer), and 22 May (Decree)). This was merely friendly litigation. Two years after the poet's death, Shakespeare's trustees conveyed the gate-house to John Greene of Clement's Inn and Mathew Morrys of Stratford, 'in performance of the confidence and trust in them reposed by William Shakespeare deceased, late of Stretford aforesaid, gent., and . . . according to the true intent and meaning of the last will and testament of the said William Shakespeare'.[34]* This was on 10 February 1618. In his testament William Hall—the father of Shakespeare's physician son-in-law—remembered this Matthew Morris as 'my man'. Morris's ties with the Halls remained close, for he named children John and Susanna.[35]

About the same time as the Blackfriars transaction, Shakespeare's company was called upon to participate in the elaborate festivities at Whitehall celebrating the nuptials, in February 1613, of James's only surviving daughter, the Princess Elizabeth, and Prince Frederick, the Elector Palatine of the Rhine. She would reign for a brief year as the Queen of Bohemia, and come to be known as the Winter Queen. But in the winter of 1613 those sad times lay ahead, unguessed at, and England toasted the marriage with plays, pageants, processions, masques, and fireworks. The King's men regaled the royal newly-weds with no fewer than fourteen plays, among them *Much Ado About Nothing, Othello, The Winter's Tale,* and *The Tempest.* For their contribution the troupe received the munificent reward of £93.6s.8d.† In comparison, the Lady Elizabeth's men, the princess's own actors, played only twice.

---

* Professor Brian Vickers has drawn my attention to a note on Shakespeare by George Colman referring to the 'house formerly situated in Black-Friars, and but lately taken down on account of the new bridge, which belonged to that Poet' (*Prose on Several Occasions* (1787), ii. 165n).

† The sum of £153.6s.8d., sometimes cited, represents payment not only for these fourteen plays but also for six other Court performances by the King's men during the same season. Joseph Quincy Adams, *A Life of William Shakespeare* (Boston and New York, 1923), p. 431, regards all twenty as contributions to the wedding celebrations, and he is not alone in doing so (cf. F. E. Halliday, *The Life of Shakespeare* (rev. ed.; 1964), p. 221).

Some historians believe that Shakespeare wrote the festive history of *Henry VIII* to celebrate the wedding of Elizabeth and Frederick. Such a performance is not mentioned in the Chamber Account, but conceivably it was the unnamed stage-play for which hundreds waited expectantly on 16 February, only to have the performance cancelled in favour of the 'greater pleasures' of a masque. Many critics, although not all, think that Shakespeare wrote *Henry VIII* in collaboration with a rising young playwright, John Fletcher. The son of the Bishop of London, bred there and (probably) Cambridge educated, Fletcher would succeed Shakespeare as the principal playwright of the King's men. Whether or not these two collaborated on *Henry VIII* we cannot say for sure, although most likely they did. That it was acted—or prepared for acting—at Whitehall after the wedding is only a pleasant, perhaps idle, supposition. But a play on the reign of Henry VIII was performed at the summer playhouse of the King's company on St. Peter's day, 29 June 1613.

On that never-to-be-forgotten occasion the thatch caught fire, a sudden wind fanned the flames, and in a little while the great Globe itself was consumed. Three days later Sir Henry Wotton, not present himself, excitedly reported the event to his nephew, Sir Edmund Bacon:

> The King's players had a new play, called *All is true*, representing some principal pieces of the reign of Henry VIII, which was set forth with many extraordinary circumstances of pomp and majesty, even to the matting of the stage; the Knights of the Order with their Georges and garters, the Guards with their embroidered coats, and the like: sufficient in truth within a while to make greatness very familiar, if not ridiculous. Now, King Henry making a masque at the Cardinal Wolsey's house, and certain chambers [i.e. pieces of ordnance] being shot off at his entry, some of the paper, or other stuff, wherewith one of them was stopped, did light on the thatch, where being thought at first but an idle smoke, and their eyes more attentive to the show, it kindled inwardly, and ran round like a train, consuming within less than an hour the whole house to the very grounds.
>
> This was the fatal period of that virtuous fabric, wherein yet nothing did perish but wood and straw, and a few forsaken cloaks; only one man had his breeches set on fire, that would perhaps have

broiled him, if he had not by the benefit of a provident wit put it out with bottle ale.[36]

Such an event is calculated to inspire a doleful ballad:

> No shower his rain did there down force
> In all that sunshine weather,
> To save that great renowned house;
> Nor thou, O ale-house, neither.
> Had it begun below, sans doubt,
> Their wives for fear had pissed it out.
>   Oh sorrow, pitiful sorrow, and yet all this is true.[37]

Puritans expectedly saw the hand of God in 'the sudden fearful burning'. But within a year a new Globe, with tiled roof, rose on the same site. On 30 June 1614 John Chamberlain called on a friend, but was told that she had 'gone to the new Globe, to a play'. As to whether the hand of God had anything to do with the miraculous restoration, the Puritans are silent. Rumour held that King James himself, with many of his noblemen, defrayed the cost of the rebuilding. In fact, however, the expense fell upon the shareholders, required by the terms of their lease to maintain and repair the theatre. Each sharer was at first assessed £50 or £60 towards the charges, but ended up having to pay much more. John Witter, already behindhand with the rent, could not put together his contribution, and bowed out from the syndicate.* We do not know what Shakespeare did. Perhaps, while pruning the vines in his Great Garden of New Place, he decided that this was a good time to sell his seventh share of the moiety in the company which he had served, to the best of his abilities, for nigh on two decades.

---

* Not a player, but the wastrel who gained control of his share in the Globe by marrying the widow of Augustine Phillips.

[15]

Stratford Again

> Graves at my command
> Have wak'd their sleepers, op'd, and let 'em forth,
> By my so potent art. But this rough magic
> I here abjure; and, when I have requir'd
> Some heavenly music—which even now I do—
> To work mine end upon their senses that
> This airy charm is for, I'll break my staff,
> Bury it certain fathoms in the earth,
> And deeper than did ever plummet sound
> I'll drown my book.

Ever since 1838, when Thomas Campbell, himself a minor poet, first made the suggestion, readers have identified the master of the revels in *The Tempest* with the master-reveller of the King's men, and interpreted Prospero's valediction, with its invocation of the supernatural potencies of art, as Shakespeare's own eloquent farewell to the stage.[1] In one respect at least, Prospero's words better suit the playwright than his puppet who speaks them. The magus of *The Tempest* has waked no sleepers from the grave, as has the author of *Richard III* and *Hamlet*. It may, however, be objected that the soliloquy has its source in the *Metamorphoses*, which Shakespeare here consulted in both Ovid's Latin and Golding's translation. Nor does a speech of such evident dramatic propriety enforce us to read into it autobiographical reverberations. Prospero's revels have indeed ended; he must relinquish his magic, discase himself, and repossess his dukedom in Milan. Anyway *The Tempest*, performed in the Banqueting House at Whitehall on Hallowmas Night, 1611, was not Shakespeare's last play. *Henry VIII* followed, and the evidence points to his having had a hand, with Fletcher, in *The Two Noble Kinsmen*, around 1613. At most, then, in *The Tempest* he is saying *au revoir* rather than *adieu*. Certainly Shakespeare did not entirely give up visiting London during his last years. As we have seen, he was there in May 1612, when he gave evidence in the Court of Requests in the Belott-Mountjoy suit; again the following March, when he bought and mortgaged the Blackfriars gate-house; and presumably also in spring, 1615, when he joined in amicable litigation over the same property. These were not his only visits. But few plays issued from Shakespeare's pen after 1610; none, so far as is known, after 1613. When all factors have been duly weighed, there seems little reason to doubt the final non-literary phase that Rowe first summed up:

> The latter Part of his Life was spent, as all Men of good Sense will wish theirs may be, in Ease, Retirement, and the Conversation of his Friends. He had the good Fortune to gather an Estate equal to his Occasion, and, in that, to his Wish; and is said to have spent some Years before his Death at his native *Stratford*.[2]

In 1611 the town rounded up subscriptions 'towards the charge of prosecuting the bill in Parliament for the better repair of the highways and amending divers defects in the statutes already made'. In this period most road building and repair were financed by local philanthropists—Sir Hugh Clopton most notably exemplifies the breed—but Stratford now wanted the national government to assume some of the burden. Perhaps the matter had been mooted when the justices of the peace surveyed the highway in Bridgetown that year, and sat down together to a light refreshment of wine, sugar, pippins, and beer.[3] In the event, seventy-one citizens lent name and purse to the cause, the chief alderman, steward of the borough, and other aldermen heading the list prepared on 11 September. The steward, 'Mr. Thomas Greene, esquire', is the only subscriber for whom a sum is mentioned; he gave 2*s*.6*d*. Near the top of the list appears, added on the right, the name of 'Mr. William Shackspere' (about a third have their names prefixed by the honorific 'Mr.'); perhaps he was in London when the sponsors first canvassed support. Bills for the repair of highways were before the Commons more than once in this period without progressing beyond the committee stage.[4] This one got nowhere too.

That season a neighbour in Henley Street, Robert Johnson, died. The inventory post-mortem, drawn up on 5 October by schoolmaster Aspinall, includes £20 for 'A lease of a barn that he holdeth of Mr. Shaxper'. Johnson, a vintner, was landlord of an inn later known as the White Lion. Probably John Shakespeare built the barn, which stood at the back of the Birthplace property, in the waste known as the Gild Pits, through which the King's highway to London passed. The back gates of the Swan Inn adjoined the barn.[5] It was still being rented by a Johnson (Michael) in 1670, when Shakespeare's granddaughter made her will. In the late eighteenth century Jordan mentions 'the large barns, built with bricks, still standing in the Gild-pits, by the side of the Birmingham road'.[6]

Shakespeare's brother Gilbert was buried on 3 February 1612. The Stratford register lists the burial of 'Gilbertus Shakspeare, adolescens', and, a year and a day later, that of Shakespeare's only remaining brother, Richard. Of the eight sons and daughters of John Shakespeare, now only the poet and his sister Joan survived.

In 1614 an unnamed preacher was entertained at New Place, the corporation paying 20d. 'for one quart of sack and one quart of claret wine' for his refreshment. He had come to deliver one of the three official foundation sermons with which the bailiff and council were edified in the chapel each year: the Oken on election day in September, the Hamlet Smith at Easter, and the Perrott at Whitsuntide. (In 1614 a fourth was established through the beneficence of John Combe.) Probably it was the Easter or Whitsuntide sermon

37. A preacher entertained at New Place, 1614.

that he preached, for the payment is recorded in the Chamberlain's Account between entries dated 21 March and 30 June 1614. Visiting clergy sometimes stopped at inns, but they found entertainment in private homes too, and New Place—just a stone's throw from the Gild Chapel—was a likely place for the stranger to spend the night. On such occasions the corporation often footed the bill for gifts of wine, sometimes accompanied by sugar.

That summer, on 9 July, a 'sudden and terrible fire' swept through the thatched houses of Stratford for the third time in living memory. Its force, the justices avouched, 'was so great (the wind sitting full upon the town) that it dispersed into so many places thereof whereby the whole town was in very great danger to have been utterly consumed'.[7] Fifty-four dwellings burnt to the ground that Saturday, as well as stables and barns stored with grain and hay. A collection was taken up for the victims. Fortunately the Shakespeare properties escaped.

Late the same summer a new crisis agitated Stratford's men of property. Enclosure was in the air again. Arthur Mainwaring (or Mannering), steward to Lord Chancellor Ellesmere, was promoting a scheme to enclose the common fields of Welcombe, and he had as his ally William Combe, who was, at the age of twenty-eight, a powerful land-holder in the neighbourhood. This Combe was the son of the Thomas Combe who dwelt at the College, and nephew of old ten-in-the-hundred, the lately deceased John Combe. A previous attempt at enclosure had failed, although the prime mover was no less a personage than Sir Edward Greville, the late lord of the manor; but Mainwaring and Combe went confidently ahead. This issue touched people's pockets, and was thus calculated to arouse fierce passions. Shakespeare's tithe-interests were affected. His name stands at the head of the list of 'Ancient freeholders in the fields of Oldstratford and Welcombe' which the Town Clerk, Thomas Greene, drew up on 5 September in response to the proposed scheme. Enclosure meant consolidating the yardlands—these were bundles of acre or half-acre strips in an open field—into larger units bounded by fences or hedges. Inevitably some boundaries would undergo alteration. The Welcombe fields were then meadowland boasting both hay for mowing and grass for pasture. If these fields

38. Greene's memorandum, 5 September 1614.

were enclosed, the arable tracts would be converted into sheep pas-
ture-land, which as a rule yielded less income per square acre than
grain and hay. Enclosure also reduced employment (sheep, as Sir
Thomas More observed, devoured men), and forced up the price of
grain. Hence the concern of the property-holders. On the other
hand, enclosure also encouraged more productive agriculture, 'since
the communal tillage of open fields was not conducted on scientific
lines, and obviously no one would spend capital on improving his
scattered and unenclosed plots for the benefit of his neighbours'.[8]
Combe clearly felt that there was profit in enclosure. Shakespeare,
wooed by both factions, seems to have kept cool.

Greene did not. As Town Clerk he looked after the minutes of
corporation meetings in the Gild Hall, and also participated in council deliberations. A solicitor (later a barrister), Thomas Greene of
the Middle Temple was Shakespeare's kinsman by blood or marriage—he speaks of himself as a cousin, and although Elizabethans
used the term loosely, perhaps he was. The two seemed to get on,
although it is curious that Shakespeare does not mention Greene in
his will. In 1609, when going about the purchase of a dwelling, he
was the Shakespeares' house-guest, and under no great pressure to
move into St. Mary's House, which George Browne was selling him,
'the rather because [he wrote] I perceived I might stay another year
at New Place'.[9] The mere suggestion of enclosure, however, made
Greene exceedingly nervous, for he had lately invested £300 in a
moiety of tithe-interests.[10] Hence the Town Clerk's several references to his tithe-holding cousin in his memoranda.

At a meeting on 23 September, Greene voiced his anxieties in the council, which voted unanimously to oppose enclosure. Two months later they agreed—with Alderman Cawdrey the lone dissenter—to use all lawful means to prevent Mainwaring's designs on the Welcombe meadowland. Meanwhile Shakespeare prudently entered into a covenant with Mainwaring's cousin, William Replingham of Great Harborough, who was the attorney acting as Mainwaring's agent. By these articles, drawn up on 28 October, Replingham undertook to compensate William Shackespeare or his heirs or assigns 'for all such loss, detriment and hindrance' with respect to the annual value of his tithes, 'by reason of any enclosure or decay of tillage there meant and intended by the said William Replingham'. At the recommendation of Thomas Lucas, Shakespeare's attorney, the covenanters included Greene's name in the agreement.

He did not rest any easier as a result. In November he was looking for Combe in London, but not finding him, called on Shakespeare, who had come up from Stratford. Greene's memorandum of the 17th shows that Shakespeare tried to calm him:

> at my cousin Shakspeare coming yesterday to town I went to see him how he did. He told me that they assured him they meant to enclose no further than to Gospel Bush, and so up straight (leaving out part of the dingles to the field) to the gate in Clopton hedge, and take in Salisbury's piece, and that they mean in April to survey the land, and then to give satisfaction and not before.[11]

Greene adds that both Shakespeare and his son-in-law, Dr. John Hall, assured him they thought nothing at all would be done. The survey, however, took place not in April but much sooner, in December, and when the Town Clerk heard of it on the 10th, he was off to the Bear Inn and New Place in search of Replingham. Greene missed him at both places.

But Greene had the corporation behind him. They made a gingerly approach to Combe, sending a deputation of six 'to present their loves and to desire he would be pleased to forbear to enclose and to desire his love as they will be ready to deserve it'. Combe thanked them for their love, but budged not an inch—he saw gain from enclosure; Mainwaring had already gone too far to turn back;

come thaw and he would begin digging his ditch and planting hedges. On 23 December the corporation dispatched letters, subscribed by 'almost all' the members, to Mainwaring and Shakespeare. 'I also writ of myself', Greene adds, 'to my cousin Shakspear the copies of all our oaths made then, also a note of the inconveniences would grow by the enclosure'. That day the council sought to enlist other local landholders in the cause: Andrew Archer of Tanworth, who held Bishopton manor and common, and Sir Francis Smith, who owned land at Welcombe.[12] The correspondence with Shakespeare has disappeared, but the corporation's letter to Mainwaring survives. They entreated him to remember the fires which had devastated Stratford, and warned that enclosure, by tending to the ruin of the borough, would bring on his head the curses of the 700 almsfolk living there.

All to no avail. The frost broke in December, and Combe's men began digging their trench, surrounded by hedge-mounds. Before long it extended over 'at least fifty perches': 275 yards. The council counter-attacked. On Greene's advice, William Walford and William Chandler bought a lease at Welcombe on 6 January 1615, thus becoming tenants with rights of common. In three days' time, having sent ahead their spades, they began surreptitiously filling in Combe's ditch. When word of the activity reached him, he was predictably enraged. Before a crowd of onlookers, Walford and Chandler were thrown to the ground by Combe's men, while their master 'sat laughing on his horseback and said they were good football players'. He also abused the corporation as 'puritan knaves and underlings in their colour [i.e. the legal pretext by which they had insinuated themselves as commoners]'. Still, righteous indignation did not prevent Combe from offering Greene £10 to buy himself a gelding, in return for propounding a peace with the council. But Greene was not to be bribed. The next day women and children from Stratford and Bishopton finished the job of filling in the ditch.

On 28 March at Warwick Assizes, upon the petition of the bailiff and burgesses of Stratford, the court issued an order restraining Combe and any other from making an enclosure—which was against the laws of the realm—unless they could show good cause at open Assizes. Mainwaring and Replingham now acknowledged defeat, but Combe, beside himself, persisted. He threatened and railed; he beat the poor tenants, imprisoned them, and impounded their pigs and sheep. By buying up land and houses, he depopulated the entire village of Welcombe, making an exception, however, for his own dwelling. In September, Greene made his most perplexing entry in his diary: 'W. Shakespeare's telling J. Greene that I was not able to bear the enclosing of Welcombe'. J. Greene was the diarist's brother John. But why should Shakespeare have communicated to John Greene a fact of which he could not have been unaware? And why did John trouble himself to pass it along to his brother? Finally, why should Thomas have regarded the intelligence as sufficiently interesting to record? Possibly 'I' was a slip for 'he'. Or possibly Greene meant to write 'bar', not 'bear'. He began by writing 'to he . . .'; maybe he intended to say 'to help', then changed his mind because of a possible ambiguity—'to help' could mean either 'to aid' or 'to remedy'.[13] For that matter, 'bear' can be taken two ways also, as 'endure' or 'justify'. Any attempt to interpret the passage is guesswork, and no more.

After the staying order the case dragged on for another year. Then, at the Lent Assizes of 1616, the Chief Justice of the King's Bench, Sir Edward Coke, advised Combe to 'set his heart at rest; he should never enclose nor lay down his common arable land'—not so long as the Chief Justice served his King. By April the force of the verdict had sunk in on Combe; he was 'out of hope ever to enclose'. But if he abandoned all hope, he did so only temporarily. In June he was offering his 'very loving friends and kind neighbours' a new set of proposals, much more conciliatory; but the corporation refused to bite. They simply asked Combe to leave them in peace.[14] He did not. Shakespeare, who seems never to have felt very keenly one way or the other about the controversy, now did not care at all. He was dead.

During his last years the retired playwright had his family with him in Stratford. So far as is known, his wife never strayed from the town, but for her the record is a blank between the baptism of her children and the drawing up of the poet's will, except for shepherd Whittington's concern about 40s. in Anne Shaxspere's hand. Her daughters' lives are more amply documented.

According to her epitaph, Shakespeare's eldest child was 'Witty above her sex' and 'Wise to salvation'—'Something of Shakespeare was in that', the memorialist, whoever he was, adds. Whether witty and wise or not, Susanna could sign her name, which is more than her sister demonstrates a capacity to do. Susanna first appears in the records, after her christening entry in the Stratford register, in the spring of 1606, just before her twenty-third birthday. That May she was cited in the act book kept by the ecclesiastical court that held 'peculiar jurisdiction' in the parish. Presided over by the vicar on his throne in Holy Trinity, with a notary present to record its acts, the court met approximately once a month. On this occasion twenty-one defendants, reported by the churchwarden and sidesmen, were charged with having failed to receive the Sacrament the preceding Easter, which that year fell on 20 April. The transgression may seem trifling, and ordinarily it was; but only six months previously a small band of fanatical Catholics had sought by violence to overthrow the government, and Parliament, having narrowly escaped being blown up in the Gunpowder Plot, was in no mood for toleration. It passed a number of vengeful statutes, including one aimed at 'persons popishly affected' who sometimes attended church 'to escape the laws in that behalf provided', but who evaded the Anglican Communion. Church papists, they were called, and the new legislation respecting non-receiving punished them with heavy fines, rising from £20 in the first year to £60 in the third and thereafter. In such an atmosphere parishioners missing Communion laid themselves open to grave suspicions of Catholicism. A third at least of the Easter Twenty-one were in fact known Catholics, or had recusant connections. There was Margaret Reynolds, for example, or Sybil Cawdrey. A 'supposed' fugitive Jesuit priest in green breeches and high shoes had once been seen at the door of Margaret and her husband Thomas. Sybil had a son in that order, and her family had been suspected of harbouring seminary priests. The list also included Shakespeare's old friends the Sadlers, who required time (Hamnet petitioned) to clear their consciences. Susanna failed to show up in the vicar's court despite a personal summons by the apparitor. (The Sadlers were guilty of a similar negligence.) The word *dimissa*, added later to the entry for her in the act book, indicates that when Su-

39. John Hall and Susanna Shakespeare married, 5 June 1607.

sanna did appear before the court her case was dismissed. Presumably she had meanwhile received the Eucharist, as we know ten of her co-defendants had, or agreed to do so.[15] A year later, on 5 June, 'John Hall, gentleman, and Susanna Shaxspere' were wed in Holy Trinity. The groom, in his early thirties, was impeccably Protestant.

The son of a well-to-do physician of Acton, Middlesex, Hall was bred in the little hamlet of Carlton in Bedfordshire. At Cambridge, thirty miles away, he proceeded B.A. from Queens' College in 1594, and three years later took his M.A. there. Around 1600 he settled in Stratford, where he soon had a thriving medical practice. If Hall ever took a medical degree, no record of it has been found—the Royal College of Physicians never licensed him, nor did he obtain a Bishop's licence to practice. But in those days the profession was very loosely regulated. No matter; Hall was a dedicated physician with a large following. 'I know by experience that he is most excellent in that art', Lady Tyrrell informed Lady Temple when the latter's husband—the same Sir Thomas Temple so desirous of vine-sets from Shakespeare's garden—had suffered a mischance. A Linacre Lecturer at Cambridge, Dr. John Bird, speaks of Hall's 'great fame for his skill, far and near', and of the 'persons noble, rich and learned' who benefited from his ministrations. Hall looked after humbler folk too —children, servants, barbers—and Catholics as well as Protestants. He did not scruple to ride forty miles on horseback to Ludlow Castle when the Earl of Northampton was down with a pleurisy contracted while following his hounds on a cold wet day. Twice the Stratford corporation elected Hall a burgess, and twice he declined because of the demands of his practice. When elected a third time he accepted, only to incur fines for missing sessions because he was out looking after his patients. One of these, Sidney Davenport, complained to the doctor that the magistrates ought not 'to lay this burden upon you whose profession is to be most abroad'.[16] So too

Hall declined a knighthood offered him in 1626 by the new monarch, King Charles I, preferring to pay a £10 fine.

Dr. Hall treated the whole gamut of human ills from measles to melancholy, and including black evacuations, cancer, bloodshot eyes, and the French pox. His medical diary records the case histories. Thus he cured the Countess of Northampton's chambermaid, laid low when her arse-gut fell out, and John Emes of Alcester, aged fifteen, unfortunately prone to 'pissing in bed'. The prescription for the latter included 'the windpipe of a cock, dried and made into powder'. When his own wife lay 'miserably tormented with the colic', Hall gave her an enema—a pint of sack, made hot—which 'presently brought forth a great deal of wind, and freed her from all pain'. Hall's best remembered patient was the Warwickshire poet Michael Drayton, whom he describes as *poeta laureatus*. Drayton often called on the Rainsfords at Clifford Chambers, only two miles from Stratford; it was probably there that Hall treated him with an emetic infusion mixed with a spoonful of syrup of violets. Some of the physician's remedies, with their cocks' guts, spider webs, and excreta, may strike moderns as more alarming than the conditions they were designed to alleviate, but this doctor let less blood than others, and was in advance of his day in his treatment of scurvy, to which Elizabethans were prone by virtue of a diet rich in salted meat and fish but deficient in seasonal fruits and vegetables. This malady Hall fought with his Scorbutick Beer. He compounded water cress, brooklime, and scurvy grass with various herbs and roots, then boiled the mixture in beer flavoured with sugar, cinnamon, or juniper berries. The beer worked; it was rich in ascorbic acid.[17]

The motto 'Health is from the Lord' fittingly precedes the English edition of Dr. Hall's Latin case-book, in which time and again he gives thanks to God for a successful cure. Nowhere is his piety more fervent than in his account of his own miraculous recovery from a debilitating fever: 'thou hast saved me . . .', he addresses his maker, 'restoring me as it were from the very jaws of death to former health, for which I praise thy name, O most merciful God, and Father of our Lord Jesus Christ, praying thee to give me a most thankful heart for this great favour, for which I have cause to admire thee'.[18] Hall showed his devotion more tangibly by giving Holy

Trinity a carved pulpit, and serving as a churchwarden. His sympathies were Puritan. He zealously reprehended parishioners who came to church late, slept there, swore, wore hats, or put their hands in ladies' plackets. Hall allied himself with vicar Thomas Wilson from Evesham (the doctor had in 1612 bought 'a close by Evesham way'), who had antagonized the corporation with his Puritanical views. The two men together sued the council in Chancery, Hall declaring that he had sold the town a lease of tithes for £100 'at the least' under their value, in order to maintain the salary of the vicar, who had six young children to worry about.[19] Two years earlier, in 1633, nineteen members of the council had voted to expel Hall 'for the breach of orders wilfully and sundry other misdemeanours contrary to the duty of a burgess . . . and for his continual disturbances at our halls'.

The Lord blessed the Halls with only one child, a daughter Elizabeth, baptized 21 February 1608. She makes a solitary appearance in her father's case-book. He describes treating her for a 'convulsion of the mouth' in January and April 1624, and, a month later, for 'an erratic fever'—'sometimes she was hot, by and by sweating, again cold, all in the space of half an hour, and thus she was vexed oft in a day'. Hall purged Elizabeth, and anointed her spine. She responded to her father's care. 'Thus was she delivered from death, and deadly diseases, and was well for many years.'[20]

The inscription on John Hall's gravestone describes Susanna as his most faithful wife (*fidissima conjux*), but that was not how John Lane, Jr., spoke of her in 1613. On 15 July, Susanna sued Lane for slander in the consistory court at Worcester Cathedral, because 'about 5 weeks past the defendant reported that the plaintiff had the running of the reins and had been naught with Rafe Smith at John Palmer'. (To have 'the running of the reins' was to suffer from gonorrhoea ('reins' = kidneys or loins); but gonorrhoea did not then necessarily denote venereal infection, although in this context that appears to be what is meant.*) Lane, then twenty-three, came of

---

* In the 'Alphabetical Table of Diseases' prefacing Hall's *Select Observations*, the first entry under 'G' is, 'Gonorrhea, see running of the reins'. The *Oxford English Dictionary* glosses the phrase under 'Running', II. 8; see also the correspondence in *The Times Literary Supplement* from A. L. Rowse (28 April

40. Susanna Hall sues John Lane, Jr., 15 July 1613.

good stock—Alveston gentry—but got into scrapes. He was sued for riot, and libelling the vicar and aldermen; the churchwardens charged him with drunkenness. Perhaps he was both drunk and pugnacious when he defamed Mrs. Hall. Ralph Smith, aged thirty-five, was a vintner's son, and by trade a hatter and haberdasher; he was Hamnet Sadler's nephew. Lane's sister Margaret was the wife of John Greene, the Town Clerk's brother, and his first cousin would marry Elizabeth Hall. His uncle, Richard Lane, in July 1613 appointed Thomas Greene and John Hall trustees of the property he settled on his son and daughter.[21] Stratford was a closely knit society, in which scandal—quick to circulate—had to be as quickly quashed. In the consistory court, Robert Whatcott, later to witness the poet's will, appeared on behalf of the plaintiff. Lane did not show at all, and in less than a fortnight found himself excommunicated. The case was closed.

Local tradition holds that the Halls lived in a handsome halftimbered house in Old Town, close to Holy Trinity, and even closer to New Place. The spacious dwelling had an ample garden in which Dr. Hall could cultivate the herbs and simples he used in his cures. Today the house is called Hall's Croft, but I have been able to find

1974, p. 447), Ernest Mehew (3 May 1974, p. 477), Audrey Eccles (17 May 1974, p. 527), and myself (24 May 1974, p. 559).

no reference to it by that name earlier than the listing of 'Hall Croft' in *Spenell's Family Almanack, Directory of South Warwickshire, and Annual Advertiser, for* 1885. It was earlier called Cambridge House, and served as a private school for girls. When Shakespeare died, the Halls moved into New Place. There they stayed for the rest of their lives.

The parish register records the burial of 'Johannes Hall, medicus peritissimus' (most expert physician) on 26 November 1635. His remains lie in the chancel of Holy Trinity. On his gravestone, the second to the right of Shakespeare's, his arms, 'Three talbots' heads erased', impale those of his father-in-law. The inscription reads:

HEERE LYETH Y.^{E} BODY OF JOHN HALL
GENT: HEE MARR: SUSANNA, Y^E DAUGH
   & coheire
TER, OF WILL: SHAKESPEARE, GENT. HEE
DECEASED NOVE^R. 25. A°. 1635, AGED 60.

The Latin epitaph which follows eulogizes his healing skill ('Hallius hic situs est medica celeberrimus arte') and loyal wife.

Hall's medical fame prompted James Cooke of Warwick, Lord Brooke's surgeon, to call on the faithful widow when he was in Stratford during the Civil War. Cooke describes the visit:

Being in my art an attendant to parts of some regiments to keep the pass at the bridge of Stratford upon Avon, there being then with me a mate allied to the gentleman that writ the following observations in Latin, he invited me to the house of Mrs. Hall, wife to the deceased, to see the books left by Mr. Hall. After a view of them, she told me she had some books left, by one that professed physic with her husband, for some money. I told her, if I liked them, I would give her the money again; she brought them forth, amongst which there was this with another of the author's, both intended for the press. I being acquainted with Mr. Hall's hand, told her that one or two of them were her husband's, and showed them her; she denied, I affirmed, till I perceived she begun to be offended. At last I returned her the money.[22]

It is odd that Susanna failed to recognize her own husband's hand. Could she read and write, or did she have learning sufficient only to

41. Thomas Quiney and Judith Shakespeare married, 10 February 1616.

enable her to sign her name? In any event, when Cooke found some spare hours he translated 178 of Hall's case-histories, from among 'no less than a thousand', and published them in 1657 as *Select Observations on English Bodies.*[23] Although the surgeon refers to two books, only one of Dr. Hall's medical diaries is known to exist. Now in the British Library, it is Egerton MS. 2065.

Judith Shakespeare fared less well matrimonially than her sister, although her husband came from an unexceptionable family. He was Thomas Quiney, son of the Richard who was Shakespeare's loving countryman. When Richard died in 1602 he left a wife, Bess, and nine children, none of them yet twenty. Of these the best hope was the eldest son, Richard Jr., who would prosper as a grocer at the Red Lion in Bucklersbury, London, and with his partner, also from Stratford, buy two plantations in Virginia. Judith however married not Richard—he took a Sadler for his wife—but his brother Thomas, baptized 26 February 1589. He achieved no comparable triumphs in trade. Thomas became a vintner in Stratford; we hear of him selling wine to the corporation in 1608. Three years later he leased, for use as a tavern, the little house called 'Atwood's' near the top of the High Street, next door to his mother. On 10 February 1616 'Tho-[mas] Queeny' was wed 'to Judith Shakspere', the assistant vicar Richard Watts probably officiating—he signed the marriage register this month. (Watts later married Quiney's sister Mary.) The groom was going on twenty-seven, the bride a mature thirty-one. One suspects she did not by then have a choice of suitors, if she ever did.

The marriage began inauspiciously. Because the ceremony took place during the Lenten prohibited season that in 1616 began on 28 January (Septuagesima Sunday) and ended on 7 April (the Sunday after Easter), the couple should have secured a special licence from the Bishop of Worcester. They did not do so, although presumably they published banns in the parish church. Without a

licence the minister was at fault in conducting the service. The up-
shot was that Thomas and Judith were cited to the consistory court
in Worcester Cathedral. Thomas did not come on the appointed
day, and was excommunicated. Possibly Judith suffered the same
fate, although the record leaves that uncertain.[24] The offence was
not serious. Others married in Lent—three weddings took place in
Holy Trinity that February—and the Quineys may have just had the
bad luck to fall victim to an apparitor hungry for a fee. Walter
Nixon, who summoned them, does not have an especially savoury
history: he had later to face accusations in Star Chamber of taking
bribes and 'subtly' forging the name of the registrar of the episcopal
court on an injunction.[25] The excommunication anyway lasted only
a short while, for before the year was out the Quineys were at the
font to have their first-born christened in Stratford church.

Excommunication was the least of Thomas Quiney's worries that
winter. Before marrying, he had got Margaret Wheeler with child,
and by February she was dangerously pregnant.[26] Scandal turned to
tragedy when, a month after the Quiney wedding, the unfortunate
woman died in childbirth, and her infant with her. The parish
register records both burials on 15 March.

Sexual delinquencies—what the homily denounced as 'whoredom
and uncleanness'—fell within the purview of the ecclesiastical court
held by the vicar of Stratford: the very court before which Susanna
had been haled for not receiving the Sacrament in Easter 1606.
Many of the cases heard by such courts of peculiar jurisdiction had
to do with fornication and the like, so they became popularly, if
somewhat disrespectfully, known as 'bawdy courts'. To the bawdy
court of Stratford the apparitor Richard Greene (he seems to have
doubled as the parish clerk, for the burial register so describes him)
summoned the newly-wed Thomas Quiney. The act book records
the hearing and sentence on Tuesday, 26 March. In open court
Thomas confessed to having had carnal copulation with the said
Wheeler (*fassus est se carnalem copulacionem habuisse cum dicta
Wheeler*), and submitted himself to correction. The judge, vicar
John Rogers, sentenced the offender to perform open penance in a
white sheet, according to custom, in the church on three successive
Sundays before the whole congregation. But the penalty was re-

42. Thomas Quiney tried for fornication, 26 March 1616.

mitted. In effect Thomas got off for 5s. This sum he gave for the use of the poor of the parish, and the vicar ordered him to acknowledge his crime, in ordinary attire, before the minister of Bishopton (*ad agnoscendum crimen in habitu suo prop[r]io coram ministro de Bishopton*). Falling as it did within Stratford parish, Bishopton had no church of its own, only a chapel; so Quiney was spared public humiliation.

His subsequent history had more downs than ups. In July 1616 Thomas exchanged houses with his brother-in-law William Chandler, and moved into the more spacious and imposing structure called The Cage at the corner of the High Street and Bridge Street. There, in the upper half, Quiney set up his vintner's shop, and also dealt in tobacco. He held several municipal offices: in 1617 he was named burgess and then constable; in 1621 and 1622 the corporation appointed him chamberlain, his pinnacle of local recognition. Quiney signed his account for 1622-3 with flourishes, and pretentiously ornamented it with a couplet in French from a romance by Saint-Gelais. Unimpressed, the council voted the account 'imperfect' in his absence, but later passed it. Quiney, no scholar, made a hash

43. Judith Shakespeare's mark, 4 December 1611.

of the quotation.[27] (His wife was even less of a scholar, if we may judge from the fact that when in 1611 she witnessed a deed of Elizabeth Quiney and her son Adrian, she twice signed by mark.*) The corporation never thought highly enough of Quiney to make him an alderman. He sued about a shipment of wine from Bristol, was fined trifling sums for swearing and suffering townsmen to tipple in his house, and was once in danger of prosecution for dispensing unwholesome and adulterated wine. Around 1630 he tried to sell the lease of The Cage, but his kinsmen stopped him, and in 1633 assigned the lease in trust to a triumvirate consisting of Dr. Hall, Hall's son-in-law Thomas Nash, and Richard Watts, now Quiney's brother-in-law and the vicar of Harbury. This move protected the interests of Judith and the children. Obviously Thomas was not to be trusted. In November 1652 The Cage lease was made over to Richard Quiney, the London grocer. When the latter died three years later, he bequeathed his brother an allowance of £12 a year and £5 for his burial. Thomas does not seem to have ever left Strat-

---

* As remarked above (p. 37), the use of a mark did not necessarily denote illiteracy. Douglas Hamer has interestingly observed that 'down to about 1840 even women who could write letters, keep domestic (and often business) accounts, and run businesses, were usually required to "sign" legal documents, including their own wills, by inscribing a cross or other mark close to their names as written by the clerk'. The document witnessed by Judith was, however, also witnessed by Lettice Greene, who signed her name. Stratford may have been neither more nor less sexist than other towns, but if the custom described by Hamer obtained there in the early seventeenth century, it would presumably have applied indifferently to both females.

ford (he was selling wine to the corporation as late as 1650), although the parish register fails to record his burial. Possibly he predeceased his wife, although he may have died in 1662-3, when the burial records are incomplete.[28]

As parents the Quineys had bad luck. Their first child, whose name Shakespeare Quiney united the two families, died in infancy on 8 May 1617. There were two more sons: Richard, christened 9 February 1618, and Thomas, christened 23 January 1620. They died within a few weeks of one another in 1639, aged respectively twenty-one and nineteen. The Quineys had no more children.

Shakespeare lived to see neither these baptisms nor burials. He died on 23 April 1616. The Stratford register records the burial two days later of 'Will Shakspere, gent.'. His brother-in-law, the hatter William Hart, who had been living in the Birthplace, was buried just eight days earlier, on 17 April.

If, as seems likely, Dr. Hall attended his father-in-law during his last illness, he may have kept notes about the progress and treatment of the ailment, although his interest as a medical diarist lay in patients who recovered rather than succumbed. The earliest dated history in the extant case-book belongs to 1617. Conceivably a second notebook exists somewhere—Cooke refers to two Hall books—and may one day surface. Meanwhile, our only information about the circumstances of the poet's death derives from the diary of John Ward. This is the Stratford vicar and physician who reminded himself 'to peruse Shakespear's plays, and be versed in them' so as not to 'be ignorant in that matter'. Ward notes that 'Shakespear, Drayton and Ben Jhonson had a merry meeting, and it seems drank too hard, for Shakespear died of a fever there contracted.'

Ward's report, half a century after the event, must be consigned to the mythos; he claims no more than to echo hearsay—'it seems' is his qualifying phrase. Whether an evening's carouse could bring on a fatal fever is not for the medical layman to say, but Ward's story is in other respects not implausible. Shakespeare might well have gathered with his fellow Warwickshireman Drayton and his old theatrical comrade Jonson (no teetotaller) for a drinking party, and Judith's wedding provided a suitable pretext for such conviviality. Ward was, moreover, still in touch with a living tradition, for Ju-

dith, now advanced in years, dwelt nearby in Stratford (he refers
to her as 'Mrs. Queeny').

During the winter of 1616 Shakespeare summoned his lawyer
Francis Collins, who a decade earlier had drawn up the indentures
for the Stratford tithes transaction, to execute his last will and testament. Apparently this event took place in January, for when Collins was called upon to revise the document some weeks later, he or
his clerk (more likely Collins) inadvertently wrote January instead
of March, copying the word from the earlier draft. Revisions were
necessitated by the marriage of Judith, with its aftermath of the
Margaret Wheeler affair. The lawyer came on 25 March. A new first
page was required, and numerous substitutions and additions in the
second and third pages, although it is impossible to say how many
changes were made in March and how many, *currente calamo*, in
January. Collins never got around to having a fair copy of the will
made, probably because of haste occasioned by the seriousness of the
testator's condition, though this attorney had a way of allowing
much-corrected draft wills to stand. Shakespeare validated each sheet
at the bottom with his signature, prefixing the last with the em-
phatic 'By me'. He describes himself as 'in perfect health and memory', a conventional phrase and not always to be taken at face value,
although perhaps apt enough in January; the law anyway would be
concerned with his memory rather than his health. In March a feeble hand held the pen. The invalid mustered all his strength for the
firm strokes of 'By me William' in the third signature, then col-
lapsed into the wavering scrawl of the surname. His two other signatures display (according to palaeographical analysis) 'weakness
and malformation'. Shakespeare was dying that March, although he
would linger for another month.

His will has given rise to even more discussion and debate than
the marriage licence bond. Yet the first to pronounce on it, the
Stratford antiquary Joseph Greene, who turned up a transcript of
the testament in 1747, was positively depressed by his discovery.
'The Legacies and Bequests therein', he informed a friend, 'are undoubtedly as he intended; but the manner of introducing them, appears to me so dull and irregular, so absolutely void of yᵉ least
particle of that Spirit which Animated Our great Poet; that it must

lessen his Character as a Writer, to imagine yᵉ least Sentence of it his production.'[29] A twentieth-century student, B. Roland Lewis, who has lovingly annotated every provision, understandably takes a different view: 'Rowe said (1709) that the spirit of the man is to be found in his works. Rather the essential spirit of William Shakespeare is to be found in his will, its preparation constituting virtually the last act of his active life only a few weeks before he died.'[30] The truth lies somewhere between these extremes. Shakespeare's will is not a poetic testament but 'a characteristic will of a man of property in the reign of James I'.[31] In such a document it is futile to seek metaphor or dark conceit, or even intimate revelation. But the will does yield a glimpse of Shakespeare's purpose in building an estate from the proceeds of his play-writing, and it enshrines the names of those he cherished most in Stratford and in London.

The will begins with a pious declaration:

> In the name of God, Amen. I, William Shackspeare . . . in perfect health and memory, God be praised, do make and ordain this my last will and testament in manner and form following. That is to say, first I commend my soul into the hands of God my Creator, hoping and assuredly believing through the only merits of Jesus Christe my Saviour, to be made partaker of life everlasting; and my body to the earth whereof it is made.

To find here a confession of personal faith is to consider the matter too curiously. The preamble is formulaic, following almost word for word a model included by William West of the Inner Temple in his *First Part of Simboleography, which may be termed the Art, or Description, of Instruments and Precedents.* West's second 'form of a will' commences, 'In the name of God, Amen. . . . sick of body but of good and perfect memory (God be praised). . . . First I commend my soul into the hands of God my maker, hoping assuredly through the only merits of Jesus Christ my Saviour, to be made partaker of life everlasting. And I commend my body to the earth whereof it is made.'[32] Shakespeare did not have to supply Collins with these phrases; he set them down automatically.

Of his several heirs, Shakespeare considers first the case of Judith—because of her, the page required recopying. 'Item. I give and bequeath unto my son-in-l[aw]'; so the lawyer took down the dying man's words, but Shakespeare caught himself—Collins (or his clerk) crossed out 'son-in-law' and wrote instead 'daughter Judyth'. She is to have £150, with strings attached. One hundred pounds go to her for a marriage portion, but for the remaining £50 she must renounce any claim to 'one copyhold tenement . . . being parcel or holden of the manor of Rowington'; this was the Chapel Lane cottage. Shakespeare further bequeaths Judith 'one hundred and fifty pounds more if she or any issue of her body be living at the end of three years next ensuing the day of the date of this my will. . . .' Should she, however, die barren during this interval, his granddaughter Elizabeth Hall (in the will called his niece)* will have £100, the other £50 going to his sister Joan and her children. If Judith, or any issue, is living after three years, then the executors will see to it that she enjoys the annual interest earned by the £150, although not the principal, so long as she stays married. Her husband can claim the sum only on condition that he 'do sufficiently assure unto her and the issue of her body lands answerable to the portion by this my will given unto her'—in other words, that he settle on his wife lands worth the £150. Later in the will, on sheet three, Shakespeare gives Judith his 'broad silver-gilt bowl'. Chambers in 1930 guessed that Shakespeare's careful provisions respecting his younger daughter argued no great confidence in Thomas Quiney, and the suspicions—which he was not the first to harbour—have been borne out by the discoveries in the act book for the Stratford ecclesiastical court. It is perhaps not too fanciful to speculate, with Hugh Hanley and E. R. C. Brinkworth, that Quiney's trial and disgrace not only motivated the alterations in the will but also constituted a shock that hastened Shakespeare's end.[33]

Lesser bequests follow. Shakespeare leaves £20 and his wearing apparel to Joan Hart, who is permitted to stay on with her family in the western house in Henley Street for a nominal yearly rent of 12d. Her three sons—he names William and Michael, but memory fails for the third, and a blank space is left for Thomas—are bequeathed £5 each. Elizabeth Hall gets all the plate, except for Ju-

* 'Niece' at this time could still carry the now obsolete sense of 'granddaughter', a usage found (Halliwell-Phillipps observes) in the Wycliffite Bible.

dith's broad silver-gilt bowl. Shakespeare, it seems, also considered providing Elizabeth with a marriage portion; but she was only eight —who knows? Susanna might bear more children—and so he changed his mind, ordering the incompletely stated clause to be struck out. The poet remembered the poor of Stratford with a donation of £10, generous enough for a man of his means; the town's richest man, John Combe, had three years earlier left £20 for the same purpose—a munificence thought worthy of mention on his monument in Stratford church.[34] Shakespeare gives his sword to Thomas, the nephew of the same Combe. The testator leaves £5 to Thomas Russell, and £13.6s.8d. to Francis Collins. (Russell, it will be recalled, was the Alderminster squire connected by marriage to the author of *Willobie his Avisa*; after his wife's death, he courted and won Anne Digges, a widow with £12,000 and two sons, Dudley and Leonard.) Money to buy memorial rings, each to cost 26s.8d., Shakespeare sets aside for old Stratford friends and neighbours: Hamnet Sadler, William Reynolds (the recusant landowner), and the Nash brothers, Anthony and John (they had witnessed Shakespeare's purchase of the Old Stratford freehold in 1602). Sadler's name replaces that of 'Mr. Richard Tyler the elder', the butcher's son of Sheep Street whom the dying man may have known from his schooldays; Tyler had just come under criticism for his handling of collections for victims of the great fire—perhaps that is why his name was deleted from the will.[35] Shakespeare does not forget his seven-year-old godson, William Walker, whom he leaves 20s. in gold. Of all those he had known in London during his years with the Chamberlain's company and then the King's men, the playwright singles out three for affectionate remembrance: 'and to my fellows John Hemynges, Richard Burbage and Henry Cundell xxvis.viiid. apiece to buy them rings'. Shakespeare neglects to mention Southampton, to whom, as an aspiring young poet, he had offered *Venus and Adonis* and *The Rape of Lucrece*; or the Earls of Pembroke and Montgomery; or, for that matter, any peer of the realm. Nor does he name any of his wife's relations, although his husbandman brother-in-law Bartholomew Hathaway—with his wife Isabel and their four offspring—lived in nearby Shottery.

His wife he failed to mention too, at least at first; but maybe he felt no specific provision was needed—the Halls, responsible folk, would look after her at New Place. But there is another, complicating factor, first publicly noticed over a century ago by the Victorian popularizer Charles Knight. English common law, Knight triumphantly disclosed, guaranteed the widow a life interest of one third in her husband's estate, as well as residence in the family domicile. Many subsequent biographers have assumed that Anne was so protected. Certainly what is sometimes called the widow's portion, or legitim, did exist, and is traceable back to the thirteenth century. If the common law gave the male partner, upon matrimony, all his wife's goods and chattels, 'shall not the husband', the anonymous author of *A Brief Discourse* rhetorically asks in 1584,

> be bound by semblable obligation of reason to leave his wife the third part of his goods, and if the law be in that respect defective (as what law in the world, except the law of God, is without his imperfections?) shall not the custom supply it in such sort that no barbarous and uncharitable or cautelous, and unkind practices by deed of gift, or otherwise, shall disappoint or defraud the same?[36]

But the writer here extols the special virtues of London, and the problem with local customs is that they are local. 'There was such a custom of dower right in London . . . ,' Miss Marchette Chute grants, but 'no such custom in Stratford.'[37] Roland Lewis is similarly positive. This question, like so many others, is however more complicated than at first appears. A widow's portion comprised both land and chattels. With respect to land, custom appears to have operated fairly uniformly, the widow's right being recognized from early until modern times (the law of property act of 1925 converted common law dower of land into an equitable interest). As regards chattels, custom varied from borough to borough. One would like to know more about Stratford practice. Wills do not provide the answer, for custom functions when the wills are silent.

Most Stratford wills of the period look after the wife, provision being covered by some such catch-all phrase as 'the residue of my estate'; and Shakespeare, as the world well knows, did not utterly ignore his Anne. The famous bequest, however, is curious: 'Item. I give unto my wife my second-best bed with the furniture' (i.e. the hangings, valance, bed linens, etc.). This provision has provoked endless, mostly unprofitable, controversy. 'His wife had not wholly escaped his memory', Malone wrote in the eighteenth century; 'he had forgot her,—he had recollected her,—but so recollected her, as more strongly to mark how little he esteemed her; he had already (as is vulgarly expressed) cut her off, not indeed with a shilling, but with an old bed.'[38] The bequest appears as an interlineation—hence Malone's reference (often echoed) to forgetfulness and recollection —but Shakespeare's will contains other interlineations: William Reynolds, for example, and the dramatist's beloved fellow-sharers are thus assured their memorial rings. Failure of memory? Perhaps. But at least as likely—so Charles Severn long ago suggested—the lawyer setting down the will, and writing rapidly, inadvertently missed these bequests, and backtracked to insert them.[39]

Nevertheless, whether an oversight or no, the bed presents a problem. Many have assumed, with Malone, that the bequest was derisive. But another school of opinion, equally long-standing, holds that the Shakespeares must have reserved their best bed for overnight guests at New Place, and that the less valuable bed was the one rich in matrimonial associations. Investigators have turned over countless Elizabethan and Jacobean wills in search of analogous bequests, and their pursuits have not gone entirely unrewarded. When Francis Russell, second Earl of Bedford, died in London in 1585, he willed his 'best bed of cloth of gold and silver', with King Henry VIII's arms, not to his wife but to his youngest daughter.[40] More to the point is the testament of William Palmer of Leamington, who in 1573 left his wife Elizabeth 'all her wearing apparel' and his 'second best featherbed for herself furnished, and one other meaner featherbed furnished for her maid'; he also doubled the income she would receive from the original marriage settlement, 'in consideration that she is a gentlewoman and drawing towards years, and that' —the testator affirms—'I would have her to live as one that were and had been my wife'.[41] This is apposite, and who would gainsay the conjugal affection informing the bequest?

It is also the case that a testator might deliberately deprive his spouse of a bed simply because of its associations: '. . . leave thy

44. Shakespeare's will, 25 March 1616: sheet three, with the bequest of
the second-best bed.

wife more than of necessity thou must, but only during her widow-
hood,' Sir Walter Raleigh advised his son; 'for if she love again, let
her not enjoy her second love in the same bed wherein she loved
thee.'[42] Others must have felt similar anxieties. But Anne's age—she
was then sixty or thereabouts—makes it unlikely that apprehension
about a second love influenced this particular bequest. The problem,
as regards the provision in Shakespeare's will, is that the scant attention paid to the wife is unusual, and what is said lacks any accompanying testamentary emotion, such as we find in the Palmer will;
but Shakespeare includes no endearing references to other family
members either, and perhaps his attorney did not encourage, or per-

mit, such flourishes. Hence our choice between cynicism and sentiment. The latter surely affords the more attractive option, but this
is a matter that can be no more than inferentially resolved.

An essential article of furniture such as the best bed qualified
as an heirloom, and would normally pass to the legal heir. So
borough custom recognised. In fourteenth-century Torksey an heir
was to have the better bed with counterpane and sheets ('meliorem
lectum cum tapeto et linthiaminis'); in Archinfield in 1663 custom
held that the eldest took possession of 'the best bed and furniture'.[43]
In the Shakespeare dispensation, the best bed would, as befitted an
heirloom, swell the value of 'all the rest of my goods, chattels, leases,
plate, jewels, and household stuff whatsoever, after my debts and
legacies paid and my funeral expenses discharged'. The 'leases' might
include Shakespeare's shares, if he still held them, in the Globe and
Blackfriars. All this he wills to his son-in-law John Hall and his
daughter Susanna.

She receives more—much more—besides: the great house of New
Place, 'wherein I now dwell',

> and two messuages or tenements with the appurtenances situate
> . . . in Henley Street within the borough of Stratford aforesaid;
> and all my barns, stables, orchards, gardens, lands, tenements, and
> hereditaments whatsoever, situate . . . within the towns, hamlets,
> villages, fields, and grounds of Stratford upon Avon, Oldstratford,
> Bushopton, and Welcombe, or in any of them, in the said county
> of Warwick; and also all that messuage or tenement with the ap-
> purtenances wherein one John Robinson dwelleth, situate . . . in
> the Blackfriers in London, near the Wardrobe; and all other my
> lands, tenements, and hereditaments whatsoever.

These properties, the bulk of the estate, are hers to have and to hold
for the rest of her natural life. After her death the premises and
appurtenances are to descend to the Halls' first son, and to that son's
lawful male heirs, and (in default of such issue) to the second son's
male heirs, and so on to the third, fourth, fifth, sixth, and seventh
sons, and their lawful heirs. 'And for default of such issue the said
premises to be and remain to my said niece Hall and the heirs males
of her body lawfully issuing. And for default of such issue, to my
daughter Judith and the heirs males of her body lawfully issu-

ing. . . .' In this way Shakespeare sought to hold together the material possessions purchased by his art. He could not have foreseen that nature would defeat his plans.

That the will lists no books or literary manuscripts has raised some eyebrows. This is not, however, as odd as might appear. Shakespeare's play-scripts were not his to dispose of—they belonged to the King's men. Books might have been separately itemized in the inventory post-mortem, but this has not come down. In any event, they would form part of the goods inherited by the Halls, and perhaps thus found a place on the doctor's shelves alongside his medical treatises. If so, a special interest attaches to the 'study of books' to which Hall refers in his nuncupative (i.e. orally declared) will of 1635, and which he bequeathed to his son-in-law, 'to dispose of them as you see good'. Two years later Susanna and her son-in-law charged in Chancery that Baldwin Brooks (afterwards to become the bailiff of Stratford) had suborned an undersheriff and some bailiffs—'men of mean estate'—to break open the doors and study of New Place, and rashly seize 'divers books' and 'other goods of great value'.[44] Brooks had been frustrated in his efforts to collect a judgement against the Hall estate.

During the Civil War, Queen Henrietta Maria, marching in triumph from Newark to Kineton with her forces, joined up with Prince Rupert and his troops in Stratford. There, in July 1643, the Queen kept her court at Stratford for three days, and for two nights slept at New Place. Maybe Susanna Hall then gave Colonel Richard Grace, chamberlain to the Duke of York, Henri Estienne's *Marvellous Discourse upon the Life of Katherine de Medicis*, for a surviving copy is inscribed in a seventeenth–century hand (not Susanna's): 'Liber R: Gracei ex dono amicae D. Susanne Hall'. Maybe too the book once formed part of her father's library. But, unfortunately for this pleasant suggestion, there is no record of Grace being in the Queen's entourage on that occasion.

Reports about Shakespeare's manuscripts first began to circulate in the next century. In 1729 John Roberts, who describes himself as 'a Stroling Player', lamented that '*Two* large *Chests* full of this GREAT MAN's *loose Papers* and *Manuscripts,* in the Hands of an ignorant *Baker* of WARWICK, (who married one of the Descendants from *Shakespear*) were carelesly scatter'd and thrown about, as Garret Lumber and Litter, to the particular Knowledge of the late *Sir William Bishop*, till they were all consum'd in the general Fire and Destruction of that Town'. Sir William Bishop (1626-1700) did live in the Shakespeare country, and a conflagration inflicted much damage on Warwick in 1694; but no descendant of Shakespeare or of the Harts is known to have then dwelt there.[45] Malone reports that in 1742 Sir Hugh Clopton, born two years after the death of the poet's granddaughter Elizabeth, told the actor Macklin of 'an old tradition that she had carried away with her from Stratford many of her grandfather's papers'.[46]

Shakespeare appointed Thomas Russell and Francis Collins overseers of his will. Five witnesses signed the document: Collins, July (or Julyns) Shaw, John Robinson, Hamnet Sadler, and Robert Whatcott. The last-named had testified for Susanna when she sued for defamation in 1613. Robinson was a labourer. Whatcott and Robinson may have been servants of Shakespeare or the Halls.[47] The Halls were the executors. A note under Shakespeare's signature on the third sheet attests that the will was proved by John Hall on 22 June 1616.

Shakespeare was laid to rest in the chancel of Holy Trinity Church near the north wall. According to a report late in the century, they 'laid him full seventeen foot deep, deep enough to secure him'; but this seems unlikely so close to where the Avon flows.[48] On the slab covering the poet's grave—'a plain free stone', Mr. Dowdall described it in 1693—appear these words:

GOOD FREND FOR JESUS SAKE FORBEARE,

TO DIGG THE DUST ENCLOASED HEARE:

BLESTE BE $\overset{E}{Y}$ MAN $\overset{T}{Y}$ SPARES THES STONES,

AND CURST BE HE $\overset{T}{Y}$ MOVES MY BONES.*

Several reporters in the late seventeenth century affirm that Shakespeare himself devised this epitaph, and ordered it to be cut on his tombstone.[49]

* BLESTE: a disputed reading, BLESE being a possible alternative.

45. William Shakespeare buried, 25 April 1616.

The malediction, expressing a conventional sentiment in commonplace phrases, solemnly forewarns not the casual passerby—he would hardly come with spade in hand—but the sexton, who, because of the limited burial space available in the church, sometimes had to dig up graves and remove the bones to the adjoining charnel-house. William Hall, who would become prebendary of St. Paul's, had something to say about the charnel-house and the curse when he wrote to 'Dear Neddy' (the noted Anglo-Saxon scholar Edward Thwaites) in 1694:

> There is in this church a place which they call the bone-house, a repository for all bones they dig up; which are so many that they would load a great number of wagons. The poet being willing to preserve his bones unmoved, lays a curse upon him that moves them; and having to do with clerks and sextons, for the most part a very ignorant sort of people, he descends to the meanest of their capacities; and disrobes himself of that art, which none of his cotemporaries wore in greater perfection.[50]

Whether or not actually written by Shakespeare, the malediction has effectively accomplished its purpose, for no sexton, clerk, or crank has moved the bones enclosed there. By the mid-eighteenth century, however, the gravestone itself (according to Halliwell-Phillipps) had sunk below floor level, and was so decayed that the overseers of the church replaced it.

There are those who suspect that Shakespeare's remains lie in the church rather than in the churchyard not because he was the celebrated poet of the London stage but because his purchase of an interest in Stratford tithes qualified him as a lay rector. However this may be, before the end of the century folk were finding their way to Holy Trinity 'to visit the ashes of the great Shakespear which lie interred in that church'. They also paused, as innumerable pilgrims have since done, before the effigy installed, about five feet above the grave, in the north wall of the chancel. As early as 1634 Lieutenant Hammond, passing through Stratford, found the 'neat monument' worthy of remark.[51] From a manuscript note in a 1653 almanac, we learn that it was made 'by one Gerard Johnson'.[52]

The name is an anglicized version, not unusual, of Gheerart Janssen, whose father (also Gheerart) had emigrated from Amsterdam to London around 1567 and set up shop as a stonemason in Southwark, not far from the Globe. Two of his five sons helped in the business, which prospered: the Janssens erected tombs in Bottesford church in Leicestershire for three Earls of Rutland, the last ordered by the same sixth Earl who bespoke an *impresa* of Shakespeare and Burbage. When the elder Janssen died in 1611, his family kept the business going. Possibly Shakespeare and his fellows knew the shop. Certainly the poet's family were acquainted with the tomb, with recumbent effigy in a gown, fashioned by Gheerart the younger for John Combe. In his will Combe had allocated £60 for this memorial in Stratford church.

For the Shakespeare monument, which is in Jacobean Renaissance style, Janssen worked mainly in white marble, with black for the two Corinthian columns, and black touchstone for the inlaid panels. The columns support a cornice on which sit two small cherubic figures, both male: the left one, holding a spade, represents Labour; the right, with a skull and inverted torch, signifies Rest. They flank the familiar Shakespeare arms, helm, and crest, carved in bas-relief on a square stone block. The design forms a pyramid at the apex of which sits another skull, chapless and hollow-eyed.

One suspects that the reverence inspired by the bust—actually a half-length figure carved from soft bluish Cotswold limestone—owes less to the execution than to the subject and setting. Wearing a sleeveless gown over a doublet, Shakespeare stands with a quill pen in his right hand, a sheet of paper under his left, both hands resting on a cushion. He looks prosperous, with unwrinkled brow, high bald dome, and thick, short neck. The side-locks are bobbed, the moustaches and beard neatly trimmed; the eyes (set too close together) stare vacantly ahead. One reminds oneself that it is unreasonable to expect lively touches of nature in a commissioned piece of funerary

46. The Shakespeare Bust.

sculpture, which tended as a class towards formalized rigidity; this effigy bears a generic resemblance to that of John Stow (d. 1605) in St. Andrew Undershaft church in London.

Dover Wilson sees 'a self-satisfied pork-butcher' peering out from under the niched arch of the monument. Maybe so; but not all middle-aged successful writers look delicately consumptive. For better or for worse, the Janssen bust is an authentic portrayal, all the rest, save one, being derivative, spurious, or in varying degrees doubt-

ful. The monument in Holy Trinity was presumably commissioned
and paid for by one or more of the surviving adult members of
Shakespeare's immediate family: the widow, the two daughters, the
two sons-in-law, and his sister. Most probably Dr. Hall looked after
the arrangements. Whoever took the responsibility, the family,
whether entirely satisfied or not, presumably found the likeness
acceptable. It is even possible that Janssen, working as he did on
Bankside, benefited from the suggestions of Shakespeare's former
colleagues in the King's men. And however burgher-like the subject
may appear, he stands before us as the poet, not the man of property, for his mouth is open to declaim his just-composed verses.

So too the tablet under the cushion celebrates the writer:

> JUDICIO PYLIUM, GENIO SOCRATEM, ARTE
>   MARONEM:
>   TERRA TEGIT, POPULUS MÆRET, OLYMPUS
>   HABET.
>
> STAY PASSENGER, WHY GOEST THOU BY SO
>   FAST?
> READ IF THOU CANST, WHOM ENVIOUS DEATH
>   HATH PLAST,
> WITH IN THIS MONUMENT SHAKSPEARE:
>   WITH WHOME,
> QUICK NATURE DIDE: WHOSE NAME DOTH
>   DECK Y^s TOMBE,
> FAR MORE THEN COST: SIEH ALL, Y^T HE HATH
>   WRITT,
> LEAVES LIVING ART, BUT PAGE, TO SERVE HIS
>   WITT.
>   OBIIT AÑO DO^I 1616
>   ÆTATIS · 53 DIE 23 AP^R.

The stone-cutter mistakenly carved 'SIEH' instead of 'SITH', but
such slips of the chisel are common enough in monumental inscriptions of all ages. A more serious blunder is made by the unknown
eulogist when he suggests that Death has placed the poet within

the monument. About all he has to offer in the way of information is that Shakespeare died on the twenty-third of April in his fifty-third year.

Around mid-century, Sir William Dugdale, born in Warwickshire on a day when (by happy omen) bees swarmed in his father's garden, visited Stratford to gather materials for his enormous *Antiquities of Warwickshire Illustrated: from Records, Leiger-Books, Manuscripts, Charters, Evidences, Tombs, and Arms: Beautified with Maps, Prospects and Portraitures*, published in a splendid folio in 1656. Although Dugdale's compilation is invaluable, the engraving made by Hollar or his assistant Gaywood from an author's sketch of Shakespeare's monument is perplexing rather than helpful, for we reconcile it with difficulty with the familiar artefact in the chancel. In the illustration in the *Antiquities* leopards' heads adorn the capitals, while on the outermost points of the cornice Rest and Labour perch precariously, the former having exchanged his torch for an hourglass. The poet has parted with quill and paper; instead, elbows akimbo, he clutches the cushion—does it represent wealth? His cheeks have shrivelled, his moustaches droop disconsolately below the tight lips. The complacent pork-butcher has metamorphosed into a melancholy tailor.[53]

We are reminded that the monument too has had a history. Over the years it deteriorated, until by 1748 the statue, several fingers amputated, required repair and beautifying which 'Mr. John Hall, Limner', supported by local contributions, accomplished the following year. Later in the century Malone, in a singular aberration, persuaded the vicar of Stratford to have the bust painted white, and for his pains was rewarded with an epigram inserted in the Stratford *Visitors' Book*:

> Stranger, to whom this monument is shewn,
> Invoke the Poet's curse upon Malone;
> Whose meddling zeal his barbarous taste betrays,
> And daubs his tombstone, as he mars his plays![54]

In 1861 a limner applied fresh colours to the bust; a healthy glow suffused Shakespeare's cheeks, his locks became auburn and his

47. The Shakespeare monument in Dugdale's *Antiquities of Warwickshire* (1656).

doublet scarlet.* That these were Janssen's colours must remain uncertain, but no amount of restoration can have transformed the monument of Dugdale's engraving into the effigy in Stratford church.† The best and simplest explanation is that the illustration, like others in the *Antiquities*, misrepresents the object, in keeping with the liberty of seventeenth-century engraving. The main interest of Dugdale, who was later to become Garter King-of-Arms, lay in pedigrees, inscriptions, and the like. In the engraving the armorial bearings are accurately delineated. (A comparison of the engraving with the drawing—perhaps still extant—on which it is based might be revealing.) The monument in Holy Trinity, with its uninspiring bust, is authentic enough.

It had been installed by 1623. In that year Leonard Digges, an Oxford scholar and translator and a Shakespeare enthusiast—he was the stepson of the Thomas Russell mentioned by Shakespeare in his will—alludes to Janssen's handiwork in his poem 'To the Memory of the deceased Author, Master W. Shakespeare':‡

> Shake-speare, at length thy pious fellows give
> The world thy works: thy works, by which, out-live
> Thy tomb, thy name must. When that stone is rent,

---

* The colours are thus described by M. H. Spielmann, 'Shakespeare's Portraiture', in *Studies in the First Folio written for the Shakespeare Association* (1924), p. 14; cited by EKC, ii. 184. Shakespeare's complexion has since darkened to a deep tan, and the eyes are almost black. On the monument Spielmann and Chambers are my principal authorities. The latter expertly sums up scholarship (ii. 182-5). Spielmann (pp. 4-5) makes the point about the Stow monument.
† It has lately again suffered desecration. On the night of 2 October 1973 intruders removed the bust from the monument by chipping out part of the plinth. The police believe they 'were seeking valuable manuscripts written by the Bard' (Birmingham *Evening Mail*, 3 October 1973). These were regrettably unforthcoming. The bust, which I examined shortly after the incident, sustained only very slight damage.
‡ There is in Balliol College Library a copy of the third edition of Lope de Vega's *Rimas* (Madrid, 1613) with a fly-leaf inscription to 'Mr. Mab' in which Digges speaks of 'this book of sonnets, which with Spaniards here is accounted of their Lope de Vega as in England we should of our Will Shakespeare' (Paul Morgan, '"Our Will Shakespeare" and Lope de Vega: An Unrecorded Contemporary Document', *Shakespeare Survey 16* (Cambridge, 1963), pp. 118-20).

> And Time dissolves thy Stratford monument,
> Here we alive shall view thee still.

The 'fellows' here applauded—in a context that brings to mind a familiar *topos* of the *Sonnets*—are Heminges and Condell, and their piety of course lies in the gathering together and publication of the plays of the First Folio. That book has indeed, as Digges foretold, made Shakespeare 'look/Fresh to all ages'.

Mr. William Shakespeare's Comedies, Histories, and Tragedies appeared at the end of 1623. The Stationers' Register entry, dated 8 November, lists sixteen plays 'not formerly entered to other men'. These include some of Shakespeare's best-loved works—*The Tempest, Twelfth Night, Julius Caesar*, and *Macbeth*—and represent all phases of his career; they are printed for the first time in the Folio. Not mentioned in the entry are *The Taming of the Shrew* and *King John*, which also find a place in the volume. Although new, they perhaps did not require registration because they passed as reprints of *The Taming of A Shrew* and the anonymous *Troublesome Reign of John, King of England*, the latter, printed in 1591, being related, probably as source, to Shakespeare's play. Heminges and Condell excluded *Pericles* and *The Two Noble Kinsmen*. A consortium of Stationers sponsored the large and expensive book, but Edward Blount and Isaac Jaggard were the final publishers. It might appear odd that Jaggard should figure in the undertaking at all, let alone so prominently, for his father William had not only offended with *The Passionate Pilgrim* but had a few years later teamed up with Thomas Pavier to bring out a dubious series of Shakespeare quartos. Jaggard and Pavier were not too fussy about the texts they selected, which included the apocryphal *Yorkshire Tragedy*, and they were ordered to desist when the King's men complained to the Lord Chamberlain. Jaggard got round the restraint by ante-dating editions, from his shop, of *The Merchant of Venice, A Midsummer-Night's Dream*, and others; thus he put the year 1608 on the title-page of the 1619 *King Lear*. Evidently Heminges and Condell, leading members of the King's company, bore no lasting grudge against Jaggard for his piratical ways. The latter died before 4 November 1623, while the Folio was being printed, and his son took over management of the shop.* A copy of the volume was bound by the Bodleian Library on 17 February 1624, this being the earliest reference to the published First Folio.

The title-page features a portrait of the author signed by the engraver, Martin Droeshout, under the lower left-hand corner.[55] Droeshout belonged to the third generation of a Flemish family of artists translated to London; his grandfather John Droeshout, a painter and joiner, had come over from Brussels in 1566. Martin was only fifteen when Shakespeare died, and twenty-two when the Folio appeared; hardly very experienced in his craft. How he obtained the commission we do not know—perhaps his fee was as modest as his gifts. As the printing of the book proceeded, Droeshout's copperplate was twice altered. In the exceedingly rare first, or 'proof', state, the ruff lacks shading under the ear. This is supplied in the second state; in the third, which is most common, a single out-of-place hair is to be detected on the right edge of the silhouette. For succeeding seventeenth-century folios, the printers used the same plate, which gradually coarsened. By 1685, when the Fourth (and last) Folio was published, a stubble covered the chin, and the complexion looked swarthy, with oily highlights.

The portrait has not gone entirely without admirers. 'What a powerful impression it gives', enthuses Dr. Rowse: 'that searching look of the eyes understanding everything, what a forehead, what a brain!'[56] But the engraver has depicted not the brain, only the forehead, described by another observer as that 'horrible hydrocephalus development'. Droeshout's deficiencies are, alas, only too gross. The huge head on a plate of a ruff surmounts a disproportionately small doublet. One eye is lower and larger than the other, the hair does not balance at the sides, light comes from several directions. It is unlikely that Droeshout ever sketched Shakespeare from the life. Probably he worked from a line drawing supplied to him. Still the Folio editors, who knew Shakespeare well, did not reject the likeness, and Jonson was able to bring himself to supply a few perfunctory lines of commendation, printed on the adjoining leaf. No doubt only

* Isaac was named City Printer on 4 November, 'in the place of . . . his late father deceased' (W. W. Greg, *The Shakespeare First Folio* (Oxford, 1955), p. 8).

48. The Droeshout engraving, 1623.

an over-subtle reader will detect a latent irony in Jonson's conclusion—'Reader, look / Not on his picture, but his book'—but the advice is sound enough.

Other preliminary leaves dedicate the Folio to William Herbert, third Earl of Pembroke (the Lord Chamberlain), and his younger brother Philip, first Earl of Montgomery, and offer commendations of the playwright in verse and prose. In an epistle 'To the great Variety of Readers', the editors praise the happy facility of their friend and fellow: 'His mind and hand went together, and what he thought, he uttered with that easiness, that we have scarce received from him a blot in his papers.' They also claim that 'as where (before) you were abused with divers stolen and surreptitious copies, maimed and deformed by the frauds and stealths of injurious impostors that exposed them, even those are now offered to your view cured, and perfect of their limbs; and all the rest, absolute in their numbers, as he conceived them'. The implications of this statement, which has inspired volumes of gloss, lie outside the biographer's province.[57] There follows Jonson's eulogy of the sweet swan of Avon, the best-known such poem in the language. It too has received much commentary, and ever since 1693, when Dryden characterized it as 'an insolent, sparing, and invidious panegyric', some readers have discerned sinister undercurrents of aspersion flowing beneath the surface of compliment. It has also been pointed out that the praise, or much of it, has a lapidary conventionality. That no doubt is true, but to the present writer, at least, Jonson's tribute seems sympathetic enough.[58] Other verse tributes—by Hugh Holland, Leonard Digges, and I. M.—follow. Then the thirty-six plays.

Although the widow lived to see Shakespeare's monument placed in Stratford church, she died just before the publication of the Folio. The brass on her gravestone, which is to the left of her husband's in

49. Anne Shakespeare buried, 8 August 1623.

50. Susanna Hall buried, 16 July 1649.

the chancel, informs us that she 'DEPARTED THIS LIFE THE 6ᵀᴴ DAY OF AUGUST: 1623 · BEING OF THE AGE OF · 67 · YEARES'. The Latin epitaph underneath fittingly memorializes the mother who gave life and milk. From the parish register we learn that she was buried on 8 August. Susanna died on 11 July 1649 at the age of sixty-six, and was interred five days later, to the right of her husband in the chancel. Dugdale records the epitaph, later erased and still later reinstated.

Judith lived on into the Restoration. On 9 February 1662, less than two weeks after her seventy-seventh birthday, 'Judith, uxor Thomas Quiney, Gent.' was buried, presumably in the churchyard. She had survived her twin brother Hamnet by sixty-six years. In this family the women outlasted their menfolk. Dowdall in 1693 reports a tradition that Shakespeare's 'wife and daughters did earnestly desire to be laid in the same grave with him', but 'for fear of the curse' nobody dared 'touch his gravestone'.

The Halls' only child Elizabeth in 1626 married Thomas Nash. He was the eldest son of the Anthony Nash remembered with a ring by the poet in his will. Thomas had studied law at Lincoln's Inn, but never seems to have practised, being comfortably off—he inherited, in addition to land, the inn called the Bear in Bridge Street. The couple presumably lived for a time in the dwelling now called Nash House, adjoining New Place. Thomas died in 1647, at the age of fifty-three, and was buried in the chancel, to the right of Shakespeare, with the combined arms of Nash, Hall, and Shakespeare

51. Judith Quiney buried, 9 February 1662.

318

carved on his gravestone. Two years later, on 5 June 1649, Elizabeth took a second husband, John Bernard (or Barnard) of Abington Manor in Northamptonshire. The wedding took place at Billesley, a hamlet four miles west of Stratford. A widowed country squire then forty, Bernard had eight children by his first wife. When her mother died, Elizabeth inherited the joint Shakespeare and Hall estates, including the Birthplace and New Place, but the couple finished their days at Abington Manor. On 25 November 1661 King Charles II rewarded Bernard with a baronetcy, for he had done the state some service during the Civil War. Lady Bernard died childless in 1670, at the age of sixty-one, and was presumably interred with other Bernards in the village church, although no monument or gravestone survives for her.* Judith Quiney's sons were dead too. 'He was the best of his family', Dowdall said of Shakespeare after visiting Stratford church in 1693, 'but the male line is extinguished.' In fact the whole direct line—male and female—was now extinct.

The Henley Street houses passed to the Harts, who remained in possession until 1806. New Place eventually returned to the Cloptons who had originally built it. In 1702 Sir John Clopton made extensive alterations along neo-classic lines. A later owner, the vicar Francis Gastrell of Frodsham, demolished New Place in 1759. Only the well and a few foundation stones remain. The vines and Shakespeare's mulberry are no longer there, but another ancient mulberry, grown from a scion of the one he reputedly planted, adorns the lawn in the Great Garden.

---

* Elizabeth was christened on 21 February 1608 and buried on 17 February 1670, so in a couple of days she would have been sixty-two.

Postscript

A Postscript must suffice for late-arriving intelligence and a few afterthoughts. Richard Hosley, cited (p. 139) for his chapter on the playhouses in *A New Companion to Shakespeare Studies* (1971), reviews the evidence again, this time more fully, in *The Revels History of Drama in English*, ed. Clifford Leech and T. W. Craik (1975-), i. 119-235. Although G. Blakemore Evans includes the 'Ill May-Day' addition to 'Sir Thomas More' in *The Riverside Shakespeare* (1974), the new orthodoxy is not yet monolithic, as two fairly recent exercises in scepticism witness: the Hays essay (cited above, pp. 341-2 n. 49) and Paul Ramsey, 'Shakespeare and *Sir Thomas More* Revisited: or, a Mounty on the Trail', *Papers of the Bibliographical Society of America*, lxx (1976), 333-46). There is a useful discussion of Lawrence Fletcher (p. 251) by Sir James Fergusson of Kilkerran in *The Man Behind Macbeth and Other Studies* (1969), pp. 13-21. On Shakespeare's Consort (pp. 91-3, 320 n. 22) I had a letter, dated 19 October 1976, from M. Jean Adhémar, the Conservateur en Chef of the Cabinet des Estampes of the Bibliothèque Nationale. He writes: 'La dame en question porte la fraise d'avant 1577; sa coiffure ne semble pas figurer dans les dessins français.' Roland Mushat Frye finds a resemblance between the drawing and works of the anonymous Master of the Countess of Warwick painted between 1567 and 1569.

In 1977 Terry Hands directed a notable revival of all three parts of *Henry VI* (see p. 161) for the Royal Shakespeare Company at Stratford-upon-Avon. These productions—with Alan Howard as Henry, Emrys James as York, and Helen Mirren as Margaret—offered reasonably full texts (the performance time for each part averaged 2½ hours), respectfully treated, and all three, especially *2 Henry VI*, were warmly received. A single marathon performance of the three plays on the same day was sold out months ahead.

Apropos of John Shakespeare's presumed illiteracy (pp. 37-8), I can share with readers a communication (24 March 1977) from David Cressy, who has been engaged in studying the problem of literacy in Tudor and Stuart England. Professor Cressy writes:

All the evidence from Elizabethan educational records suggests that children learned to write only after they had mastered the primary skill of reading. Thus, it is not very surprising that many people of humble education, including the likes of John Shakespeare, were unable to write their names, even though they could probably read. In most cases a mark signifies incomplete literacy, or illiteracy. In the mid-seventeenth century, where there is good evidence, some 70% of all English men could not sign their names. Their sisters and wives were much worse, about 90% illiterate. These figures represent an improvement over the mid-Tudor period. William Shakespeare's generation was much more literate than his father's. The Elizabethan educational revolution bore fruit in improving literacy among all social classes. By 1600, the literacy picture can be summarized thus, with the percentages representing these unable to sign:

Clergy and Professions	0%
Gentry	2%
Yeomen	35%
Tradesmen and Craftsmen	44%
Husbandmen	79%
Labourers	85%
All Women	89%

Among craftsmen, I find approximately 44% of the glovers unable to sign. These figures are all derived from East Anglia, both Norwich and the surrounding rural area, but I would guess they apply equally to Stratford and Warwickshire.

About John Shakespeare's literacy—or lack of same—Professor Cressy has since expressed firm views in his *Literacy and the Social Order: Reading and Writing in Tudor and Stuart England* (1980). 'People in Tudor and Stuart England used marks when they did not know how to write their name', he remarks; 'it was a question of capacity, not of choice. The only exception was when people who had been fully literate grew senile or infirm and lost the ability to perform a signature, and in those cases we usually find a simple scrawl rather than a pictogram vibrating with symbolism' (p. 58). Cressy cites Charles Sisson's essay, 'Marks as Signatures', in *The Library*, ix (1928), 5-12.

Like others of his class, John Shakespeare, as I noted originally, more than once entered the courtroom to sue or be sued (p. 32). Four more cases involving him have lately come to light in the Exchequer court; see D. L. Thomas and N. E. Evans, 'John Shakespeare in the Exchequer', *Shakespeare Quarterly*, xxxv (1984), 315-18. They reveal the Stratford glover as engaged in subsidiary wool dealings and moneylending transactions deemed illegal by the Tudor parliaments. In buying wool John had violated legislation restricting such activities to manufacturers or merchants of the Staple. In the sixteenth century—as in later periods—trade depended upon the availability of credit, but anachronistic statutes held usury 'a vice most odious and detestable', and subject to prosecution. Infractions were unsurprisingly widespread. Lacking means to enforce its regulations, the government relied upon private individuals to bring damaging information into the royal courts, the informers being rewarded with half the penalties assessed. Thus, in Hilary term 1570, one of the barons of the Exchequer exhibited an information by Anthony Harrison of Evesham in Worcestershire claiming that John 'Shakespeare' of 'Stratford upon Haven' had lent the substantial sum of £100 to John Mussum of 'Woltun' in Warwickshire for £20 in interest. In the same term James Langrake of Whittlebury, Northamptonshire, reported that John 'Shappere alias Shakespere' of Stratford had lent John Musshem of Walton D'Eiville, a village not far from Stratford, the sum of £80, also with £20 due in interest. This Langrake, a professional informer, had been accused of raping one of his maidservants; he had been imprisoned for accepting considerations from the unfortunates he informed against, and was subsequently fined and prohibited from bringing further informations for a twelvemonth. In the first case there is no further record of proceedings after the recital of the accusation; in the second, John was fined 40s. The same pestiferous Langrake in 1572 informed the court that John 'Shaxspere' of 'Stretford super Haven' and John Lockesley of the same place had illegally bought 200 tods (i.e., 5,600 pounds) of wool, at a price of 14s per tod, from Walter Newsam and others. Later that year John was accused—once again by Langrake—of buying 100 tods of wool at the same price from Edward and Richard 'Graunte' and other unidentified individuals. In both instances the accused apparently wound up compounding with the informer.

About John Shakespeare's partners in his transactions little is known, but Edward Grant was a Catholic landowner in Snitterfield who had a manor house at nearby Northbrook. Recusants dangerously resorted to his house. His wife's nephew, John Somerville, plotted against the Queen in 1583, and his grandson John Grant would in the next reign be implicated in the Gunpowder Plot. John Shakespeare's usurious activities cast a curious sidelight on his playwright-son's *Merchant of Venice*, written a quarter of a century later.

Like father, like son, when it came to business dealings? One may ask—as Professor Honigmann recently has asked, in his paper ' "There is a world elsewhere": William Shakespeare, Businessman' at the World Shakespeare Congress in West Berlin (1986)—whether Richard Quiney was prepared to pay interest on the loan he solicited in his undelivered letter of 25 October 1598 (see pp. 238-40) and whether his 'loving good friend and countryman' would have expected to receive it. Like other prospective lenders, Shakespeare may well have. 'And now but persuade yourself so, as I hope,' Quiney promised, 'and you shall not need to fear, but with all hearty thankfulness I will hold my time and content your friend'—presumably, if Shakespeare should himself have to borrow the money for the loan—'and if you bargain further you shall be the paymaster yourself.' No explicit reference is made by Quiney to the payment of a fee, so we cannot certainly say whether any such payment would have been involved; but the possibility—to Professor Honigmann, the likelihood—is certainly there. Richard's father Adrian, a well-to-do mercer and Henley street neighbour of the Shakespeares, wrote to his son around 1 November, 'If you bargain with William Shakespeare and receive money there'—i.e. at his hands—'bring your money home that you may buy such wares as you may sell presently to profit'. Friendly neighbours the Quineys and Shakespeare may have been, but neighbourly fellow-feeling need not—then as now—have sentimentally affected the outcome of business practicalities. The 'indifferent conditions' for which Abraham Sturley hoped (see p. 239) may, in the event, have proved to be hard conditions.

If there is something to the speculations respecting a Lancaster connection for Shakespeare (see pp. 112-15), he would have been no more than fifteen or sixteen when he began to teach. There is precedent for such precocity. Richard Mather (1596-1669), who haled from Lowton, near Liverpool, and would win fame in the New World as a Congregational clergyman, taught at a grammar school in Lancashire at the age of fifteen. His grandson—the even more celebrated Cotton Mather—entered Harvard College at the age of twelve, and was teaching at fifteen. Simon Forman's youthful—although not quite so youthful—induction into schoolmastering has already been noted (p. 111).

With respect to the will of Alexander Hoghton (see p. 112), Professor David George, who has been collecting and editing the Lancashire materials for the *Records of Early English Drama* series, notes that Hoghton's musical instruments in fact no doubt went to Sir Thomas Hesketh (c. 1518-1588), as may be seen from the inventory of the property of his son Robert drawn up in 1620. Most likely Sir Thomas accepted both instruments and players—Fulke Gyllome surfaces as a Hesketh servant in 1591. In *The Annotator* (1954), Alan Keen and Roger Lubbock observe that the musical instruments itemized in the Hesketh inventory 'could well have suited a small orchestra'. These consisted of viol, violins, virginals (a smaller version of the harpsicord), sackbut (trombone), oboe, cornetts, cittern (a plucked string instrument resembling a lute), and taber (a small drum). A single musician, however, might be able to play all these instruments, the drums being strung from the shoulder or wrists. The term 'play-clothes' suggests that the players mentioned in Sir Thomas's will were indeed actors. That only two are cited by name is something of a puzzlement, unless the other members of the household troupe were not specified by the testator, the troupe possibly being made up of the eleven servants elsewhere named by Hesketh in the document.

Regarding deficiencies in Shakespeare's Biblical knowledge (p.

58), Lawrence J. Ross argues against the evidential significance of Shakespeare's conflation of Satan and Lucifer; Ross notes too that the salutation 'All hail!' occurs in Coverdale's 'Fruitful Lessons upon the Passion', and also in Samuel Rowlands's *Betrayal of Christ* (1598), the greeting being 'sometimes rendered in this form in order to contrast Mary and Judas' ('Two Supposed "Defects in Shakespeare's Biblical Knowledge"', *Notes and Queries*, cciii (1958), 462-3).

About overindulgence as the cause of Robert Greenes's death (see p. 149): so the contentious Gabriel Harvey sneeringly averred, but Greene was more likely done in by pestilence than pickled herring, for a particularly savage onslaught of plague had lately overtaken London (see pp. 167-9). The next year 11,000 deaths were reported. In *The Impact of Plague in Tudor and Stuart England* (1985), Paul Slack calculates the plague mortality in the forty-seven parishes in the city and liberties of London at 8,716 for 1593—approximately 2,000 fewer than Stow reports. For the even more virulent epidemic which marked the year of James's accession (see p. 251), Slack places the number of plague deaths at 13,436.

The 1563 indenture between Bott and Clopton (p. 236) is Folger Shakespeare Library MS, Z.c.36 (100), and refers to 'all that his capital messuage and garden thereunto belonging' in Chapel Street. This information I owe to Mark Eccles.

As regards Thomas Quiney's delinquency (see pp. 293-4), the church canons of 1604 specified such offences as 'adultery, whoredom, incest, drunkenness, swearing, ribaldry, usury', and any other 'uncleanness and wickedness of life' as liable to presentment before the appropriate subordinate ecclesiastical court. Such courts, which had come down from the Middle Ages, numbered over 250 in this period. Although they remained active, few offenders were in fact subjected to the public humiliation of standing in white sheets. In his informative chapter on the bawdy courts in *Society and Puritanism in Pre-Revolutionary England* (1964), Christopher Hill notes that 'penance was often commuted for money, at the discretion of the judges, even in very serious cases' (p. 311). So it was for Quiney. In 1664 the Presbyterian divine Richard Baxter, surveying the previous half century, wrote that—'except in the space when bishops were down'—he had heard of only two in Worcestershire who had to stand in white sheets for adultery.

It is a question whether New Place was rebuilt by John Clopton (see p. 319) or his second son Hugh, to whom the father had conveyed it, subject to a life interest, on 20 January 1700. There appears to be more to this family affair than the several deeds, preserved in the Shakespeare Birthplace Records Office, relate; but it seems reasonable to infer that Sir John had the work done, although probably with borrowed money which Hugh undertook to repay. For this interpretation of the complicated and sometimes confusing sequence of events I am obliged to the Birthplace Records Office archivist, Robert Bearman, who followed up my inquiries with patient thoroughness.

In 1985 Her Majesty's Stationery Office issued *Shakespeare in the Public Records*, with text and selection of documents by David Thomas, and a section by Jane Cox on the will and signatures. Concerned with the documents relating to Shakespeare and his family reposited in the Public Record Office in London—the documentation to be found in the records of the Central Government and the law courts—the book expertly reproduces many of these items in facsimile. There is also a useful list of the records, with all casemarks supplied. The book replaces, without rendering obsolete, the pamphlet of the same title by N. E. Evans issued as a Public Record Office Handbook in the quatercentenary year. Most interest attaches to Miss Cox's discussion of the six Shakespeare signatures customarily regarded as authentic. 'It is obvious at a glance', she writes, 'that these signatures, with the exception of the last two, are not the signatures of the same man. Almost every letter is formed in a different way in each. Literate men in the sixteenth and seventeenth centuries developed personalized signatures much as people do today and it is unthinkable that Shakespeare did not.'

Which of the signatures then, is the genuine article? According to Miss Cox, that is anybody's guess. She finds a clue, however, in Sir Hilary Jenkinson's essay, 'Elizabethan Handwriting', in *The Library*, 4th Ser., vol. iii, no. 1 (1922), 1-34. Jenkinson believes that clerks taking down the evidence in law suits often signed the deponents' names themselves, for verisimilitude using a different hand from the one in the body of the text. 'If this was the practice in the equity courts', Miss Cox asks, 'why should it not also have been the practice of attorneys' clerks when drawing up conveyancing documents?' Shakespeare, after all, was possibly not even in London to sign the mortgage deed and the deed of purchase for the Blackfriars Gate-house. She even queries the authenticity of the will signatures, although their shakiness points to a gravely ill signator holding the pen. 'Until the Statute of Frauds of 1667 there was no necessity for a will to bear the testator's signature at all. Manuals of the period indicate the form preferred by the doctors of civil law, namely that a will should be signed on every page and witnessed, but virtually any form was acceptable so long as it seemed to be a true representation of the dying man's wishes.' Even the names of the three witnesses to Shakespeare's will—Shaw, Robinson, and Sadler—look suspiciously similar to Miss Cox. She finds numerous instances of 'forgeries' of witnesses' signatures among fifty-five wills proved in the Prerogative Court of Canterbury in the same month as Shakespeare's. Scholarship is process, and, as has often happened in the past, a sceptical inquirer has made necessary a re-examination of comfortable assumptions. Miss Cox has deigned to milk a sacred cow.

Inadvertently, I failed to include any mention of 'The Phoenix and Turtle', one of several commendatory poems (the others are by Jonson, Chapman, and Marston) appended to Robert Chester's fantastical compilation, *Love's Martyr, or Rosalin's Complaint, allegorically shadowing the truth of love, in the constant fate of the Phoenix and Turtle* (1601). Subscribed "William Shakespeare", the poem appeared also in the stationer John Benson's 1640 collection, *Poems: Written by Wil. Shake-speare*, not all of which, however, were actually written by Shakespeare. A much discussed curiosity, the 67-line elegy in trochaic tetrameter celebrates ideal love, and begins with a summons of other birds to assemble to mourn the death of the phoenix—that legendary Arabian bird which rose from its own ashes—and the turtle dove, a bird renowned for its amatory fidelity:

Postscript

Love and constancy is dead,
Phoenix and the turtle fled
In a mutual flame from hence.

The poem shows Shakespeare in the unfamiliar role of nonce poet.

Notes

1. STRATFORD TOWN AND STRATFORD CHURCH

1. On Stratford history I have profited mainly from Levi Fox, *The Borough Town of Stratford-upon-Avon* (Stratford-upon-Avon, 1953), and, only slightly less, from Sidney Lee, *Stratford-on-Avon from the Earliest Times to the Death of Shakespeare* (rev. ed., 1907); also R. B. Wheler, *History and Antiquities of Stratford-upon-Avon* (Stratford-upon-Avon, [1806]), and Philip Styles, 'Borough of Stratford-upon-Avon', in *The Victoria History of the County of Warwick* (1904-69), iii. 221-82. A. L. Rowse, *William Shakespeare* (1963), is evocative on the Warwickshire context.

2. William Harrison, *The Description of England*, in Raphael Holinshed, *The First and Second Volumes of Chronicles* [1587], i. 202.

3. John Leland, *Itinerary*, ed. Lucy Toulmin Smith (1907-10), ii. 48.

4. The quoted phrase is the first reference to brick in Stratford; brick did not become popular, except for chimneys, until after the Restoration (*Victoria History*, iii. 223).

5. A detailed account (which I have found most valuable) of Holy Trinity is J. Harvey Bloom, *Shakespeare's Church, otherwise the Collegiate Church of the Holy Trinity of Stratford-upon-Avon* (1902); see also the more technical description in the *Victoria History*, iii. 269-76.

6. *A Short History of Stratford-on-Avon, Written in Ballad Form by an Old Warwickshire Boy* (Privately Printed, 1926), verse 12. This anonymous ballad was composed by A. C. Hands.

7. So William Hall reported in a letter (1694) to Edward Thwaites (Bodleian Library, MS. Rawlinson D. 377, f. 90; SS, item 205, p. 251).

8. See ch. 3, 'Offspring'.

9. *The Registers of Stratford-on-Avon, in the County of Warwick*, ed. Richard Savage (Parish Register Society, 1897-1905), i, pref., pp. vi-vii; ME, 51.

10. *Registrum Annalium Collegii Mertonensis 1483-1521*, ed. H. E. Salter (Oxford Historical Society *Publications*, lxxvi; Oxford, 1923), pp. xxxiv, 98; noted in a letter to *The Times* from Sir Robert Birley, 3 May 1976.

2. THE SHAKESPEARES: FROM SNITTERFIELD TO STRATFORD

1. For a more detailed account of Snitterfield see L. F. Saltzmann, 'Snitterfield', *The Victoria History of the County of Warwick* (1904-69), iii. 167-72. On Richard Shakespeare and his sons, ME (7-12) concisely sums up knowledge.

2. The Public Record Office document (E 202/327, 2 Eliz.), not previously known to students, was found by the late Tangye Lean.

3. Henry Swinburne, *A Briefe Treatise of Testaments and Last Willes* (1590), f. 220; cited by J. O. Halliwell-Phillipps, *Outlines of the Life of Shakespeare* (7th ed., 1887), ii. 245.

4. See Charles Isaac Elton, *William Shakespeare: His Family and Friends* (1904), pp. 349-50.

5. F. P. Wilson, *The Plague in Shakespeare's London* (Oxford, 1927), p. 26.

6. Edgar I. Fripp, *Shakespeare: Man and Artist* (1938), i. 73.

7. See G. R. French, *Shakespeareana Genealogica* (1869), pp. 416-524; EKC, ii. 28-32; and ME, 12-5. The last also deals authoritatively with the Ardens of Wilmcote (15-23).

8. For a more technically detailed description of the house, see Philip Styles, 'Aston Cantlow', *Victoria History*, iii. 32-3.

3. OFFSPRING

1. Bretchgirdle's will and inventory were transcribed by Richard Savage and printed by Edgar I. Fripp, *Shakespeare Studies, Biographical and Literary* (1930), pp. 23-31. On Dyos and Bretchgirdle, see *Minutes and Accounts of the Corporation of Stratford-upon-Avon*, ed. Richard Savage and Edgar I. Fripp; Publications of the Dugdale Society (Oxford and London, 1921-30), i, pp. xlvii-xlviii, 101-2; ii. 110; Fripp, *Shakespeare: Man and Artist* (1938), i. 37-8, 41-2.

2. Sidney Lee, *A Life of William Shakespeare* (4th ed. of revised version, 1925), p. 8.

3. On the birth-date I am principally indebted to EKC (ii. 1-2), who authoritatively recapitulates and analyses preceding scholarship, but I have also consulted Fripp, *Shakespeare: Man and Artist*, i. 38; and Charles Isaac Elton, *William Shakespeare: His Family and Friends* (1904), pp. 22-5, is still too useful to be ignored.

4. Fripp, *Shakespeare*, i. 40.

5. William Shakespeare, *Plays and Poems*, ed. Edmond Malone (1790), vol. i, pt. 1, p. 124n. Malone's flight proved too much for one contemporary reader, the Revd. John Horne Tooke; in his copy he scrawled alongside the passage, 'Alack aday Mr Malone!', and after it expressed his distaste with a single forcible expletive: 'Boh!' (Folger Shakespeare Library, PR 2752. 1790c. Sh. Col., copy 4).

6. J. O. Halliwell-Phillipps (*Outlines of the Life of Shakespeare* (7th ed., 1887), ii. 298) found this suit in the Coram Rege rolls. Unable to locate Gilbert Shakespeare in the St. Bride's register or in the books of the Worshipful Company of Haberdashers (which however, contain a Gilbert Shepheard, who took up his freedom in 1579), and unprepared 'to wade through the six volumes of closely-written contracted Latin cases that make up the Coram Rege Roll of 1597', Mrs. C. C. Stopes concluded that Halliwell-Phillipps must have erred (*Shakespeare's Environment* (1914), pp. 64-5). But she is wrong, and he is right.

7. ME, 108.

8. See below, pp. 43, 281.

9. Stopes, *Shakespeare's Environment*, pp. 333-4, brings together a number of such entries.

10. The vicissitudes of the Henley Street houses are authoritatively recounted by Levi Fox, 'The Heritage of Shakespeare's Birthplace', *Shakespeare Survey 1* (Cambridge, 1948), pp. 79-88.

11. E. R. C. Brinkworth, *Shakespeare and the Bawdy Court of Stratford* (1972), pp. 110, 141. Mark Eccles, reviewing Brinkworth, makes the suggestion about the nature of the offence (*Modern Language Review*, lix (1974), 373).

12. G. E. Bentley, *Shakespeare: A Biographical Handbook* (New Haven, 1961), p. 81.

13. *The Great Frost; cold doings in London* (1608); cited by Fripp (*Shakespeare*, ii. 687), who speculates on Shakespeare's role in the funeral arrangements.

4. RISE AND FALL

1. Edgar I. Fripp, *Shakespeare: Man and Artist* (1938), i. 36. Fripp does not document the transfer. ME (p. 8) merely notes that 'John

Shakespeare probably sold his copyhold, since he does not appear in the next court rolls, for 1574 and later years.'

2. Samuel A. Tannenbaum prints the complete text of this document in 'A Neglected Shakspere Document', *Shakespeare Association Bulletin*, vi (1931), 111-2. ME (32) mistakenly gives the date as 19 July 1586 instead of 1587.

3. This document, which is among the Sackville papers deposited in the Kent Archives Office, was made public by Hugh A. Hanley, 'Shakespeare's Family in Stratford Records', *The Times Literary Supplement* (21 May 1964), 441.

4. Sir Richard Phillips, in *The Monthly Magazine; or British Register*, xlv (1818), 2; EKC, ii. 299.

5. Leslie Hotson, 'Three Shakespeares', *Shakespeare's Sonnets Dated and Other Essays* (1949), p. 231. Hotson discovered the action.

6. Two of Higford's four attempts have been previously noted by Edgar I. Fripp (see *Shakespeare: Man and Artist* (1938), i. 71n). The other two are described in the papers of Tangye Lean, who gives the references: Public Record Office, CP 40 1352, Hilary 20 Eliz., and CP 40 1356, Easter 20 Eliz.

7. *Minutes and Accounts of the Corporation of Stratford-upon-Avon*, ed. Richard Savage and Edgar I. Fripp; Publications of the Dugdale Society (Oxford and London, 1921-30), i, pp. xxi-xxii, xxxiv-xxxv; see also *The Taming of the Shrew*, Induction, sc. ii, 83-6.

8. Fripp, *Shakespeare*, i. 34; *The Victoria History of the County of Warwick* (1904-69), iii. 254.

9. Fripp, *Shakespeare*, i. 43. I am chiefly indebted to Fripp for the details of corporate life and local custom.

10. The Shakespeare Birthplace Trust preserves a specimen of a glover's 'donkey' in the museum collection at Mary Arden's House.

11. John Ferne, *The Blazon of Gentrie* (1586), the first part, *The Glorie of Generositie*, pp. 58-60; cited (in part) by EKC, ii. 25.

12. See below, pp. 227-8.

13. ME, 29-30.

14. Ibid., p. 31.

15. Curiously, three names used by Shakespeare in *Henry V*—Fluellen, Bardolph, and Court—appear in the list, with Fluellen and Bardolph among the nine, and Court in the next grouping.

16. ME, 33-4. I have found ME invaluable throughout on John Shakespeare's career.

17. Council Book, cited by Fripp, *Master Richard Quyny* (Oxford, 1924), p. 132. Douglas Hamer draws attention to economic conditions in his review of my *Shakespeare's Lives* (Oxford, 1970) in *Review of English Studies*, n.s., xxxii (1971), 483-4.

18. Lewis Bayly, *The Practise of Pietie* (1613 ed.), p. 551; cited

(in 1699 ed.) by Fripp, *Quyny*, p. 101. By 1842 this edifying treatise had gone through seventy-five editions. On the two Stratford fires see also Fripp, *Shakespeare*, i. 402-3, 419.

5. JOHN SHAKESPEARE'S SPIRITUAL TESTAMENT

1. ME, 36-7.
2. Letter, dated 14 June 1784, cited in J. O. Halliwell-Phillipps, *Outlines of the Life of Shakespeare* (7th ed., 1887), ii. 399.
3. William Shakespeare, *Plays and Poems*, ed. Edmond Malone (1790), vol. i, pt. 2, pp. 161-2.
4. Ibid., pp. 162-6. I have modernized these articles and the next.
5. Malone, *An Inquiry into the Authenticity of Certain Miscellaneous Papers and Legal Instruments* (1796), pp. 198-9.
6. The questions are put by James G. McManaway in 'John Shakespeare's "Spiritual Testament"', *Shakespeare Quarterly*, xviii (1967), 197-205; reprinted in McManaway, *Studies in Shakespeare, Bibliography, and Theater*, ed. Richard Hosley, Arthur C. Kirsch, and John W. Velz (New York, 1969), pp. 293-304.
7. Sidney Lee, *A Life of William Shakespeare* (4th ed. of revised version, 1925), p. 647.
8. *Testamento o Ultima Voluntad del Alma hecho en Salud para assegurarse el christiano de las tentaciones del Demonio, en la hora de la muerte*; Herbert Thurston, 'A Controverted Shakespeare Document', *The Dublin Review*, clxxiii (1923), 165. I give Thurston's translation.
9. Cited by John Henry de Groot, *The Shakespeares and 'The Old Faith'* (New York, 1946), p. 88.
10. *The Contract and Testament of the Soule*, pp. 45-50. The unique copy of the *Testament*, now in the Folger Shakespeare Library (shelfmark: STC 5645.5), is reproduced in facsimile in SS, 44-5 (item 52).
11. Thomas Wilkes, Clerk of the Council, quoted by Peter Milward, *Shakespeare's Religious Background* (Bloomington and London, 1973), p. 21.
12. *Minutes and Accounts of the Corporation of Stratford-upon-Avon*, ed. Richard Savage and Edgar I. Fripp; Publications of the Dugdale Society (Oxford and London, 1921-30), i. 138; ii, pp. xxv, 47, 49, 54.

6. FAITH AND KNOWLEDGE

1. That he was chaplain is the reasonable supposition of EKC, ii. 256.

2. Articles of Grindal and Sandys, issued in 1571; quoted by the Revd. Ronald Bayne in his chapter 'Religion', in *Shakespeare's England* (Oxford, 1916), i. 63. Bayne furnishes a compendious survey of the subject.

3. On this passage Bayne remarks, 'The words seem to recognize some pride in the refusal to don the surplice and yet to imply a respect for the zeal which distinguished the wearers of the black gown' ('Religion', i. 56).

4. Richmond Noble, *Shakespeare's Biblical Knowledge and Use of the Book of Common Prayer as Exemplified in the Plays of the First Folio* (1935), pp. 14-5.

5. Articles of Grindal and Sandys, quoted by Bayne, 'Religion', i. 63.

6. Noble, *Shakespeare's Biblical Knowledge*, p. 20. On Shakespeare's use of the Bible I am especially indebted to Noble.

7. Ibid., pp. 69, 86-7.

8. Edgar I. Fripp, *Shakespeare: Man and Artist* (1938), i. 85-6.

9. Alfred Hart, *Shakespeare and the Homilies* (Melbourne, 1934), pp. 9-76; see, esp., p. 67.

10. A. L. Rowse, *William Shakespeare: A Biography* (1963), p. 43.

11. Ibid., p. 451.

12. See B. Roland Lewis, *The Shakespeare Documents* (Stanford, 1940), ii. 481-2; also below, p. 298. The point had been earlier made by J. O. Halliwell-Phillipps in his *Outlines of the Life of Shakespeare* (7th ed.; 1887), i. 263-4. Catholics of course would be conscious of the fact that their wills would be probated before Anglican authorities.

13. See below, pp. 286-7.

14. See Roland Mushat Frye's valuable Appendix, 'The Roman Catholic Censorship of Shakespeare: 1641-1651', to *Shakespeare and Christian Doctrine* (Princeton, 1963), pp. 275-93, esp. 282-8. The expurgations were made in a copy of the 1632 Folio for the benefit of pupils in the English College at Valladolid, Spain.

15. Frank Mathew, *An Image of Shakespeare* (1922), p. 391; cited by John Henry de Groot, *The Shakespeares and 'The Old Faith'* (New York, 1946), p. 170. I am mostly obliged to de Groot for, in his phrase, 'positive indications of Shakespeare's esteem for the Old Faith', but I have also profited from the more recent study by Peter Milward, *Shakespeare's Religious Background* (Bloomington and London, 1973), although the latter, a work of special pleading, should be consulted with caution.

16. Frye, *Shakespeare and Christian Doctrine*, pp. 262-3.

17. Milward, *Shakespeare's Religious Background*, pp. 24, 78.

18. Alexander Nowell, *A Catechisme, or first Instruction and Learning of Christian Religion*, transl. T. Norton (1570), sig. B1.

19. On the education of women, see the chapter on that subject in Carroll Camden, *The Elizabethan Woman* (Houston, 1952), pp. 37-58.

20. The comprehensive account is T. W. Baldwin, *William Shakspere's Petty School* (Urbana, Ill., 1943).

21. The most convenient and reliable account of these pedagogues is in ME, 54-8; see also Fripp, *Shakespeare*, i. 89-92.

22. John Brinsley, *Ludus Literarius: or, The Grammar Schoole* (1612), p. 88; cited (from 1627 ed.) by Baldwin, *William Shakspere's Small Latine & Lesse Greeke* (Urbana, Ill., 1944), i. 567.

23. Fane MS., f. 177, printed by E. M. Martin, 'Shakespeare in a Seventeenth Century Manuscript', *English Review*, li (1930), 484-9; see also Fripp, *Shakespeare*, i. 401-2, and ME, 57.

24. John Clarke, *An Essay upon the Education of Youth in Grammar-Schools* (1720), pp. 86-7; cited by Baldwin, *Shakspere's Small Latine*, i. 594n.

25. *Colloquia Mensalia: or, Dr Martin Luther's Divine Discourses . . .* , transl. Henry Bell (1652), p. 532; cited by Baldwin, *Shakspere's Small Latine*, i. 609.

26. Brinsley, *Ludus Literarius*, p. 191; cited (from 1627 ed.) by Baldwin, *Shakspere's Small Latine*, i. 380.

27. See Philip J. Finkelpearl, *John Marston of the Middle Temple: An Elizabethan Dramatist in His Social Setting* (Cambridge, Mass., 1969).

28. Baldwin, *Shakspere's Small Latine*, ii. 663. Baldwin must be reckoned the principal authority for any account of grammar-school education in this period. The subject has been much discussed. Of earlier treatments, Joseph Quincy Adams's chapter, 'Schooling', in *A Life of William Shakespeare* (Boston and New York, 1923), pp. 48-60, if now expectedly somewhat dated, provides a useful overview and conveniently includes many of Shakespeare's references to schooling. An excellent later essay by M. H. Curtis, 'Education and Apprenticeship', *Shakespeare Survey* 17 (Cambridge, 1964), pp. 53-72, places the educational system in context: the 'coherent, well-articulated system' of schools in Tudor England represented an effort 'infused and inspired by the genius of the age'.

29. Bodleian Library, MS. Arch. F. c. 37 (formerly Aubrey MS. 6, f. 109); SS, item 57, p. 58.

30. The possibility is tentatively suggested by ME, 62. Shakespeare bequeathed Richard Tyler the elder 26s.8d. to buy a ring, but afterwards replaced his name with that of Hamnet Sadler; see below, p. 300.

7. EARLY EMPLOYMENT AND MARRIAGE

1. Nicholas Rowe, 'Some Account of the Life, &c. of Mr. William Shakespear', in Shakespeare, *Works*, ed. Rowe (1709), i, pp. ii-iii.

2. Thomas Elyot, *The Boke Named the Governour* (1531 ed.), f. 60 (sig. H4). Quoted by Joseph Quincy Adams, *A Life of William Shakespeare* (Boston and New York, 1923), pp. 61-2.

3. Bodleian Library, MS. Arch. F.c. 37 (formerly Aubrey MS. 6, f. 109); SS, item 57, p. 58.

4. I am here obliged to Douglas Hamer's review of my *Shakespeare's Lives* (Oxford, 1970) in *The Review of English Studies*, n.s., xxxii (1971), 484.

5. Edgar I. Fripp, *Shakespeare: Man and Artist* (1938), i. 79-80.

6. Joseph William Gray, *Shakespeare's Marriage* (1905), remains the fullest and most authoritative treatment of the subject, although I have equally profited from EKC (ii. 43-52) in the paragraphs that follow. ME (63-70) is also valuable. On this episode the biographer is well served.

7. Sidney Lee, *A Life of William Shakespeare* (4th ed. of revised version, 1925), p. 29. Lee allowed this passage (which appeared in the 1898 ed.) to remain intact in this last edition during his lifetime, despite the fact that twenty years earlier Gray had refuted Lee's inferences in *Shakespeare's Marriage*, pp. 48-57.

8. For a more detailed description of Anne Hathaway's Cottage, see *The Victoria History of the County of Warwick* (1904-69), iii. 235; less technical but no less reliable are the descriptions by Levi Fox in his 'Pictorial Guide', *Anne Hathaway's Cottage* [1964], and *The Shakespearian Properties* (1964).

9. J. O. Halliwell-Phillipps refers to a 'Mrs Ann Shakespeare' as cited in 'a contemporary transcript' of the burial entry (*Outlines of the Life of Shakespeare* (7th ed., 1887), ii. 372).

10. See ME, 63, for these and other examples.

11. The Worcester seals are studied by Gray in *Shakespeare's Marriage*, pp. 33-5.

12. Anthony Burgess, *Shakespeare* (New York, 1970), pp. 57-60. The banns were of course read once, not twice.

13. Lee, *Life of William Shakespeare*, p. 31.

14. On Frith, see ME (66), whose transcriptions I quote. Temple Grafton is described, in characteristic detail, by Philip Styles in the *Victoria History*, iii. 94-100.

15. S. W. Fullom, *History of William Shakespeare, Player and Poet: with New Facts and Traditions* (1862), p. 202.

16. For an acount of Fullom's vagaries, see S. Schoenbaum, *Shakespeare's Lives* (Oxford, 1970), pp. 479-82.

17. Gray, *Shakespeare's Marriage*, p. 236.

18. William Harrington, *The Commendations of Matrimony* (n.d.), sig. A4^v.

19. On Alice Shaw and William Holder, and the depositions in their action, see Halliwell-Phillipps, *Outlines*, i. 64-5; Gray, *Shakespeare's Marriage*, pp. 190-2; ME, 66.

20. Andrew Gurr, 'Shakespeare's First Poem: Sonnet 145', *Essays in Criticism*, xxi (1971), 221-6.

21. See F. W. Bateson's postscript to Gurr, p. 226.

22. On the Colgate portrait see George M. Friend, 'A Possible Portrait of Anne Hathaway', *Philobiblon*, No. 9 (Spring 1972), 44-51. To Douglas Hamer, writing more recently, 'The drawing is a tracing of a portrait almost certainly by Clouet (d. 1572), and is French, not Tudor.' This is an interesting, if rather positively couched, speculation. I have shown the drawing to Dr. Harold Joachim, Curator of Prints and Drawings at the Chicago Art Institute; he does not think it self-evidently a Clouet, or (for that matter) self-evidently French in origin.

23. ME, 70.

24. Cited by ME, 51.

8. *THE LOST YEARS*

1. William Shakespeare, *Works*, ed. Sir Thomas Hanmer (2nd ed., 1770), vi, *Glossary*, s.v. *Wincote*; EKC, ii. 288.

2. 'Letter from the Place of Shakespear's Nativity', *British Magazine, or Monthly Repository for Gentlemen and Ladies*, iii (1762), 301.

3. John Jordan, from 'a manuscript written about the year 1770', printed by J. O. Halliwell-Phillipps, *Outlines of the Life of Shakespeare* (7th ed., 1887), ii. 326. The manuscript is now in the Folger Shakespeare Library (shelfmark: S.a. 118), but the text is incomplete.

4. Samuel Ireland, *Picturesque Views on the Upper, or Warwickshire Avon* . . . (1795), p. 233.

5. R. B. Wheler, *Collectanea de Stratford*, p. 202, in Shakespeare Birthplace Trust Records Office; shelfmark: MS. ER 1/8.

6. Nicholas Rowe, 'Some Account of the Life, &c. of Mr. William Shakespear', in Shakespeare, *Works*, ed. Rowe (1709), i, p. v.

7. Ibid., i, pp. xvii, xviii.

8. A. L. Rowse, *The Elizabethan Renaissance: The Life of the Society* (New York, 1971), p. 205, notes the Elizabethan fondness for poaching, and cites clerics and Balliol scholars who indulged in the pastime.

9. Shakespeare, *Plays and Poems*, ed. Edmond Malone (1790), vol i, pt. 1, pp. 106-7n. Malone printed the passage again in the Variorum, this time unequivocally labelling as spurious the verses of 'a songstress in Stratford' (ii. 144). The manuscript 'History of the Stage' seems to have disappeared.

10. Shakespeare, *Works*, ed. George Steevens (1778), i, *The Merry Wives of Windsor*, p. 223n.

11. 'William Shakespeare', *Biographia Britannica* (1747-66), vol. vi, pt. 1, p. 3628. Reprinted in EKC, ii. 287. A manuscript note on the title-page of the Bodleian copy identifies 'P' as Philip Nichols, who contributed a number of articles to the *Biographia Britannica*. The shaft referred to in the passage is *The Merry Wives of Windsor*.

12. Mary Elizabeth Lucy, *Biography of the Lucy Family, of Charlecote Park, in the County of Warwick* (1862), pp. 12-13

13. Henry James, *English Hours* (1905), p. 201. This chapter, 'In Warwickshire', is dated 1877.

14. The house and its setting are evocatively described by Alice Fairfax-Lucy, *Charlecote and the Lucys: The Chronicle of an English Family* (1958), pp. 10-11, 68ff. This delightful and informative book has furnished me with many facts and details for the present chapter. A very great deal has been written on Lucy and the deer-poaching episode. Of the earlier authorities, Malone is most useful (Shakespeare, *Plays and Poems* (1821), ii. 118-49); the most authoritative modern account is, as so often, in EKC, ii. 18-21, to which (along with the others) I am indebted. I have also profited from John Semple Smart, *Shakespeare: Truth and Tradition* (1928), pp. 89-104.

15. William Blackstone, *Commentaries on the Laws of England* (1765-9), ii. 38; cited by Edmond Malone in *The Life of William Shakspeare* (Shakespeare, *Plays and Poems*, ed. Malone (1821), ii. 147).

16. Samuel Ireland, *Picturesque Views on the Upper, or Warwickshire Avon* . . . (1795), p. 154.

17. *The Journal of Sir Walter Scott*, ed. W. E. K. Anderson (Oxford, 1972), p. 454.

18. Fairfax-Lucy, *Charlecote and the Lucys*, p. 9.

19. The date is given as 1584 by ME, 76; 1583 by Fairfax-Lucy, *Charlecote and the Lucys*, p. 85. Perhaps the distinction between Old Style and New Style in dating is responsible for the discrepancy.

20. Cited by Fairfax-Lucy, *Charlecote and the Lucys*, p. 13. I have transcribed the epitaph directly from the tomb.

21. For other escutcheons with luces, see Leslie Hotson, *Shakespeare versus Shallow* (1931), p. 92.

22. Fairfax-Lucy, *Charlecote and the Lucys*, pp. 129-30.

23. Ibid., p. 5.

24. Folger Shakespeare Library, MS. V.a.74; SS, item 218, p. 262.

25. 'An Attempt to Ascertain the Order in which the Plays of Shakspeare Were Written', in Shakespeare, *Plays and Poems*, ed. Edmond Malone (1790), vol. i, pt. 1, p. 307; see also p. 104n.

26. John Campbell, *Shakespeare's Legal Acquirements Considered* (1859), p. 23.

27. William J. Thoms, 'Was Shakespeare Ever a Soldier?', *Three Notelets on Shakespeare* (1865), p. 136. The Rowington muster roll entry was first noted by Robert Lemon of the State Paper Office, and by him communicated to J. Payne Collier, who discusses the record, without reaching any positive conclusion, in the second edition of 'The Life of William Shakespeare' in his 1858 *Shakespeare* (i. 181).

28. Bodleian Library, MS. Arch. F.c.37 (formerly Aubrey MS. 6, f. 109); SS, item 57, p. 58.

29. In G. E. Bentley's considered judgement; see his account of Beeston in *The Jacobean and Caroline Stage* (Oxford, 1941-68), ii. 363-70.

30. So EKC suggests (i. 22).

31. Thomas Fuller, *The Holy State and Profane State* (Cambridge, 1642), p. 109; cited by Joseph Quincy Adams, *A Life of William Shakespeare* (Boston and New York, 1923), p. 93.

32. *Autobiography*, cited by ME, 73-4. Forman's *Autobiography* is reprinted by A. L. Rowse, *Simon Forman* (1974), pp. 267-78.

33. ME, 83; he makes the apposite reference to *The Two Gentlemen of Verona*.

34. On William Shakeshafte see Oliver Baker, *In Shakespeare's Warwickshire and the Unknown Years* (1937), pp. 297-319; E. K. Chambers, 'William Shakeshafte', *Shakespearean Gleanings* (1944), pp. 52-6 (the essay, dated 1943, was first published in this collection); Leslie Hotson, 'John Jackson and Thomas Savage', *Shakespeare's Sonnets Dated and Other Essays* (1949), pp. 125-40 (first printed in this volume); Robert Stevenson, 'William Shakespeare and William Shakeshafte', *Shakespeare's Religious Frontier* (The Hague, 1958), pp. 67-83; Douglas Hamer, 'Was William Shakespeare William Shakeshafte?', *The Review of English Studies*, n.s., xxi (1970), 41-8; Peter Milward, *Shakespeare's Religious Background* (Bloomington and London, 1973), pp. 40-2. Also, on Richard Shakeschafte-Shakstaff, see John Pym Yeatman, *The Gentle Shakspere: A Vindication* (Birmingham, 1911), p. 172; C. C. Stopes, *Shakespeare's Environment* (1914), p. 16; EKC, ii. 27; ME, 7-8. The quotation from Milward appears on p. 42.

35. [Robert Laneham], *A Letter: Whearin, part of the entertainment untoo the Queenʒ Majesty, at Killingwoorth Castl, in Warwik Sheer in this Soomerʒ Progress 1575. iʒ signified* . . . (n.d.), p. 43.

36. EKC, i. 39-41.

37. The discovery of the slaying of William Knell we owe to ME, 82-3, whose account I follow.

9. LONDON AND THE THEATRES

1. Bodleian Library, MS. Arch. F.c.37 (formerly Aubrey MS. 6, f. 109); SS, item 57, p. 58.

2. For the itinerary I mainly follow Henry B. Wheatley, 'London and the Life of the Town', *Shakespeare's England* (Oxford, 1916), ii. 153, but Charles Isaac Elton, *William Shakespeare: His Family and Friends* (1904), pp. 179-93, has furnished some details. On Elizabethan London generally, I have found most useful two older accounts, T. Fairman Ordish, *Shakespeare's London* (2nd ed., 1904) and H. T. Stephenson, *Shakespeare's London* (New York, 1905); and of course Stow (see n. 9) has been invaluable, while Wheatley's compendious survey has provided a number of particulars.

3. John Taylor, *Taylor on Thame Isis: or the Description of the Two Famous Rivers of Thame and Isis* . . . (1632), sig. B1ᵛ.

4. *The Diary of Henry Machyn*, ed. John Gough Nichols (Camden Society, 1848), p. 196; quoted by A. L. Rowse, *The England of Elizabeth* (1950), pp. 213-4. I have found very helpful Rowse's chapter 'London and the Towns'.

5. Michael Drayton, *Polyolbion* [1613], p. 259.

6. *Paul Hentzner's Travels in England, During the Reign of Queen Elizabeth*, transl. Richard Bentley (1797), p. 3. The title-page erroneously ascribes the translation to Horace Walpole.

7. Frederick, Duke of Württemberg, 'A True and Faithful Narrative of the Bathing Excursion. . .', *England as Seen by Foreigners in the Days of Elizabeth and James the First*, transl. and ed. William Brenchley Rye (1865), p. 9. The narrative of the Duke's travels was in fact written by his companion and private secretary, Jacob Rathgeb.

8. Not poorly erected, but erected with ill consequences. I have profited in this paragraph from Rowse, *The Tower of London in the History of the Nation* (1972).

9. John Stow, *A Survey of London reprinted from the text of 1603*, ed. C. L. Kingsford (Oxford, 1908), i. 59; Wheatley, 'London', p. 157.

10. The familiar episode is effectively retold by Rowse, *Tower of London*, pp. 74-5.

11. G. B. Harrison, *Shakespeare under Elizabeth* (New York, 1933), pp. 310-11.

12. Leslie Hotson, *Mr. W. H.* (1964), pp. 244-55.

13. See below, pp. 170, 180, and S. Schoenbaum, *Shakespeare's Lives* (Oxford, 1970), pp. 456-8, 683-8, 739-40, *et passim.*

14. Stow, *Survey*, ii. 71.

15. Ibid., ii. 70.

16. *Hentzner's Travels*, p. 31.

17. Cited by Kingsford in Stow, *Survey*, ii. 368.

18. On the conditions that encouraged the spread of plague I have found most valuable F. P. Wilson, *The Plague in Shakespeare's London* (Oxford, 1927).

19. For a fuller—and delightful—account of the flora of London, see the chapter 'Nature and London', in Ordish, *Shakespeare's London*, pp. 83-134.

20. Stow, *Survey*, i. 93, ii. 236; E. K. Chambers, *The Elizabethan Stage* (Oxford, 1923), ii. 363.

21. Stow, *Survey*, ii. 73, 262; Chambers, *Elizabethan Stage*, ii. 363.

22. Thomas Heywood, *An Apology for Actors* (1612), sig. F3.

23. *Hentzner's Travels*, p. 29.

24. Ibid., pp. 29-30.

25. Quoted in *England as Seen by Foreigners*, p. 88; see also Chambers, *Elizabethan Stage*, ii. 358.

26. The Answer of Cuthbert Burbage, Winifred Robinson, and William Burbage, *c.* 1 August 1635; Public Record Office, LC/5/133, pp. 50-1 (SS, item 81, p. 104). On the Theatre and other early playhouses I am principally indebted to Chambers, although I have also profitably consulted an earlier study, Joseph Quincy Adams, *Shakespearean Playhouses* (Boston, 1917). Chambers (*Elizabethan Stage*, ii. 384-6) provides the topographical details in this paragraph and elsewhere.

27. 'Robin Goodfellow', *Tarltons Newes out of Purgatorie* (1590), pp. 1-2, 52; quoted by Chambers, *Elizabethan Stage*, ii. 386n.

28. T[homas] W[hite], *A Sermon preached at Pawles Crosse on Sunday the thirde of November 1577. in the time of the Plague* (1578), p. 47; Chambers, *Elizabethan Stage*, iv. 197.

29. William Harrison, MS. 'Chronologie', quoted by Chambers, *Elizabethan Stage*, iv. 269.

30. Ernest Schanzer, 'Thomas Platter's Observations on the Elizabethan Stage', *Notes and Queries*, cci (1956), 466.

31. Adams, *Shakespearean Playhouses*, pp. 119-22.

32. For a recent reconstruction of the early history of the Newington Butts playhouse, see William Ingram, 'The Playhouse at Newington Butts: A New Proposal', *Shakespeare Quarterly*, xxi (1970), 385-98.

33. Chambers, *Elizabethan Stage*, ii. 405; iv. 313.

34. C. W. Wallace, *The First London Theatre, Materials for a*

History, in Nebraska *University Studies,* xiii (1913), 2. Wallace never got round to publishing his source for this assertion.

35. On prostitution in this district, see David J. Johnson, *Southwark and the City* (1969), pp. 64-7.

36. On the significance of this term, see *Henslowe's Diary,* ed. R. A. Foakes and R. T. Rickert (Cambridge, 1961), pp. xxx-xxxi.

37. Chambers, *Elizabethan Stage,* ii. 411.

38. On this episode see below, pp. 198-200.

39. Frances A. Yates suggests these possibilities in her fascinating, if wayward, study, *Theatre of the World* (1936); see, esp., pp. 125-6.

40. Adams, *Shakespearean Playhouses,* pp. 167-8. For the complete Latin text of De Witt's note, see 'A Note on the Swan Theatre Drawing', *Shakespeare Survey 1* (Cambridge, 1948), pp. 23-4; also Chambers, *Elizabethan Stage,* ii. 361-2. Richard Hosley expertly describes the drawing in 'The Playhouses and the Stage', *A New Companion to Shakespeare Studies,* ed. Kenneth Muir and S. Schoenbaum (Cambridge, 1971), pp. 23-4. A valuable earlier detailed analysis (with other matter interspersed) is in Chambers, *Elizabethan Stage,* ii. 524-47.

10. THE UPSTART CROW

1. See above, p. 109; SS, item 218, p. 262.

2. Nicholas Rowe, 'Some Account of the Life, &c. of Mr. William Shakespear', in Shakespeare, *Works,* ed. Rowe (1709), i, p. vi.

3. *The Lives of the Poets of Great Britain and Ireland, To the Time of Dean Swift* . . . . 'By Mr Cibber' (1753), vol. i, pp. 130-1. The Johnsonian source is suggested by EKC, ii. 285.

4. William Shakespeare, *Plays,* ed. Samuel Johnson (1765), i, p. c.

5. EKC, i. 60.

6. Shakespeare, *Plays and Poems,* ed. Edmond Malone (1821), ii. 164.

7. *Supplement to the Edition of Shakspeare's Plays Published in 1778 by Samuel Johnson and George Steevens,* ed. Malone (1780), i. 67. Malone added the words '*Call-boy,* or' before 'prompter's attendant' in his 1790 edition of Shakespeare (*Plays and Poems,* vol. i, pt. 1, p. 107).

8. Shakespeare, *Plays and Poems,* ed. Malone (1821), ii. 166-7.

9. Here the most useful authority is EKC, i. 27-56. G. M. Pinciss gives a detailed, full account of 'The Queen's Men, 1583-1592', in *Theatre Survey,* xi (1970), 50-65.

10. Chambers, *The Elizabethan Stage* (Oxford, 1923), ii. 118-9.

11. British Library, MS. Harley 3885, f. 19.

12. Greene's life is recounted more fully by J. Churton Collins in his introduction to his edition of the *Plays and Poems* (Oxford, 1905), which, despite its deficiencies, remains the fullest account in English. A more recent study is René Pruvost, *Robert Greene et ses romans* (1558-1592) (Paris, 1938).

13. 'Cuthbert Cunny-Catcher', *The Defence of Conny Catching* (1592), sig. C3^{r-v}.

14. [Gabriel Harvey], *Foure Letters, and certaine Sonnets* (1592), p. 4. To Harvey we are obliged for small benefactions; from this pamphlet we gather that Greene's wife was named Dorothea, for he addresses her as 'Doll' in his deathbed letter as published in the *Foure Letters* (p. 12).

15. Robert Greene, *Groats-worth of witte, bought with a million of Repentance* (1592), sig. A3^v.

16. A. L. Rowse, *Shakespeare the Man* (1973), p. 60.

17. Greene, *Groats-worth*, sig. F1^v.

18. Greene, *Francescos Fortunes: Or the second part of Greenes Never too Late* . . . (1590), sigs. B4^v-C1.

19. Arthur Freeman draws attention to the Brathwait passage in 'Notes on the Text of "2 Henry VI", and the "Upstart Crow" ', *Notes and Queries*, ccxiii (1968), 129-30.

20. J. Dover Wilson, 'Malone and the Upstart Crow', *Shakespeare Survey 4* (Cambridge, 1951), p. 65. I have profited much from Wilson's valuable close analysis of the passage.

21. Thomas Nashe, *Pierce Penilesse his Supplication to the Divell*, in *Works*, ed. Ronald B. McKerrow (rev. F. P. Wilson; Oxford, 1958), i. 154.

22. Henry Chettle, *Kind-Harts Dreame* [1592?], sigs. A3^v-4.

23. Dover Wilson, *The Essential Shakespeare: A Biographical Adventure* (Cambridge, 1932), p. 62.

24. See William A. Ringler, Jr., 'Spenser, Shakespeare, Honor, and Worship', *Renaissance News*, xiv (1961), 159-61.

25. Warren B. Austin, *A Computer-Aided Technique for Stylistic Discrimination. The Authorship* of Greene's Groatsworth of Wit (U.S. Department of Health, Education and Welfare, 1969).

26. J. Payne Collier first suggested that Chettle 'possibly' wrote the *Groatsworth of Wit* in his 1844 *Life of William Shakespeare*, and J. O. Halliwell[-Phillipps] picked up the suggestion in his *Life of William Shakespeare* (1848), p. 143. The Folger Shakespeare Library has a copy of the *Life* (shelfmark: PR2894.H28.1848) with a marginal comment by C. M. Ingleby alongside the passage: 'An absurd conjecture. Greene's work is full of genius, whereas Chettle was a poor stick, & could hardly write English.' At the least Austin has shown that the conjecture is not so absurd as Ingleby thought.

27. For the several strictures, see the reviews of Austin by R. L. Widmann, *Shakespeare Quarterly*, xxiii (1972), 214-5, and by T. R. Waldo, *Computers and the Humanities*, vii (1972), 109-10. The *Shakespeare Newsletter* (December 1974, pp. 47, 49) reports a University of Cologne dissertation by Barbara Kreifeltz in support of the Austin theory.

28. *Greenes Funeralls*, ed. McKerrow (1911), p. 81.

29. Austin, 'A Supposed Contemporary Allusion to Shakespeare as a Plagiarist', *Shakespeare Quarterly*, vi (1955), 373-80.

30. John Semple Smart, *Shakespeare: Truth and Tradition* (1928), p. 196.

31. The point is made by EKC, i. 58.

11. PLAYS, PLAGUE, AND A PATRON

1. See above, p. 71.

2. The details of Brome's 1635 contract, revised and renewed in 1638, are known from *Heton* v. *Brome*, a suit in the Court of Requests in 1640. Anne Haaker published transcripts of the documents in 'The Plague, the Theater, and the Poet', *Renaissance Drama*, n.s., i (1968), 283-306. See also G. E. Bentley, *The Profession of Dramatist in Shakespeare's Time 1590-1642* (Princeton, N.J., 1971), pp. 113-44, 264-8. The latter is a full and authoritative account of the playwright's vocation.

3. Thomas Nashe, *Pierce Penilesse his Supplication to the Divell*, in Nashe, *Works*, ed. Ronald B. McKerrow (rev. F. P. Wilson; Oxford, 1958), i. 212.

4. Marchette Chute, *Shakespeare of London* (1951), p. 85. She is one of the ablest popular biographers of Shakespeare; see S. Schoenbaum, *Shakespeare's Lives* (Oxford, 1970), pp. 757-9.

5. This reasonable suggestion is made by Peter Alexander, *Shakespeare's Henry VI and Richard III* (Cambridge, 1929), p. 8.

6. *Ben Jonson*, ed. C. H. Herford and Percy and Evelyn Simpson (Oxford, 1925-52), vi. 16.

7. The point is made by J. C. Maxwell in his New Arden ed. of *Titus Andronicus*, 1953, introd., p. xxvii.

8. Edward Ravenscroft, Address 'To the Reader', *Titus Andronicus, or The Rape of Lavinia* (1687), sig. A2; in EKC, ii. 254-5.

9. William Shakespeare, *Titus Andronicus*, ed. J. Dover Wilson (The New Shakespeare; Cambridge, 1948), p. 99; see also Wilson, '*Titus Andronicus* on the Stage in 1595', *Shakespeare Survey 1* (Cambridge, 1948), pp. 17-22.

10. W. Moelwyn Merchant, *Shakespeare and the Artist* (1959),

p. 13. In *Shakespeare and his Players* (1972), pp. 150-4, Martin Holmes informatively discusses the armour shown in the drawing, but he is more positive than the evidence warrants when he asserts that the sketch 'illustrates a production by Henslowe's company'.

11. A. W. Pollard suggests that Shakespeare was affiliated to the Queen's men in his introduction to Alexander's *Shakespeare's Henry VI and Richard III*, pp. 13-21. More recently the argument has been ably pursued by G. M. Pinciss, 'Shakespeare, Her Majesty's Players and Pembroke's Men', *Shakespeare Survey 27* (Cambridge, 1974), pp. 129-36.

12. Alexander cites several such duplications (*Shakespeare's Henry VI and Richard III*, pp. 191-2); see also the New Arden *1 Henry VI*, ed. Andrew S. Cairncross (1962), p. xxxiii.

13. Shakespeare, *2 Henry VI*, ed. J. Dover Wilson (The New Shakespeare; Cambridge, 1952), pp. xii-xiv.

14. See *Extracts from the Letters and Journals of William Cory*, ed. Francis Warre Cornish (1897), p. 168; EKC, ii. 329.

15. Mary Edmond, 'Pembroke's Men', *Review of English Studies*, n.s., xxv (1974), 129-36.

16. Quoted by F. P. Wilson, *The Plague in Shakespeare's London* (Oxford, 1927), p. 52.

17. E. K. Chambers, *The Elizabethan Stage* (Oxford, 1923), iv. 313.

18. Ibid., iv. 314-5.

19. See Mario Praz's article, 'Italy', in *The Reader's Encyclopaedia of Shakespeare*, ed. Oscar James Campbell and Edward G. Quinn (1966), pp. 388-93; also John S. Smart, 'Shakespeare's Italian Names', *Modern Language Review*, xi (1916), 339. The *traghetto* plied between Venice and the mainland.

20. Smart (p. 339) remarks on Bassanio and Lucchese. The latter is an emendation (first suggested by Capell) for *Luccicos*, which Smart and others take to be a misprint. The topographical examples in my next paragraph are noted by Praz (p. 391).

21. See A. L. Rowse, *Shakespeare the Man* (1973), pp. 106 ff. He silently revises his account of Emilia in *Simon Forman* (1974), pp. 99-117. Stanley Wells corrected 'brown' (*The Times Literary Supplement*, 11 May 1973, p. 528).

22. John Sanford, *Apollinis et Musarum Euktika Eidyllia* (Oxford, 1592), cited and trans. G. P. V. Akrigg, *Shakespeare and the Earl of Southampton* (1968), p. 36. Akrigg and Rowse (*Shakespeare's Southampton, Patron of Virginia* (1965)) furnish compendious modern biographies.

23. Nashe, *The Unfortunate Traveller*, in *Works*, ed. McKerrow, ii. 202.

24. Shakespeare, *Works*, ed. Alexander Dyce (1857), i. p. xlv; cited

by Hyder Edward Rollins in the New Variorum edition of *The Poems* (Philadelphia and London, 1938), p. 385.

25. For an excellent, full account of Field, see A. E. M. Kirwood, 'Richard Field, Printer, 1589-1624', *The Library*, 4th Ser., xii (1931), 1-39.

26. C. C. Stopes, *Shakespeare's Environment* (2nd ed., 1918), p. 155. Mrs. Stopes gives Mrs. Field's christian name as Jacquinetta, thus conflating the printer's wife with the country wench of *Love's Labour's Lost*.

27. *The First Part of the Return from Parnassus*, in *The Three Parnassus Plays* (1598-1601), ed. J. B. Leishman (1949), pp. 185, 192-3.

28. See, for example, Joseph Quincy Adams, *A Life of William Shakespeare* (Boston and New York, 1923), p. 238; also Rowse, *Shakespeare the Man*, p. 75.

29. EKC, i. 61-2.

30. *The Second Part of the Return from Parnassus*, in *Three Parnassus Plays*, ed. Leishman, p. 244.

31. Nicholas Rowe, 'Some Account of the Life, &c. of Mr. William Shakespear', in Shakespeare, *Works*, ed. Rowe (1709), i., p. x. Unaware of the existence of *The Rape of Lucrece*, Rowe describes *Venus and Adonis* as 'the only Piece of his Poetry which he [Shakespeare] ever publish'd himself'.

32. Rowse, *Shakespeare the Man*, p. 215; see also the same author's *Shakespeare's Southampton*, p. 85, where the Earl's munificence to the poet is described as an authentic tradition.

33. See Akrigg, *Shakespeare and the Earl of Southampton*, pp. 38-9, 47.

34. Shakespeare, *The Sonnets*, ed. Rollins (New Variorum; Philadelphia and London, 1944), ii. 53.

35. Henry Willobie, *Willobie his Avisa* (1594), sigs. L1ᵛ-L2.

36. See Arthur Acheson, *Mistress Davenant* (1913) and *Shakespeare's Sonnet Story* (1922).

37. B. N. De Luna, *The Queen Declined: An Interpretation of Willobie his Avisa* (Oxford, 1970), pp. 5-43. Her theories are mercilessly anatomised in *The Review of English Studies*, n.s., xxii (1971), 335-40, by Douglas Hamer, who thinks 'W. S.' resided in the vicinity of Mere, Wiltshire; possibly he was 'a William Stourton, but evidence is difficult to obtain'.

38. Willobie, *Willobie his Avisa*, sig. A4.

39. See below, pp. 185-6.

12. THE LORD CHAMBERLAIN'S MAN

1. G. E. Bentley, *Shakespeare: A Biographical Handbook* (New Haven, 1961), p. 119. The 'director' as a theatrical functionary did not then exist.

2. Kenneth Muir makes this point in *Shakespeare the Professional* (1973), pp. 3-4.

3. *Gesta Grayorum: or, the History of the High and Mighty Prince, Henry Prince of Purpoole . . .* (1688), p. 22.

4. William Shakespeare, *A Midsummer Night's Dream*, ed. Stanley Wells (New Penguin Shakespeare; 1967), introd., pp. 13-4.

5. Francis Meres, *Palladis Tamia. Wits Treasury* (1598), sig. A2.

6. Don Cameron Allen succinctly analyses Meres's sources in his introduction to the Scholars' Facsimile edition of *Palladis Tamia* (New York, 1938), pp. vii-viii. See also Allen's *Francis Meres's Treatise 'Poetrie': A Critical Edition* (Urbana, Ill., 1933).

7. Meres, *Palladis Tamia*, ff. 281ᵛ-2.

8. T. W. Baldwin, *Shakspere's Love's Labour's Won: New Evidence from the Account Books of an Elizabethan Bookseller* (Carbondale, Ill., 1957), p. 15. *All's Well that Ends Well*, as we have it, is tentatively dated 1603-4 by G. K. Hunter, who surveys the evidence disinterestedly in his introduction to the New Arden edition (1959), pp. xviii-xxv.

9. Leslie Hotson, 'Love's Labour's Won', *Shakespeare's Sonnets Dated and Other Essays* (1949), pp. 37-56.

10. Augustus Ralli, *A History of Shakespearian Criticism* (1932), i. 1.

11. C. S. Lewis, *English Literature in the Sixteenth Century Excluding Drama* (Oxford History of English Literature; Oxford, 1954), p. 430; see also Bentley, *Shakespeare*, pp. 199-203.

12. Thomas Fuller, *The Church-History of Britain: from the Birth of Jesus Christ, until the year 1648* (1655), bk. iv, cent. xv, p. 168.

13. Fuller, *The Worthies of England* (1662), ii. 253. He died in 1661.

14. 'N.D.' [Nicholas Dolman, pseudonym of Robert Persons], *The Third Part of a Treatise, Intituled: of three Conversions of England: An Examen of the Calendar or Catalogue of Protestant Saints . . . by John Fox* (1604). *The Last Six Monethes* (1604), p. 31; quoted in EKC, ii. 213.

15. See below, pp. 270-1.

16. Bodleian Library, MS. James 34; SS, item 101, p. 143.

17. Nicholas Rowe, 'Some Account of the Life, &c. of Mr. William Shakespear', in Shakespeare, *Works*, ed. Rowe (1709), i, p. ix.

18. John Dennis, Epistle Dedicatory 'To the Honourable George Granville, Esq.', in *The Comicall Gallant: or the Amours of Sir John Falstaffe* (1702), sig. A2.

19. Dennis, *The Person of Quality's Answer to Mr. Collier's Letter* (1704), p. 4; quoted by EKC, ii. 263.

20. Rowe, 'Account', in Shakespeare, *Works*, ed. Rowe (1709), i, pp. viii-ix.

21. Charles Gildon, 'Remarks on the Plays of Shakespear', in Shakespeare, *Works* (1710), vii. 291.

22. Shakespeare, *The Merry Wives of Windsor*, ed. H. J. Oliver (New Arden Shakespeare; 1971), introd., p. xlv.

23. The problems, often complex, connected with this play are ably treated by William Green, *Shakespeare's* Merry Wives of Windsor (Princeton, N.J., 1962).

24. Hotson, *Shakespeare versus Shallow* (1931), p. 24. He fully describes the personages and legal procedures.

25. On Shakespeare's London residences, see below, pp. 220-3.

26. John Davies of Hereford, *The Scourge of Folly* (n.d.; Stationers' Register: 8 October 1610), Epig. 159, p. 76.

27. *Historia Histrionica: an Historical Account of the English Stage . . . In a Dialogue, of Plays and Players* (1699), p. 4.

28. Rowe, 'Account', in Shakespeare, *Works*, ed. Rowe (1709), i, p. vi.

29. Shakespeare, *Plays*, ed. Samuel Johnson and George Steevens (1778), i. 204.

30. Edward Capell, *Notes and Various Readings to Shakespeare* [1779], vol. i, pt. 1, p. 60.

31. Sir Walter Scott, *Kenilworth*, ch. xvii.

32. Rowe, 'Account', in Shakespeare, *Works*, ed. Rowe (1709), i, pp. xii-xiii.

33. Richard Ryan, *Dramatic Table Talk; or Scenes, Situations, & Adventures, Serious & Comic, in Theatrical History & Biography* (1825), ii. 156-7.

34. These are not overlooked by Bentley (*Shakespeare*, p. 9), whose analysis covers the same points as my own.

35. British Library, MS. Harley 5353, f. 29^v; SS, item 115, p. 152.

36. On the building of the Globe, as on the other playhouses, my principal sources are E. K. Chambers, *The Elizabethan Stage* (Oxford, 1923), ii, and Joseph Quincy Adams, *Shakespearean Playhouses* (Boston, 1917).

37. [Edward Guilpin], *Skialetheia, or, a shadowe of Truth, in certaine Epigrams and Satyres* (1598), sig. D6.

38. C. W. Wallace, *The First London Theatre: Materials for a History*, in Nebraska *University Studies*, xiii (1913), 278-9.

39. This was the old name for what is now St. Saviour's parish.

40. John Stow, *A Survey of the Cities of London and Westminster . . . Corrected, Improved, and very much Enlarged . . . by John Strype* (1720), vol. ii, bk. iv, p. 28; quoted by Adams, *Shakespearean Playhouses*, p. 243.

41. Wallace, *First London Theatre*, pp. 275-6.

42. Ernest Schanzer, 'Thomas Platter's Observations on the Elizabethan Stage', *Notes and Queries*, cci (1956), 466.

43. The action, *Witter* v. *Heminges and Condell*, was discovered in the Public Record Office by Charles William Wallace, who announced his findings in 'Shakespeare's Money Interest in the Globe Theatre', *The Century Magazine*, lxxx (1910), 500-12. Wallace printed the texts of the ten documents comprising the action the same year in the Nebraska *University Studies*, x ('Shakespeare and his London Associates as Revealed in Recently Discovered Documents'). The most authoritative discussion of Shakespeare's financial interests in the Globe and Blackfriars is in EKC, ii. 52-71; Chambers gives, in abridged form, the Answer of Heminges and Condell in the suit. The same material is discussed, with transcripts, in B. Roland Lewis, *The Shakespeare Documents* (Stanford, 1940), ii. 508-20.

44. The Folger Shakespeare Library, MS. V.a. 292 (formerly MS. 2073.5), f. 140; SS, item 116, p. 155.

45. Sidney Lee, *A Life of William Shakespeare* (4th ed. of revised version, 1925), p. 315.

46. M. M. Reese, *Shakespeare: His World and his Work* (1953), p. 365. He is more cautious earlier when he describes the fate of the dramatist's holdings in the Globe and the Blackfriars as 'one of the unsolved mysteries of Shakespeare's life' (p. 214).

47. Arthur Collins, *Letters and Memorials of State . . . written and collected by Sir Henry Sydney, Sir Philip Sydney, Sir Robert Sydney, &c.* (1746), ii. 175; quoted by EKC, ii. 322.

48. British Library, MS. Harley 5353, f. 12^v; SS, item 117, p. 156.

49. Sir Edward Maunde Thompson, quoted by R. C. Bald, 'The *Booke of Sir Thomas More* and its Problems', *Shakespeare Survey 2* (Cambridge, 1949), p. 55. This essay is a masterly survey of the problems. Another important review, more recent, is Harold Jenkins's Supplement to Greg's edition of 'Sir Thomas More', published in the 1961 lithographic reprint of the volume, and also in Malone Society *Collections*, vi (1961 (1962)), pp. 179-92. Jenkins, it may be noted, favours c. 1594-5 as the date for the revision. Michael L. Hays, 'Shakespeare's Hand in *Sir Thomas More*: Some Aspects of the Paleographic Argument', *Shakespeare Studies VIII* (1975), 241-53, appeared too late to

be more than cited here, but the questions Hays raises about the validity of the palaeographical evidence deserve, at the least, thoughtful consideration.

50. See R. W. Chambers, 'The Expression of Ideas—Particularly Political Ideas—in the Three Pages and in Shakespeare', in Alfred Pollard et al., *Shakespeare's Hand in the Play of Sir Thomas More* (Cambridge, 1923), pp. 142-87, esp. 158-60. For the commonplace, see F. P. Wilson, 'Shakespeare's Reading', *Shakespeare Survey 3* (Cambridge, 1950), pp. 19-20.

51. *The Book of Sir Thomas More*, ed. W. W. Greg (Malone Society Reprints, 1911), ll. 584-92; cited by Bald, p. 53.

52. J. Dover Wilson, *The Essential Shakespeare: A Biographical Adventure* (Cambridge, 1932), p. 103.

53. EKC, ii. 326-7.

54. Wilson, *Essential Shakespeare*, pp. 104-7.

13. A GENTLEMAN OF MEANS

1. Alexander Pope, *Imitations of Horace*, ed. John Butt (2nd ed., 1953), p. 199 (The Twickenham Pope, vol. iv).

2. A *Life of William Shakespeare*, in Shakespeare, *Works*, ed. J. O. Halliwell-Phillipps (1853-65), i. 151.

3. The five documents discussed in this section are analysed in detail by M. S. Giuseppi in 'The Exchequer Documents Relative to Shakespeare's Residence in Southwark', *Transactions of the London and Middlesex Archaeological Society*, N.S., v (1929), 281-8. This remains the standard treatment, although EKC (ii. 88-90) is essential. N. E. Evans, *Shakespeare in the Public Records* (1964), pp. 9-12, is helpful; nor should B. Roland Lewis, *The Shakespeare Documents* (Stanford, 1940), i. 262-71, be ignored. On the history of subsidies, and the system of grants of fifteenths and tenths to which they are related, Stephen Dowell, *A History of Taxation and Taxes in England* (2nd ed., 1888), ii. 67-71, although in some respects outdated, is still concisely informative.

4. Stow supplies most of these details; see also A. L. Rowse, *William Shakespeare* (1963), pp. 280-1.

5. This information I owe to Professor William Ingram.

6. Edmond Malone, *An Inquiry into the Authenticity of Certain Miscellaneous Papers and Legal Instruments* (1796), pp. 215-16.

7. See below, pp. 260ff.

8. Arthur H. Nethercot, *Sir William D'Avenant, Poet Laureate*

and Playwright-Manager (Chicago, 1938), p. 20. Nethercot describes the Taverne in detail (pp. 16-20).

9. Joseph Spence, *Observations, Anecdotes, and Characters of Books and Men, Collected from Conversation*, ed. James M. Osborn (Oxford, 1966), i. 184.

10. Bodleian Library, MS. Hearne, Diaries 20, f. 127; SS, item 126, p. 165.

11. Shakespeare, *Plays*, ed. Samuel Johnson and George Steevens (1778), i. 203-4.

12. Spence, *Observations*, ed. Osborn, i. 185.

13. Reprinted in *All the Works of John Taylor the Water-Poet* (1630), p. 184 (sig. Qq4^v).

14. Gerard Langbaine, *The Lives and Characters of the English Dramatick Poets* . . . , ed. Charles Gildon [1698], p. 32.

15. William Chetwood, *A General History of the Stage* . . . (1749), p. 21n.

16. The point is made by Raymond Carter Sutherland in his informative essay, 'The Grants of Arms to Shakespeare's Father', *Shakespeare Quarterly*, xiv (1963), 379-85.

17. The second draft, with missing words supplied from the first, as in EKC (ii. 19).

18. In the judgement of C. W. Scott-Giles, *Shakespeare's Heraldry* (1950), p. 33. In these paragraphs I am especially indebted to Mr. Scott-Giles's unpretentiously authoritative account (pp. 27-41). He makes the apposite reference to *A Midsummer-Night's Dream* (see below, p. 230).

19. Charles Crisp, 'Shakespeare's Ancestors', *Coat of Arms*, vi (1960), 105-9; cited by Sutherland, p. 384.

20. J. O. Halliwell[-Phillipps], *An Historical Account of the New Place, the Last Residence of Shakespeare* (1864), p. 10; ME compendiously summarises the history of New Place (86-9). On the Underhill family see J. H. Morrison, *The Underhills of Warwickshire* (Cambridge, 1932), esp. pp. 152-6, 183-5.

21. This episode was discovered by Tangye Lean, among whose private papers I found the relevant transcriptions from Public Record Office documents. The shelfmark for the Wheler deposition is SP 12/79. The volume in which it is bound consists of documents in Alford *v.* Greville and Porter, and is dated June 1571.

22. A hearth-tax return for 1663 establishes the number of fireplaces; see Halliwell[-Phillipps], *Historical Account*, p. 162.

23. Stowe MSS. in the Huntington Library; 'A Document Concerning Shakespeare's Garden', *The Huntington Library Bulletin*, i (1931), 199-201; ME, 91. I follow ME's transcription.

24. Joseph Quincy Adams, *A Life of William Shakespeare* (Boston

and New York, 1923), p. 259. Sturley was not in fact, as formerly thought, Quiney's brother-in-law.

25. Sturley's letter (Shakespeare Birthplace Trust Records Office, Misc. Doc. I, 136) was badly damaged by water leakage during the Second World War. Ultra-violet light failed to render the writing legible, nor was I able to track down a photograph. Halliwell-Phillipps, however, printed a line-block facsimile of an extract (*Shakespearian Facsimiles* . . . (1863), Plate IX, item 1); in *Outlines of the Life of Shakespeare* (7th ed., 1887), ii. 59-60, he gives the complete text. The letter was first published in the appendix to Malone's posthumous *Life of William Shakspeare* in the 1821 Variorum (ii. 569-72). There is a partial transcript in EKC, ii. 103; ME, 95, gives an extract. Another Sturley letter to Quiney (Misc. Doc. I, 135; EKC, ii. 101-2) was similarly affected.

26. See below, pp. 292-6.

27. See above, pp. 81, 82.

28. On these actions see EKC, ii. 113-18; ME, 91-2, 107.

29. Malone, *Supplement to the Edition of Shakspeare's Plays Published in 1778 by Samuel Johnson and George Steevens* (1780), ii. 369-70: George Steevens's note to *Sir John Oldcastle*.

30. Shakespeare, *Plays*, ed. Johnson and Steevens (1778), i. 205.

31. Nicholas Rowe, 'Some Account of the Life, &c. of Mr. William Shakespear', in Shakespeare, *Works*, ed. Rowe (1709), i, p. xxxvi.

32. *A Relation of a short Survey of 26. Counties . . . By a Captaine, a Lieutennant, and an Ancient. All three of the Military Company in Norwich*, British Library, MS. Lansdowne 213, f. 332ᵛ; EKC, ii. 243.

33. Francis Peck, 'Explanatory & Critical Notes on Divers Passages of Shakespeare's Plays', in *New Memoirs of the Life and Poetical Works of Mr. John Milton* (1740), pp. 222-3.

34. MS. in the Shakespeare Library, Birmingham Public Library; shelfmark: S977, pp. 25-6. Jordan set down the story more than once; see EKC, ii. 293-4.

35. Edward Dowden is apparently the first to treat Hamlet's reflections in relation to his creator's real-estate interests (*Shakspere: A Critical Study of his Mind and Art* (1875), p. 35); see also S. Schoenbaum, *Shakespeare's Lives* (Oxford, 1970), pp. 492ff.

36. ME, 103.

37. EKC, ii. 125.

38. *Huband* in earlier biographies. On the spelling see ME, who assembles the facts about Hubaud (105).

39. A third witness was William Hubaud.

14. HIS MAJESTY'S SERVANT

1. Some have gone so far; they are forcefully rebutted by Richard Levin, 'The King James Version of *Measure for Measure*', *Clio*, iii (1974), 129-63. The topical allusiveness of the play is argued by, among others, David Lloyd Stevenson, in 'The Historical Dimension in *Measure for Measure:* The Role of James I in the Play', an appendix to *The Achievement of Shakespeare's* Measure for Measure (Ithaca, N.Y., 1966), pp. 134-66.

2. For a detailed account of the entry see David M. Bergeron, *English Civic Pageantry 1558-1642* (1971), pp. 66-89.

3. B. Roland Lewis, *The Shakespeare Documents* (Stanford, 1940), ii. 368.

4. The inventory of the envoy's titles is given by Joseph Quincy Adams, *A Life of William Shakespeare* (Boston and New York, 1923), p. 364, and the occasion is described in detail by Ernest Law, *Shakespeare as a Groom of the Chamber* (1910).

5. G. E. Bentley, 'Shakespeare and the Blackfriars Theatre', *Shakespeare Survey 1* (Cambridge, 1948), p. 40.

6. Advertisement to Lintot's Edition of Shakespeare's *Poems* (*c.* 1709), sig. A2ᵛ.

7. EKC, ii. 280.

8. John Davies, *Microcosmos* (1603), p. 215; quoted by EKC, ii. 213.

9. William Barksted, *Mirrha the Mother of Adonis: or, Lustes Prodegies* (1607), sig. E1; quoted by EKC, ii. 216.

10. Bodleian Library, MS. Arch. F.c.37 (formerly Aubrey MS. 6, f. 109); SS, item 57, p. 58.

11. Nicholas Rowe, 'Some Account of the Life, &c. of Mr. William Shakespear', in Shakespeare, *Works*, ed. Rowe (1709), i, pp. viii, xxxv-xxxvi.

12. I have dealt more largely with this subject in 'Shakespeare and Jonson: Fact and Myth', *The Elizabethan Theatre II*, ed. David Galloway (Toronto, 1970), pp. 1-19. See also below, p. 317. For the anecdotes cited see British Library, MS. Harley 6395, f. 2 (L'Estrange); Bodleian Library, MS. Ashmole 38, p. 181 (Burgh); MS. 25, ff. 77, 161, in the Plume Library at Maldon, Essex (Plume); SS, items 167-9, p. 206.

13. Thomas Fuller, *The History of the Worthies of England* (1662), 'Warwickshire', p. 126.

14. Ben Jonson, *Timber: or, Discoveries; Made upon Men and Matter* (1641), in Ben Jonson, *Workes* (1640 title-page), pp. 97-8.

15. I. A. Shapiro analyses this legend in 'The "Mermaid Club" ', *Modern Language Review*, xlv (1950), 6-17.

16. See below, pp. 273-4. Leslie Hotson has investigated Johnson's career ('Shakespeare and Mine Host of the Mermaid', *Shakespeare's Sonnets Dated and Other Essays* (1949), pp. 76-88).

17. The references in this paragraph to Silver Street and environs are from John Stow, *A Survey of London*, ed. C. L. Kingsford (Oxford, 1908), i. 291ff. The quoted phrases about Paul's Walk are from John Earl, *Microcosmographie* (1628), sig. I11ᵛ. A. L. Rowse, *Shakespeare the Man* (1973), p. 197, has also furnished a few details.

18. A. L. Rowse has brought these facts to light ('Secrets of Shakespeare's Landlady', *The Times*, 23 April 1973, p. 6). See also Rowse's *Simon Forman: Sex and Society in Shakespeare's Age* (1974), pp. 98-9.

19. C. W. Wallace, 'New Shakespeare Discoveries: Shakespeare as a Man among Men', *Harper's Monthly Magazine*, cxx (1910), 489-510. In the same year Wallace published transcripts of the twenty-six documents he had found pertaining to the suit ('Shakespeare and his London Associates as Revealed in Recently Discovered Documents', *Nebraska University Studies*, x (1910), pp. 261-360). EKC gives extracts from the principal documents, and analysis (ii. 90-5), and Adams, *Life of William Shakespeare*, has a useful account (pp. 378-87, 393-95).

20. Adams, *Life of William Shakespeare*, pp. 380-1.

21. The public and private playhouses, their audiences and repertoires, are analysed by Alfred Harbage in his influential *Shakespeare and the Rival Traditions* (New York, 1952).

22. G. E. Bentley, *Shakespeare and his Theatre* (Lincoln, Neb., 1964), p. 88. For a recent searching critique of Bentley, see J. A. Lavin, 'Shakespeare and the Second Blackfriars', *The Elizabethan Theatre III*, ed. David Galloway (Toronto, 1973), pp. 66-81.

23. Bodleian Library, MS. Ashmole 208, ff. 200-13; EKC, ii. 337-41. Forman's notes on *Cymbeline* are reproduced in SS, item 176, p. 215.

24. EKC, ii. 62-71.

25. Prefatory Epistle to *Troilus and Cressida*, 1609, sig. ¶2.

26. Peter Alexander, *Shakespeare* (1964), p. 247.

27. Shakespeare, *Works*, ed. Richard Grant White (Boston, 1865), i. 152; cited by Hyder Edward Rollins in the New Variorum *Sonnets* (Philadelphia and London, 1944), ii. 166.

28. Hotson, *Mr. W. H.* (1964).

29. Thomas Heywood, *An Apology for Actors* (1612), sig. G4ʳ⁻ᵛ.

30. Logan Pearsall Smith, *The Life and Letters of Sir Henry Wotton* (Oxford, 1907), ii. 17; quoted by EKC, ii. 153.

31. Hotson, *Shakespeare's Sonnets Dated*, pp. 111-40, 207-17. An epitaph on Elias James, ascribed to 'Wᵐ: Shakespeare', appears in Bodl.

Rawlinson Poet. MS. 160, f. 41, and is dated 'about 1650' in the *Catalogue*; EKC gives the text (i. 551).

32. This legal opinion was given by Charles Elton, Q.C., to Sidney Lee (*A Life of William Shakespeare* (4th ed. of revised version, 1925)), p. 488n.

33. Ibid., pp. 488-9.

34. Halliwell-Phillipps, *Outlines of the Life of Shakespeare* (7th ed., 1887), ii. 36-7. On the gate-house purchase see EKC, ii. 154-69.

35. ME, 112.

36. Smith, *Wotton*, ii. 32-3.

37. E. K. Chambers, *The Elizabethan Stage* (Oxford, 1923), ii. 421.

15. STRATFORD AGAIN

1. William Shakespeare, *Dramatic Works*, ed. Thomas Campbell (1838), p. lxiv. For a discussion of Campbell on Shakespeare, see S. Schoenbaum, *Shakespeare's Lives* (Oxford, 1970), pp. 312-15.

2. Nicholas Rowe, 'Some Account of the Life, &c. of Mr. William Shakespear', in Shakespeare, *Works*, ed. Rowe (1709), i, p. xxxv.

3. The suggestion is made by ME, 133, whose chapter, 'The Final Years' (131-44), is, like the rest, authoritatively succinct.

4. Chambers notes that highway bills died in committee in 1610 and 1614; EKC, ii. 153.

5. Richard Savage describes the position of the barn in *The Athenæum*, 29 August 1908, p. 250.

6. *Original Collections on Shakespeare & Stratford-on-Avon, by John Jordan, the Stratford Poet . . .* , ed. J. O. Halliwell-Phillipps (1864), p. 50. See also ME, 133.

7. ME, 135-6.

8. On the Welcombe enclosure see EKC, ii. 141-52; C. M. Ingleby, *Shakespeare and the Enclosure of Common Fields at Welcombe* (Birmingham, 1885); ME, 136-8.

9. Shakespeare Birthplace Trust, Corporation Records, Misc. Doc. XII, 103; Halliwell-Phillipps, *Outlines of the Life of Shakespeare* (7th ed., 1887), ii. 378. Greene dated his memorandum 9 September.

10. Edgar I. Fripp, *Shakespeare: Man and Artist* (1938), ii. 806, gives Greene's investment as £300, but his figure seems too small: in 1617 he was asking £590 for the lease, but settled for £400 (ME, 129).

11. Shakespeare Birthplace Trust Records Office, Corp. Rec., Misc. Doc. XIII, 26a; SS, item 190, p. 233.

12. ME, 137.

13. The point is made by ME, 138.

14. Ingleby, *Shakespeare and the Enclosure of Common Fields*, gives complete texts for Combe's letter and the corporation's reply (pp. 16-18). Greene records Combe's April despair in his diary (Ingleby, p. 12).

15. This plausible interpretation is offered by E. R. C. Brinkworth, *Shakespeare and the Bawdy Court of Stratford* (1972), p. 46. Brinkworth's book, which is helpfully informative on the proceedings of the parish ecclesiastical court, follows up the important article by Hugh A. Hanley, 'Shakespeare's Family in Stratford Records', *The Times Literary Supplement*, 21 May 1964, p. 441.

16. ME, 115.

17. Hall's work as a physician is analysed by Harriet Joseph, *Shakespeare's Son-in-Law: John Hall, Man and Physician* (Hamden, Conn., 1964); see also ME, 114-15.

18. John Hall *Select Observations on English Bodies* . . . , transl. James Cooke (1657), pp. 227-8.

19. Fripp, *Shakespeare*, ii. 885-91.

20. Hall, *Select Observations*, pp. 47-51.

21. ME, 113.

22. Hall, *Select Observations*, sig. A3^{r-v}.

23. The collection comprised 200 'observations' altogether, the remainder not being by Hall.

24. ME, 139.

25. Public Record Office, Star Chamber Proceedings, James I, 26/10, *m*. 2; cited by Fripp, *Shakespeare*, ii. 824, and by ME, 140. Fripp and ME are, in general, the most useful authorities on the Quineys, as well as on the Halls.

26. For the Wheeler episode and its aftermath, as for Susanna's non-receiving, my sources are Hanley ('Shakespeare's Family in Stratford Records') and Brinkworth (*Shakespeare and the Bawdy Court*).

27. See Fripp, *Master Richard Quyny* (Oxford, 1924), pp. 206-7; also his *Shakespeare*, ii. 833.

28. ME, 140-1.

29. British Library, MS. Landsdowne 721, f. 2. The existence of the will was known earlier.

30. B. Roland Lewis, *The Shakespeare Documents* (Stanford, 1940), ii. 471.

31. G. E. Bentley, *Shakespeare: A Biographical Handbook* (New Haven, 1961), p. 61.

32. William West, *The First Part of Simboleography* . . . (1615 ed.), Sect. 643.

33. Brinkworth, *Shakespeare and the Bawdy Court*, pp. 80-3.

34. It is fair to add that Combe left an additional £5 for the poor of Warwick, and £5 for the poor of Alcester.

35. ME, 136.

36. *A Brief Discourse . . . of the Laudable Customs of London* (1584), pp. 24-5. On the perplexing legal issue of the widow's portion I have profited from the expert advice of the Revd. Eric McDermott of Georgetown University, and Dr. Levi Fox and Mr. Robert Bearman of the Shakespeare Birthplace Trust.

37. Marchette Chute, *Shakespeare of London* (1949), p. 279.

38. *Supplement to the Edition of Shakespeare's Plays Published in 1778 by Samuel Johnson and George Steevens*, ed. Edmond Malone (1780), i. 657.

39. *Diary of the Rev. John Ward . . .*, ed. Charles Severn (1839), p. 56.

40. Elaine W. Fowler, 'The Earl of Bedford's "Best Bed" ', *Shakespeare Quarterly*, xviii (1967), 80.

41. ME brings the will to notice and cites the salient bequest (164-5n).

42. Cited by G. R. Potter, 'Shakespeare's Will and Raleigh's Instructions to his Son', *Notes and Queries*, clviii (1930), 364. The passage appears in Raleigh's posthumous 'Remains'.

43. *Borough Customs*, ed. Mary Bateson (*Publications* of the Selden Society, 21;1906), ii. 142-3, 144.

44. For the text of 'The Joint and several Answers of Susan Hall, widow, and Thomas Nashe, gent.', see Frank Marcham, *William Shakespeare and his Daughter Susannah* (1931), pp. 66-71.

45. *An Answer to Mr. Pope's Preface to Shakespear . . . By a Stroling Player* (1729), pp. 45-6; EKC, ii. 272.

46. William Shakespeare, *Plays and Poems*, ed. Malone (1790), vol. i, pt. 1, p. 136.

47. ME, 142.

48. The report is by William Hall, Bodleian Library, MS. Rawlinson D. 377, f. 90; SS, item 205, p. 251. Chambers makes the point about the improbability of a seventeen-foot grave (EKC, ii. 181).

49. Mr. Dowdall (SS, item 218, p. 262) and Hall both have Shakespeare composing the epitaph, as does the author of an anonymous manuscript note 'written towards the end of the seventeenth century' in a copy of the Third Folio. Halliwell-Phillipps prints the note in his *Outlines* (ii. 357), and EKC reprints it (ii. 261).

50. Bodleian Library, MS. Rawlinson D. 377, f. 90; SS, item 205, p. 251.

51. EKC, ii. 242-3; British Library, MS. Lansdowne 213, f. 332^v; see also above, pp. 242-3.

52. The note was set down by Dugdale; see *The Life, Diary, and*

Correspondence of Sir William Dugdale, ed. William Hamper (1827), p. 99.

53. It is Chambers who thinks of a melancholy tailor (EKC, ii. 185).

54. R. B. Wheler, *The Gentleman's Magazine*, lxxxv (1815), 390.

55. On the engraving, as on the monument, I have profited most from Chambers and Spielmann.

56. A. L. Rowse, *The English Spirit: Essays in Literature and History* (rev. ed.; 1966), p. 6.

57. For a masterly brief account of the First Folio, see Charlton Hinman's introduction to the Norton Facsimile, *The First Folio of Shakespeare* (New York, 1968). Authoritative studies on a large scale are W. W. Greg, *The Shakespeare First Folio*, and Hinman, *The Printing and Proof-reading of the First Folio of Shakespeare* (Oxford, 1963), 2 vols. Hinman (i. 248-9) describes the three states of the Droeshout engraving.

58. For a different view, see T. J. B. Spencer, 'Ben Jonson on his beloved, The Author Mr. William Shakespeare', *The Elizabethan Theatre IV*, ed. G. R. Hibbard (Toronto, 1974), pp. 22-40.

Acknowledgements of Facsimiles

Belvoir Castle (by permission of the Duke of Rutland): 36 (Rutland MSS. iv. 494).

Bodleian Library (by permission of the Curators): 11, 16 (Fulman MS. xv (Corpus Christi College, Oxford, MS. 309)), 33 (Aubrey MS. 8, f. 45^v), 47.

British Library (by permission of the British Library Board): 24 (Harley 5353, f. 12^v), 25 (Harley 7368, f. 9), 29 (Portland Loan 29/246, p. 18; by permission of the Duke of Portland), 34 (Harley 6395, f. 2), 40 (Harley 4064, f. 189), 48.

Colgate University Library, Hamilton, New York: 13.

Fitzwilliam Museum, Cambridge (by permission of the Syndics): 21.

Folger Shakespeare Library: 2 (Art Vol. d75, no. 27c), 10, 17, 22 (V.a.460, f. 9), 23 (V.a.292 (formerly 2073.5), f. 140), 28 (V.a.350 (formerly 423.3), p. 28), front endpaper, frontispiece (c.b.7).

Greater London Record Office (by permission of the Corporation of Wardens of the Parish of St. Saviour, Southwark): 4 (P92/SAV/3001 (register), P92/SAV/370/10 (fee book)).

Kent County Archives Office, Maidstone (by permission of Lord Sackville): 42 (U 269 Q 22).

Longleat (by permission of the Marquess of Bath): 20 (Harley Papers, vol. i, f. 159^v).

Plume Library, Maldon, Essex: 5 (MS. 25, f. 161).

Public Record Office (by permission of the Controller of Her Majesty's Stationery Office): 8 (S.P., 12/243, no. 76), 26 (E. 179/146/354), 32 (A.O. 3/908/13), 35 (Req. 4/1), 44 (Prob. 1/4).

Shakespeare Birthplace Trust Records Office (by permission of the Trustees and Guardians of Shakespeare's Birthplace): 6 (Misc. Doc. VII, 56), 7 (Corp. Rec., Council Book A, p. 368), 30 (ER 27/4), 37 (Corp. Rec., Chamberlain's Accounts 1585-1619, p. 266), 38 (Misc. Doc. I, 94), 43 (ER 27/11).

Shakespeare Birthplace Trust Records Office (by permission of the Vicar and Church Wardens of Holy Trinity Church): 3, 9, 14, 15, 27, 31, 39, 41, 45, 49, 50 (DR 243/1); 51 (DR 243/2), rear endpaper.

Utrecht University Library: 18 (1198, f. 83), 19 (842, f. 132).

Worcestershire Record Office (by permission of the County Archivist): 12 (b716.093 BA 2648/10(i)).

York Public Library: 1.

Index

To facilitate consultation, the spelling of proper names is regularized.